FIGHTING
FIFTEEN

ALSO BY STEPHEN L. MOORE

Beyond the Call of Duty: The Life of Colonel Robert Howard, America's Most Decorated Green Beret

Strike of the Sailfish: Two Sister Submarines and the Sinking of a Japanese Aircraft Carrier

Blood and Fury: The World War II Story of Tank Sergeant Lafayette "War Daddy" Pool

Patton's Payback: The Battle of El Guettar and General Patton's Rise to Glory

Battle Stations: How the USS Yorktown Helped Turn the Tide at Coral Sea and Midway

Rain of Steel: Mitscher's Task Force 58, Ugaki's Thunder Gods, and the Kamikaze War off Okinawa

Uncommon Valor: The Recon Company That Earned Five Medals of Honor and Included America's Most Decorated Green Beret

As Good as Dead: The Daring Escape of American POWs from a Japanese Death Camp

The Battle for Hell's Island: How a Small Band of Carrier Dive-Bombers Helped Save Guadalcanal

Texas Rising: The Epic True Story of the Lone Star Republic and the Rise of the Texas Rangers, 1836–1846

Pacific Payback: The Carrier Aviators Who Avenged Pearl Harbor at the Battle of Midway

Battle Surface!: Lawson P. "Red" Ramage and the War Patrols of the USS Parche

Presumed Lost: The Incredible Ordeal of America's Submarine POWs During the Pacific War

Relic Quest: A Guide to Responsible Relic Recovery Techniques with Metal Detectors

Savage Frontier: Rangers, Riflemen, and Indian Wars in Texas, Volume IV: 1842–1845

Last Stand of the Texas Cherokees: Chief Bowles and the 1839 Cherokee War in Texas

War of the Wolf: Texas' Memorial Submarine, World War II's
Famous USS Seawolf

Savage Frontier: Rangers, Riflemen, and Indian Wars in Texas,
Volume III: 1840–1841

Spadefish: *On Patrol with a Top-Scoring World War II Submarine*

Savage Frontier: Rangers, Riflemen, and Indian Wars in Texas,
Volume II: 1838–1839

Eighteen Minutes: The Battle of San Jacinto and the Texas
Independence Campaign

Savage Frontier: Rangers, Riflemen, and Indian Wars in Texas,
Volume I: 1835–1837

Taming Texas: Captain William T. Sadler's Lone Star Service

The Buzzard Brigade: Torpedo Squadron Ten at War
(with William J. Shinneman and Robert Gruebel)

FIGHTING FIFTEEN

The Navy's Top Ace and the
Deadliest Hellcat Squadron
of the Pacific War

STEPHEN L. MOORE

CALIBER

CALIBER

An imprint of Penguin Random House LLC
1745 Broadway, New York, NY 10019
penguinrandomhouse.com

LIBRARY OF CONGRESS CATALOGING-IN-PUBLICATION DATA
has been applied for.

ISBN 9780593475867 (hardcover)
ISBN 9780593475874 (ebook)

Printed in the United States of America
1st Printing

The authorized representative in the EU for product safety and compliance is
Penguin Random House Ireland, Morrison Chambers, 32 Nassau Street,
Dublin D02 YH68, Ireland, https://eu-contact.penguin.ie.

Dedicated to the valiant warriors of Fighting Fifteen,

the U.S. Navy's true top guns of World War II

CONTENTS

PROLOGUE

October 12, 1944

S pike Borley had never wished for a reason to abort a mission. Until
now.

Orange-magenta rays of light were just filtering through the low
gray scud as sixteen Grumman F6F Hellcats effected their rendezvous
high above the fleet carrier USS *Essex* (CV-9). Two of the glossy sea blue–
colored fighter planes signaled that they were returning to the ship due to
mechanical failures. One had a windshield spattered black with oil from a
troubling engine leak.

A fouled engine would be a perfect reason to return to base, but Ensign
Borley's eighteen-cylinder Pratt & Whitney engine was purring perfectly.
The reason for his apprehension this morning was the nature of his squad-
ron's mission. VF-15 was going in to execute a fighter sweep over central
Formosa (modern Taiwan), to clear the air of any enemy aircraft before
waves of task force bombers and torpedo bombers arrived to attack.

What troubled young Borley was the fact that the only visuals his
squadron had of the large Japanese-held island of Formosa were from submarine periscope photos. Intelligence warned that the Japanese might
have as many as two dozen airfields on the island and more than three
hundred aircraft to greet their strike group.

Clarence Borley was just two years removed from the ranches of Yakima, Washington, where he had been raised. Following his high school
graduation in 1942, he had taken a bus to Seattle, where he enlisted in the

Navy and was soon accepted into flight school. In the spring of 1944, he had been assigned to VF-15 in Hawaii, shortly before the squadron deployed on the carrier *Essex*.

In the months since Fighting Fifteen had made its first combat flights in May 1944, Borley had been credited with only one aerial victory, a Zeke fighter he'd shot down just two days before. His flight today was loaded with bona fide aces: the thirteen VF-15 pilots launched from *Essex* had scored more than four dozen kills, and six of the pilots with him had already shot down five or more enemy aircraft. Lieutenant Commander George Duncan and Lieutenant (junior grade) George Carr each had 9.5 kills to their credit, and squadron skipper Jim Rigg had nine.

One hour out from the ship, as the VF-15 flight approached Formosa's outer islands, the action commenced. Numerous enemy aircraft were tallyhoed at 23,000 feet. (The radio call of "Tallyho!" originated from the British air force, whose pilots had used the old fox hunting call since the late 1930s to announce their spotting of enemy aircraft.) Lieutenant Commander Rigg called for his Hellcat pilots to begin climbing. It was time to engage the Japanese fighters who were awaiting them.

Rigg, Carr, and Duncan each added another kill to their personal tallies. Four junior *Essex* fighter pilots made their first kills on the mission. But the action was not one-sided: two VF-15 planes were lost.

Attaining ace status this day was far removed from Borley's thoughts as he entered the big aerial melee. And yet, in a series of twisting, diving engagements, he did just that with judicious bursts of his .50-caliber wing guns. Borley shot down four enemy fighter planes. Suddenly he became the youngest American ace in the Navy, having reached the age of twenty only in July.

As the action waned, Borley and his wingman joined a larger formation of Hellcats turning for home. Spotting Japanese aircraft taking off from Keishu Airfield on Formosa, Borley made a strafing run on an anti-aircraft position. As he pulled out of his run, he was flying fast across the island at 2,000 feet. That's when his good luck finally ran out.

An antiaircraft shell, estimated to be of 40mm size, struck his F6F. His cockpit filled with smoke and his left leg throbbed with pain from embedded shrapnel. His cockpit smelled of burning rubber, and his external belly tank was ablaze. Fearing his Grumman could explode at any moment, Borley struggled to get the fuel tank to release.

Finally, it dropped. By this time he had a bigger problem. His engine seized up and quit. His only hope was to try to reach the open ocean before his powerless Hellcat dropped onto the enemy island. Borley had just cleared the coastline when he slammed into the ocean, still making 90 knots.

His plane broke up on impact, but Borley was able to scramble free. He quickly inflated his yellow Mae West life jacket and began swimming. He feared becoming a prisoner of war, so he pushed hard toward the open water.

But his worst fears were soon realized. A small Japanese fishing vessel along the coast veered toward him. As it approached, he could see Japanese men topside looking at him. Borley pulled out his .38-caliber sidearm and raised it at the oncoming enemy.

He had no idea if the gun would even fire after having been submerged in salt water. But Spike Borley was not going to become a POW if he could help it.

In late March 1944, the pilots of VF-15 were treated to a dinner party on Oahu, hosted by Countess Alexa von Tempsky Zabriskie. In her personal scrapbook, the VF-15 pilots added their "Satan's Playmates" squadron logo and all of their autographs. Weeks later, VF-15 was at war on their carrier, Essex. *Many of the pilots who signed this page would not survive.*

JOHN BARRY III

ONE

DASHING DAVE

September 15, 1942
Near Guadalcanal

Dave McCampbell never saw it coming.

A half hour earlier, he had simply been doing his job. As the primary landing signal officer (LSO) on board one of the U.S. Navy's newest aircraft carriers, he was in charge of directing and managing the landing of all combat airplanes. Lieutenant McCampbell, standing on a platform at the very aft end of the 19,000-ton carrier USS *Wasp* (CV-7), had used his special canvas-covered signal paddles to coach in eight Grumman F4F Wildcat fighter planes and three Douglas SBD Dauntless dive-bombers.

If a pilot was too low or too high to safely make his landing on *Wasp*'s teakwood flight deck, McCampbell directed him up or down. A pilot coming in too fast or endangering another aircraft still on deck would be given a "wave-off," or a refusal to be taken on board. When a plane was properly aligned above the deck, he gave them the "cut"—a paddle across his throat to signal that the pilot should chop his throttle. Once McCampbell had brought the group of fighters and bombers in, his job was complete for a while. As plane handlers (called "airedales") struck these planes below the flight deck via the amidships aircraft elevator, McCampbell made a quick trip down to his cabin, located one deck above the hangar deck.

After a brief break, he headed topside again, back to his duty station. He climbed up a steel ladder to reach *Wasp*'s flight deck. As he walked aft,

Lieutenant Dave McCampbell (on platform with LSO paddles) in 1942 while serving as the landing signal officer on the carrier Wasp. *Standing behind him is his assistant landing signal officer, Ensign George E. "Doc" Savage.*

NATIONAL ARCHIVES, 80-G-K-687

McCampbell was greeted by the carrier's arresting gear officer. There was a problem. One of the steel cables used to snag the tailhooks of landing planes was badly frayed, and the officer recommended that McCampbell's deckhands should replace it.

The time was 1444.

As the two officers strolled across the flight deck, an unseen menace was unleashing a deadly attack. The skies were clear blue with unlimited visibility as the Japanese fleet submarine *I-19*, skippered by Commander Takakazu Kinashi, fired a full nest of six torpedoes at the American carrier fleet. His precision could not have been better. Three warheads struck *Wasp*. Two missed ahead of the flattop, with one exploding in the destroyer USS *O'Brien* (DD-415). The sixth torpedo passed astern or under *Wasp* and ran another seven minutes before exploding into the side of the battleship USS *North Carolina* (BB-55).

The incoming torpedoes were spotted, but the carrier's skipper, Captain Forrest Sherman, only had time to order hard left rudder. Before his mighty warship could twist out of the way, two torpedoes exploded almost simultaneously directly beneath the forward five-inch gun galleries on the starboard side. *Wasp* was whipped violently as smoke, debris, and flames belched skyward.

As the first warhead exploded, McCampbell assumed that *Wasp* had been struck by a dive-bombing attack. He and the other officer scrambled into the catwalk lining the flight deck. Peeking up to see where the bomb had exploded, McCampbell saw nothing. At that instant, a third torpedo exploded, and the number two elevator was blown ten feet into the air.

Dave jumped to his feet and sprinted aft on the flight deck toward his LSO station. The carrier vibrated so violently that it knocked him to the flight deck. Picking himself up, he raced back to his abandon-ship station.

The power went out, so McCampbell heard no communications. *I-19*'s torpedo hits were disastrous. Fueled and armed aircraft on *Wasp*'s hangar deck caught fire and exploded. Twenty minutes after the third torpedo hit, ruptured fuel lines triggered another massive internal explosion that cooked off other torpedoes, bombs, and fuel on the hangar deck. The devastation was extensive, and *Wasp* was soon a raging inferno. Thousands of rounds of .30- and .50-caliber machine-gun ammunition began exploding. Firefighting efforts were in vain as fire swept through the ship. By 1520, Captain Sherman climbed to the bridge to apprise the task force commander, Rear Admiral Leigh Noyes, that it was time to abandon ship. Lack of communication power meant that the order was passed verbally, and it took some time for many to receive the word.

McCampbell was surprised just a half hour after the explosions to see sailors starting to go over the fantail. Dozens of knotted lines were dangling over the sides, and men began dropping toward the ocean. Many enlisted flight deck personnel had gathered near him. He and one of his dive-bomber pilots, Lieutenant (jg) Spencer Wright, began working to lower an eighteen-man lifeboat suspended from the overhang of the stern of the ship. As they eased it toward the water, Wright suddenly released the line on his side. As the lifeboat plunged the remaining distance to the water below, McCampbell was jerked off the deck into the pulley before he released the line.[1]

McCampbell then remained at his station, ensuring that all his people

McCampbell survived the sinking of the Wasp *after she was torpedoed off Guadalcanal by a Japanese submarine in November 1942.*   U.S. NAVY PHOTO

made it over the side from the stern or went down to the hangar deck to climb down lines there. He finally decided it was time to go. He removed his shirt and shoes and then prepared to execute something he had always wanted to do: a 1.5 flip dive with a full twist. In his youth, he had been a championship diver.

When the time came, he climbed atop a square loudspeaker box and surveyed the ocean below. To his disappointment, he saw too many people in the water and too much floating debris to dive safely. "I held my nose with one hand and my family jewels with the other, and I jumped," he recalled.[2]

As he leapt, thoughts rushed through his head. *This might be it for me. Well, at least my insurance is paid up.* The fall was longer than he imagined: close to sixty feet due to the starboard list of *Wasp.* He plunged deep beneath the waves and then scrambled back to the surface. The burning, exploding carrier drifted down on him, and McCampbell fought to swim clear.

As he made his way around to the starboard side of the ship, McCampbell found three men he knew on a makeshift life raft fashioned from their belts and floating lumber. Seeing that their little raft wouldn't support four people, McCampbell set off swimming for a destroyer about three hundred yards away. It got underway before he reached it, leaving him stranded again. At one point McCampbell took a rest on the edge of a floating mattress that Captain Sherman was on.[3]

Spotting another destroyer, he started swimming for it. En route, he was scooped up by the crew of a motor whaleboat from the destroyer USS *Farenholt* (DD-491). After more than three hours in the ocean, he found himself in the same rescue vessel as Rear Admiral Noyes. Mc-Campbell quickly advised Noyes of having seen *Wasp*'s Captain Sherman clinging to a large floating mattress earlier. The whaleboat motored over and rescued the carrier's skipper before depositing all three men on *Farenholt*.

After cleaning some of the oil off his body with kerosene, McCampbell got a shower. He walked out on deck naked, hoping to find some clothes. He instead spotted a wounded shipmate floating on a raft down below *Farenholt*. McCampbell and a destroyer officer jumped overboard and helped get the wounded man into a stretcher to be brought aboard. Before the task group cleared the area that evening, Admiral Noyes directed one of his destroyers to finish off his flagship, *Wasp*, with torpedoes to prevent her from falling into enemy hands.[4]

During the return to port, McCampbell was offered the destroyer executive officer's cabin and some oversized clothing. McCampbell ultimately secured passage on a troop transport back to San Diego. In October 1942, he learned of his promotion to lieutenant commander and thirty days of survivor leave that would enable him to visit his family in Norfolk.

By the time his leave ended, McCampbell had received new orders. His naval aviation career was still relatively young, but that would soon change.

DAVE MCCAMPBELL'S FASCINATION with aviation began with Jenny at age nine.

Manufactured by the Curtiss Aeroplane and Motor Company of Buffalo and Hammondsport, New York, "Jenny" was the nickname for the company's JN-4 model of biplanes. In 1916, Curtiss began building the twin-seat propeller planes as training aircraft for the American and Canadian militaries. Following World War I, thousands of surplus Jennys—with forty-four-foot wingspans and a maximum speed of 75 miles per hour—were sold at bargain prices to private owners.

Dave's maternal grandfather, a wealthy wholesale and retail hardware businessman, bought a Jenny and offered several rides to his young grandson. His love of aviation began.[5]

David McCampbell was born on January 16, 1910, in the town of Bessemer, Alabama, to Andrew Jackson and Elizabeth LaValle Perry McCampbell. His father, the son of an Alabama farmer, worked in the family hardware business during his early years. Young Dave made extra money by mowing grass and delivering milk from the family's ten cows. As a child, he developed a love for swimming that became his passion later in school.

In 1920, Andrew McCampbell moved his family to West Palm Beach, Florida, to start his own furniture store. In 1923, David entered the prestigious Staunton Military Academy in Staunton, Virginia, where he was educated on military discipline. He then enrolled in Georgia Tech in 1928, aspiring to earn his engineering degree with hopes of later working as a civil engineer for his uncle's road construction firm. He began to date Sara Jane Heliker, a black-haired young woman his age with flashing eyes. An outstanding dancer who was later schooled in New York to become a photographic model and professional dancer, Heliker was nicknamed "Jill" by McCampbell.

At Georgia Tech, McCampbell tried his hand on the freshman football team, but at a mere 156 pounds he didn't have the bulk to compete against the bigger players. He turned to his love of swimming, competing on the collegiate team as a backstroker and a diver. By 1929 the family business had expanded to three stores and was doing quite well—until the crash of the New York Stock Exchange that year plunged America into the Great Depression.[6]

With the economic boom now a bust, young Dave knew his parents could not continue to afford his schooling. "I figured it was an undue burden on my family to continue my education, when I could get a free education at the Naval Academy," he recalled. During his time with the ROTC at Georgia Tech, McCampbell had made a reserve cruise over the summer. The Navy suited him just fine, and his local Florida senator recommended him for an appointment to Annapolis.[7]

Upon receiving his appointment, Dave was given a ten-day break in 1929 to drive to Miami to take his entrance examinations. This offered him a chance to drive to West Palm Beach to visit Jill, whom he had not seen in months, at her home. He passed the test and enjoyed his days with her before heading to the academy in Maryland.[8]

McCampbell was an average student at the academy, where he spent all four years on the diving team. During his third year, he won the Eastern Intercollegiates and was runner-up in his senior year. He was prevented from competing in the 1932 Olympics due to his poor grades in Spanish. Dave also pursued his interest in aviation at the academy, obtaining several familiarization flights in seaplanes. His relationship with Jill Heliker took a back seat during these years, and he eventually heard from her that she had married another man, Gilbert Kahn, the son of a wealthy banker.[9]

Upon his graduation from Annapolis in June 1933, Dave was honorably discharged due to congressional legislation limiting commissions in the U.S. Navy that year. McCampbell tried to enter flight training with the Army Air Corps but was medically declined due to hyperphoria of the right eye, a condition that left vision in that eye slanted upward. McCampbell remained in the reserves, taking a job as an assembly mechanic with an Alabama construction company. By May 1934, the Navy had transferred him back to full service, and he was commissioned an ensign. He served on the cruiser USS *Portland* (CA-33) and later was her aircraft gunnery observation officer for Scouting Squadron Eleven.[10]

The handsome dark-haired, blue-eyed aviator had no trouble finding company with ladies during his off time. In later years he would jestingly sign his name as "Dashing Dave" without adding his surname. But McCampbell's bachelor days came to an end when he began dating Susan Rankin from Glendale, California. They were soon engaged and married on June 26, 1936, spending their honeymoon in Honolulu while *Portland* was in overhaul.

McCampbell applied for flight duty again that year but was again turned down due to his eye. After a six-month cruise on *Portland*, he was finally cleared for flight school by a different flight surgeon. In June 1937, he reported to the naval air station (NAS) in Pensacola, Florida, for flight training. He proved to be a natural, having spent countless hours flying as an observer off *Portland*. "I was comfortable in the air," McCampbell recalled. At times his pilot had allowed him to take the controls. In Squadron One, the first stage of his flight training, McCampbell was the first pilot of his class to complete a solo flight.[11] Four more stages of flight training followed; during them the young students mastered various trainer aircraft, from floatplanes to seaplanes to multi-engine torpedo planes.

Life in Pensacola was grand for the young married aviation student, who continued to gain confidence with each passing month. McCampbell was pinned with his golden wings on April 23, 1938. With a high class standing, he requested and received orders to a fighting squadron, Fighting Squadron Four (VF-4) on the carrier USS *Ranger* (CV-4).

McCampbell learned to fly the Grumman F3F biplane fighter, which had a wingspan of thirty-two feet and a maximum speed of 264 miles per hour. He found the biplane to be very maneuverable, with a good rate of climb and a solid gunnery platform. Ensign McCampbell earned the "E" for excellence mark for both his gunnery and bombing marksmanship. "They used to call me a hotshot, but I really wasn't that hot," he recalled. He would later credit his tactical skills to an excellent cadre of instructors and senior section leader pilots.[12]

Tailhook landings on the early flattops were a learning experience. During his early qualification landings on *Ranger*, McCampbell failed to lower his hook. His F3F slammed into the barrier with enough force that his nose received a permanent scar after his face rammed into the gunsight. McCampbell served two years with VF-4 on *Ranger* before being assigned to the new carrier *Wasp* as she was put into commission in 1940. Dave's flight time decreased during 1941 as he transitioned into the role of assistant landing signal officer for *Wasp*'s air group, eventually working his way up to senior LSO.[13]

During the early months of World War II, *Wasp* participated in convoy escort duty, including two trips to Malta to deliver Supermarine Spitfire

Mk Vb fighters. Following the Pacific carrier battles of the Coral Sea and Midway in 1942, the carrier shifted to the Pacific theater in time to support the U.S. invasion of Guadalcanal in the Solomon Islands. *Wasp*'s service in the campaign was brief, ended by the three torpedoes from the submarine *I-19*. Throughout the early months of war, McCampbell had not lost the urge to get out from behind his paddles and into a cockpit to fight. "I always had that desire, even when we weren't in combat," he later stated.[14]

After his survival leave, McCampbell was assigned to the operational training command for new aviators in Jacksonville, Florida. After brief stints at NAS Cecil Field and NAS Fort Lauderdale, McCampbell was ordered to the newly commissioned NAS Melbourne, a sprawling base for advanced training of carrier-based fighter pilots. Lieutenant McCampbell was the senior landing signal officer, tasked with training a new cadre of LSOs. "I let them do most of the work, and I'd supervise every day," he recalled.[15]

Because he was a veteran of the carrier fleet, his services were essential. But the ensuing months of training work did not satisfy McCampbell. He was teaching men he knew had the opportunity to achieve great success in aerial combat. His first class of twelve at Melbourne included two men who would wind up becoming top U.S. Navy fighter aces, Alex Vraciu and Gene Valencia. Like McCampbell, Valencia had been pulled into instructional work in 1942 but he managed to talk his way into a new squadron in 1943, VF-9 on board the new carrier *Essex*.

Through the first half of 1943, McCampbell expressed his desire to escape fighter training responsibilities and get into combat. At age thirty-three, he was already pushing the limits on the age for a fighter pilot in the wartime Navy. But he worked his contacts in the Bureau of Aeronautics and the Navy's personnel bureau in hopes of returning to fleet aviation with his own command.[16]

At Melbourne, McCampbell was contacted by others who had similar desires. One of the men he heard from was his nephew-in-law Bert De-Wayne Morris, who was married to his niece Patricia Ann O'Rourke. For Morris, it was his second marriage. After graduating high school, he had played football at Los Angeles Junior College and then worked as a forest ranger. Returning to his college, Morris studied acting there and at the acclaimed Pasadena Playhouse, where he was discovered by a Warner Bros. talent agent and signed in 1936.

Under the screen name Wayne Morris, he fit the role of the blond-haired boy-next-door type and was cast in the starring role for the 1937 film *Kid Galahad*, a film about a prizefighter that included stars Bette Davis and Humphrey Bogart. In 1938, he filmed *Brother Rat,* with Ronald Reagan, Eddie Albert, and Jane Wyman. In 1939, Morris starred with Bogart in another film, the science fiction–horror movie *The Return of Doctor X*.

Morris's popularity soared. In 1939, he married Leonora "Bubbles" Schinasi, the eighteen-year-old stepdaughter of a New York tobacco baron. Their marriage did not survive the glitz of Hollywood by 1941, but it produced one son, Bert DeWayne Morris III. Bubbles later changed her son's first name to Michael, and he later adopted his stepfather's last name. She went on to become a journalist and children's book author under the name Leonora Hornblow.[17]

While filming *Flight Angels* in 1940, Morris became interested in flying and earned his private pilot's license. He joined the Naval Reserve, went through flight training in Pensacola in 1942, and left his Hollywood career for the time being to become a flight instructor at Hutchinson, Kansas. On February 25, 1942, he married Dave McCampbell's niece Patricia, an actress who had recently appeared in *The Jungle Book* under the screen name Patricia O'Rourke. Tired of being a flight instructor, he reached out to McCampbell asking for his help to get into fighters. "Give me a letter," McCampbell advised. With his uncle-in-law's assistance, Morris was reassigned to operational training command in Jacksonville and then to Melbourne for fighter training.

By early 1943, McCampbell had filed for divorce from his wife, Susan, who retained custody of their young daughter, Frances Ann. During his months of instructing in Florida, he reunited with his old girlfriend, Jill Heliker. Jill's first marriage, like Dave's, had ended in divorce, leaving her with one son and an adopted daughter. Although a dozen years had passed, the two began dating again and would remain in correspondence even after McCampbell was given orders to a new command.[18]

His persistence in requesting active flight command finally paid off in July. Orders arrived for McCampbell to report by August 1 to NAS Atlantic City in New Jersey, to stand up a new fighter unit to be designated Fighting Fifteen (VF-15). Wayne Morris was equally eager to get into McCampbell's forming squadron. "Stay in touch," Dave advised. "I'll keep you in mind."[19]

Now a lieutenant commander, McCampbell eagerly packed his bags and departed Florida. His dreams of flight command were finally in motion.

TWO

DUZ, DUFFY, AND JIGS

Wendell Van Twelves was ready for the next step.

His thick black hair was neatly tucked under his leather flying helmet. His hazel eyes flashed with exhilaration as he adjusted the goggles on his face and gunned the throttle on his Piper J-3 Cub. In Provo, Utah, after six hours of training, Twelves had made his first solo flight. His whole family had been at the airstrip in the fall of 1941, collectively holding their breath and saying prayers, as their son and sibling went around the field for his five required solo landings.[1]

Now he was tasked with making his first open-country flight. It would be from Salt Lake City to Fairview, Utah, where he would land, have his logbook signed, and then fly on to Salt Lake City Airport No. 2. There, he would have his logbook signed again and refuel before flying back to Provo to complete his three-legged flight.

His Piper Cub roared to life as he pushed the stick forward and rumbled down the crushed-gravel surface. Seconds later he was off the ground, flying solo on his final primary training assignment. He made it to Fairview—a flight distance of only forty-three miles—without a hitch. But upon landing and taxiing up to the hangar, he saw no one.[2]

Don't shut down, he told himself.

These little J-3s required hand cranking, spinning the wooden propeller by hand. There was no one in sight on the field or in the hangar to help. Twelves tied the stick back with a safety belt, put a pair of chocks under the wheels, and left his Cub idling. The thought of his first solo flight going unrecorded troubled him.

Wendell Van Twelves at the Provo, Utah, airport in late 1941. "Duz" Twelves is standing beside the Piper J-3 Cub prop plane in which he made his first solo flights at age twenty. VAN TWELVES

Twelves spotted a farmer plowing the adjacent field. With no other choice, the lanky, five-foot-eleven pilot hurried across the uneven field and flagged down the farmer. He was only too happy to sign the young aviator's logbook as a witness before Twelves scurried back to his idling J-3. As he returned to the skies, he made a point of buzzing low over the gracious farmer to waggle his wings as he passed by. The farmer stood in his seat and waved his straw hat in salute.

Although unorthodox, Wendell Twelves's first three-legged flight was a success.

BORN IN SPANISH FORK, Utah, Wendell was one of hundreds of young pilots aspiring to become a naval aviator. His dreams dated back to his childhood, when a local pilot had taken Twelves and a buddy aloft to herd cattle in a 150-horsepower Alexander Eaglerock biplane. "It was the most beautiful old airplane I'd ever seen," Twelves recalled. "From that day on, I knew I had to fly."[3]

His family joked that his first flight had actually taken place when he was even younger. During a visit to family, Wendell slipped while playing on a fire escape. He was not seriously injured when he slammed onto the landing one floor below, but his family would long kid him that it had been his first "air time."

Wendell's interest in flying went unchecked until he started college at Brigham Young University in the fall of 1941. With World War II looming on America's doorstep, thousands of young men felt the urge to partake in flight training. For those like young Wendell without the luxury of formal military training, the Civilian Pilot Training Program (CPTP) was a natural course of action. Wendell began the CPTP at age twenty at the small Provo, Utah, airport in the Piper Cub.

In 1942, Wendell moved on to tackle ground school training at Utah State Agricultural College in Logan and further flight training out at Cache Valley Airport in a WACO UPF-7. With a 220-horsepower Continental engine, the UPF-7 was large but fast and nimble. After the finish of every hop, Twelves's instructor put the plane through varying loops and spins—known as Immelmanns, chandelles, spins, Cuban eights—before returning to the strip. "He could see that I was eating this up, and he liked a cadet who liked to do that kind of thing," Twelves recalled.[4]

From there, Twelves went before the Naval Aviation Cadet Selection Board in San Francisco in the summer. He was assigned to begin at one of the Navy's five designated training schools, the Naval Aviation Pre-Flight School at St. Mary's College in Moraga, California, near Oakland, on October 15. The rigorous three-month program was a physical weeding-out process that included hand-to-hand combat training in addition to ground school and continuing college courses. Twelves was told by senior officers from the beginning that there were three ways to go about doing things: the right way, the wrong way, and the Navy way. It became his motto. "As soon as I learned to fly the 'navy way,' I was able to progress quite rapidly through primary training," Twelves remembered.[5]

The demand for new pilots was high at the onset of World War II. Only 17,614 Army Air Corps cadets were in training as of December 1941, but by

the end of 1942, this figure had ballooned to 94,003. The USN's pilot training program graduated 10,869 aviators in 1942, but this number doubled
to 20,842 graduates by the end of 1943.[6]

At St. Mary's, Twelves made good friends with men with whom he
would continue through his aviation training. Among them were cadets
James Antony "Jimmy" Wakefield, a twenty-two-year-old former Colorado State College student who hailed from Fort Collins, and George
Henry Rader, a twenty-one-year-old who had studied at the University of
California. With auburn hair, Rader inevitably became known as "Red" to
his buddies. With the name Twelves, in reference to "dozen," Wendell
earned the nickname "Duz" for short.

In March 1943, Duz and his companions were assigned to NAS Corpus
Christi, which had focused on cadet training in May 1941. Its primary
training plane was the Vultee BT-13 Valiant, a loud, rattling aircraft that
Duz and others quickly dubbed the "Vibrator." The cadets were informed
that if they ever had to make a forced landing outside of Kingsville, they
were to avoid touching down on the massive King Ranch nearby. If the
ranch was unavoidable, the pilot should stay in his aircraft. "Those long-
horn Texas cattle will sure 'getcha,'" the instructor advised.[7]

One of the students Twelves came to know was cadet Jim Duffy, a lean,
dark-haired Californian with a hearty smile. His family was originally
from Oklahoma, where his father had been a sharecropper when the Great
Depression hit. Then the family moved to Southern California, where Jim
went to school. "I was a relatively happy kid but did have an Irish temper,"
he admitted. "I would not let any other kid bully me around, which resulted in getting several black eyes."[8]

Like many young boys, Duffy grew up reading about Charles Lind-
bergh and building model planes to fly around his neighborhood. He had
his first flight at age eighteen when a buddy took him up in a Beechcraft
Staggerwing. But years would pass before his desire to become a pilot had
a realistic chance. Duffy was working at an aircraft company while attending Pasadena City College, one month shy of his twenty-second birthday, when Pearl Harbor was attacked.[9]

Duffy first went to the Army Air Corps, but they could not guarantee
him that he would learn to fly. Minus that promise, he told the Army he

Ensign Jim Duffy in his F6F.
KATHY DUFFY KALOHI

was not interested just before he was sworn in. His recruiting sergeant yelled at him, telling him he would be getting a draft notice and would spend the war as a foot soldier. "That scared me enough that I enlisted in the Navy the next day," he said. Duffy entered the Navy's V-5 pilot training program on April 7, 1942, and went through civilian pilot training while awaiting his spot at preflight school.[10]

His first flights over the California desert and at the Oakland school were in Piper J-3 Cubs and Stearman N2S Kaydet biplanes, learning loops, spins, and snap rolls. His first introduction to Navy flying came during Los Alamitos, California, primary training. "They were marching us down to get the flight gear and two planes crashed and burned in front of us," Jim remembered. "Needless to say, it was an eye-opener."

Duffy racked up plenty of solo hours while awaiting his next orders. He had already selected fighter pilot as his desired training plan. Upon arriving at Corpus Christi, he joined the ranks of numerous others working to earn their wings, flying BT-13s while learning formations and other basics. During his time at Corpus and Kingsville, Texas, he had the chance to form a strong friendship with Duz Twelves and others.

Another cadet who became friends with Twelves and Duffy was twenty-one-year-old Ralph Foltz from San Francisco. Like Duffy, Ralph had grown up building model airplanes, and he went to college to learn aircraft construction after high school. Foltz joined the U.S. Army Air Corps to work on bombers and fighters and eventually transferred to Elmendorf Field in Anchorage, Alaska. Spotting a squadron of Navy Grumman F4F Wildcat fighters landing one day, Foltz decided, "That's for me!"[11]

But an Elmendorf doctor informed him that he was unable to fly because of a deviated septum. Foltz instead hopped a ride on a Douglas C-47 to Kodiak, where he found a Navy doctor willing to give him a favorable physical. Joining the Navy in August 1942, Foltz completed his preflight training at St. Mary's College with Duz Twelves, Jim Duffy, and others. As with many cadets, he quickly picked up a nickname. Someone began calling him "Zigs" because of his short, zigzag-style haircut. Another pilot mistakenly called him "Jigs," which drew even more snickers. It stuck, and throughout the rest of his flight training, Ralph Foltz was simply "Jigs."[12]

During the more advanced training at Corpus, Twelves and his comrades moved to the Navy SNJ* trainer, the North American Aviation T-6 Texan. For Duz, this single-engine, dual-cockpit plane was as close as he had been so far to flying a fighter. "It was extremely acrobatic," he recalled. "Still, you had to stay ahead of it. You learned it

Ensign Ralph "Jigs" Foltz in March 1944.

DOYLE BARE COLLECTION, COURTESY OF RITA BARE

wasn't going to forgive you for all your mistakes." Jim Duffy recalled, "We practiced glide bombing, simulated carrier landings, slow rolls, and gunnery practice, which I really enjoyed." Plenty of other cadets washed out during this phase of training, and others were killed or seriously injured in various mishaps.[13]

The training was completed in stages, which became progressively harder for those lucky enough to advance. By the program's end, Twelves had accumulated 199.6 flight hours. His last flight was on June 23, at which time he was pinned with his golden wings and was commissioned an ensign in the U.S. Navy. His three closest buddies—Jimmy Wakefield, Dave Johnson, and Red Rader—were all commissioned during the same week. The quartet longed to join a new squadron, but instead found yet another training session in store for them.

Next up was advanced operational flight training in fighter planes at NAS Miami, flying from U.S. Naval Reserve Air Base Opa Locka. Instead of the more modern Grumman F4F Wildcat, the ensigns learned to fly the Brewster F2A Buffalo, the Navy's first monoplane fighter. To Twelves, it

---

* The North American AT-6 Texan was technically an "Army Trainer" plane, but the U.S. Navy's variant of the Texan was known as the SNJ: "S" for Scout, "N" the Navy's designation for a trainer aircraft, and "J" indicating it had been built by North American.

was a "beer can with wings"—a stubby little round fuselage with wings jutting out.[14]

Duz found the brakes on the Buffalo to be so bad that he was generally off the runway and onto the grass before he could stop the squatty fighter. At the grassy end, he often had to unlock his tail wheel just to wheel the F2A around to avoid going into a nearby drainage canal. In the air, the Brewster handled well enough, but Twelves was always happier when he was able to do flights in the SNJ trainers also available at Opa Locka.

Jigs Foltz found the F2A's sheet metal landing gear "crunched real good in a hard landing." He learned to improvise with the temperamental fighter. Once, when his landing gear failed to lower properly, he simply pulled a pair of wire cutters from his pocket and snipped the hydraulic lines, causing the undercarriage to drop automatically.[15]

Finally, on September 1, 1943, Duz Twelves, Rader, Wakefield, and Johnson each received their orders to a squadron. The destinies of Jigs and Duffy were on similar, parallel courses. The training phase was finally over after more than nine grueling months.

Now things are going to start paying off, thought Twelves. *This is the glory day!*[16]

THREE

HELLCATS AND SATAN'S PLAYMATES

August 1943
Atlantic City, New Jersey

Two years of disappointment melted away in an instant as John Strane read through his orders. He finally had his wish. He had been assigned to join a brand-new Navy fighter squadron forming in New Jersey in August 1943.

The twenty-two-year-old Duluth, Minnesota, native had entered the Civilian Pilot Training Program while attending his local junior college. Training in summer and winter, Strane and his fellow students landed both on wheels and skis, learning in biplane Fleet Model 1s and Meyers OTWs and WACO UPF-7s. Fully convinced that flying would be his life, Strane applied and was accepted for Navy flight training at NAS Pensacola in early 1941.[1]

Strane longed to fly fighter planes. But the fighter training program was overcrowded, and Strane was assigned to multi-engine patrol boats. He was commissioned an ensign on October 1, and was thereafter retained to serve as an instructor in the "P-boat" training squadron. As America went to war, he was bitterly disappointed. "Most of us could see the handwriting on the wall, and knew that the place we wanted to do our flying was in the fleet squadrons," he remembered.

By a stroke of good luck, he was instead assigned by his sympathetic personnel officer to instruct new fighter pilot cadets. He built up plenty of flight hours in fighters and gained considerable experience during the next two years. When his orders finally arrived to join the new Fighting Squadron Fifteen (VF-15), Strane was overjoyed. He reported in to his new skipper, Lieutenant Commander Dave McCampbell, and was soon appointed as the squadron's radio communications officer.

Like Strane, McCampbell had finally escaped from instructor duties at NAS Melbourne. At his age, he was pushing the limits to become a squadron commander, but he had the energy of a teenager. McCampbell was pleased with the new airfield at NAS Atlantic City, where his unit would be trained. The naval air station was built on 2,400 acres of land leased in Egg Harbor Township, New Jersey, ten miles northwest of Atlantic City. The base had been newly transformed into a fighter training facility, and McCampbell's unit was among the first three to train there. The concrete runways were new, and proper Navy aircraft hangars and barracks buildings had recently been completed.

McCampbell's first week was consumed with organizing the keymen who would help him fill out the squadron. His unit would be part of the composite Air Group Fifteen slated to go on board a new fleet carrier for service upon completion of training. America had scraped by during 1942 with only a handful of aircraft carriers in four battles with Japanese carrier forces that year. But in 1943, new fleet carriers were coming from the shipyards, and squadrons to fill their rosters were in high demand. The first Air Group Fifteen officer to arrive for duty on September 9 was North Carolinian Lieutenant Paul F. Maness, who would serve as the AG-15 flight surgeon. In the absence of other staff officers, "Doc" Maness was temporarily assigned to McCampbell's fighter squadron.[2]

Two of his original officers, Lieutenants Joe O'Brien and Bob McReynolds, were nonflying ground officers Dave had known at Melbourne. O'Brien became the squadron's administrative officer while McReynolds would be the air combat intelligence officer (ACIO). Another former instructor McCampbell drew from NAS Pensacola was Lieutenant Arend Grothaus, a six-foot-three former basketball center from Ohio University who had been nicknamed "Stretch." Lieutenant John Randolph "Jack" Ivey, a 1940 graduate of Georgia Tech with a mechanical engineering degree, was pulled from instruments teaching at NAS Atlanta.[3]

McCampbell also recruited his own nephew-in-law Bert Morris, who had been begging him to help move him toward a combat role. The former Hollywood star known to the world as Wayne Morris gladly took on the role of flight officer for the squadron. At age twenty-nine, he was seven years older than the average pilot who would join his squadron, but he had no more flight hours amassed than many of these youngsters. "Bert was a jaygee with the flying hours of an ensign, but he was determined, and that mattered," McCampbell recalled.[4]

Another senior officer joining McCampbell's fleet of former instructors was Lieutenant James Francis Rigg. Age twenty-eight, Jimmy Rigg hailed from Saginaw, Michigan, and had attended the University of Michigan before beginning his naval aviation training in July 1937. Prewar, he served in VF-2, VF-7, and in *Wasp*'s VF-72. After the U.S. entered World War II, Rigg served as a flight instructor until September 1942, when he reported on board USS *Wolverine* (IX-64), a converted aircraft training carrier. Because of Rigg's seniority and tenure as an instructor, he became McCampbell's second-in-command, or executive officer (XO) of the fledgling squadron.

McCampbell and his early officers were slowly joined by other Air Group Fifteen staffers. It was not until September 15 that William M. Drane, the senior officer, or commander air group (CAG), assumed his duties. Commander Drane was from Clarksville, Tennessee, and served as the former skipper of Composite Squadron Nine (VC-9) on the escort carrier *Bogue* (CVE-9) until detached to join AG-15. With only eight officers originally present, Fighting Squadron Fifteen was formally placed into commission on September 1, as McCampbell read his orders. The ceremony was followed by a dinner at the Seaview Country Club in nearby Absecon. Formalities and cocktails concluded, recruiting and training for the new squadron began in earnest the next day.

Lieutenant George Duncan, a twenty-six-year-old from Washington State, was one of the original eight officers. He became the squadron's operations officer, placing him third in command of VF-15. Born and raised in Tacoma, he had been inspired to join the Navy by a cousin who was an academy graduate. Upon his own graduation from the academy in Annapolis in 1939, Duncan had served his obligatory postgraduation surface duty on the battleship USS *West Virginia* (BB-48). He entered flight training at Pensacola in September 1941 and earned his golden aviator's wings in February 1942.[5]

Duncan served in the aviation unit of the cruiser USS *Louisville* (CA-28) for the next year. His small contingent flew the vulnerable catapult-launched SOC Seagull scout biplanes. During the naval bombardment of the Japanese-held island of Kiska, he was flying air support when he encountered a Japanese float Zero. His SOC was badly holed by the enemy fighter and he received an Air Medal for nursing his aircraft back to *Louisville*. "I was glad to get back to the ship," Duncan recalled. "I knew I was a fighter pilot from then on."[6]

He would get his wish soon enough. During the fall of 1942, after a bout with malaria, he was sent stateside to enter fighter training. "It was the best thing that ever happened to me, because that got me off the ship," he recalled. Following his operational training in F4Fs in Florida, Duncan was assigned to McCampbell's new unit in late August.[7]

Following the commissioning, McCampbell and Jim Rigg flew to other bases to recruit men they believed had the guts to make their squadron great. As with any new naval aviation unit, the lion's share of their men would be newly commissioned ensigns fresh from flight school. But VF-15's senior leaders were able to score a handful of seasoned pilots. During one visit to NAS New York (Floyd Bennett Field in Brooklyn), they interviewed twenty-plus former Royal Canadian Air Force (RCAF) pilots for possible selection into their squadron and sent orders for three of them: George Carr, Jim Bruce, and Walter Lundin.

Ensign Lundin was a first-generation American from Queens, New York, whose parents had emigrated from Sweden. In high school, he was known as "Jake" and had served as the varsity quarterback until cartilage damage in his knee sidelined him from athletics. Determined to become a pilot, Jake went to Montreal in May 1941 and enlisted in the Royal Canadian Air Force.[8]

By April 29, 1942, Lundin had received his wings and commission in the RCAF. "In Canada at that time, only the top one-third of the class were commissioned," he recalled. Lundin and many other pilots were shipped over to England and then on to Northern Ireland for training in Wellington bombers.

Unsatisfied with the prospect of patrolling the Indian Ocean, Jake and others learned in the fall of 1942 that the U.S. military was accepting transferees from the RCAF. On November 9, he was commissioned by the U.S. Navy. Along with Bruce, Carr, and others, Lundin was ordered back to NAS Jacksonville on January 16, 1943. After a crash course in United States naval aviation training, the trio was commissioned as ensigns and received their golden wings.

A mixed bag of former Florida flight instructors and three former RCAF pilots, Fighting Fifteen quickly became a tight, well-blended family. "Friction among the various officer backgrounds was non-existent," Jake recalled. "Each and every one of us knew we could rely on one another completely."[9]

Duz Twelves, Jim Duffy, and Jigs Foltz each joined VF-15 at NAS Atlantic City.

Ensign Twelves arrived in early September along with his three closest flight training buddies: Jimmy Wakefield, Dave Johnson, and Red Rader. The F6F Hellcat was a new plane to this quartet, but Twelves was excited to make his first familiarization hop on September 8. One of the plane's most important features to him was the armor plating, including reinforcement behind the pilot's seat intended to deflect enemy machine-gun bullets in combat. "Leroy Grumman's theory was to make it strong, make it work, make it simple," he later stated. "Once you got used to flying the Hellcat, and got familiar with it, everything was right where it should be, and it worked."[10]

During his first ten days with VF-15, Twelves made seventeen flights. Each averaged only an hour and a half due to the number of new pilots and available planes. He quickly took a liking to this new fighter. "The Hellcat was a beautiful airplane to fly," Twelves said. "It had a tendency to forgive you, but it could kill you."

When Ensign Duffy reported in at Atlantic City, he was initially impressed to be met by former movie actor Bert Morris.[11]

Morris led the ensign to the flight line, where Duffy had his first view of the Hellcat, which towered above him. He couldn't believe it was a fighter plane: *It must be a bomber. It's huge!*

Duffy's buddy Jigs Foltz arrived days later as just "a boot-ass ensign flying tail-end to a lot of good pilots." At NAS Atlantic City, Foltz saw a familiar face: "Lo and behold, there was Jim Duffy, a friend with whom I'd attended junior college," Foltz recalled. Within the next two months, Duffy and Foltz would end up flying in the same four-plane division under Lieutenant John Strane.[12]

Before the men were able to fly the F6F, all new VF-15 pilots had to learn all of the cockpit controls well enough to identify them even while blindfolded. Upon their arrival, they were each given a F6F-3 handbook by squadron operations officer George Duncan and told to learn the manual thoroughly. After Duffy and Foltz passed the blindfold test and proved they had memorized the instrument panel, it was time to crank up the engine and take off. "No instructor in the back to bail you out if you messed up," recalled Duffy. He was anxious, feeling he was in over his head. As he raced down the runway, he knew this was no SNJ trainer. It took little effort to control the direction of this Grumman. "As far as I was concerned, the Hellcat was the Navy's best kept secret!"[13]

The new pilots joining Fighting Fifteen came from all over the country. Ensign Albert Slack had been a journeyman bricklayer working with his father in Lufkin, Texas, before the war broke out. In his youth, he had often walked miles to the local East Texas airport just to watch an old WACO biplane take off and fly around. After finishing high school in 1940, he went to work on a major hospital project in Temple, Texas. He and a buddy had saved up enough money to purchase a light, two-seater Aeronca Chief touring aircraft to fly the 170-mile distance to their project. "I'd take my brick tools and suitcase out there . . . work a week, and then, Friday afternoon, fly that thing home," Slack recalled.[14]

By the late summer of 1942, Slack decided he would take the naval air cadet test with a buddy, hoping to avoid becoming a drafted foot soldier. As he awaited his orders after being accepted, he took preflight courses at the University of Georgia. Slack was, admittedly, "a poor, ignorant country boy. . . . I really had to study . . . because I . . . lacked academic skills." But he finished in the middle of his class of 250 and moved on to primary training at NAS Dallas.[15]

By the time he finished primary, Slack was convinced that he wanted to be a fighter pilot. As his training progressed through Pensacola and Opa Locka, he flew SNJ trainers and old Brewster Buffalo fighter planes. When he arrived in Atlantic City in late September 1943, he was impressed with the modern F6F Hellcat. "That was like going from a T-Model to a Cadillac," Slack remembered. "I never had felt so much power the first time I took off."[16]

McCampbell had first checked out the new Grumman F6F Hellcat while teaching at Melbourne when he and another instructor flew F6Fs cross-country to NAS Glenview in Illinois for checkout landings on USS *Sable* (IX-81) and *Wolverine*. Dave found the Hellcat easy to fly and easy to land. "It was not like the Wildcat, which some people found very difficult to land, until I taught them better," he recalled. McCampbell coached his pilots against braking hard with either the starboard or port brake in order to prevent ground looping. "If you stayed off your brakes, you had plenty of directional control through your rudder."[17]

Grumman's New York factories ramped up production of the new plane, with a record-setting four hundred Hellcats built during November 1943. Larger in size and faster than Grumman's previous F4F Wildcat model, the F6F was also faster in level flight than the dreaded Japanese Mitsubishi A6M2 "Zero" fighter. At airspeeds below 230 mph (200 knots), the lighter Zero could outmaneuver a Hellcat with tighter turns. But the rugged F6F could withstand greater g-force pressure in prolonged dives and held maneuvering advantages over the Mitsubishi at higher speeds.[18]

Each Hellcat could carry 250 gallons of fuel in its internal tanks and could be fitted with an additional 150-gallon jettisonable external belly tank. The current model supplied to VF-15 was the F6F-3 variant, which sported six Colt-Browning .50-caliber machine guns, with four hundred rounds per gun. The F6F was equipped to carry either depth charges or various bombloads as great as a single 1,000-pound bomb. Powered by an eighteen-cylinder Pratt & Whitney R-2800 Double Wasp radial engine, the Hellcat had an operating range of more than a thousand miles of flight. Most new F6F-3s were painted an overall gloss sea-blue finish.

Unlike the Wildcat, the newest Hellcats built during late 1943 included an extra power-boost option. The Hellcat's throttle could be pushed more than 100 percent of the engine's normal rated power for a matter of minutes, during which time water injected into the intake air provided a temporary density/horsepower boost known as WEP (war emergency power) to the Pratt & Whitney engine. Dave McCampbell's Hellcat jockeys would come to love the water-injected boost of WEP in future dogfights.

The squadron's first operational loss came on September 18, during a scheduled tactics hop. Ensign Jimmy Wakefield was killed when his F6F crashed five miles northwest of New Gretna, New Jersey, during dive-bombing practice on field targets.

As one of Wakefield's flight school buddies, Duz Twelves was tasked with boxing up his personal belongings. Since he had met the young pilot's family previously, Twelves was also assigned to accompany the casket on the long train ride back to Colorado for the service. He was rattled when Mrs. Wakefield insisted that the casket be opened so she could say goodbye to her son.[19]

"No, you don't want to do that," Twelves said to the father, William Wakefield. "It was a very bad crash, and his remains do not look like you remember him."

For Duz, it was the hardest moment of his young aviation career. He finally convinced Wakefield's mother to leave the casket closed. It was a somber train ride back to Atlantic City. When Twelves returned to his squadron, he was saddened to learn that VF-15 had lost another young pilot on September 20. Ensign Donald Fred Hoffman, new to the squadron, had crashed while making his very first familiarization hop in a Navy SNJ-4 trainer.

These losses were offset by the volume of new pilots Dave McCampbell was receiving. By September 15, the squadron had grown to thirty officers. Two weeks later, the roster was filled out with forty-seven pilots and three ground officers, with the addition of Lieutenant (jg) John "Bob" Hoffman as the nonflying material officer.

Among the late-September arrivals was Lieutenant (jg) John Edmund Barry Jr. from Wilmington, North Carolina. Sporting a thick head of hair and an athletic build, he had earned his wings one year prior. During his prewar schooling, John had lettered in football and baseball while doubling as a cheerleader at the all-boys Belmont Abbey College. During his flight training and subsequent assignment as a flight instructor at NAS Corpus Christi, John remained in contact with a beautiful brunette from North Carolina named Olive Elizabeth Hennessee. By the time he received orders on September 6, 1943, to report to the commander, Naval Air Force Atlantic in Norfolk, the couple had become engaged.[20]

The next three weeks were a whirlwind for Barry. After a brief leave, he reported to NAS Norfolk in time to witness one of the deadliest noncombat disasters of the war. "Twenty-four depth charges blew up, wrecking parts of the Naval Air Station," he wrote to Olive. "Between fifty and a hundred sailors were killed, with more than 400 injured." John anxiously awaited orders to a fighter squadron that next week. They arrived on Thursday, September 23, just two days before his scheduled wedding to twenty-four-year-old Olive in Pinehurst, North Carolina.[21]

Following their Saturday wedding and reception, John and Olive loaded their belongings in his 1941 Hudson convertible. Their journey to NAS Atlantic City was broken by an overnight in Richmond, Virginia, where they spent their first night together in the Jefferson Hotel's honeymoon suite. They reached Atlantic City on Sunday evening and checked in at the Claridge Hotel. The following morning, September 27, Barry reported in to Lieutenant Commander Dave Mc-Campbell and VF-15. During his early checkouts, he was equally impressed with the squadron's new fighter and its most famous officer. "I could not ask for a better plane to fly," Barry recalled. "Wayne Morris the movie star is now starring in our squadron."[22]

Lieutenant John Barry was married two days prior to reporting to VF-15. Barry kept a detailed journal of his combat cruise with the squadron. JOHN BARRY III

By October 1, Barry was sporting two full bars on his shoulder scales to denote his promotion to full lieutenant. During the next six weeks of training, he would receive only one six-day leave to spend with his new wife, Olive. The rest of his time was consumed with aerial training, precision landing, machine-gun practice, and Hellcat tactics. Lieutenant Barry's early period with VF-15 found him attached as second section leader for the division led by Lieutenant Jack Ivey. Their four-plane fighter division also included former RCAF pilot George Carr from Bogalusa, Louisiana, and Ensign Joe Power. Rail-thin and slight in stature, Power hailed from Jacksonville, Florida, and would become Barry's regular wingman. During his time away from his wife, John Barry would write letters almost daily to Olive describing his daily routines. As a further log of his experiences, he kept a secret journal detailing his life as a fighter pilot in training.

As the weeks progressed, McCampbell and his senior officers pulled the pilots into regular divisions. Ensign Duffy was assigned as wingman to Lieutenant John Strane, whose division also included the second section of Ensigns Jigs Foltz and Warren "Red Bird" Clark from Canby, Minnesota.[23]

Upon his return from Colorado, Duz Twelves settled in as wingman for Lieutenant George Duncan. Their second section leader was Lieutenant (jg) William "Bud" Henning, a fun-loving Pennsylvania native who kept his own convertible on base for squadron use. Most of McCampbell's new division leaders were former naval aviation instructors or pilots who had previous fighter experience with other squadrons.

Among these was Virginian Lieutenant (jg) Mel Roach, who had flown with VF-5 on the carrier USS *Saratoga* (CV-3) during the August 1942 Guadalcanal offensive. After *Saratoga* was torpedoed and sent stateside for repairs, Roach and VF-5 served with the Cactus Air Force. By November, Roach had achieved two aerial kills against Japanese planes. His flight suit was hard pressed to contain the rotund aviator, but Roach was also solid in spirit. After ditching in October 1942, he had spent two days evading Japanese captors before he was rescued by a J2F flying boat. Recipient of a Distinguished Flying Cross (DFC) for his tenure on Guadalcanal, Mel Roach was a natural VF-15 division leader.[24]

Roach's division included two former RCAF pilots, Jake Lundin and his buddy Jim Bruce, plus two new ensigns, Norm Berree and Ken West. Fighting Fifteen was regularly assigned thirty-six fighter planes. Divided out, this allowed for nine regular four-plane divisions, or "combat teams." With forty-five aviators, McCampbell's squadron thus organized into teams of five—four pilots plus a spare per team, allowing one junior pilot to rotate in as needed.

Several of McCampbell's new division leaders had previous carrier experience. Lieutenant Edward "Ted" Overton, a graduate of Williams College, had served on the carrier *Wasp* with McCampbell in 1942 as an assistant gunnery officer. Following the sinking of *Wasp*, Overton had entered flight school in January 1943, and was assigned to VF-15 in October. Overton's professionalism and flight proficiency earned him high marks with his new skipper.

Fighting Fifteen's only bona fide "ace" pilot was Lieutenant (jg) John Carlos Cleves Symmes, who had graduated from the University of Pennsylvania in 1938 with an economics degree. A descendant of Colonel John Cleves Symmes of Revolutionary War fame, "Jack" Symmes left his pursuit of a Harvard Law School degree behind in September 1941 to enter naval flight training. Symmes was commissioned as an ensign in August 1942 and the following year flew combat in F4F-4 Wildcat fighters with VF-21 from Guadalcanal.

During June and July 1943, Symmes was credited with 5.5 aerial victories against Japanese "Zeke" (Zero) fighters and a "Betty" (Mitsubishi G4M) twin-engine bomber. In forty-three combat missions, he had earned a Distinguished Flying Cross and surpassed ace status—an honorary title for a pilot who had destroyed at least five enemy aircraft in aerial combat. One of Jack's VF-21 squadron mates from Guadalcanal, Ensign Charles Milton, was assigned to VF-15 as well. Milton, who hailed from the small town of Jasper, Florida, went by either his middle name, Baynard, or "Milt." An able pilot, he had survived two water landings in his F4F but had not achieved an enemy kill. Milton became second section leader for Symmes and would later lead his own division.

Milton's wingman was tall, dark-haired, athletic Ensign George Pigman. Navy life was in his blood. His father had been a Navy commander, and his grandfather, Rear Admiral George Wood Pigman, had attended the Naval Academy during the Civil War. Born in Washington, DC, in 1923, George attended Jesuit, the most prestigious Catholic high school in the New Orleans area. He had been a member of Jesuit's state championship basketball team. He left his studies at Tulane University to begin pilot training in 1942. Pigman had a great sense of humor and took little offense when Milton began referring to his wingman as "Porkchop."[25]

ANY GOOD FIGHTER SQUADRON had swagger, and a nickname worthy of its characters.

In between flights and ground training—a total of 4,926 hours on 3,544 sorties—the Hellcat pilots got to know one another and each man's colorful background. In the air, formal names and ranks were dispensed with in favor of radio call signs derived from personal characteristics or squadron nicknames. Duz Twelves and Jigs Foltz had already been tagged with monikers. Others, like George "Red" Rader, were nicknamed after their hair color or ancestry. Ensign Thorolf Thompson, being of European descent, was inevitably dubbed "Swede." Ensign Claude "Bud" Plant carried over his minor-league-baseball nickname.

The feisty squadron soon adopted the nickname "Satan's Playmates." A national contest was held for a squadron insignia, and the hands-down winner was cartoonist Milton Caniff of *Terry and the Pirates* fame. Caniff's graphic captured a dark Hellcat face with sharp teeth and flames blazing above golden aviator wings. "Satan's Playmates" patches were soon created from the new logo, and the pilots had them stitched on their leather flight jackets.[26]

McCampbell had his pilots read action reports from other fighter squadrons who had been up against Japanese planes, as well as an intelligence report on the flight capabilities of the Japanese Zero based on tests conducted on a Japanese fighter that had been seized in the Aleutians the previous year. Tough on his pilots during training, skipper McCampbell was equally tough on himself.[27]

Dashing Dave found it difficult to fall back into precise gunnery after his prolonged period as a landing signal officer and instructor. His F6F pilots were required to achieve at least a 10 percent hit ratio when firing on a target sleeve towed by another plane. The bullets in each pilot's plane were painted a different color so that hits on the sleeve could be counted once the tow plane landed. McCampbell initially scored only 8 percent on his best run. Lieutenants John Strane and George Duncan, wishing to keep their beloved skipper on the team, had their bullets painted the same color as McCampbell's for the next gunnery hop. When the two aircraft returned to the field, the maintenance crews recorded the skipper's gunnery score as 15 percent.[28]

On November 15, Satan's Playmates moved their unit and its planes from NAS Atlantic City south to Naval Auxiliary Air Station Pungo, near Norfolk, Virginia, a newly commissioned training field. McCampbell was pleased that his squadron had one field all to itself, alleviating the usual congestion found at other large air stations. The officers lived in long, army-style single-story barracks, each heated by a stove-furnace in the center of the room. "From the niceties of Atlantic City, we went to the basic necessities, the crude form of living," McCampbell recalled of Pungo. The only positive attribute he could find for their miserable living conditions was that his squadron would look forward to moving on board a fleet carrier as soon as possible.[29]

Pungo was an auxiliary airfield operating in conjunction with the larger NAS Norfolk base, which was still in the process of rebuilding after a horrific mishap. Lieutenant John Barry and Ensign Jigs Foltz—the latter briefly stationed at the Norfolk base before being assigned to VF-15—had been present on the morning of September 17, 1943, when the tragedy occurred. Foltz and other boot ensigns were just lining up for their first instructions when a massive explosion shook their building. Racing outside, Jigs was shocked by the carnage he witnessed.

A group of sailors had been tasked with moving 355-pound depth charges from a hangar to ready PBY Catalina anti-submarine patrol planes. The silver canisters, each the size of a garbage can, were being towed on trailers behind a truck toward the ready aircraft. En route, one of the canisters slipped from its perch, became wedged between the next cart in the train, and started creating sparks along the concrete. By the time the driver was flagged down, the depth charge and its 252 pounds of Torpex—an explosive element that extended the pulse of its shock wave with enough power to crack a submarine's hull—was smoking.

The canister exploded, igniting every bomb on the trolley and a nearby truck filled with aviation fuel. The ensuing blast punched a crater five feet deep in the concrete runway and sent a blast of fire up five hundred feet. The boom turned heads twenty miles away in the town of Suffolk. Thirty-three aircraft, nearby buildings, and more than two dozen personnel were lost in the massive explosions, which wounded more than two hundred others.

One of the aviation ordnance mechanics, William Chester "Chet" Owens, was just putting a chock under the wheel of an aircraft. "I was thrown 300 feet beyond a seaplane hangar," he recalled. "Twenty-six of my shipmates were killed right behind me. The Good Lord spared me." Owens spent the next two weeks in the hospital, recovering from three shrapnel wounds.[30]

After recuperating that winter, Owens learned of an opening within Fighting Fifteen. Owens went to the base and asked to see the skipper.

"Why do you want to be in my fighter squadron?" McCampbell asked.

"Sir, I would rather be killed by the Japs than my own shipmates," Owens stated.

Baffled, McCampbell listened to the sad story of the ordnance explosion at Norfolk that had devastated the young man's unit. McCampbell admired Owens's spirit and promised to secure papers for his transfer. McCampbell's mechanics and ordnancemen quickly developed as loyal a following for their skipper as the young pilots had. "Right away, all of us got the feeling that our skipper knew what he was doing and that we would be in good hands," aviation ordnanceman Elmer Cordray, a teenager from St. Louis, wrote in the secret diary he maintained.[31]

SKIPPER DAVE MCCAMPBELL worked hard during late November to bring his squadron into operational strength. He had received word that his unit would be part of a new air group slated for service on the carrier USS *Hornet* (CV-12), whose construction was almost complete. Fighting Fifteen would eventually be joined by Bombing Squadron Fifteen (VB-15) and Torpedo Squadron Fifteen (VT-15).

McCampbell demanded precise formation flying from his group. One morning, McCampbell ordered all thirty-six of his fighters into the air for what they dubbed a "group grope." Jim Duffy found himself flying in the rearmost position of the group, a position the pilots referred to as the "tail-end Charlie" slot. Duffy felt like he was on the end of a whip, making it very challenging to maintain proper airspeed and position within the

Fighting Fifteen (VF-15) in its first formal photo at NAS Norfolk, Virginia, in late 1943. Lt. Cdr. Dave McCampbell, the first squadron skipper, is seated in the front row, seventh from left. Front row, left to right: Lt. Arend Grothaus, Lt. (jg) Mel Roach, Lt. Bert Morris, Lt. John Barry, Lt. George Duncan, Lt. Joe O'Brien, Lt. Cdr. David McCampbell, Lt. Jim Rigg, Lt. Bob McReynolds, Lt. George Crittenden, Lt. John Strane, Ens. Jim Duffy, Lt. (jg) Gilbert, Lt. (jg) Alfred Jones, and Lt. (jg) John Symmes.   JOHN BARRY III

formation. "McCampbell would go to full throttle, back down to almost idle, and then back to full," he remembered. "By the time his inputs got back to me, I was practically falling out of the sky."[32]

Duffy pulled out a little wider from his division leader, John Strane. He hoped to give himself a little breathing room. It also helped to keep him in a reasonable position. Duffy's radio was apparently malfunctioning. As the squadron skipper continued to make wide turnouts and pull back in, Duffy continued to lag behind. Calls from McCampbell for him to close up were neither heard by the junior ensign nor acknowledged. "I think he had eyes in the back of his head!" Duffy recalled.

Annoyed, McCampbell finally did a big wingover (a steep, climbing turn) and pulled his F6F up alongside Ensign Duffy. The skipper shook his fist at Duffy and motioned for him to get back into proper position. "I never moved faster as I slid back in," he later related. Back on the ground, McCampbell never said a word about the incident. His point had been made, and Duffy never straggled out of position again. In hindsight, he felt Dave McCampbell was fair and understanding. But failure to follow direction was not tolerated. "If you screwed up, you had a fair chance of getting an ass-chewing," said Duffy. "He was eager to get the squadron in the best possible shape for combat in the Pacific."[33]

Two of McCampbell's pilots, Ensigns Roy Nall and Art Singer, attended photographic training school to learn the art of aerial photography. Fighting Fifteen had been assigned a pair of F6F-3P ("photo") variants, Hellcats equipped with a British-built F24 camera mounted in the rear fuselage just behind the wing for photoreconnaissance. Images obtained from photo hops would later be vital intelligence sources for damage assessment of strikes and for strip mapping of lesser-known Japanese-held islands. Dubbed "Photo Joe" missions, these flights would require precise, smooth aircraft operation while Singer and Nall used cockpit-mounted timers to trigger their cameras to take a series of images.

On November 29, a *Hornet* commissioning party was held. The after-party in the Portsmouth Navy Yard officers' club was recorded in VF-15's history as "the most successful party in squadron annals."[34]

John Barry and his wife of two months, Olive, enjoyed touring the new aircraft carrier. They had settled into a thirteen-bedroom rented house in Virginia Beach. During their free time, when John was not training, they often spent time with other married couples from VF-15, including Ted and Nonnie Overton and George and Ann Crittenden. On December 20, VF-15's pilots were given leave until the end of the year to enjoy the holidays. John and Olive departed for Pinehurst, North Carolina, for a carefree period with their families.[35]

Returning to Virginia Beach on December 28, John and Olive rang in the New Year with a celebration that evening at the NAS Norfolk officers' club with the Crittendens, the Overtons, and other senior pilots like Jim Rigg and Jack Ivey. Fighting Fifteen's enlisted men also enjoyed their R & R time during the holidays, even if some wished to be with their families on a more permanent basis. Deployment was coming soon. "'White Christmas' and 'I'll Be Home for Christmas' played havoc on our morale," mechanic Elmer Cordray noted of the popular holiday tunes filling the airwaves.[36]

———

STARTING ON JANUARY 1, 1944, Air Group Fifteen began a ten-day period of more intensive flight training and multi-squadron group exercises. These included more gunnery practice, weather hops, and additional carrier landing practice off the coast of Norfolk.

On January 7, Air Group Commander Bill Drane made the first landing on *Hornet* for AG-15. Fighting Fifteen skipper Dave McCampbell took the chance on board ship to call on *Hornet's* new skipper, Captain Miles Browning. During their first meeting, McCampbell was already aware of the tense relationship that existed between Browning and key members of his air group. A forty-six-year-old Annapolis graduate, Browning was a "brown shoe," a naval aviator who had earned his wings in 1924 and had first served on the carrier USS *Langley* (CV-1). And the airman expected more leniency from a fellow brown shoe, as opposed to a surface fleet commander who wore the traditional black shoes with dress uniform. But Browning, who had commanded *Langley's* air group and served as a flight instructor, was known for his harsh mannerisms, snarling orders, and micromanagement of everyone's business.

During the early months of war in 1942, Browning had served as chief of staff to Admiral William Frederick "Bull" Halsey, and he was promoted to captain for his intelligence in directing operations. With Halsey sidelined with an ailment during the pivotal Battle of Midway, Browning helped direct the victory. As technically brilliant as he was, Browning was equally irritating, prone to insulting behavior. He was temperamental, disrespectful, and given to outbursts when drinking. Secretary of the Navy Frank Knox advised Halsey to dispose of his chief of staff for his disrespectful behavior, but the admiral resisted. Admiral Ernest King, the chief of naval operations, finally tempted Browning away from Halsey by offering him command of the new carrier *Hornet*.[37]

During their first meeting, Browning was quick to instruct McCampbell that his Hellcats were not to be trained in dive-bombing. "But I knew they were being used for that out in the Pacific to a certain extent, so I went ahead anyway," McCampbell later admitted. Browning was soon despised by nearly all of Air Group Fifteen. "He was really a mean, wild man," recalled George Duncan. "The whole ship was scared to death of him. He trained hard. He didn't want to have any liberty or anything. He wanted to get the ship out there and into the war."[38]

Hornet began loading stores on January 13 in Norfolk and sortied two days later for her two-week shakedown cruise near Bermuda. What should have been a golden opportunity to shape out the new Air Group Fifteen proved to be a period filled with challenges that would result in a shake-up within the air group's command.

It was a bitterly cold day as wives and girlfriends stood on the dock waving goodbye. Nonnie Overton and Ann Crittenden were among them. John Barry wrote a letter to his wife that evening: "This is our first night apart since our marriage and I do not like it one bit. It was an ugly day to start a cruise."[39]

The weather became so foul that there was no flying on January 16 or 17. Ensign Jim Duffy's quarters were in "Boys' Town," a multi-bunk stateroom for many of the most junior pilots. With little else to do during the storm, he passed his downtime playing bridge and Ping-Pong.

When flight duty resumed, Air Group Fifteen got off to a rough start. CAG Bill Drane had been remiss in fully training all of his squadrons together as a team, and their lack of carrier operation experience quickly gave Captain Browning reason to distrust Drane. The largest problem among his air group proved to be the pilots and aircraft of VB-15, under Lieutenant Commander Irvin L. "Ike" Dew, a U.S. Naval Academy classmate of Dave McCampbell. His pilots had flown SNJ trainers and SBD Dauntless dive-bombers before receiving their new SB2C Helldivers. When their air operations commenced on *Hornet*, most VB-15 pilots had no more than fifteen flight hours in the SB2C, which they had only received on December 20. Throughout the shakedown cruise, the new dive-bombers suffered tail-hook failures and a number of crashes.

On January 19, an Avenger* ran into a five-inch gun mount upon landing, shearing off a wing. No sooner had the deck crew cleared this mess than an F6F went into the catwalk and caused another forty-five-minute

---

* The Grumman TBF and the General Motors TBM are both designations for the same aircraft, the Avenger torpedo bomber.

delay. John Barry wrote, "Every time that planes return to the carrier to land, everyone dashes up to watch the landings, as accidents are frequent and freakish." The bridge area above the flight deck became known as "Vulture's Row," a popular place for the pilots not making landings to watch how their comrades fared. Barry noted a number of blown tires as pilots landed heavily on the wheels.[40]

In late January, a young new VB-15 ensign drowned when he was forced to make a water landing due to plane difficulties. Two other SB2Cs suffered barrier crashes that day. The following day, Ensign Andrew Peterson and his radioman were killed when their Helldiver failed to recover from a dive during a simulated attack on the carrier. Within the next three days, three other SB2Cs suffered deck crashes, further irritating Captain Browning.[41]

Jim Duffy of VF-15, who witnessed many of these mishaps, was outraged. "You couldn't have gotten me to fly one of those airplanes with a direct order," he recalled. George Duncan wondered how many Helldivers would survive the cruise. "We were losing one a day," he recalled.[42]

McCampbell's fighter squadron had its own share of mishaps during the shakedown cruise. On January 22, John Barry noted in his diary: "One of the fighters had a tail-hook pull out when he landed. The plane hit the barrier and broke in half." On January 23, Ensign Red Bird Clark of VF-15 was forced down into the water astern of Hornet. Clark was scooped from the ocean by the plane guard destroyer USS Forrest (DD-461) and was returned to his carrier the following morning during refueling. On January 29, Ensign Ken West swerved off Hornet's port side after a run of 160 feet on takeoff. His F6F spun in on its port wing at low altitude. West was picked up by the destroyer Forrest with only minor injuries and was returned to his carrier a half hour later.[43]

The string of crashes frustrated Miles Browning. He had instructed McCampbell and other squadron commanders that he wanted his planes to use no more than four hundred feet of the flight deck—less than half of the 844 feet—for takeoffs. But the heavy and underpowered SB2C Helldivers were suffering.

"What the hell's going on here?" Browning demanded. "Why are these dive-bombers hitting the water as soon as they take off?"[44]

"From my experiences as a landing signal officer on the *Wasp*, if we found that happening, we would give them more 'run' down the deck," McCampbell replied.

He recommended that Browning ease up on the four-hundred-foot order and allow them at least another hundred feet of takeoff space. With this issue resolved, the shakedown cruise continued. *Hornet* returned to Norfolk on January 31, but Captain Browning was not in good spirits. His new air group was struggling, and he was not about to shoulder the blame for their string of losses. He planned to make a point.

Changes were in store for Air Group Fifteen.

FOUR

CAST ASHORE

John Barry's twenty-seventh birthday on February 1, 1944, was spent on board *Hornet* with squadron duty while his comrades went ashore. All damaged Hellcats that could not be repaired were removed as the carrier slipped into the Norfolk Navy Yard for post-shakedown repairs and alterations during the first week of February. One day later, John's wife, Olive, picked him up to celebrate his birthday by sharing the news that they were expecting their first child. She joked that it would be twins, but John simply hoped for a boy.[1]

Captain Browning used his carrier's repair time to work the chopping block, taking out his frustrations against Air Group Fifteen's poor showing the previous two weeks. First to go was Commander Bill Drane. Then the squadrons were ordered to tighten up their numbers in preparation for embarking on the ship, resulting in VT-15 cutting two of its Avenger pilots to bring the flying roster to an even two dozen TBM pilots. Dave McCampbell was tasked with cutting five of his Satan's Playmates fighter pilots to achieve Captain Browning's quota.

He opted to let his squadron make the decision in the form of a secret ballot, assuming they would naturally cut those who were most difficult to get along with. "Every pilot got to vote who they'd like to go to combat with the most," McCampbell remembered. "Everybody was given a sheet of paper with a roster on it." Although he held the final decision, Dave was pleased to find his officers to be very much in sync on their thoughts. Five pilots were issued new orders without any commotion.[2]

In the meantime, Browning detached VB-15 skipper Ike Dew, who had been too ill even to participate in flight duties during the carrier's shakedown cruise. On February 8, Captain Browning promoted Lieutenant Commander Dave McCampbell to CAG, commander of all Air Group Fifteen squadrons. Although happy in his new role, he was immediately challenged with finding a replacement for Ike Dew.

"Get me a new bombing squadron commander," said Browning.[3]

McCampbell first suggested Lieutenant Commander Arthur Giesser, who was training dive-bomber pilots on the East Coast. When Giesser politely declined the offer, Browning returned to his new CAG and asked for other choices. The only other man that came to mind for McCampbell was Lieutenant Commander James Haile Mini, whom he remembered as being on the Naval Academy football team during his early years in Annapolis. Mini, a former dive-bomber pilot with squadrons on the carriers *Saratoga* and *Ranger*, was pulled from his position at NAS Quonset Point in Rhode Island.

The skipper of VT-15 was Lieutenant Commander Valdemar Greene Lambert, from Lake Charles, Louisiana. A Naval Academy graduate and an experienced naval flight instructor, Lambert was known to his friends simply as "VeeGee" in short for his initials. During his six weeks in command of VT-15, Lambert had thus far proven himself to be an able skipper in McCampbell's eyes.

McCampbell's own VF-15 was in turn delivered a new skipper in the form of Lieutenant Commander Charles Walter Brewer. Hailing from Clinton, Oklahoma, Charlie Brewer was a 1935 Naval Academy graduate. The son of a banker, he was tall, with sandy hair and a sincere disposition. After two years of surface duty, he went through flight training and was assigned as a fighter pilot with VF-4 on the carrier *Ranger* in 1937. Promoted to lieutenant commander on March 1, 1943, Brewer commanded composite squadron VC-13 on board the escort carrier USS *Core* (CVE-13). He twice earned the Distinguished Flying Cross for strafing attacks on German U-boats made in conjunction with dive-bombers from *Core*'s air group.

While Charlie Brewer was a newcomer to VF-15, he was quickly ac-

cepted by virtue of his command experience. "He was a good guy," Mc-
Campbell recalled. "He was well prepared." Ensign Jim Duffy found
confidence in Brewer's gunnery skills. With scores that often reflected 30
percent efficiency, Duffy considered his new skipper to be the best shot in
the squadron.[4]

McCampbell had several key officers as part of his CAG team to support his work. Lieutenant Paul "Doc" Maness would continue as the flight
surgeon for all squadrons, and Lieutenant John Smith Miller served as the
nonflying ACIO for the air group. Although most air group commanders
in early 1944 opted to fly TBM torpedo bombers, McCampbell was an exception. He was simply more comfortable flying the Hellcat than one of
the lumbering "turkeys" of the torpedo squadron. "It was a good plane,
but it didn't have the performance that the fighter did," he reasoned. In
time, his strategy of flying a fighter as CAG would be adopted by other
group commanders.[5]

Hornet's post-shakedown repairs were completed by February 11, and
the next three days were spent loading ammunition, stores, aircraft, and
her revamped air group. She sortied with a pair of destroyers from the
East Coast on February 14, bound for Cristóbal in the Panama Canal
Zone, and ultimately to the Pacific theater of operations.

New air group commander Dave McCampbell found one of his first
tasks to be that of qualifying his new VB-15 skipper, Jim Mini, in SB2C
carrier landings. Although he had spent his previous months training
dive-bomber pilots in the SBD Dauntless, Mini had no experience in the
newer Helldiver variant. He arrived on board *Hornet* just hours before
she sailed. "We'd had no chance to give him training on the field," Mc-
Campbell recalled. "The first two landings he made, he cracked up,
crashed the barrier."[6]

With his former experience as an LSO, Dave coached Mini on his mistakes.

"You're holding the plane off," he advised. "Come on in. The signal officer will put you in a good position. Just relax on the stick, let the nose
drop down, and kind of ease back on it when you actually touch down,
and you'll be all right." McCampbell was pleased that his new VB skipper
soon improved on his landings.

The next evening, all air operations were shut down on *Hornet* as her little task group encountered a nasty storm near Cape Hatteras. One SB2C was blown overboard, and five others were so severely damaged that they would require major overhauls. Lieutenant George Duncan received notice en route to Panama that his wife had given birth to their first son on February 15. During his time ashore at Panama, he bought several boxes of cigars.[7]

As *Hornet* approached the Canal Zone, her air group was flown ashore to New France Field to lighten the ship's weight for the transit. During the morning of February 18, as *Hornet* and her escort destroyers began the transit of the Panama Canal locks, McCampbell's Air Group Fifteen conducted a simulated attack mission against the Gatun locks and dams of the canal. The air group began launching at 0800 in clear weather and the squadrons were effectively rendezvoused within a half hour. As the planes approached their target area, they were "intercepted" by a dozen P-39 fighters acting as enemy aircraft.[8]

Lieutenant Commander Brewer, Bert Morris, and Jack Ivey led three divisions of VF-15 to escort eight of VeeGee Lambert's Avengers of the low bombing group, with ACIO Bob McReynolds flying passenger in one of the TBMs. CAG Dave McCampbell, Ted Overton, Lieutenant John Collins, and George Duncan led another four divisions of fighters to escort the Helldivers. Skipper Brewer's wingman, Ensign Otus Garwood Lippincott Jr., began maneuvering against one of the P-39s. His Hellcat No. 13 went into a stall and others watched in horror as his plane crashed into the jungle.

By the evening of February 19, *Hornet* had reached Balboa, where there was evening liberty before the ship sortied into the Pacific. Air Group Fifteen landed back on board *Hornet* as she departed Balboa the next day. Unfortunately for new air group commander McCampbell, VB-15's woes continued during the week of transit northwest toward San Diego. One Helldiver was damaged in a barrier crash, and three SB2Cs and three men were lost to other operational mishaps.

The continued mishaps and personnel losses further infuriated Captain Browning. By the time *Hornet* arrived in San Diego on February 27, he was reaching the breaking point. His carrier was loaded with provisions and a large detachment of Marine fliers and ground personnel before sailing for the Hawaiian Islands on February 29. On March 4, Lieutenant John Barry was topside as his carrier eased up the channel into Pearl Harbor. He listened to the lofting strains of "Aloha" from the base band and marveled at the enormous size of the U.S. Pacific Fleet anchored around Ford Island. But *Hornet*'s skipper had other thoughts on his mind. Scuttlebutt around the air group had it that Miles Browning planned to boot his air group off *Hornet*. Tensions were high between Dave McCampbell and Browning. Lieutenant George Duncan was present for one exchange between his CAG and the *Hornet* skipper.

"I'm glad your group won't be on my ship any longer," Browning said.[9]

"We're damned glad to get off!" McCampbell snapped.

Duncan believed Browning removed the entire air group based largely on the continued poor performance of Bombing Group Fifteen. In their place, Air Group Two reported on board *Hornet* and took over the aircraft of AG-15. Being cast ashore without a ship and minus the planes they had worked so hard to break in was a major blow to McCampbell. "Captain Browning felt that they weren't well trained and prepared to go into combat," he recalled.[10]

McCAMPBELL RECEIVED WORD that Air Group Fifteen would be sent temporarily to NAS Kaneohe Bay on Oahu for extended training. Aviation chief ordnanceman Alfred Henry Mason, Elmer Cordray, and several other VF-15 mechanics loaded the squadron's equipment onto army trucks for the cross-island journey.[11]

In the interim, John Barry, Jim Rigg, and Jack Ivey made the most of their free time. Borrowing a vehicle, they drove over Mount Pali to sightsee around Honolulu. Aside from daily flights from Kaneohe Bay, the trio was free to stop for drinks at Trader Vic's and visit the Royal Hawaiian Hotel. By March 10, orders were received that Air Group Fifteen would be moved to NAS Pu'unene on Maui for its extended training in the Hawaiian Islands.

For Barry, Rigg, Ivey, and the majority of McCampbell's pilots, this required an interisland flight from Kaneohe Bay to Maui. They were the fortunate ones. Fighting Fifteen's enlisted men, along with ACIOs John

Miller and Bob Hoffman, were loaded onto the seaplane tender USS *Swan* (AVP-7) for seaborne transport to their new island base. Without enough F6Fs for every pilot assigned to the squadron, Jim Duffy and eight other fighter pilots endured the *Swan* voyage with squadron gear piled high on the vessel's fantail.

Swan reached Kahului Harbor on the morning of March 11, and the process of moving gear and personnel to NAS Pu'unene commenced. McCampbell's air group was destined to spend the next six weeks at this remote air base, which had just been vacated by outgoing Air Group Eight. NAS Pu'unene was only a year old, constructed in cane fields leased from the Hawaiian Commercial & Sugar Company.

The first week was all business at Pu'unene, filled with numerous training flights. By the second week, Commander McCampbell relaxed the pressure enough to issue two-day passes for his men so they could explore the island. In between ground school and intensive daily flight training, the pilots and their enlisted airmen would make the most of their new tropical home. Evening life at Pu'unene included the base officers' club, movies, or the chance to venture to the club at nearby NAS Kahului. Others frequented the nearby town of Wailuku for shopping and its bistros.

Back at base, the bachelor officers' quarters at Pu'unene included small private rooms for each pilot, each with a small desk. Lieutenant Barry spent most evenings dashing off letters to his wife amid the blaring radios and swarms of mosquitoes that infiltrated his new quarters. His new routine became morning and early-afternoon flights, followed by exercise in the base gym and two hours of downtime from 1600 to 1800 in the base officers' club. Many evenings, he found himself playing bridge with fellow pilots Jim Rigg, Ted Overton, and George Crittenden.[12]

Outside of training time, VF-15's pilots made the most of their time on Maui. One of the squadron's highlights involved dinner parties held at the mountain homestead of one of the island's wealthier locals, Countess Alexa von Tempsky Zabriskie, at her estate high on the slopes of nearby Mount Haleakalā. John Barry and seven VF-15 comrades were invited to a meal on March 26. Afterward, Barry wrote to wife, Olive, that the countess was so charming that she "could almost make you think you were the host and she the guest. She entertains only naval aviator officers. Admiral Nimitz has been her guest on numerous occasions."[13]

Mount Haleakalā, a dormant volcano whose tallest peak pierced the clouds at more than 10,000 feet, was also a popular hiking spot for Barry and many others from his squadron. Station wagons could be checked out from the base transportation pool for sightseeing. Twenty-three-year-old Ensign James Bare—a former Eagle Scout who hailed from rural Wetumka, Oklahoma, and was known by his middle name, Doyle—was popular due to his personal camera. He documented much of VF-15's time on Maui. Bare snapped group photos with XO Jim Rigg and his own division mates—Jack Ivey, Red Rader, Dave Johnson—in their leather flight jackets on top of the world among the clouds.

As new planes were broken in, VF-15 received two new F6F-3P Hellcats. McCampbell decided he needed a third pilot to help rotate the duties with the two photoreconnaissance Hellcats when the squadron got into the combat zone. Art Singer and Roy Nall had already undergone special training, so Ensign Jigs Foltz volunteered and was put through a crash course at Barbers Point to be the third "Photo Joe" pilot. Jigs quickly mastered the process and his cool cartography skills were appreciated. "He was the best photo pilot we had," George Duncan later said of Foltz.[14]

One of the drills that McCampbell worked on at Pu'unene was simulated night carrier landings on the fields. As a former landing signal officer, he conducted these until he was pleased with the performance of his unit. Other drills, known as "group gropes," involved blended flight with aircraft from the three main squadrons going out to make dive-bombing attacks on the island of Kaho'olawe. There were minor mishaps along the way. Ensign Tom Tarr made a forced landing in the ocean when he had engine trouble, but he was picked up uninjured.[15]

The first fatality for Fighting Fifteen's Maui training came on March 12. The squadron was conducting a battle exercise in which some Hellcat divisions were caught in a mock attack by an "enemy" team of other divisions. Duz Twelves, flying wing on George Duncan, was in one of the divisions attacked by the other group. As the "enemy" F6Fs bounced their formation, Duz and Duncan went into a defensive maneuver. Tragedy ensued as their second section, Lieutenant Stretch Grothaus and Ensign Bob Stime, attempted to do the same.

The right wing of Grothaus's Hellcat clipped the horizontal stabilizer of Stime's F6F. Grothaus's Hellcat spun out of control and crashed into the ocean in flames, leaving only an oil slick on the water. Stime's plane was relatively undamaged and he was able to return to base. No blame was assigned to either pilot, but it was a costly loss.

By March 14, VF-15 had been joined at NAS Pu'unene by both VB-15 and VT-15. Jim Mini's dive-bomber group benefited greatly during the next month on Maui. Although there were mishaps among the SB2C pilots, there were no fatalities. The divisions of Satan's Playmates became solid, and the five pilots assigned to each became like family. New skipper Charlie Brewer took on Ensign Dick Fowler as his regular wingman, and CAG Dave McCampbell settled on Ensign Wesley Burnam as his regular slot man. Having studied at Texas Christian University in the Fort Worth metroplex before the war, Burnam was a popular member of his squadron and a solid wingman for the air group commander.

For his part, Commander McCampbell used the flight time at NAS Pu'unene to sharpen his gunnery skills. Squadron mates no longer needed to sneakily assist his scoring. During one gunnery flight, he led two divisions against an eighteen-foot canvas target sleeve pulled by a tow plane. During his first overhead run, the CAG neatly laced the pennant with so many bullets that he cut it in half. He called to Lieutenant (jg) Roy Rushing over the radio with a hearty laugh. "Roy, take charge," he ordered. "I can't do any better than that."[16]

Fighting Fifteen's second month of training on Maui was marred by another flight tragedy. On April 1, Ensign George Francis Butler from Philadelphia was killed when his plane crashed on the ground immediately following a predawn takeoff at 0554 at NAS Pu'unene. His engine cut out just after he became airborne and his fighter slammed into a sugarcane field. John Barry, who served as a pallbearer at Butler's funeral, was greatly troubled by this loss and that of Stretch Grothaus just weeks before. "The death of our pilots left me in a very depressive mood which found me fearing death," he confided in his journal.[17]

Due to the loss of Butler and Grothaus, VF-15 received two replacement pilots at Maui—Ensigns Len Spencer Hamblin and Clarence Alvin Borley. Hamblin was one of three brothers from Wyoming who had all entered the service to become fighter pilots. Hailing from ranchlands near Yakima, Washington, Borley had a fascination with flight that stemmed from two events: his father taking him as a kid to watch barnstormers, and watching the summer 1941 Errol Flynn movie *Dive Bomber*. Nicknamed "Spike" by his fellow aviators, Borley finished his carrier flight training at NAS Willow Grove, Pennsylvania, before being shipped to Hawaii as part of the replacement pilot pool.[18]

At age nineteen, Ensign Borley was the youngest member of VF-15. He was assigned as the fifth pilot for Lieutenant Rigg's division, while Hamblin was assigned to Lieutenant John Collins. The next two weeks of training progressed without further serious accidents, save a sprained ankle suffered by Lieutenant Commander Brewer during a squadron softball game at the base. On April 19, Brewer and McCampbell gathered the officers of VF-15 for a squadron photo beside one of their Hellcats. John Barry arrived just in time, fresh from a swim in the ocean and three sets of doubles tennis with Ted Overton, "Critt" Crittenden, and Jim Rigg. Barry's only regret with the photo session was that it negated his planned afternoon of body-surfing on the local Maui beach during his day off.[19]

The following day, McCampbell passed the word that Air Group Fifteen had finally been assigned to an incoming new carrier, *Essex*. Commissioned on December 31, 1942, the carrier had entered Pacific service in May 1943. Most recently, her air group had participated in raids on Truk, Saipan, Tinian, and Guam in February. *Essex* had then gone to San Francisco for an overhaul and was just returning to Hawaii to begin her next war cruise.

On April 24, *Essex* departed Pearl Harbor for a three-day training cruise with her new air group conducted in company with the light carrier USS *San Jacinto* (CVL-30) and her Air Group Fifty-One. Dave McCampbell was familiar with *Essex*'s skipper, Captain Ralph Ofstie, a 1918 Naval Academy graduate, former fighter squadron commander, and most recently staffer for Admiral Chester Nimitz. In his first meeting with Ofstie, McCampbell discussed expectations for his air group. Unlike

VF-15 squadron photo, taken at NAS Pu'unene on Maui on April 19, 1944.
Back row, left to right: George Crittenden, John Strane, John Barry,* Joe O'Brien, George Duncan, Jim Rigg, Ted Overton, Charlie Brewer,* David McCampbell, Robert Stearns,* John Collins, John Ivey,* Bert Morris, and Mel Roach.*
Second row, left to right: Baynard Milton, Kenneth Flinn,* Jim Bruce,* Dick Fowler, Leo Kenney,* Roy Bruninghaus, Carleton White, John Symmes, George Carr, Jake Lundin, John Hoffman, and Claude Plant.*
Third row, left to right: Wesley Burnam,* Jim Duffy, Dave Johnson,* Thorolf Thompson,* Norm Berree, Wendell Twelves, Ken West, Bill Henning,* George Rader,* Alfred Jones,* Clarence Borley, and Art Singer.
Front row, left to right: Tom Tarr,* Bob Johnson, Al Slack, Robert Stime, Warren Clark, Doyle Bare, George Pigman, Roy Rushing, Ed Mellon, and Joe Power.*
* Indicates a pilot killed or taken as a POW during VF-15's tour of duty.   JOHN BARRY III

Miles Browning, who had inflicted harsh treatment on the air group, Ofstie had only one main concern for McCampbell's aviators: he expected them to utilize strict radio discipline, using open-air communication only when absolutely essential.[20]

McCampbell had an immediate feeling of respect for his new carrier's senior officers. The newly appointed *Essex* air officer, Commander David L. McDonald, was already an old friend. The two had known each other in Florida during their time of operational pilot training at NAS Pensacola.

Air Group Fifteen made its first landings on their new home carrier on April 25. "Landing aboard a carrier has not lost any of [its] zest or thrill," John Barry wrote to his wife. Barry was assigned a two-man stateroom in "Officers' Country" with Lieutenant John Collins, the same division leader he had roomed with on *Hornet* months earlier. Right away, Barry felt that *Essex* was a smoother-operating ship and that his squadron was greatly improved in its efficiency.[21]

Fighting Fifteen's pilots treated their second chance at carrier operation seriously. Having been cast ashore on Maui by Captain Browning, they had little desire to disappoint their new skipper, Captain Ofstie.

During the brief training cruise on *Essex*, Dave McCampbell's air group conducted both day and night flight operations. Air Group Fifteen now sported a brand-new contingent: a six-plane night fighter Hellcat unit. Under the command of Lieutenant Commander Robert M. Freeman, Night Fighter Squadron Seventy-Seven, or VF(N)-77, had been formed on December 1, 1943. During its early training in January 1944, Freeman's Hellcats were installed with new AIA aerial radar devices. By the end of February, his unit included thirty-two officers and fifty-nine enlisted men, utilizing both F6Fs and a six-plane detachment of radar-equipped TBMs.[22]

During March, VF(N)-77 was transported to Oahu. Once deemed ready for Pacific service, Bob Freeman's squadron, known as the "Wild Cats," was broken up for deployment on several carriers. Detachment B was assigned to the new USS *Yorktown* (CV-10), Detachment C to the new carrier USS *Wasp* (CV-18), and Detachment A, or Headquarters Detachment, to *Essex*.

Freeman's "bat men" took to the skies long after dark in late April to practice night interceptions via radar to prove their value to McCampbell and the *Essex* air group. The unit included its own night fighter director officer (FDO), Lieutenant Harold Seigler; radar officer Lieutenant Sam Lundquist; and a nonflying ACIO, Lieutenant Inman Brandon. Night fighter contingents were new to the Pacific carrier fleet, and would become a mainstay for U.S. carrier operations.

To make room for the new night Hellcat detachment, CAG McCampbell and his air officer, Dave McDonald, made changes. Jim Mini's VB-15 was downsized from thirty-six to thirty Helldivers on *Essex*, requiring a cut of two pilot officers. By the completion of its first training cruise on its new carrier, Air Group Fifteen's composition was as follows:

Air Group Fifteen, USS *Essex*

April 29, 1944

Unit	Commander	No. Pilots	No. Planes
CAG-15	Cdr. David McCampbell	1	1 F6F-3
VF-15	Cdr. Charles W. Brewer	46	2 F6F-3Ps, 34 F6F-3s
VB-15	Lt. Cdr. James H. Mini	43	30 SB2C-1Cs
VT-15	Lt. Cdr. Valdemar G. Lambert	26	18 TBF-1Cs and TBM-1Cs
VF(N)-77	Lt. Cdr. Robert M. Freeman	6	6 F6F-3Ns

Upon return to Pearl Harbor, *Essex* began loading stores for the war zone. The pilots of VF-15 made the most of their final days in Hawaii that afternoon. At the "O Club," Jim Rigg and George Duncan bought numerous rounds of drinks for their comrades to celebrate their dual promotions to lieutenant commander. John Barry for one felt the effects of a few too many Tom Collinses before the afternoon's celebration was complete.[23]

On May 2, the final day before departing Pearl Harbor, some of VF-15's division and section leaders adorned their Hellcats with nicknames. Barry had *Olive* painted on the sides of his fuselage near the cockpit of Hellcat No. 7 in honor of his pregnant wife. Former movie star Lieutenant Bert Morris choose to paint the name *Galahad* on his F6F in reference to his starring role in the film *Kid Galahad*. Duz Twelves and his plane captain, Aviation Machinist's Mate 2nd Class Victor W. Lain, had *Lady La Rhea* painted on their F6F for Twelves's fiancée. Bill "Bud" Henning had *Little Duchess* applied to his fighter, and air group commander Dave McCampbell's personal Hellcat was painted with the nickname *Monsoon Maiden*.

Thus far in World War II, Army Air Corps pilots had received greater press coverage than their Navy counterparts for their aerial victories against Japanese navy and army combatants. The Army's air wing had a long-running race to find the first pilot who could break World War I ace Eddie Rickenbacker's long-held record of twenty-six kills. In late 1942, Rickenbacker had even offered a case of Scotch to the first pilot who could surpass him. Stateside newspapers were filled regularly with the latest news on the "ace chase."

First to match Rickenbacker's record was Marine captain Joe Foss of VMF-121. The World War II "ace of aces" record was tied on January 3, 1944, by Major Gregory "Pappy" Boyington, skipper of the famed "Black Sheep" Corsair squadron VMF-214. But on the day he tied with Rickenbacker and Foss, Boyington was shot down near Rabaul. The Black Sheep skipper would also earn the Medal of Honor, but he spent the remainder of the war in Japanese POW camps. Then, on April 12, 1944, over Hollandia, Major Richard Bong reached twenty-seven kills and became the U.S. military's new ace of aces.[24]

Within the U.S. Navy, its pilots were nowhere close to surpassing Eddie Rickenbacker or Dick Bong as of April 1944. By the beginning of 1944, only twenty-seven pilots had even achieved ace status. Those numbers would increase dramatically in a year that saw greater numbers of carriers entering the Pacific offensive.[25]

The first carrier raids on the Japanese base of Truk Atoll proved to be very productive against Japanese aircraft. One of Dave McCampbell's former flight school students, Alex Vraciu, made four kills, raising his overall tally to nine. On the same day, Hamilton McWhorter became the first Navy pilot to achieve ten kills (double ace) while flying the Hellcat. Just a month prior, Donald Eugene Runyon had become the Navy's first double ace on January 4, 1944, with his kills coming in both F4F Wildcats and F6F Hellcats. By early February, two land-based Navy pilots, Lieutenant Commander John Thomas Blackburn and Lieutenant (jg) Ira Kepford, had reached double-kill figures while flying F4U Corsairs with VF-17.[26]

Many VF-15 pilots had the itch to become aces, even if most kept it to themselves. Satan's Playmates had only one bona fide former ace, Lieutenant (jg) Jack Symmes. The next-highest-scoring veteran with VF-15 was

Lieutenant (jg) Mel Roach, who had achieved two kills in 1942 while flying from Guadalcanal. The majority of Charlie Brewer's fighter pilots were aerial combat virgins eager to cut their teeth.

Their chance to change their status was finally within sight as Air Group Fifteen lifted off from Oahu on the morning of May 3, 1944. Their new carrier *Essex* was already underway from Pearl Harbor, steaming in company with the carriers *Wasp* and *San Jacinto*, cruisers USS *San Diego* (CL-53) and USS *Reno* (CL-96), and two destroyers. Around 1100, Dave McCampbell's AG-15 was jockeying for landing positions in the groove as their task group cut white wakes toward Majuro Atoll in the Marshall Islands chain.

Air group commander McCampbell was first to trap (land), in his *Monsoon Maiden* F6F. Seven dozen more Hellcats, Helldivers, and Avengers followed as *Essex* pushed out into the Pacific. For Air Group Fifteen, their new home on CV-9 marked a second lease on life.

For Dave McCampbell and Satan's Playmates, their chances to enter the elite race of aces would come soon enough.

FIVE

FIRST COMBAT

May 8, 1944
Majuro Lagoon

Duz Twelves knew he was in the big leagues now. Majuro, one of the largest of the sixty-four islands making up the Marshall Islands chain, had a 114-square-mile aquamarine lagoon filled with carriers, cruisers, battleships, destroyers, tankers, and other amphibious vessels staging for the next major operation of the Pacific War.

Temperatures were in the mid-eighties, but the humidity was high. Duz had been assigned stateroom 271 belowdecks, which he shared with fellow rookie ensigns Dick Fowler, Red Rader, and Jigs Foltz. Although the officers had their own bunks and small locker spaces and they shared writing desks—a far cry above the racks of bunks *Essex* enlisted men had for personal quarters—the living area in Officers' Country was hot and stuffy in the tropics. Duz looked for any chance he could get to be up on the flight deck or in VF-15's air-conditioned ready room.

Ensign Twelves was anxious for his first combat. He had little knowledge of the larger plans being devised for the upcoming assault on the Mariana Islands chain. His Air Group Fifteen and *Essex* were newcomers to the party, as the majority of the carrier air groups staging out of Majuro had been in action for months against Japanese bases like those on Truk, Palau, and Hollandia. While in Majuro's lagoon, the pilots had ground school each morning, followed by free time in the afternoon and an evening movie. Aside from shore leave to swim, snorkel, and drink, those on board ship listened to the latest propaganda on the radio from Tokyo Rose.

Command of the U.S. naval forces in the Central Pacific Force was under Admiral Raymond Spruance, one of the masterminds of the 1942 carrier victory at Midway. By May 8, Spruance's fast carrier fleet was known as Task Group 58, commanded by sun-weathered Vice Admiral Marc "Pete" Mitscher. A longtime naval aviator and fellow brown shoe commander, Mitscher was respected by his aviators. He roamed the bridge in a duck-billed cap, smoking cigarettes and eagerly listening to reports from pilots. His fleet call sign was "Bald Eagle."

Captain Ralph Ofstie was briefed by Mitscher's staff on their plans for *Essex* and her task group. The Marianas invasion was about a month out, but Air Group Fifteen was green. It had become something of a tradition for new carrier groups to "break in" their squadrons with raids against the westernmost Japanese-occupied islands in the Pacific: Marcus and Wake Islands. With Marcus Island located about 1,000 miles southeast of Tokyo and just about that far from Saipan in the Marianas, no naval vessels were expected to be encountered. It was about the safest on-the-job training in a real war zone that Dave McCampbell's fledgling air group could have hoped for.

On May 15, *Essex* sortied from Majuro at 0730 as part of Rear Admiral Alfred Eugene Montgomery's temporary task group, TG 58.6. It included three carriers with new air groups: *Essex*, *Wasp*, and *San Jacinto*. They were accompanied by five cruisers and eleven destroyers. Making his flagship on board *Essex* was Rear Admiral William Keene Harrill, who would eventually command TG 58.1 as part of Pete Mitscher's Carrier Division One. Harrill was soon found to be overly cautious in his war methods. The *Essex* aviators, learning of his love for a certain libation during off-duty hours, dubbed their new admiral "Whiskey" Harrill.[1]

During the three-day run toward their first target area, Commander McCampbell's air group prepared for combat. Fighting Fifteen skipper Charlie Brewer and his exec, Lieutenant Commander Jimmy Rigg, lectured the Hellcat pilots on flight discipline, formation flying, and other expectations. In the event of being shot down, the F6F pilots were each issued bolo knives and other survival gear. Engineering officer Jack Ivey worked closely with his enlisted mechanics to tune motors and sight in their machine guns, while flight officer Bert Morris drew up the initial flight rosters. Brewer, Rigg, Ivey, Morris, and five other lieutenants—John Collins, Ted Overton, John Strane, George Duncan, and Mel Roach—coached their divisions.

As the task group was en route to Marcus Island, the prospect for enemy encounters became real. On May 18, the task force spent the day refueling from fleet oilers. Now just a mere 150 miles from the Japanese-held island, Lieutenant John Barry was primed for action when he took off on a four-hour scouting hop. "We all thought that enemy planes would be out scouting but none were sighted, much to our regret," Barry wrote in his diary.[2]

MARCUS ISLAND STRIKES

May 19, 1944

Ensign Jim Duffy was snoozing hard when the duty sailor tapped on his stateroom door at 0230. Anxious for his first combat, the Hellcat pilot raced to don his khakis and flight gear before heading to the wardroom for breakfast. Most VF-15 pilots felt the same nervous excitement, which they displaced by shoveling in platefuls of steaming-hot breakfast.

Their new air group commander, Dave McCampbell, was quite the opposite. In what would become his preflight routine, he simply skipped breakfast in favor of a morning cigarette while downing black coffee. Once in a while he would stop by the wardroom for a glass of orange juice. Then it was off to the ready room for paperwork until it was time to man the planes.[3]

By the time McCampbell reached the VF-15 ready room on the port side of the carrier below the flight deck, it was already filled with anxious chatter and clouds of bluish smoke. The spacious compartment was dark, with only red overhead lights used at times to help vision adjust before going topside. Duffy slid into his leather chair and began updating his chartboard with the latest info: ship's heading, proper combat radio frequencies, target distance, and expected task force positions.

Ensign Spike Borley, another rookie VF-15 pilot assigned to the morning strikes, had his leather flight helmet ready and had already pulled on his yellow Mae West life vest over his flight suit. "You could cut the tension in the ready room with a knife," Borley recalled. To ease the anxiety, CAG McCampbell stood and launched into a foul joke that caught everyone by surprise. It worked. The nervous pilots erupted in laughter. They were then ready to listen as skipper Charlie Brewer ran through the day's strike plans. "These jokes became a tradition of pre-strike briefings for the rest of the cruise," said Borley.[4]

Lieutenant Bob McReynolds, the ACIO for VF-15, ran through the available intelligence on the island. His shipboard roommate, Bert Morris, handed out the flight assignments. McCampbell trusted McReynolds to give him the latest intelligence. On this day and many others, Dashing Dave would speak before his former fighter squadron, but he never offered briefings for VT-15 or VB-15.

McReynolds continually drilled his fighter pilots on proper recognition of enemy aircraft silhouettes. He would flash various types of planes and ships on a screen very briefly, then call on pilots to answer what it was. At first, McReynolds had to tell them what the proper answer was, but they improved over time.[5]

The first planes to launch from *Essex* were held until daybreak. Lieutenant Commander Bob Freeman's VF(N)-77 was slated to be first off the deck during the early hours of May 19. But his planes found insufficient wind for takeoff at 0500, forcing them to delay their departure for another ninety minutes. By the time the night fighters were launched, the flight deck was buzzing with activity as the first fighter sweep Hellcats were readied. When the word to man planes was received in VF-15's ready room, the pilots buckled on the four snaps that held their parachute straps in place. Jim Duffy double-checked the .38 Special pistol in his shoulder holster as he filed out the small corridor at the rear of the ready room on the gallery deck.

He raced up a steel ladder to the flight deck, where he was greeted by a stiff gust in his face as *Essex* plowed into the wind. Duffy and the other eleven pilots made quick surveys of their assigned F6Fs. Dave McCampbell always made a point to check his rudder and elevators before climbing onto the wing and into his plane. Beyond that, he had complete faith in his plane captain, E. E. "Ed" Carroll, to make sure everything was in order. Dave's *Monsoon Maiden* Hellcat even had a special ashtray that Carroll had had welded inside the cockpit. "Every time I made a flight, he always had a fresh pack of cigarettes in there for me," McCampbell recalled.[6] Carroll wanted to become an aviator himself, and in time his CAG would see to that taking place.

At 0630, on the heels of Freeman's night fighters, a dozen F6F engines coughed to life as clouds of black smoke belched skyward above swirling yellow-tipped propellers. Behind McCampbell's command division, Jim Rigg and John Strane followed with their divisions. Next off *Essex* were eight bomb-armed Avenger torpedo planes of VeeGee Lambert's VT-15 and fifteen of Jim Mini's SB2C Helldivers, each of the latter fitted with five-hundred-pound bombs and small antipersonnel hundred-pounders under their wings. For their first combat operation, the Satan's Playmates fighters carried no ordnance other than their full complement of 2,400 bullets per plane.

The flight to Marcus Island went without a hitch. Over the target area, McCampbell orbited with his fighter division until the main strike group approached from the west. He then directed in the *Essex* and *Wasp* warplanes through the scattered cloud cover. To start the show, McCampbell sent his Hellcats in first to suppress enemy gunfire. Due to the cloud cover, the F6Fs made flatter dives than they would have preferred, subjecting them to antiaircraft fire as the gun crews defending Marcus came to life.

The VF-15 pilots found only a dismantled twin-engine Japanese plane in a revetment during their dives over the enemy airstrip. The *Essex* dive-bombers and torpedo planes unloaded their bombs on a concrete building and other structures. Tracers zipped past Air Group Fifteen's planes like hail. The water below them was filled with little splashes as they retired. Flying wing on Lieutenant Commander Rigg, Spike Borley noted flak rising toward his F6F like big, slow golf balls before suddenly zipping past his canopy like tiny red rockets.[7]

Jim Duffy followed his division leader, Lieutenant Strane, on a strafing run against enemy gun positions. He watched his tracers and incendiaries hit the ground and create flashes—and he also spotted muzzle flashes from Japanese gunners. In that instant, a strange flash of anger swept over Duffy. *You dumb sons of bitches!* he thought. *Don't you know you're supposed to hide? I'm trying to kill you!*[8]

The Japanese gunners were effective: four *Essex* Hellcats were hit, along with three Avengers of VT-15 and two SB2Cs of VB-15. Each of McCampbell's strikers returned to base, although the carrier's maintenance crews would have long hours repairing some of the damage. The only injury was to Lieutenant Bob Stearns of VF-15, who suffered abrasions to his neck from a 40mm AA burst that struck his Hellcat.

DUZ TWELVES WAS spotted on deck around 1020 as part of *Essex*'s second Marcus Island strike group.

Twelves and plane captain Victor Lain made a proper preflight check around his F6F, scanning for any hydraulic, oil, or gasoline leaks. Lain then helped the ensign adjust his straps as Twelves checked his cockpit's instruments. The order was passed to start engines, and Lain stepped clear as the props windmilled from their idle position into deadly whirling disks. Squadron skipper Charlie Brewer led the second strike's fighter contingent, his F6F followed off the deck in short order by ten others from VF-15.

Duz was next in line behind his division leader, George Duncan. As the flight deck officer whirled his wands, Twelves revved up his engine to full power while standing on the brakes. He checked his fuel mixture control, ensured that the prop pitch lever was full forward, and eased on the throttle to check his engine instruments. His oil temperature was normal, and his manifold pressure was a full fifty-four inches. He waved his hand to the launching officer to signal his readiness.

The officer dropped his arm, pointing down the flight deck. Twelves released the brakes and went racing down the deck at full throttle. As soon as his wheels cleared the deck, he raised his landing gear, cranked his canopy closed, and closed his flaps. He was airborne on his first mission, his eyes shifting about to find his division for their aerial rendezvous above the task force. For Ensign Twelves and most of his companions, this was a first: launching with a 350-pound depth bomb strapped beneath each of their fighters.

Seemingly an unorthodox armament choice, the depth bomb was capable of cratering enemy airstrips or blasting apart antiaircraft emplacements. Brewer's divisions were tasked with escorting in twenty-three bomb-laden Avengers and Helldivers to continue pounding enemy installations on Marcus.

Brewer's second group damaged a small merchant ship with strafing and with their depth bombs. Duncan's and Jack Ivey's divisions were first down on Marcus, ordered to strafe Japanese antiaircraft emplacements on the island's northern side. Duz Twelves followed Duncan as they made their dives on a gun emplacement. Twelves strafed heavily until he toggled his own depth bomb. Before he pulled out, he noted the blast of the bomb ahead of him. Climbing back to altitude, he made his second pass, triggering his .50s against the winking fire of enemy guns below him. "Narrowly escaped AA by pulling steeply into clouds," Twelves noted in his journal that evening.[9]

Two of VF-15's depth bombs flattened a pair of small buildings. Section leader John Barry toggled his depth bomb on his first dive and found enemy AA fire to be more intense as he commenced a second strafing run. "To say I was nervous is putting it mildly," he wrote. "My nervousness reached a point at times when I thought I would suffocate." Barry's port wing was hit by flak, but he regained altitude and made a third strafing run in support of the Helldivers and Avengers as they went in to drop their ordnance.[10]

Another ten *Essex* planes were hit by shrapnel or AA bursts on this strike, including four other VF-15 Hellcats. The only loss was the VB-15 dive-bomber piloted by Ensign Thomas A. "Al" Woods, whose engine was struck by an AA burst during his dive. He was able to make a successful water landing just off Marcus, where he and his gunner bobbed about in their life raft until the duty "lifeguard" submarine, USS *Sturgeon* (SS-187), could be called in. By 1944, rescue duty was commonplace for U.S. submarines operating in the vicinity of carrier air strikes. Such heroic work was much appreciated by the aviators, who avoided capture and possible execution had the Japanese gotten to them first. By day's end, the busy *Sturgeon* crew had also rescued a *Wasp* rear seat gunner who had bailed out of his damaged VT-14 TBM.[11]

DAVE MCCAMPBELL TOOK to the air again at 1325 to lead the third *Essex* strike group against Marcus Island. Eight Hellcats carried 350-pound depth bombs, while two photo F6Fs were without ordnance. As the strike group approached Marcus, the morning's foul weather only worsened, eliminating all views of the target area until the pilots descended below 1,000 feet.

The danger in flying lower was that their planes became much easier targets for the frenzied Japanese AA gun crews. McCampbell's leading division was the first to pay the price. He pushed his *Monsoon Maiden* over from 12,000 feet, plunging through the heavy cumulonimbus banks until his F6F emerged at low altitude for his strafing run against the enemy batteries. McCampbell made it to the other side of the island before he hit a wall of 20mm and 40mm AA fire. The CAG felt his F6F shudder twice as shells punctured his lower-rear fuselage, severing his rudder controls.

McCampbell's wingman, Ensign Wes Burnam, was less fortunate. His plane, No. 8, was hit in the main fuel tank or cockpit area, sending his fighter plunging into the ocean in flames. As McCampbell retired from the area, he was followed by his nephew-in-law Bert Morris, flying as his second section leader for this hop.

"Dave, your belly tank's on fire!" Morris radioed.[12]

"Thanks, Bert!"

McCampbell dropped his external tank and retired toward the air group's rendezvous spot away from the island after his fires subsided. With smoke and fluid streaming from his Hellcat, the CAG circled until the balance of his flock returned from delivering bombs and rockets against Marcus targets. In addition to Wes Burnam, VB-15 had lost Ensign Jared Hunt Dixon and his rear seat gunner. Their Helldiver had been hit in a wing, sending it spinning out of control into the ocean, where it disintegrated upon impact.

With three aviators lost in action, McCampbell signaled to his squadron leaders to head for base. Seven other aircraft aside from his own suffered varying degrees of damage. They reached the task group around 1530, whereupon Dave ordered the dive-bombers and Avengers to land

Left to right: *Ens. Wes Burnam, Lt. Jack Ivey, Ens. George Carr, and Ens. Tom Tarr. On May 20, 1944, Burnam was killed in action. Ivey and Tarr would also be killed later.* Doyle Bare collection, courtesy of Rita Bare

first. Bert Morris remained with the CAG until all others were safely on board *Essex*. With his rudder destroyed and one dive flap shot up, Dave had a new problem: "I found that I couldn't lower my wheels in the normal manner," he recalled. Using the manual crank, McCampbell lowered his gear and ordered Morris into the groove ahead of him.[13]

Atop the carrier's island structure, Vulture's Row was packed to watch the air group commander bring in his bird. Senior LSO Charles Iarrobino expertly coached McCampbell into the groove before giving him the paddle slash that indicated he was cleared to land. Dashing Dave was none the worse for wear, but his *Monsoon Maiden* was finished. Airedales hauled the Grumman to an elevator and lowered it to the hangar deck. Mechanics found it unworthy of repair. They stripped valuable replacement parts and photos were taken of the shell holes. Someone even thought to extract the Hamilton standard clock from the dashboard before AG-15's command fighter was pushed overboard.

Air Group Fifteen sent in a fourth and final strike on Marcus to blast the Japanese runway and shore installations. This group returned without plane loss, but plenty of lessons had been learned in the first combat hops for most of *Essex*'s pilots. Each squadron was tasked with writing detailed air combat action (ACA) reports for each strike. In the case of VF-15, this task fell upon ACIO Bob McReynolds and his staff of enlisted yeomen. Each pilot was interviewed for specific details, which were then compiled into the report. This in turn was forwarded to skipper Charlie Brewer for his review and approval.

With VB-15 and VT-15 also involved in the strikes that day, a cohesive action report was compiled and was submitted to CAG McCampbell for his blessing. "The three squadrons would make different determinations of what they attacked and what damage they'd done," McCampbell recalled. "I would try to put it all together so it would be consistent if there were any deviations."[14]

Maintenance crews and plane captains worked late into the night patching aircraft to be able to fly again the following morning. Rear Admiral Montgomery had directed that Task Group 58.6 would hit Marcus again at first light.

McCampbell's *Monsoon Maiden* had not survived her maiden day of combat. Hoping for better luck from his next F6F, Dave conferred with two of the leading men assigned to maintain his fighter: Ed Carroll and Chet Owens. It was a frequent choice of other pilots to paint the name of their wife or girlfriend on the fuselage of their plane. In McCampbell's case, he had a choice. He was corresponding with two girls back home: Mary Louise Wiener from Milwaukee and the woman he had known longer, Sara Jane "Jill" Heliker of Florida.

He and his crew opted for *The Minsi* for his new F6F-3. Before shipping out from the East Coast with VF-15, McCampbell had been dating twenty-two-year-old Mary Louise, whose nickname was Minsi. The stepdaughter of a member of the Blatz brewery family, Mary had married a naval aviator, Joseph Prentice Willetts, in March 1942. When Dave began dating her in the fall of 1943, she was newly widowed after Willetts was killed in the crash of a Mariner patrol plane off Long Island on August 18, 1943.[15]

McCampbell was first off the deck in his new F6F around 0630 on May 20. He took four divisions of VF-15 up to escort fifteen Helldivers and

Avengers. Enemy AA fire was again intense as the fighters made strafing runs to help protect the air group bombers. Foul weather again hampered results, but the group claimed damage to additional buildings and AA emplacements. In return, eight aircraft were damaged. The most serious from VF-15 was that of Ensign Red Rader, flying F6F No. 32, who lost his left stabilizer and elevator, with additional damage to his right side. Buddy Duz Twelves noted in his diary that his roommate Rader "got aboard with tail shot half off."[16]

Ensign Red Rader returns to Essex *with tailhook dangling and half his tail shot away on May 20, 1944.*   U.S. NAVY, NARA

John Barry made only one bombing-and-strafing run in support of the bombers and felt that his efforts were better than on the previous day. "The experience yesterday left me much calmer and cooler today in my attack," he wrote in his journal.[17]

The second *Essex* strike on May 20 was equally costly, as another ten planes suffered varying degrees of damage. Lieutenant Bob Stearns returned with an F6F so shot up that only one wheel of his landing gear was functional. He still managed to make a beautiful landing that ended up with his fighter skidding across the deck. Lieutenant (jg) Leo Kenney suffered a 40mm burst that struck his wheel well and main tank, knocking out his landing gear. With burns on his leg and forehead, Kenney managed to nurse his crippled F6F No. 20 back toward the fleet, where he made a smooth water landing alongside a TF 58 destroyer, USS *Cowell* (DD-547), which picked him up uninjured. He returned to *Essex* the following day.[18]

TASK GROUP 58.6 retired from Marcus on May 21, moving more than eight hundred miles to the east-southeast toward lonely Wake Island, which had been seized by the Japanese in late December 1941. Beginning in the fall of 1943, passing U.S. carrier task forces frequently pounded the scant Japanese installations on Wake en route to other campaigns.

As Admiral Montgomery's task group refueled from fleet tankers on May 22, Charlie Brewer and Dave McCampbell reviewed lessons learned at Marcus with their new fighter squadron. The *Essex* CAG headed the first predawn strike on May 23, with three divisions of VF-15 launched at 0531 to shepherd sixteen TBFs and SB2Cs to the island base. The first strike group arrived over Wake Island at 0650, with McCampbell leading in his Hellcats on a high-speed approach from 14,000 feet.

With the bombing units close behind, the F6Fs strafed and dropped their five-hundred-pound bombs on antiaircraft emplacements. No enemy fire was taken during the initial dives, as the Japanese were apparently caught completely off guard. The Helldivers and Avengers targeted various buildings with their bombs, but enough targets of opportunity remained that *Essex* was already sending her second strike group out at 0728.

VF-15 skipper Charlie Brewer led his men on strafing-and-bombing runs through fairly light enemy machine-gun and small-arms fire. Air Group Fifteen's only loss from this flight was the Helldiver of Ensign Conrad Crellin, although he and his gunner were rescued by a task force destroyer, USS *Bradford* (DD-545). Barry found the enemy's AA fire to be inaccurate and "meager in comparison to Marcus."[19]

Dave McCampbell led strike number three with *The Minsi*, returning to the skies just over two hours after trapping (catching an arresting wire) from his dawn strike. His F6Fs, TBFs, and SB2Cs blasted buildings and revetments without loss. The only mishap during their return involved a pair of VF(N)-77 night fighters that had been launched on a special mission to provide cover for a U.S. lifeguard submarine. Shortly after 1300, Ensign Bonner Davis crashed in the ocean after receiving a wave-off from the LSO about forty-two miles south of Wake Island. Although the destroyer *Bradford* was quickly dispatched to the scene, there was no evidence Davis had escaped his sinking fighter.

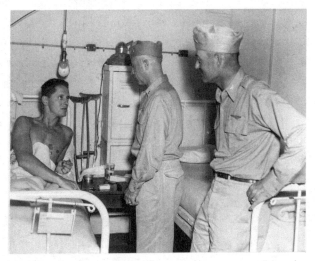

John Collins in sick bay receiving a Purple Heart from Rear Admiral
Alfred Montgomery (center) and Captain Ralph Ofstie (right).
NATIONAL ARCHIVES, 80-G-352993

Two more strike groups were launched from *Essex* in the afternoon. The final group of twenty-three AG-15 aircraft and eight AG-51 *San Jacinto* planes was led by Commander McCampbell, marking his third mission of the long day. During their low-level strafing-and-bombing runs, the Hellcat of division leader John Collins was hit by 12.7mm antiaircraft rounds. Shrapnel and bullets pierced his wing stub, landing gear, ailerons, fuselage, fin, rudder, and stabilizer. The remaining pilots rendezvoused west of the target area while McCampbell escorted Collins back to the carrier. Collins's airspeed indicator and other instruments were knocked out, and he was in considerable pain from shrapnel that had entered his right thigh.

"Just get on my wing and follow me," McCampell radioed. Upon returning to *Essex*, Collins was worried about landing, but his CAG ordered him in. "He made it all right, with no strain," McCampbell remembered. "I led him in, to give him an indication of the airspeed, so on the follow approach, he could get the throttle set, then all he had to do when he got the cut, was throttle it back."[20]

The only problem was that the flak damage prevented Collins from lowering his landing gear. Crash crews stood ready as the lieutenant executed a wheels-up slam into the teakwood deck. Enlisted men scrambled onto the wings to help the bloodied pilot from his cockpit. He was hustled down to sick bay in a stretcher, sporting a weak grin beneath his dark crew cut. Captain Ofstie and Rear Admiral Montgomery visited the wounded VF-15 pilot in sick bay to present him with a Purple Heart. "It scared the hell out of him," McCampbell recalled. He put Collins on light duty for the next two weeks as a squadron duty officer, but his division leader would return to combat duty soon enough.

By the day's end, Air Group Fifteen had completed eleven strike missions on Wake and Marcus Islands in five days. They had lost five aircraft in action, operationally or damaged beyond repair. Another sixty-three aircraft required damage repair from bullets or landing mishaps. Five men had been wounded or injured and another five had been killed. As much as was possible, McCampbell had rotated an equal number of flights for each pilot except for squadron COs and XOs, who flew every other strike. "This arrangement provided the maximum combat experience for the Air Group as a whole and should prove its value in future assignments," McCampbell wrote. Although his pilots had

Former movie star Wayne Morris, now Lt. Bert Morris, seen after making his fifth combat flight in May 1944. It was his third mission of the day. National Archives, 80-G-240270

gained considerable experience, Dave felt that the damage inflicted on the enemy installations was not commensurate with the efforts involved and the losses incurred on personnel and aircraft.[21]

His air group emerged from these first two atoll strikes with much-needed experience. As young pilot Jim Duffy recalled, "Strafing and raising hell with the Japanese garrisons helped build our confidence."[22]

SIX

TO THE MARIANAS

May 27, 1944
Majuro Atoll

U pon returning to Majuro on May 26, *Essex* spent the next few days taking on provisions. For Lieutenant John Barry, it was a chance to catch up on mail from home and dash off letters to his wife, Olive, now five months pregnant. Barry was not alone in being an expectant father. Squadron mates Leo Kenney and Bert Morris expected birth news any day now, and George Crittenden's wife, Ann, was pregnant with their first child. Lieutenant Morris would soon learn that his first daughter arrived on May 30.[1]

With the air group now broken in, Rear Admiral Montgomery left Rear Admiral Harrill formally in command of Task Group 58.4. It included *Essex* as his flagship, along with the carriers *Langley* and USS *Cowpens* (CVL-25), cruisers *San Diego* and *Reno*, and seven destroyers. After a day at sea on May 31 for training exercises, *Essex* returned to Majuro to wait out the next big sortie of Vice Admiral Pete Mitscher's Task Force 58.

Ensign Duz Twelves found little respite from the routine during these days save for a trip to Reta Island in a motor launch with several enlisted mechanics on June 3 to secure spare parts and supplies for VF-15. Unknown to him, major plans were in the works for Admiral Ray Spruance's Fifth Fleet. Although the invasion of Europe via Normandy was but a week away, the U.S. military was also focused on the Japanese-held Mariana Islands in the Pacific. The island of Saipan would be the starting point of the offensive that would be code-named "Operation Forager." The capture of Saipan's airfields would offer the U.S. Army its first chance to put big bombers within range of the Japanese home islands.

Admiral Soemu Toyoda, commander in chief of the Japanese Combined Fleet, had already begun an operation called "A-Go" in early May. Although the Americans were initially expected to strike at the Caroline Islands first, A-Go called for a major portion of the Imperial Japanese Navy (IJN) to crush Mitscher's carrier fleet. Vice Admiral Jisaburo Ozawa, commander of the First Mobile Fleet, had been busily assembling every major warship and aircraft carrier he could muster for this operation. The potential for the world's fifth-ever carrier-versus-carrier sea battle was brewing.

The D-day Marine landings on Saipan had been set for the morning of June 15. In advance of boots hitting the shore, Mitscher's Task Force 58 was charged with crippling Ozawa's land-based air strength—more than five hundred planes—to gain air supremacy and remove the danger of the Japanese using Marianas airfields to assault the amphibious forces.

One hundred and eleven warships sortied from Majuro on June 6 beneath drizzly gray clouds. Fifteen fleet carriers of TF 58 carried nearly a thousand warplanes, supported by more than 96,000 men serving aboard the various ships in the armada. From other ports, battleships, cruisers, destroyers, escort carrier groups, and various ships of an amphibious landing force got underway toward the Philippines—some 535 vessels in total—in what would prove to be the largest sea battle yet fought in World War II.[2]

As *Essex* headed toward her next combat, John Barry flew a combat air patrol on June 9. "Damn but those four-hour hops are hard on one's seat," he wrote. He resorted to pouring water on his head and flying with his canopy open just to keep alert.[3]

The following day, Bob Freeman's VF(N)-77 suffered its second casualty within three weeks. Returning from a mission at 1005 on June 10, Ensign Daniel Kelly's F6F spun into the ocean. Although task force destroyers combed the area thoroughly, his body was not recovered.

Freeman's unit was now down to only four radar-equipped night fighters, with little hope of obtaining such a specialized replacement aircraft soon. Charlie Brewer's VF-15 had thirty-seven operable Hellcats, but his unit remained aerial kill virgins. In nearly a month of Pacific operations, Satan's Playmates had yet to tangle with Japanese aircraft.

With D-day on Saipan fast approaching, and Vice Admiral Ozawa's carrier fleet poised to attack, heated action was imminent.

MARIANAS STRIKES COMMENCE

June 11, 1944

Operation Forager was still days away from the scheduled D-day landings on Saipan, but Task Force 58 had other duties first. Marc Mitscher's staff believed the Japanese would expect the usual dawn fighter sweep over the Marianas airfields. He decided to surprise his enemy by sending out more than two hundred Hellcats on the afternoon of June 11.

Fleet CAPs downed two Japanese snoopers that morning as the big carriers steamed toward their afternoon launch point. On board *Essex*, Charlie Brewer and Dave McCampbell reviewed last-minute plans with their fighter squadron during the noon hour. Each *Essex*-class fleet carrier was scheduled to launch sixteen fighters, and each task group's smaller *Independence*-class escort carriers would contribute an even dozen. Around 1245, the *Essex* flight deck was alive like a rattled hornets' nest as starter cartridges kicked the big cylinders into motion of the Grumman F6Fs' Pratt & Whitney engines.[4]

CAG McCampbell would serve as the overall strike coordinator, not only for his *Essex* bunch but also for twenty-four planes contributed from his Task Group 58.4: twelve VF-25 Hellcats from *Cowpens* and another dozen VF-32s from *Langley*. In addition to his command division, three other VF-15 combat teams would launch: those of skipper Charlie Brewer, squadron XO Jim Rigg, and Mel Roach.

The first *Essex* fighters raced down the flight deck at 1259, although one of the sixteen would be scrubbed. Lieutenant John Barry had spent the morning writing letters to his wife up until it was time to report to the ready room. When the call came after lunch to man planes, he raced to the flight deck in his parachute harness with all his gear. To his chagrin, another pilot had manned his plane by mistake. Old No. 7, painted on both sides of its canopy with his wife's name, Olive, was already rumbling and rolling toward the starting line. This, the first day where VF-15 might actually engage enemy fighters, would be a disappointing day on the sidelines for Barry.[5]

Strike coordinator Dave McCampbell and his F6Fs rendezvoused with a pair of VB-15 Helldivers equipped with additional survival gear in the event any fighter pilots were shot down and in need of rescue. His fighters could not have been any more eager for action. Prior to launch, Admiral Mitscher had sent a message to each Hellcat squadron: "Cut their damned throats. Wish I could be with you."[6]

The flight to Saipan was 188 miles, with the group flying low to avoid enemy radar until a short distance from their target area. The *Essex* air group commander was flying this day with his newest wingman, twenty-two-year-old Lieutenant (jg) Roy Rushing. Born in Macon, Missouri, Rushing had attended Northeast Junior College in Monroe, Louisiana, before entering flight training in 1942. He had been with VF-15 since its early days in New Jersey. After the loss of wingman Wes Burnam weeks prior, Rushing had been tapped by skipper Charlie Brewer to fly wing on the CAG.

He and McCampbell quickly became inseparable. In flight, Rushing followed every move his air group commander made. "He'd stick so close sometimes I'd have to wave him back to give me a little more freedom to operate," McCampbell recalled. The pair created their own radio-free style of communicating in flight using a Morse code system. McCampbell would wave Rushing in close alongside his F6F and then pound on his dashboard with a dit-dot-dot-dot rhythm to share his intentions.[7]

As McCampbell arrived over Saipan Island, his division flew "mattress," meaning they remained at high altitude above the heavy cloud cover below them. He directed his other three divisions to make their first strafing-and-bombing runs while his F6Fs covered them. Commander Brewer led in seven fighters armed with 350-pound depth bombs, approaching their target area—a seaplane base on Flores Point in Tanapag Harbor—from 12,000 feet.

Brewer's division, and that of Lieutenant Roach, commenced their pushovers from 11,000 feet, moving east to west over the island from seaward.

Each pilot dropped his depth bomb at around 2,500 feet, strafing in line before releasing. Brewer's bomb was seen by his wingman, Ensign Dick Fowler, to make a direct hit on the seaplane ramp, in the center of two Kawanishi H8K flying boats (code-named "Emilys") and an Aichi E13A Reisu long-range reconnaissance seaplane (code-named "Jake"). All three aircraft were wrecked by the ensuing explosion.

The other six pilots following Brewer landed hits on the ramp and installations, starting fires. Fighting Fifteen claimed six total planes demolished, in addition to other Emilys and a Kawanishi H6K Navy flying boat (code-named "Mavis") damaged or destroyed by strafing. The remaining eight fighters acted as cover during the bombing attack and then followed with their own strafing runs. Enemy antiaircraft fire was intense and moderately accurate. Three F6Fs were damaged, and Lieutenant (jg) Leo Kenney's plane was hit solidly during his initial dive over Tanapag Harbor. Kenney, one of the squadron's newest fathers, did not survive. His Hellcat continued straight into the Japanese-occupied harbor.

Recovering from his attack run, Brewer was rejoined by wingman Fowler about five miles northwest of Marpi Point. There they encountered an Emily flying boat and commenced their attacks immediately. Brewer scored hits in the plane's port stub wing and its No. 2 engine on his highside beam approach. The plane, simultaneously under attack by Jim Rigg and other pilots, began smoking heavily and trailing flames. Fowler made a flat side run, hitting the burning Emily around the cockpit. Twenty seconds after Brewer's firing, the Emily struck the water and exploded, credited as a shared kill—the first aerial victory for VF-15.

Lieutenant Commander Rigg, after making his first strafing run and helping to shoot up the Emily, next latched onto a Nakajima Ki-44 Shoki single-seat fighter plane (code-named "Tojo") and began firing. His bullets stitched the cockpit and the fuselage aft of it. The Tojo skidded right but then continued straight until it hit the water and disintegrated. Climbing back to altitude, Rigg encountered a Zeke head-on. Japanese pilots more commonly referred to their Mitsubishi A6M fighter as a "Zero" due to its "Type 0" naming convention, but U.S. Navy pilots in the Pacific had adopted the code-name "Zeke" for the Zero fighter. The opposing pilots held their courses until the Zeke finally pulled up. Closing fast, Rigg scored hits in the Zeke's engine, sending it diving to port in flames before it crashed into the ocean.

Bert Morris, leading McCampbell's second section, was next to score. He sighted a dark, brindle-brown-colored Kawanishi H6K flying boat that had just taken off from the harbor. Pushing over, he fired in bursts down to just two hundred feet above the ocean, causing the plane to burst into flames and crash on the reef. "It has four engines, and I tried to get credit for four planes," Morris later joked.[8]

Morris's wingman, Ensign Ken Flinn, pursued a Zeke he encountered five miles west of the southern tip of Saipan. His opponent proved difficult to line up on until Flinn got directly astern. The Zeke made a steep diving spiral to the right, but Flinn managed to hit its engine, cockpit, and wing roots. Fires erupted and the Japanese fighter flipped on its back and slammed into the water.

Dave McCampbell, flying cover at 10,000 feet above the mattress layer of clouds, spotted a Zeke at 1430 diving through the overcast astern of his F6Fs. It pulled up in a high wingover onto McCampbell's port beam. The Essex CAG made a flipper turn into him and gave it one short burst from seven hundred to eight hundred feet distance. The Zeke made a left wingover, but McCampbell retained his belly tank, followed, and gave him another short blast. Following through, he added a burst on his tail. The Zeke made another right wingover but did not recover. Dashing Dave had scored his first shoot-down.

Roy Rushing followed McCampbell's victim down toward the water, firing until it hit. Rushing had already attacked three Zekes off the tip of Saipan. He encountered one head-on, and although the fighter tried to scissor out of the assault, a five-second burst from Rushing caused it to explode. He saw the pilot bail out, his parachute opening at 2,000 feet, seconds before his Zeke disintegrated upon slamming into the ocean.

Ensigns Dave Johnson and Red Rader from Rigg's division combined to flame another Zeke near the northern tip of Tinian. Johnson landed the first hits on the fighter, which burst into flames as Rader began scoring his own. The Japanese pilot bailed out, his chute opening just as his plane hit the water. Johnson and Rader shared the kill.

By the time McCampbell's group headed for base, they had destroyed eight enemy aircraft. It was the squadron's first blood. In return, they had lost Leo Kenney to flak. Other fighter squadrons from Task Groups 58.1, 58.2, and 58.3 had their share of enemy aircraft encounters over Saipan, Tinian, Guam, and Pagan Island. Total aerial victories claimed on June 11 were ninety-eight, three times the number the Japanese would officially admit to losing. In any event, Task Force 58 had flexed its muscles, exhibiting aerial dominance over the enemy airfields in exchange for eleven Hellcats lost.[9]

June 12, 1944

Pete Mitscher's surprise attack the previous afternoon had been a success. He followed up on the morning of June 12 with a more traditional predawn fighter sweep launch for Task Force 58 against the Japanese airfields. Flight quarters came very early for Air Group Fifteen that morning. By 0400, Captain Ofstie had *Essex* steaming into the wind as a deckload strike commenced launching in full darkness.

Overnight, his carrier had closed to within eighty-three miles of Saipan in order for his flyboys to shock the enemy with their first attacks preceding daybreak. CAG Dave McCampbell led with two dozen Hellcats from six divisions. They were followed off the deck by fifteen bomb-armed SB2C Helldivers under Lieutenant Commander Jim Mini of VB-15 and eight Avengers, each carrying a dozen hundred-pounders, under Lieutenant Commander VeeGee Lambert.

After a rendezvous in the night sky, McCampbell took the lead as strike commander of both his *Essex* air group and another twenty-five planes from *Cowpens*. By 0545, the *Essex* planes were making bombing runs on antiaircraft gun positions near the Marpi Point airstrip. Other planes cratered the runway with bomb hits and started several fires. No enemy aerial opposition was encountered during this strike, but McCampbell's fighters located six freighters while searching the vicinity. Some of these merchant ships were attacked during the return to *Essex*, with VF-15 pilots claiming to have left the vessels burning and trailing oil and at least two small ones sinking.

Charlie Brewer served as strike coordinator for the second *Essex* strike group, launched around 0645. He led his dozen Hellcats on strafing runs on the airfield on Pagan Island, demolishing a Mitsubishi G3M medium bomber (U.S. designation "Nell") and a single-engine plane, and damaging a second Nell. On their second pass, they strafed aircraft installations and miscellaneous buildings while photo pilots Jigs Foltz and Roy Nall documented the island. As *Essex* Helldivers and Avengers dropped their bombloads, Brewer took his F6Fs down to strafe and sink two small barges in the harbor. Antiaircraft fire damaged one VT-15 plane, but its pilot, Lieutenant (jg) John Chambers, nursed his Avenger close enough to the task group that he and his enlisted crewmen were recovered by a destroyer.

The third *Essex* strike was launched at 0900. Thirty-six planes raced down the deck, including four fighter squadron (VF) divisions led by CAG McCampbell. Eight of the Hellcats carried 350-pound depth bombs, while the others escorted the torpedo bomber squadron (VT) and dive-bombing squadron (VB). The Hellcats had been loaded to attack antiaircraft gun emplacements. But just before launching, McCampbell was notified to search out an enemy convoy that had been reported.

McCampbell had his fighters spread out into scouting lines until the convoy was located. Officially Japanese Convoy No. 4611, it consisted of about thirty-seven ships, including an old destroyer, troop transports, freighters, a torpedo boat, subchasers, and other small escort vessels. Convoy 4611 had gotten underway around 0400 in fear of the imminent Allied invasion of Saipan.[10]

Fighting Fifteen split into divisions and sections to help escort the dive-bombers and torpedo bombers in their attacks on these ships. The Hellcat pilots made numerous strafing runs, and the Japanese convoy scattered as the attacks commenced. "Direct hits from 350 lb. DBs by VFs were quite scarce against maneuvering, relatively small targets," McCampbell assessed.[11]

The SB2Cs and TBMs hit various ships with bombs, rockets, and bullets. When the attacks ended, McCampbell reported that three freighters and two escorts had been sunk. Another four ships were deemed probably sunk, while the remaining twenty ships had suffered varying degrees of damage. The only loss was the SB2C of Ensign John Foote, who crashed at sea after a wave-off. His crew was rescued by a destroyer.

By the time McCampbell's strikers returned to their task force, *Essex* had already dispatched a fourth strike group at 1100. It consisted of ten F6Fs to accompany nineteen VB-15 and VT-15 bombers to hit enemy aircraft and installations at Pagan Island. But the launch was marred by a fatal crash. Lieutenant Mel Roach sped down the flight deck, only to lose power as his F6F cleared the bow.

Witnesses saw Roach's plane No. 34 settle slowly off the bow and head for the waves. Roach made a water landing, but before he could climb from his cockpit, the droppable fuel tank below his fuselage suddenly exploded. "As we passed, the whole thing blew up as he was crawling out of the cockpit," pilot Al Slack recalled. A cloud of black smoke rose from the location as *Essex* continued launching her strike planes. A destroyer raced to the scene, but there was no evidence Roach had survived the horrific explosion.[12]

"Roach's loss was felt by everyone, as he was well liked. He left a bride of two months in Norfolk," John Barry wrote that night.[13]

Barry and Jake Lundin, two members of Roach's second division, proceeded with the mission at hand. The strikers flew at 12,000 feet until they reached Pagan Island. Only three previously destroyed aircraft were noted on the ground, so VF-15 strafed installations, barracks, and a radio direction finder station on Pagan. Two Hellcats were hit by 7.7mm antiaircraft rounds; one of them was flown by Ensign Duz Twelves, who collected an enemy round in his cockpit enclosure.

Ten miles west of Pagan, the *Essex* strike group found fourteen small cargo boats and made four strafing attacks on them. One dive-bomber, that of Ensign Clarence Vanderwall, exploded and crashed with no survivors after being hit by an AA round in midair. Four vessels were left burning fiercely and in a sinking condition, with another six dead in the water and trailing oil. "What a picnic we had with them," Barry wrote of the merchant ships. "All were streaming oil when we left except two."[14]

Convoy No. 4611 was next pounced on by another *Essex* strike group that had been launched at 1500. Led by Lieutenant Commander Charlie Brewer, it included three divisions of VF-15 and fifteen SB2Cs. Arriving over the battered convoy at 1620, Brewer assigned various targets to the divisions of George Duncan and George Crittenden. Many ships were burning, others were trailing oil, and some still seemed battle-worthy.

Brewer initially selected what he deemed to be a newer, *Fubuki*-class Japanese destroyer for his division. His target was actually the 960-ton *Otori*, officially classified as a torpedo boat, a smaller destroyer of the *Matsu* class. Carrying three torpedoes, four dozen depth charges, and a full array of antiaircraft guns, *Otori* was manned by a crew of 129 sailors. She was sleek and nimble, capable of making 30 knots at full speed. Excited by the prospect of knocking out an enemy warship first, Brewer called Duncan's division to join him on this target.

Brewer's Hellcats swept in first, each pilot walking his six streams of .50-caliber bullets into the destroyer's superstructure. Duncan's combat team followed, as did Jim Rigg's, and the F6Fs largely silenced *Otori*'s gunners with their own lethal fire. Ensign Al Slack heard Duncan order his team to concentrate on the rear guns after the forward batteries had been silenced. Climbing back to altitude, the divisions began making repeated runs on the warship. "We set his after deckhouse on fire, so we concentrated on that," Duncan recalled.[15]

After several runs, *Otori*'s guns were silenced and she was burning heavily. The tail-end Charlies of the strafing Hellcats were flown by Al

The Japanese destroyer Otori *burning and sinking after VF-15 strafing attacks on June 12, 1944.* U.S. Navy, NARA

Slack and wingman Doyle Bare. Slack and Bare had become close friends since meeting as aviation cadets in 1943. "I was shooting all six right into the base of that turret, and coming low enough to see them hitting," said Slack. As he pulled clear from his final strafing run, Slack saw fire leaping from the destroyer's after turret. Just as he swept past, *Otori* suddenly erupted into flames, possibly from her own torpedoes exploding. The force of the concussion flipped his F6F on its side. "My first thought was Doyle caught in that huge explosion," Slack recalled. As he righted his Grumman, he looked back and saw a towering ball of fire climbing from the remnants of *Otori*.[16]

He opened up on his radio. "Doyle! Doyle! Are you okay?"

He heard nothing but silence for long seconds. "Doyle, are you all right? Answer me!"

Finally, Slack heard the deep baritone voice of his undersized Oklahoma wingman. "I'm all right," Bare replied.

"When the smoke cleared, there wasn't anything but an oil slick," Slack remembered. Photos taken by the *Essex* planes later confirmed that this Japanese destroyer had been sunk solely by fighter pilot strafing, which caused the massive explosion.

Charlie Brewer made his next dive on a 3,000-ton freighter. He and his wingman scored only near misses with their five hundred-pound bombs, so Brewer made a second dive. This time he toggled his drop tank and was pleased to see it land amidships. The aviation fuel was seen by other pilots to start a furious fire. Ensign Bud Plant was also credited with a direct hit that helped to sink this medium-sized cargo ship.

The remaining pilots of VF-15 escorted VB-15 Helldivers in strafing and bombing a dozen ships of varying sizes. Lieutenant (jg) Richard Glass of VB-15 landed a five-hundred-pounder at the waterline off the fantail of a small freighter, leaving it in a sinking condition. By the end of the attack, the *Essex* group had sunk the destroyer *Otori*, left two merchant ships as probably sunk, and inflicted additional damage to seven other vessels. Based on the reports of seven Japanese and Korean survivors later picked up by Task Force 58 and transferred to *Essex* for interrogation, their convoy's losses had been severe. A half dozen ships were seriously damaged. Ten transport and cargo ships were sunk, along with an auxiliary netlayer and the aircraft transport *Keiyo Maru* (beached on Saipan but destroyed on June 13).

Rear Admiral Harrill made plans to finish off the convoy's cripples the following morning. Flight quarters sounded early on June 13, and the *Essex* flight deck was alive with activity long before dawn. CAG Dave Mc-Campbell and the first of his fighters roared off the deck at 0500, a thirty-seven-plane strike group loaded with bombs, depth bombs, and rockets. By 0630, McCampbell's scouting line had the remnants of Convoy No. 4611 in sight.

A small Japanese freighter burning after Air Group Fifteen rocket hits on June 13, 1944. U.S. NAVY, NARA

As his strike group approached from 7,000 feet, McCampbell led his fighters down to make four strafing runs on a freighter of about five hundred tons. Two of the four Mark 47 depth bombs dropped by the Hellcats were damaging near misses as the tiny ship maneuvered radically to avoid them. Torpedo Fifteen moved in next, pounding the ship with up to seventeen five-inch rocket hits. This ship was seen to sink stern first within five minutes of Air Group Fifteen's attack. It was a massive showing for one minor sinking.

During the return to base, two of McCampbell's fighter divisions were flying only a thousand feet above the water. At 0900, Ensign Walter Fontaine of VB-15, flying above at 8,000 feet, suddenly reported a shiny

Japanese plane trailing their formation. It was a Nakajima Ki-49 Donryu twin-engine heavy bomber (code-named "Helen"). Fontaine made a high-side firing run, striking the Helen and sending it fleeing toward the clouds.

"He turned right, poured on coal, and I chased him from astern," Mc-Campbell related. The enemy plane was two miles away, but the CAG caught him in 2.5 minutes at full throttle. McCampbell's entire division engaged with firing runs, with Dave making three. On his third firing pass, the Helen exploded fifty feet above the water. Brand-new, with very bright paint, the plane was possibly being ferried south.[17]

The *Essex* air group made additional strikes on Saipan through the day. Charlie Brewer led the VF-15 contingent on strike number two, which strafed enemy guns and three small cargo boats offshore. Lieutenant Commander Jim Rigg handled the third flight fighter escort. This force pounded buildings and AA emplacements but found no aerial opposition. During an afternoon strike headed by George Duncan, Hellcats and their accompanying SB2Cs attacked another crippled freighter from Convoy No. 4611. Additional hits from Hellcat depth bombs and VB-15 bombs left the ship sinking. Duncan moved his force on to Pagan Island, where two divisions made strafing runs on the airfield.

At 1600, during the group's low-altitude return to base, a twin-engine Betty bomber was tallyhoed by Ensign Ken West.

The mottled brown bomber, sporting large red Japanese Rising Sun flags (irreverently known as meatballs) on its sides, was a prime target as it flew high above at 8,000 feet. Lieutenant John Barry and his wingman, Ensign Joe Power, quickly reversed course and began climbing to attack. Within four minutes they were in position and commenced their assault. Power made the first run, but was too far for his bullets to strike home. Alerted to the previously unseen threat, the Betty pilot made a sharp maneuver to the right and went into a dive.

Closing in from astern, Barry was primed for his first chance to engage an enemy aircraft. "I was so damn eager to get at the Betty that I threw caution to the winds," he admitted. Coming in from straight behind, his plane was an easy target for the bomber's rear tail stinger. Barry's F6F was hit in the port wing, tearing it open and leaving hydraulic lines and electrical lines destroyed.[18]

Unfazed, Barry flew up on the Betty's tail, firing all the way until he silenced its rear gunner. He observed parts flying off the Betty's port wing and flames erupt in its wing root. Now down to 5,000 feet, the Betty fell off to port and dived straight into the sea.

Upon returning to base, Barry could not lower his port wheel. The LSO waved him off, bringing in wingman Joe Power first. It was not the first time an *Essex* F6F had come in hot with only one wheel of the landing gear operational, so Charlie Iarrobino coached him in. Barry chopped the throttle and set the Hellcat down gingerly on its starboard wheel. The plane then dropped onto its port wing, collapsed, and skidded to a stop. Barry climbed out uninjured and watched as plane handlers hauled his No. 7 to the hangar deck to be surveyed and stripped for spare parts. Due to its extensive wing damage, his beloved *Olive* was jettisoned over the side the next day.

Ensign Duz Twelves, wingman for Duncan, was later pinned with a Purple Heart for his actions that day. While strafing an enemy ship, his plane took an AA round that blew off half his canopy. Pierced in the chest and head with shrapnel, Twelves found his injuries to be minor enough that he was patched up on board ship and was flying again the next day.

During the afternoon, *Essex* launched pairs of Helldivers and Hellcats on joint scouting/attack missions. Each SB2C, loaded with a pair of 250-pound bombs, was escorted by a VF-15 pilot. During the preflight briefing, Lieutenant John David "Jig" Bridgers of VB-15 was paired with Ensign Bud Plant, the prewar baseball star pitcher whom Bridgers found to be less than gifted as a student. As he finished his own navigational plot in the wardroom, he saw that Plant's chartboard was blank—void of calculations or even the carrier's "Point Option," or where she was to be found upon their return from the scouting mission.[19]

"Okay, Plant," said Bridgers. "Let's compare our figures."

"Don't give me that bullshit, Jig," Plant replied. "Just show me your numbers."

Although irritated, Bridgers handed over his chartboard for Plant to copy down times and headings he would need in the event the two became separated during their flight.

Their five-hundred-mile round-trip mission was highlighted by two bombing-and-strafing runs the pair made on Japanese ships during their return leg. One of their 250-pounders damaged a troopship's rudder. Plant and Bridgers sent position reports, then strafed a motor whaleboat loaded with Japanese soldiers in green uniforms. "Our blood was up," Bridgers later reflected in defense of his actions. "My conscience has never since been at ease with our ruthlessness."[20]

THE AMERICAN CARRIER strikes against the Marianas had not gone unnoticed. Vice Admiral Ozawa wondered at first if the June 11 strikes had been a diversionary tactic by the enemy to take his focus away from landings in Biak. Reports of continued raids and U.S. carrier forces operating near Saipan convinced him that Task Force 58 was out in force. But further reports of American battleships shelling Saipan on June 13 convinced Ozawa that Biak was not a real target. He followed his original intent to move his own carrier forces to Guimaras, closer to the American showing of strength.

Ozawa's Mobile Fleet sortied from Tawi Tawi on the morning of June 13, stalked by the submarine USS *Redfin* (SS-272). By evening, *Redfin's* contact report alerted Admirals Nimitz, Spruance, and Mitscher that six Japanese carriers, four battleships, and several cruisers and destroyers were on the move. That afternoon, Ozawa sent the order "Prepare for A-GO Decisive Operation." In response, the heavy force of battleships *Yamato* and *Musashi*; cruisers *Myoko, Haguro,* and *Noshiro*; and their destroyers prepared for a rendezvous with Ozawa's fleet.[21]

Ozawa's carrier fleet reached Guimaras in the early afternoon of June 14 and began taking on fuel. The admiral continued to monitor intelligence, poised to mobilize his warships the following day. By the morning of June 15, he received word that U.S. Marines were storming ashore on Saipan. He passed the word that his Combined Fleet would attack the enemy in the Marianas and "annihilate the invasion force." Just five minutes later, a strong directive was received from Admiral Toyoda: "The rise and fall of Imperial Japan depends on this one battle. Every man shall do his utmost."[22]

Essex and the other fleet carriers had a relaxed day on June 14, officially

D minus one (D-1) day. With troops scheduled to go ashore on Tinian, Guam, and Saipan in the morning, the task group refueled from fleet oilers. The *Essex* Hellcats saw no action, but two Betty bombers were splashed that morning by other fighter jockeys. One fell to McCampbell's former flight school student Lieutenant (jg) Alex Vraciu of VF-6 from USS *Lexington* (CV-16), raising his victory tally to an even dozen.

On the morning of June 15, U.S. Marines commenced their landings on Saipan, covered by six dozen Grumman fighters launched from Task Force 58. By afternoon, more than 20,000 Marines were ashore to begin one of the bloodiest assaults they had yet endured. Two task groups, those of William Keene Harrill and Joseph James "Jocko" Clark, had been detached from the Saipan landings to instead knock down potential Japanese aerial resistance from the island of Iwo Jima in the Bonins.

The first sweep from *Essex* launched at 1330 on June 15. Strike coordinator Dave McCampbell had twenty-two Hellcats, plus additional F6Fs from *Yorktown* and USS *Bataan* (CVL-29). Charlie Brewer, George Duncan, George Crittenden, and John Strane led the other VF-15 divisions as the combined fighter sweep covered the 137-mile flight in toward Iwo Jima and the two airfields they were assigned to work over. Inbound, the strikers hit a solid wall of weather, with high surface winds, rain squalls, and cloud cover extending up to 28,000 feet.

"It was without a doubt the worst hop that I have ever been on," wrote John Barry. "The high winds blew us north of the island, so we flew south for twenty minutes, then located the island." It was a full two hours after departure before the *Essex* planes had their target area in sight and began climbing to 8,000 feet to commence strafing runs. For Satan's Playmates, it was a dream come true: more than a hundred Japanese aircraft were spread out on the ground.[23]

McCampbell led the strafing parade down, with twenty-one other Hellcats close on his tail. Their bullets chewed through twin-engine Bettys and Nells, and dozens of fighter planes: Zekes, Hamps (Mitsubishi A6M3 Model 32s), and Tojos. At 1535, just five minutes into the assault on the Iwo fields, Commander McCampbell spotted his first airborne enemy. It was a lone Zeke approaching from his port beam. "I turned into him and gave him a long burst head-on," McCampbell recalled. "He continued straight and level until dangerously close, and I pulled out above and to right before he did."[24]

The *Essex* CAG pursued the Zeke as he headed into cloud cover, firing a long burst from 2,500 feet astern. Popping back out of the clouds, Dave found him dead ahead. Jockeying to get back on his tail, McCampbell made a vertical flipper turn to the right and "grayed out" (temporarily losing his peripheral vision and color perception) due to the extreme g-force on his body. He managed a short burst before the Zeke made an abrupt wingover and locked onto McCampbell's tail. Wingman Roy Rushing, having followed the action, saw the enemy fighter latch onto his CAG's tail. Before Rushing could fire, the Zeke pulled back into the clouds. The plane was not seen again, although two other pilots reported seeing a splash in the ocean. McCampbell hoped it was the Zeke, but some thought it could have been a discarded belly tank.

Five miles southwest of the field, Charlie Brewer downed a Zeke by closing to a mere hundred feet before blasting it into the sea. George Duncan found four olive drab–colored Zekes three miles east of the island, and chased them for about ten miles. By turning on his water injection for a quick WEP boost, Duncan was able to catch the rear Zeke and shoot it into the ocean.

Back at the airfields, all VF-15 divisions made at least three strafing runs from 7,000 feet, pulling out as low as 200 feet. More than fifty aircraft were burned or wrecked on the ground.

Rolling black smoke climbed into the skies, adding to the innumerable black puffs of antiaircraft fire dotting the gray skies. "It was a frightening but exhilarating picture," Barry recalled. Japanese gunners winged eight VF-15 Hellcats, including that of Lieutenant George Crittenden. The division leader heard 7.7mm bullets banging into his fuselage and then felt the sharp sting of a bullet that embedded in his left leg.

Crittenden, bleeding heavily, retired to the squadron rendezvous area while other divisions continued to work over Iwo for a full hour. The only loss for Brewer's squadron came during the third strafing run made by Lieutenant (jg) Alfred "Ack-Ack" Jones. Caught in an intense AA cross fire, Jones's F6F was hit. He was seen to pull up slightly about halfway across the runway before rolling over onto his back. His plane slammed into the ocean, killing Jones.

The *Essex* fighters claimed at least twenty-five Japanese aircraft destroyed on the ground, plus the three aerial kills. McCampbell and his division of Rushing, Bert Morris, and Ken Flinn made six total strafing runs before retiring to the rendezvous spot. He sent the balance of his group home while remaining on the scene to act as aerial coordinator for the second strike group. It reached the target area at 1615, forty-five minutes after the first *Essex* group had arrived over Iwo Jima.

Led by squadron XO Jim Rigg, the group included two VF-15 divisions to cover thirty dive-bombers and torpedo planes from *Essex* and *Langley*. The enlarged, inverted A–shaped airfield on the southern part of Iwo Jima was very difficult to see from the air, as it blended well into the dark-colored earth. The new strip to the north was brown in color but more easily discernible. There were numerous medium bombers parked on the ground, some packed close together like aircraft on a carrier, making a beautiful target.

Rigg led both divisions down from 13,000 feet. Their strafing efforts caused two Betty bombers to burst into flames. Five other aircraft were damaged, but the antiaircraft fire took a toll on Air Group Fifteen. One SB2C and two VT-15 Avengers were knocked down, with the loss of their crews.

VF-15 photo Hellcat pilots Art Singer and Roy Nall and their wingmen broke off from covering the bombers to make their photo sorties of the entire island. After Singer had completed his vertical coverage at 5,000 feet, he was making dicing shots of the beaches at two hundred feet. About a hundred yards off the shoreline, he suddenly encountered an olive drab–colored Zeke with random yellow streaks in its color pattern. The enemy fighter was on a parallel course in the opposite direction 1 o'clock up.

Singer turned into a climbing approach with full throttle and water injection, pulled up on the Zeke's tail, and fired into the cockpit and wing roots. He overshot the Zero and pulled up. Wingman Lieutenant (jg) Jim Bruce then came into position on the Zeke's tail ready to fire, but the Zeke went out of control and crashed into the water just after the pilot bailed out. Singer and Bruce saw the poor Japanese pilot being dragged downwind as his plane plowed under the waves.

Heavy weather caused Admiral Mitscher to cancel flight operations on the morning of June 16, allowing the aviators some extra sack time. The weather was marginally improved by noon, permitting the launching of routine patrols and several strike groups. Included among them was a forty-plane *Essex* group launched at 1340 in company with sixteen *Cowpens* strikers.

Dave McCampbell led eleven VF-15 Hellcats that covered the bombers and torpedo planes while George Duncan led another seven fighters to concentrate on Iwo without escort duties. McCampbell's men faced heavy antiaircraft fire as they strafed several gun emplacements. Repeated strafing runs were made on AA positions, aircraft on the ground, fuel dumps, and buildings. VF-15 claimed destruction of eighteen medium bombers and ten fighters on the ground, many already damaged from the previous day's strikes.

McCampbell's wingman, Roy Rushing, had his Hellcat's hydraulic system knocked out by AA shrapnel that ripped through his wings and fuselage. Without instruments and with one aileron shot away, Rushing nonetheless limped back to *Essex*, where his Grumman was later repaired by the deck crews. Duncan's divisions found no aerial opposition, so they also strafed gun positions and aircraft on the ground. Duncan's wingman, Duz Twelves, wiped out a Japanese 40mm gun emplacement with his strafing efforts. By the time the group departed, fires from burning planes and shore installations created heavy smoke covering almost half of Iwo Jima.

John Barry, one of the five men making up Lieutenant Jack Ivey's division, was not assigned to this strike. He later heard the results from three others who flew with Ivey this day: Joe Power, George Carr, and Glenn Edward Mellon. During his dive over the Iwo airfield, Ivey's F6F was struck by flak as he dropped down to 2,500 feet on his strafing pass. Shrapnel entered the left side of his head, completely blinding his left eye and severely damaging his right eye.

Although vision-impaired, Ivey somehow managed to pull out of his dive and climb away from the island. He jettisoned his plotting board and turned toward base. It was an eighty-five-mile flight back to *Essex*, but Ivey was flying mainly on reflexes as he suffered through the shock and pain of his horrific head wounds. Carr and Mellon eased their Hellcats up alongside the division leader and helped shepherd him slowly back toward the fleet. It was immediately apparent that Ivey was in very bad shape.

At times, Ivey's plane drifted off on a course away from Task Force 58. Carr had to use his own wingtips to gently nudge the lieutenant back onto the proper heading. Ivey's radio was shot out and he was clearly fighting to stay conscious. He was only able to communicate with Carr and Mellon via hand signals. They implored him to bail out and save himself, but Ivey continued to stagger along, his plane nudged back on the proper course each time he strayed.

As the trio reached the fleet, Carr was ordered to land aboard *Essex*, while the duty CAP team was vectored out to continue working with the semi-coherent lieutenant. Jack Ivey was clearly in no shape to land, but he made no effort to ditch. His Hellcat was last seen flying into a cloud bank. The CAP fighters lost him but soon found a dye marker streaking the water below the heavy clouds. No sign of his F6F remained save for a spreading oil slick. Ivey had simply hit the water at some point, unseen by his comrades.

John Barry, upset at not being included on this flight, mourned the loss of his division leader that evening as he wrote in his diary: "Jack was a prince of a fellow. Steady, conservative, intelligent boy."[25]

June 17, 1944

The first five days of action in the Marianas had been tough on Fighting Fifteen. Mel Roach, Jack Ivey, and Ack-Ack Jones were gone, leaving three divisions minus their leaders or section leaders. But business was business, and Whiskey Harrill's task group was charged with making another strike against Pagan Island on the afternoon of June 17.

With the loss of two division leaders, Charlie Brewer elevated other men within their divisions to take acting command. Roach's division was split up, with sections from his group now flying with others. George Carr, second section leader for Ivey's division, became an acting division leader, although he would at times fly as a section leader for other divisions in a pinch.

Lieutenant Commander Jim Rigg headed out at 1426 with fifteen fighters, eleven Helldivers, and eight Avengers to attack enemy aircraft and installations on the island. Six of his F6Fs armed with bombs dropped their twelve-hour-delay ordnance (set to explode during night hours) on Pagan airfield's runway, while the balance of the fighters strafed parked aircraft, barracks, and a radio station. All of the aircraft found had been previously shot up and destroyed during TF 58's June 12 raids.

Vice Admiral Pete Mitscher was aware that Ozawa's Mobile Fleet had departed Guimaras on the morning of June 15. His movements were reported by coastwatchers that day as his carriers moved into San Bernardino Strait, but it would be two days before this news reached Admiral Spruance. Fortunately, intelligence from Vice Admiral Charles Lockwood's Silent Service moved swifter. The submarine USS *Flying Fish* (SS-229) counted three carriers, three battleships, and many cruisers and destroyers on the afternoon of June 15. Hours later, Lieutenant Commander Slade Cutter's USS *Seahorse* (SS-304) reported a heavy warship force that included the super-battleships *Yamato* and *Musashi* two hundred miles east of Surigao Strait.[26]

During the afternoon of June 16, Admiral Matome Ugaki's battleship force made rendezvous with Ozawa's carriers, and the entire Mobile Fleet was finally joined. The force refueled from fleet tankers through the following morning. A little over 750 nautical miles from Saipan by the afternoon of June 17, Ozawa bided his time. His staff believed that the Japanese military's land-based squadrons could severely damage Task Force 58 while he temporarily stayed out of range. Outnumbered nine carriers against fifteen American carriers, Ozawa hoped to lie in wait for some of them to be knocked out before he charged down against Mitscher's flattops.[27]

Aerial snoopers and submarines continued to stalk the Mobile Fleet as the waiting game continued. The fifth carrier engagement between Japan and the United States was brewing, and it was just a matter of time before things exploded.

Long-ranging American search planes launched from Saipan and the Admiralty Islands roamed the seas in search of the Japanese Mobile Fleet. Mitscher's carriers sent up their own search groups on the morning of June 18. From *Essex*, three teams of Helldivers and Hellcats took to the air at 0535. Each fighter/bomber team was tasked with flying narrow search legs out as far as 325 miles from the fleet in the direction Mitscher believed Ozawa's fleet would be found. They did not locate any Japanese warships during their five-hour flights, but the teams did encounter a handful of enemy airplanes out doing their own probing.

First to make contact at 0755 was the *Essex* team of Ensign Jim Duffy and Lieutenant (jg) Raymond Turner of VB-15. Flying at 1,000 feet, Duffy suddenly noticed Turner rocking the wings of his Helldiver to get his attention. Turner pointed toward a single-engine plane at about their altitude, five miles off their starboard bow. Duffy snugged in close on his SB2C companion and they began climbing to make an attack.

Duffy's first thoughts were that it might be a scout plane, but he quickly realized there was no fighter escort with this aircraft. As he pulled in closer behind and below the bandit, he was surprised to see red meatballs on its sides. "My adrenaline started to flow," Duffy remembered. He believed it to be a Nakajima B5N carrier-based torpedo bomber (code-named "Kate"), but it was later determined to be a similar, newer model Nakajima B6N Tenzan torpedo plane (code-named "Jill"). Less than a half mile away, they were spotted by the Japanese pilot. As Duffy closed the range on a beam run, the Jill made a diving turn to port. Duffy swung wide to keep from overrunning it. He came up on the Jill at 7 o'clock and commenced firing.[28] Its port wing root flamed, and the pilot pulled up as Turner started his run from astern and below. Turner fired a hundred rounds, sending the Jill spinning into the ocean before Duffy could participate in the kill. "I was amazed how fast a fight would develop and then how fast it would subside," Duffy recalled.[29]

Search Team 2 also had an enemy encounter ninety minutes later. At 0930, Lieutenant (jg) William S. Rising sighted a Betty bomber at about 1,500 feet altitude, thirteen miles ahead. His fighter escort, Ensign Ken

Flinn, made five firing runs and caused the Betty's port wing tank to blaze. As Flinn completed his final run, the big bomber's port wing dipped into the ocean, causing the plane to explode, with debris flying high. Flinn was disgusted to find upon returning to *Essex* that his gun camera magazine had jammed and failed to capture his second kill on film.

With VF-15's two victories this day, the squadron's total now stood at fifteen confirmed kills since entering the Pacific combat zone in May.

Other teams from Task Force 58 added a few more shoot-downs through the day on June 18, but the Mobile Fleet remained undetected by American aircraft. Japanese scout planes proved more effective. Two different contact reports of the U.S. carrier fleet reached Ozawa. He prudently elected to keep the distance extreme between his force and Mitscher's, staying just on the fringe of the range his carrier aircraft could fly to hit his enemy. The Mobile Force included only 69 warships pitted against some 138 U.S. combat vessels deployed in the near vicinity. Ozawa had about 440 carrier-based aircraft on his nine flattops to go against some 900 planes on Mitscher's carriers. But Ozawa knew that he had a slight advantage when counting 630 additional land-based planes ashore in the Marianas and from bases within range of Task Force 58.[30]

Ozawa flew his flag on the 34,600-ton carrier *Taiho*, which had just been completed in March. His Carrier Division (CarDiv) One also included the fleet carriers *Zuikaku* and *Shokaku*, the only flattops that had participated in the surprise attack on Pearl Harbor in December 1941 still above the waves. The other four had been sent to the bottom of the ocean by Dauntless dive-bombers during the June 1942 Battle of Midway.

CarDiv Two, under Rear Admiral Takaji Joshima, included the 26,900-ton sister carriers *Junyo* and *Hiyo*, plus the 16,700-ton *Ryuho*, which had been converted to a carrier in 1942. Rear Admiral Sueo Obayashi's CarDiv Three was built around the light carrier *Zuiho*, which had been damaged in the carrier Battle of Santa Cruz in October 1942, and two light carriers that had originally been constructed as seaplane tenders: *Chitose* and *Chiyoda*.

The Japanese and American task forces continued to probe for better intelligence on each other's locations. During the overnight of June 18–19, they were a mere three hundred miles apart at one point. Admiral Spruance, a surface sailor by trade, did not trust his intelligence enough yet. Although Pete Mitscher's staff urged Spruance to allow Task Force 58 to charge west toward Ozawa's Mobile Fleet, Spruance prudently opted to keep his carriers guarding the invasion beaches on June 19.[31]

Mitscher could do little to soothe his frustration. Orders were orders. Flight operations and searches would resume the next day. A clash of carriers seemed inevitable.

The only question was when.

SEVEN

TURKEY SHOOT'S FIRST RAIDS

June 19, 1944

In his stateroom, John Strane was startled from a deep sleep. It was 0200, and the duty sailor who nudged him whispered that it was time for him to prepare for flight duty. There was the entire Japanese Mobile Fleet out there to find, and flight scheduler Bert Morris had assigned Lieutenant Strane to help locate it.

Donning his flight suit, Strane hurried to the wardroom for a quick breakfast and then made his way up to the squadron ready room, located just one deck below the main flight deck. Skipper Charlie Brewer prepped his pilots while Lieutenant Morris handed out the assignments. "I was told that I was to fly escort on an SB2C Helldiver and that we would fly a high-speed search in hopes of finding units of the Jap fleet," Strane recalled.[1]

Ensign Spike Borley was more excited than Strane for this day. He had been scheduled for the predawn first combat air patrol launch. He knew enemy action was expected, and this might be his first chance to engage in a dogfight. When his alarm rang at 0345, he rolled out of bed wide-awake, dressed quickly, and raced to down a hasty breakfast. "As the newest and youngest ensign in the squadron, I was anxious to be on time and to do all that I had been trained for," Borley remembered.[2]

Assigned to Lieutenant Commander Jim Rigg's CAP division, Borley was one of four Hellcats launched by catapult around 0500. They rendezvoused in complete blackness and then began climbing to 26,000 feet to orbit around the fleet. "The sunrise was spectacular!" Borley recalled. "It lit up the scattered cumulus clouds in a variety of colors and reflected off the ever-changing white-capped sea."

Next off *Essex* were the search teams. Three hours after waking, John Strane crawled into the cockpit of his Helldiver and ran through his launch checklist. Everything was in order and his engine coughed to life minutes later, shortly before the first rays of sunlight had the chance to illuminate his task group. "Although our squadrons had been in the combat area for over a month, a lot of us had yet to see our first enemy plane and, of course, were anxious to do so," recalled Strane. He was equally anxious for his own chance, and the prospect of pasting a red Japanese Rising Sun flag on the side of his own F6F.[3]

Three Helldivers, each in company with a VF-15 Hellcat, climbed into the dark and proceeded toward their three search sectors. Flying at around 1,000 feet over the vast Pacific, Strane positioned himself just slightly behind and on the starboard flank of the Helldiver flown by Lieutenant (jg) Don McCutcheon, a twenty-four-year-old who hailed from New Jersey. Strane would fly in a protective position, shepherding his SB2C crew as their Search Team 1 flew in strict radio silence. Two hours out from *Essex*, Strane and McCutcheon were nearing the limits of their outbound leg at 0725. McCutcheon then spotted a bandit about ten miles away, approaching at about 150 knots to the left of the search team.

McCutcheon drifted back alongside Strane and hand-signaled to the fighter pilot to join up closer on him. Three hundred feet below was a Zero floatplane (Navy Type Zero Reconnaissance Seaplane), an Aichi E13A, which the U.S. military had code-named "Jake." Strane found the Japanese pilot to be blissfully unaware of his danger. The bluish black–colored Jake continued on its course until he passed almost directly underneath McCutcheon's Helldiver.

Strane quickly charged his six wing guns. As the floatplane passed aft of him, it was now flying perpendicular to his own course. Strane kicked his Hellcat around to port and made a hard, diving left turn to attain a firing position on his enemy's port beam. The dull search flight had suddenly turned into John Strane's first opportunity to attack an enemy aircraft. "My heart was really thumping," he recalled. "I was about as excited as a person could be."[4]

Strane's first dozen .50-caliber bullets were right on the money. They thumped into the Jake's cockpit and fuselage, causing pieces to fly off from both sides as the plane immediately burst into flames. The Japanese pilot attempted to pull up about five hundred feet, but his floatplane was mortally wounded. Strane watched the Jake fall into a spin down at a 75-degree angle and slam into the ocean. Circling the wreckage, Don McCutcheon saw only one of the plane's two pontoons floating on the water.

One burst, one kill. Lieutenant Strane was now on the board, a blooded fighter pilot who had achieved his first victory. He rejoined his Helldiver crew, and ten minutes into their reverse course for home, at 0741, Strane spotted another bandit. This one proved to be a dark brown Japanese "Kate" carrier torpedo bomber. It was flying just below the cloud bank at about 1,500 feet, almost their same level.

The Kate pilot continued his approach until his course put him in the 2 o'clock position, just to the right side of Search Team 1. The Japanese aviator apparently then spotted the American team, as he abruptly pulled up sharply into an opposite course to reach the cloud cover. "I broke immediately and climbed to get into a shooting position," Strane recalled. "He passed over our intended track, so he was now on my left side."[5]

He chased the Kate through cloud cover, turning on his emergency power water injection to narrow the range. As he made his first firing pass, Strane noted the plane had a torpedo dangling below its belly and that its rear canopy enclosure was in the open position. Winking red bursts of tracers made it clear to Strane that the Kate's rear gunner was fully alert. He was firing back at the menacing Hellcat, although the Kate's port wing tank had burst into flames. Fortunately, his shots missed. The opponents lost sight of each other for desperate seconds as they tore through the cloud bank. When they emerged on the other side, the Japanese plane was dead ahead of Strane.

He opened fire again with another short burst. He saw more flames erupt in the Kate's port wing and could see the rear gunner slumped over the right canopy rail, now lifeless. As Strane overshot his stricken opponent, he saw that the pilot also appeared to be dead, slumped over his control stick. The Kate then stalled out and went into a spin from 3,000 feet altitude before it slammed almost vertically into the ocean with terrific impact.

Strane and McCutcheon then proceeded back toward *Essex*. With use of his Zed-Baker navigational aid, Strane located *Essex* some sixty miles from her Point Option. When they finally landed after the task group had escaped an enemy air attack, Strane was summoned to the bridge to offer a report to Rear Admiral Harrill.[6]

It was still early morning of June 19, a day that would make history both for Task Force 58 and for VF-15. But John Strane had already begun to make his contributions. His F6F had earned the right to be adorned with two Rising Sun stickers.

Essex Search Team 3 made no enemy encounters this morning, but Search Team 2 was just as deadly as Strane's scout group had been. Comprising VB-15's Lieutenant (jg) Clifford Jordan and VF-15's Ensign Doyle Bare, the team spent its first three hours searching in vain. But things changed quickly as Team 2 headed back toward base.

It was 0834 when rear gunner Aviation Radioman 2nd Class (ARM2c) Stanley Whitby called up to his pilot that he had spotted an enemy plane lurking near the edge of a cloud base. Bare climbed for altitude against what proved to be a dark blue Jake floatplane. Bare squeezed his trigger and fired his first burst into its tail. On his second pass, Bare put twenty rounds into the Jake, causing it to explode into flames and dive into the ocean. Jordan was first to spot their next quarry at 0912, a Kate torpedo bomber. It was two miles away, flying at about 150 knots. Jordan waggled his wings to attract the attention of Bare, then pointed toward the plane.

Jordan locked in on the target first, and his long burst sent the Kate blazing into the drink. At 0935, Jordan spotted another Kate, this one heading away from the search team at high speed in the opposite direction. Ensign Bare turned and climbed to follow. Using full military power for about five minutes, Bare was able to reach a position about five hundred feet above the torpedo plane. The Kate nosed down, but Bare hung with him, firing from behind. Only one of his wing guns would fire, but he pressed in and was soon able to get smoke and fire from the Kate's port wing.

Bare recharged his guns as Jordan's SB2C Helldiver moved in to add additional bursts. His run caused no apparent damage, but Bare was quickly into his next pass, firing from above and behind the Kate. As he closed to less than a thousand feet distance, the torpedo bomber began blazing. It pulled up sharply and the pilot attempted to bail out. His chute had barely opened by the time he hit the water.

Two of the three *Essex* search teams had scored in the early morning of June 19 in what would prove to be an epic aerial battle in the Philippine Sea. Bombing Squadron Fifteen had claimed one victim, while Strane and Bare of VF-15 had each scored two kills. By the time the six *Essex* searchers returned to the carrier at 1014, their task force was embroiled in a major fight.

RAID I INTERCEPTS: "HEY, RUBE!"

By 0600, Pete Mitscher's Task Force 58 was less than ninety miles northwest of Guam. Carrier operations were ideal: a bright sun was beginning to warm the air to a temperature that would climb into the low eighties. Visibility was excellent, but the Bald Eagle still had no lock on the enemy's fleet from his early snoopers.

His carriers were 330 miles north-northeast of the Japanese van force, and another hundred miles from Admiral Ozawa's Carrier Division One and Joshima's CarDiv Two. At 0730, Jake floatplanes from the Mobile Fleet were first to spot Whiskey Harrill's Task Group 58.4. From his nine carriers, Ozawa commenced launching the first of his strikes against the American flattops at 0800. Eventually labeled "Raid I" by his opponents, Ozawa's first force was dispatched from the light carriers *Chitose*, *Chiyoda*, and *Zuiho* of CarDiv Three. It included sixty-nine planes: forty-five Zero fighter-bombers, sixteen escort planes, and eight Jill torpedo planes.[7]

Nearly two hours would pass before Ozawa's Raid I was close enough to be picked up by TF 58 radar. Mitscher's carriers had filled the air surrounding his task groups with fighter CAP teams, each lying in wait for word on enemy air strikes. From *Essex*, eleven of twelve F6Fs had launched successfully at 0910. Charlie Brewer's division was one short, with only three Hellcats, but George Duncan and George Carr each had complete four-plane teams. Carr, one of the three former RCAF veterans, had become acting division leader after the death of Jack Ivey days prior. Upon completing the rendezvous, the VF-15 divisions began climbing for altitude.

High in the island superstructures of Mitscher's carriers, radio and radar sets were dutifully manned by electronics experts in each combat information center (CIC). At 0937, while still climbing, Duncan's division was vectored out toward a bogey. They made a tallyho at 0950 on a TBF that was returning without its Identification of Friend or Foe unit working. The rest of their flight was uneventful. For Duncan, the morning flight was one of frustration. The only enemy plane his division encountered was a lone Yokosuka D4Y Suisei dive-bomber (code-named "Judy") that was already under fire from another group of Hellcats. "I never got to him because he was low on the water and scooting as fast as he could go with people shooting at him," Duncan said.[8]

. The other two CAP divisions, under Brewer and Carr, soon had their hands full. At 1000, Mitscher received radar intelligence and pilot reports of Japanese planes taking off from Guam. By 1013, Ozawa's Raid I was picked up on radar screens, closing from a distance of about 118 miles. Assuming that his carriers were about to be worked over, Mitscher had his FDOs begin recalling his roving CAPs from the island with an old circus barker's slang phrase for calling in patrons: "Hey, Rube!" At 1023, the FDOs began clearing flight decks of bombers and scrambling all available fighter planes. Within fifteen minutes, some two hundred Hellcats were airborne or climbing toward their stations.[9]

On *Essex*, Lieutenant Bert Morris and his four-plane division was launched via catapult by 1025. His quartet would help cover as TG 58.4 CAP while the FDOs directed two of Commander Brewer's divisions at 1024 on a vector to intercept Raid I. Although Morris and his three pilots would receive one vector about twenty minutes after launching, their group did not become involved with intercepting the inbound Japanese force.

Charlie Brewer and George Carr had taken their divisions to 24,000 feet (Angels 24). Each pilot had donned his mask and was inhaling pure oxygen—required when their F6Fs surpassed 10,000 feet in altitude. When their vector was received at 1024, each pilot ran though his pre-combat checklist, adjusting his Mark VIII sight rheostats, checking his shoulder harness, and arming his six Browning .50-caliber machine guns. Each gun carried four hundred rounds, totaling 2,400 rounds of ammunition per Grumman fighter. The ammo for each gun was belted in sequence of armor-piercing (AP) incendiary, tracer, and ball bullets. A trigger-happy pilot could empty all four hundred rounds from a wing gun with only thirty seconds of trigger time.[10]

Conservation was the name of the game.

As fate would have it, Satan's Playmates were the first of any squadron to sight Ozawa's Raid I bandits. Squadron skipper Brewer gave the tallyho call at 1035. In fighter lingo, enemy carrier planes were designated as "rats" (fighter planes), "hawks" (bombers), or "fish" (torpedo planes). Brewer identified his quarry as comprising twenty-four rats and sixteen hawks, with no fish, flying below at 18,000 feet. He felt he was facing a combination of A6M3 Hamp and A6M2 Zeke fighters mixed with Judy dive-bombers, although the Judys were actually Jill torpedo planes. Fighting Fifteen's biggest challenge was at hand, and the fight commenced.

Brewer signaled to his second section leader, Jake Lundin, to prepare. Their combat team and that of Carr would make an overhead run on the enemy formation. Lundin noted a division of Hamp fighters slightly to the rear of the sixteen bombers. Another sixteen Zekes were stacked 1,000 to 2,000 feet above the bombers. The VF-15 pilots had the advantage of altitude, and Brewer wasted no time.

He plunged down into the Jills, opening fire on his first torpedo plane from eight hundred feet. The first burst of Brewer's .50s ripped into a Japanese plane, and it exploded immediately. Passing through the flames and debris, the skipper pulled up, shooting into a second Jill. Pieces flew off, and the plane flamed before diving into the ocean minus half of one wing. Brewer then pushed over to overtake a Zeke. He chased it until he got on its tail, and he was able to shoot up its wing roots. As Brewer closed to about four hundred feet, the Zeke flamed and spun into the ocean, marking Brewer's third kill in short order. Following this encounter, Brewer found a Zeke diving on his Hellcat. In the dogfight that ensued, the VF-15 skipper worked his way onto the Zeke's tail. At each burst of his guns, Brewer watched the crafty Zeke pilot maneuver violently. He half rolled; then, after staying on his back briefly, the Zeke pulled through sharply, following with barrel rolls and wingovers.

This is no rookie, Brewer thought. But he stayed with his opponent, landing hits in his fuselage, wings, and cockpit until the Zeke caught fire. Going into a tight spiral, the Japanese fighter slammed into the ocean. In a matter of minutes, Brewer had brought down two Zekes and two Jills. Combined with his prior 1.5 victories, Brewer had become VF-15's first ace of the tour.

His wingman, Ensign Dick Fowler, was equally effective during this melee. He followed Brewer into the action. As Brewer fired on his third opponent, a Zeke, Fowler noted the Zeke's wingman stall or make a diving right turn in front of his F6F. Fowler broke away and began firing at the Japanese fighter at long range. As he closed in on the Zeke's tail, he began firing short bursts.

The Zeke began smoking from Fowler's bullets, finally starting a fast, steep spiral to the left before hitting the ocean. Now at 10,000 feet altitude, Fowler spotted two Zekes in a tight Lufbery circle. Named for World War I fighter pilot Major Raoul Lufbery, this maneuver was essentially a defensive tactic in which planes flew in a ring so that each could protect the tail of the plane ahead.

Ensign Dick Fowler scored four kills on June 19, 1944, during the Turkey Shoot.
DEBBIE FOWLER BAATSTAD

Fowler charged into the Lufbery circle, making multiple firing passes. In short order, his bullets sent two Zekes plunging into the drink. Recovering from this action, Fowler started to join on two other F6Fs just as they were making a run on a Hamp. The Hamp continued into a cloud and the other Hellcats pulled off him. Noting the Hamp emerge from the other side of the cloud bank, Fowler applied throttle and gave pursuit. He started firing at 1,500 feet.

His hits were going into the Hamp's fuselage and cockpit when all but one of Fowler's guns ceased firing. But the Hamp caught fire and spun in.

Unfazed, Fowler next found two Jills flying in a section, made two overhead runs with one gun firing, and saw hits on the second overhead. Pieces flew from the fuselage and cockpit, but the Jill appeared to stay in formation, leaving Fowler with a final score of one Jill damaged plus three Zekes and a Hamp destroyed.

Commander Brewer's second section, Lieutenant Ted Overton with wingman Ed Mellon, engaged in their own separate melees. Struggling with a slow F6F, Overton soon fell behind the rest of the division. Alone, he flamed the engine of a Jill and watched it explode in midair. Overton then shot up a Zeke enough to create smoke and flames, but he was forced to dive for safety as another Japanese fighter latched onto his tail. He was credited with a kill and a probable. For his part, Mellon downed a Jill and landed hits on another Japanese torpedo plane that was being assaulted by another Hellcat.

In just minutes, skipper Brewer's lead division had racked up ten kills and a probable. During this same time, Lieutenant (jg) Carr's second division bracketed the same enemy formation and was equally effective.

Carr's first Jill victim exploded immediately. Dodging through the flames and aerial debris, he executed a wingover and caught a second Jill at the top of his maneuver. A high-side sitting duck, this Jill burst into flames and spiraled toward the ocean. Carr then found what he deemed a Hamp (actually a Zeke) on his tail. He pushed into a 90-degree dive, with 430 knots (nearly 500 mph) indicated, and made an aileron roll to the right. Although his heater and defrosters were on, Carr's windshield fogged badly in the moist tropical air.

Carr outdistanced the Zeke, climbed back to altitude, and found himself all alone. His wingman, Ensign Norm Berree, was nowhere to be found. Spotting a Jill approaching him, Carr put a short burst into its engine and wing roots and exploded his opponent. In the process, he collected a direct hit in his own bulletproof windshield. As he pulled up from this pass, Carr found two more Jills ahead and up about 2,000 feet on a parallel course.

He made a stern run on the Jill off his port wing. Something left the plane—he thought it might have been the pilot—but there was no time to watch. Carr skidded left sharply to get on the tail of the second Jill. One long burst started a fire aft of its engine. He then split-S'ed to catch the Jill on its way down, but it exploded before he could get it in his sights. In the same instant, he saw the first of his two Jills splash into the ocean with no parachutes evident.

At low altitude, Carr began climbing. At this point he could find no other enemy aircraft airborne. He began to count oil slicks and visible splashes in the ocean below. He was up to seventeen victims from the melee when two other F6Fs went by. Carr joined them and returned to the *Essex*, having become an "ace in a day" by downing five Jills in a single mission—at the same time that his skipper was attaining ace status with his morning's four kills.

Ensign Berree, separated from division leader Carr during the scrap, shot down two Hamps and a Jill. In his first pass, he blasted an unsuspecting Hamp on the starboard side of the enemy formation. It caught fire, but he continued firing until it exploded. As Berree pulled out of his dive, the first Hamp's wingman was on his tail. Pushing into a dive with a sharp right turn, he shook his opponent.

Now at 10,000 feet, Berree spotted a third Hamp on a parallel course on his level. The Japanese and American pilots turned toward each other. As Berree commenced firing, the Hamp rolled onto its back. Each pilot held his course until a collision appeared unavoidable. At the last instant, the Hamp pilot broke underneath Berree, smoking badly. Berree's own water injection system was hit at this time as bullets raked his F6F. "The Hellcat's armor plate protection saved my butt," Berree recalled. He cartwheeled to follow his brazen opponent, but the Hamp exploded and disintegrated before he could fire again.[11]

By this point the fight had dissolved, so Berree rejoined the other pilots of Carr's division to return to base. Carr's second section, consisting of Jake Lundin and Jim Bruce, had also plowed into the enemy formation. On their first run, Lundin and Bruce each had to check fire as another F6F entered their sights. Climbing back up, Lundin made a second pass and came down on a Zeke. He fired up the tail and fuselage past the cockpit.

Lundin watched his shots stitch all the way up the Zeke's back until his opponent suddenly exploded.

Lundin and Bruce then attacked a lone Jill they encountered on an opposite course, apparently running away from the deadly fray. Lundin landed hits in its wings and started the Jill smoking. The torpedo plane began diving for the water, pulled into a wingover, and crashed vertically into the sea. As he was climbing to join the action, Lundin saw seven planes in the air burning or in spirals at the same time. Bruce, soon separated from wingman Lundin, managed to shoot up a Zeke that was last seen smoking.

Eight Hellcats from *Cowpens* arrived at the attack scene shortly after VF-15 and made more kills. As George Carr's triumphant division returned to Task Force 38, they were ordered to remain on CAP duty. At 1151 they were vectored out to intercept a lone bogey, seen to be approaching slowly from thirty miles out. This lone Judy (or possibly Jill) was pursued by Norm Berree, but he overshot his opponent on the first pass. Winging over, he then landed hits in its engine from above, dead astern. The Judy flamed, lost altitude, and crashed into the water, raising Berree's scorecard to three kills for the morning.

Other Task Force 58 fighters tore into the balance of Japanese carrier Raid I. The VF-8 of *Bunker Hill* (CV-17) claimed two Zekes and a bomber at the price of one Hellcat pilot forced to ditch his shot-up mount and be recovered by a destroyer. *Hornet*'s VF-2 claimed nine Zekes and three Jills, while VF-27 Hellcat pilots from the light carrier USS *Princeton* (CVL-23) knocked down bombers and fighter-bombers. USS *Enterprise* (CV-6) and USS *Monterey* (CVL-26) fighters scored additional kills, but a handful of the Japanese strikers survived long enough to make attacks.[12]

One Zero landed a bomb hit on the battleship USS *South Dakota* (BB-57), and the destroyer USS *Hudson* (DD-475) suffered two sailors killed by friendly fire from American warships blazing away at diving enemy planes. In the end, forty-two Japanese aircraft from Raid I were lost, while overzealous fighter pilots turned in claims for more than twice that many downed. In the frenzied heat of battle, some pilots no doubt submitted claims for the same blazing Japanese plane that another pilot felt was his kill.

The most important outcome of the first aerial battle for Pete Mitscher was that none of his precious carriers had been hit. Meanwhile, Charlie Brewer's VF-15 emerged from the combat without loss and sporting claims of twenty aerial victories—by far their greatest showing to date in their young combat tour.

RAID II INTERCEPTS

Admiral Ozawa's scout planes had been busy. With fresh contact reports of American carriers in hand, he had already launched a second large assault group at 0900. From the carriers *Taiho*, *Shokaku*, and *Zuikaku*, he dispatched 128 planes: 53 Judy dive-bombers with 550-pound bombs, 27 torpedo-laden Jills, and 48 Zeke fighters. More than 20 were forced to abort the mission for various difficulties, but it was still a formidable force.[13]

Ozawa's Raid II was still effecting its rendezvous above the carrier force when disaster struck. Commander James Blanchard's submarine, USS *Albacore* (SS-218), had eased into position near the Japanese force and launched six torpedoes. One of the freshly launched Jill pilots gave his own life by diving his strike plane directly into one of the onrushing white torpedo wakes. But his sacrifice did not save *Taiho* from being slammed with a torpedo on her starboard side. Damage control parties shored her up well enough that she would later contribute strike planes to two other raids on June 19. But dangerous aviation gasoline vapors began accumulating, making *Taiho* a ticking time bomb.

The balance of Raid II's strike force that made its approach on Task Force 58 numbered 109 Judys, Jills, and Zekes. One saving grace for Admiral Mitscher was that the Japanese strike leader squandered precious time in circling his planes some distance out to provide them with last-minute instructions. The American flattops had been busily rotating CAPs since the initial intercepts of Raid I, and this extra time proved to be a godsend in their next successful intercepts.

CAG Dave McCampbell had remained on board *Essex*, listening intently to the intelligence as Brewer's and Carr's divisions fought the early battles. Three divisions of Satan's Playmates were spotted on deck, armed and fueled for the next menace. Suited up in the ready room near him was Ensign Ralph "Jigs" Foltz, one of VF-15's three photo Hellcat pilots. Having never encountered an enemy aircraft in combat, Foltz was "chomping at the bit to fly."[14]

Around 1030, McCampbell was ordered into the air to provide task force coverage to spell the early teams. He raced out onto the flight deck with his division and those of Lieutenant Commander Jim Rigg—the VF-15 executive officer—and Lieutenant (jg) Jack Symmes. For Spike Borley and his companions from Rigg's division, this was already their second flight of the day. Their predawn CAP duty had been uneventful, but Borley had high hopes now. "The flight deck looked like utter chaos," he recalled. Aircraft were being hastily positioned for launch as pilots raced topside to find their assigned Hellcats. As he strapped into his F6F, Borley was given the latest positions on where his carrier was expected to move while he was aloft. Seconds before being catapulted off, Borley heard an excited voice shout, "The Japs are coming!"[15]

Ensign Al Slack was in the officers' mess having coffee when the general quarters sounded. Horns blared and the PA system repeated the call, "Fighter pilots, man your planes!"

Racing up the steel ladders to the hangar deck, Slack found his regularly assigned Hellcat parked close to the rear elevator. His plane captain had his parachute ready as Slack jumped into his cockpit and ran through his preflight checklist. Engines coughed to life, and he heard the rush of other airplanes beginning to take off. Slack received the signal to start his Pratt & Whitney engine as plane handlers jockeyed his F6F onto the elevator platform and swung its tail out.[16]

As the large slab of steel elevator rose level with the flight deck, Slack felt a strong breeze through his open cockpit. *Essex* was heading into the wind at full speed, flinging fighter planes skyward as fast as her launching officer could ready them. Given the rev-up signal, Slack gunned his throttle and turned his Grumman to face the bow. As his wheels cleared the deck, he began retracting them as he raced to join Commander McCampbell's group ahead of him. He was the last fighter launched from his ship. "I could barely see the last plane ahead of me," he recalled.

Slack chased after the F6Fs ahead of him, all the while listening intently to his radio. *Essex* fighter director officer Lieutenant John Connally, the future governor of Texas, was offering instructions to McCampbell. Not waiting to make a proper rendezvous, the CAG division was simply barreling ahead. Slack bent on his throttle and pushed his Grumman to catch up with the climbing Hellcats ahead of him.[17]

By 1037, a dozen Hellcats had successfully launched. Minutes later, *Essex* plane handlers continued clearing the deck by helping to launch a group of VB-15 Helldivers. They were ordered to use their payloads to crater the runways at Orote Field on Guam.

The three VF-15 divisions launched prior to the dive-bombers were unable to operate in unison. McCampbell rendezvoused his fighters and began climbing to 25,000 feet (Angels 25) in the bright sun. As Jim Rigg reached Angels 20, his Pratt & Whitney began cutting out badly. Although frustrated, he had little choice. He and his wingman, Ensign Dave Johnson, were forced to remain at that lower altitude and would operate independently through the balance of their flight. Rigg's second section—Ensigns Spike Borley and Red Rader—continued with McCampbell's main bunch, joining up on the tail end of Jack Symmes's third division.

McCampbell had Jigs Foltz as his wingman, with his second section of Ensigns Bud Plant and Joe Power. Symmes's division included wingman Al Slack, second section leader Charles Baynard Milton, and his wingman, George Pigman. Adding the two stragglers from Rigg's division, CAG's main attack body numbered ten F6Fs. Their time waiting for action was brief.

By 1107, *Lexington*'s radar team sniffed out the first blips of what would prove to be Raid II. Within two minutes, the Japanese force was reported to be 112 miles out and apparently circling, preparing for their assault. At 1123, the raid ceased circling and was seen on radar to be approaching. McCampbell's fighters had reached Angels 25 at 1126 when his radio crackled to life with welcomed orders: "Vector 245 degrees, distance eighty miles."

VF-15's pilots poured on the throttle and raced to intercept. "I pushed that engine harder than I'd ever pushed before," recalled Slack. "The heat gauge was showing hotter and hotter, but I couldn't let up." Over his radio, he began hearing plenty of excited chatter. It was like the minute before the opening kickoff in a national championship ball game. "We were heading for the big shoot-out at last," recalled Jigs Foltz.[18]

Satan's Playmates had been the first fighters to intercept Raid I, and VF-15 was again first to find Raid II. At 1139, about forty miles west of the U.S. battleship force and more than sixty miles from his own carriers, McCampbell's flight tallyhoed the incoming Japanese raiders. He estimated Raid II to be composed of about fifty planes—mainly Judys and Zekes—flying at 180 knots down lower at 5,000 feet, about two miles away. It appeared to be one large formation of three-plane sections and divisions.

The actual Japanese force was twice the size McCampbell could see, but it was no matter. With dozens of opponents before him, he acted quickly.

Immediately upon Campbell's group sighting the enemy formation, a high-speed closing approach was initiated by nosing over and converting altitude advantage to speed. McCampbell left four planes at high altitude while the remaining six dived into action.

Symmes, leading the third division, suffered from a radio that cut out. He turned the lead over to Milton. For the opening minutes of the fight, Milton's division maintained high cover at 22,000 feet.

CAG's first target was a Judy on the left flank, about halfway back in the enemy formation. "It was my planned intention after completing the run on this plane to pass under it, retire across the formation and take under fire a plane on the right flank with a low altitude attack," McCampbell related.[19]

The first plane he fired at exploded in his face. The other planes then commenced a pullout above the entire formation. He felt he could not reach the other side fast enough. Every rear gunner in the formation seemed to have his fire directed at the CAG Hellcat, *The Minsi*. On his second attack, McCampbell hit a Judy on the right side of the formation. After one long firing burst, it was burning "favorably" and fell away from the formation, out of control.

Having dropped two enemy planes in his first sweep, McCampbell retired below and ahead of the Japanese group. He made every effort to maintain his speed while working himself into position to attack the Japanese group leader.

Pulling up and to the side, McCampbell obtained firing position on the Japanese leader, who was snugged tightly against his wingman. After his first pass on the leader, Dave saw no visible damage. He pulled out below and to the left. He quickly decided to take on the leader's port wingman. Sliding in behind this plane, he made his next pass and caused the wingman to explode in flames. Breaking away and to the left, McCampbell then got on a lower-rear firing run on the leader. "I worked onto his tail and continued to fire until he burned furiously and spiraled downward out of control," McCampbell related.[20]

The *Essex* CAG suffered from gun stoppages during this last run. Both his port and starboard guns were charged in his attempt to clear them before firing again.

The first glimpse of action Jigs Foltz had was that of bits of wings tumbling down in the distance, small explosions, and aircraft flying in arcs. As Commander McCampbell began his attacks, Foltz spotted a pair of Judys descending in a 45-degree dive. He nosed down sharply in a steep bank and closed on the tail of one of the Judys. "I was in gun range with a clean tail shot," he recalled. His first burst blasted the plane's cockpit and engine. Spinning and smoking, the Judy burst into flames and spun in. "I realized we were both diving like a bat out of hell, and almost straight down," he said.[21]

Foltz pulled back hard on the stick and leveled off, low on the water, making high speed. Seconds later, he was in a dogfight with a Zeke that had slid onto his tail. He pulled away by applying full throttle, rpm, and fuel injection. Foltz then climbed and joined two other F6Fs as a hit in his engine caused oil to begin fouling his windshield. Through the blur, he saw that he was closing on a Judy. Pushing his stick forward, Foltz squeezed his trigger, and caused the Judy to explode right in front of his plane. "I ducked my head as I flew through the debris," Foltz recalled. With failing oil pressure, he opted to abandon the fight and limp toward home.[22]

From McCampbell's second section, Bud Plant tore into the Japanese fighters, burning a Zeke on his first run. It burst into flames and spiraled down into the ocean. Plant then put a burst into another Zeke, which flamed, pulled up, and fell off into a spin toward the water. The third Zeke he encountered was attacking another Hellcat at low altitude. Plant turned and jumped onto its tail, firing a long burst that stitched its cockpit and engine. Parts from the fighter's stabilizer broke off and its forward end began flaming.

The pilot, seen slumped over his stick, appeared to be dead. His plane spun out of control and crashed. Plant's fourth encounter was with four Zekes. He attacked the nearest one, firing many bursts from a high-side run. The Zeke pulled into a tight turn, but Plant clung to its tail, firing numerous bursts. Although the Zeke did not burn, he "descended crazily, [like] a cockeyed falling leaf, into the water."[23]

The fifth Zeke that Bud Plant took on was not as easy. As he attacked it from level altitude from behind, the Zeke pulled left into a tight circle. Plant fired many rounds by dropping down and then pulling up in order to get a lead on his quarry. Watching his tracers arc toward his target, he felt sure the trailing slugs were scoring hits. During these runs, Plant was pounced on by another Zeke that opened up on his tail.

Frantic maneuvering by Plant failed to shake the trailing Zeke. Twenty-millimeter cannon slugs and 7.7mm rounds began slamming into his F6F. He could hear bullets splattering off his armor plate. Other rounds tore through his fuselage, wings, cockpit, engine, prop, and water injection tank. Plant was spared only by the grace of a fellow F6F pilot who finally shot the Zeke off his tail. The other Hellcat was also badly shot up. The wounded pair joined up and headed home together. Both had shot-out radios, and they could only communicate by hand signals. Both were out of ammunition, but Plant had four Zeke kills to his credit.

Plant's wingman, Ensign Power, had first attacked a Zeke. It disintegrated completely, with only the wingtips and empennage floating down toward the water. After recovery, Power saw another Zeke on his same level, and both pilots turned in to each other. The Hellcat and Zeke each suffered hits in the wing roots, but the Zeke flamed and went into a high-speed dive in a gradual left turn into the sea. One of the Zeke's 20mm rounds exploded in Power's starboard wing root, and a piece of shell en-

Left to right: *Jim Duffy, Red Rader, and Al Slack. All three buddies took part in the June 19, 1944, Turkey Shoot, but Rader was killed in action.*
DOYLE BARE COLLECTION, COURTESY OF RITA BARE

tered his leg. Power dived to the water, pulled out at 1,500 feet in a right turn, and headed for the carrier with his leg wound.

After the first two divisions made several runs, Milton and Symmes led their sections down from the high-cover position to help mop up on the attackers. Symmes entered the flight with six planes: his own, those of his three division mates—Al Slack, Baynard Milton, and George Pigman— and the two remaining planes of Rigg's division: Borley and Rader. All six reached the tallyho point, with Borley and Rader trailing.

The first Judy attacked by Symmes burst into flames and crashed into the ocean. He next rolled into a Zeke below him and exploded it. He followed by turning right and firing into another Zeke that was being fired on by another Hellcat, piloted by VF-15's Milton. This fighter exploded also, and Symmes shared the kill with Milton. Milton passed so close during this firing pass that expended brass cartridges from his wing guns bounced off Symmes's windshield.

Symmes then spotted another Zeke and landed hits in its fuselage and tail. Unable to witness its demise, he concluded his combat with a scorecard of one Judy and 1.5 Zekes destroyed, plus another Zeke damaged.

During this action, Milton became separated from his wingman,

Pigman. Milton joined up with Symmes but missed his first target. On his second pass, Milton damaged a Zeke. Seeing Japanese planes burning all around him, Milt became angry with himself. On his next attack run, he bore in to within mere feet of his quarry before breaking off. On his next pass, he fired into a Zeke until part of the fighter broke off and the Zeke crashed into the water. Latching onto another Zeke, Milton followed it through violent skids, firing until his opponent slow-rolled into the sea.

Spike Borley dropped his auxiliary fuel tank and charged into the fight. In the swirl of diving planes and slashing attacks, Borley quickly became separated from his section leader, Red Rader. "All hell broke loose," he recalled. "The scene was chaotic beyond description. Every aircraft seemed to be firing at somebody else."[24] Rader was not seen again after entering his first attack. He had apparently fallen victim to a Zeke.

Meanwhile, a Zeke flashed down, firing at Borley in a high-side pass. The Japanese pilot overshot the Hellcat, but his recovery brought the Zeke right alongside the VF-15 Grumman. "We stared at each other from forty feet," said Borley. "He just as quickly broke violently right as I rolled to the left in a stalling turn." Upon completing his turn, Borley found the enemy fighter was nowhere to be seen.

During the ensuing minutes, he worked to attain position on other Japanese planes. Around him, Borley saw aircraft exploding and falling toward the sea. Several parachutes dotted the skies as opposing pilots bailed out of their wrecked aircraft and drifted toward the whitecapped blue water below. Almost as suddenly as the fight had begun, Borley found the skies clear of enemy planes. His comrades had done their part, even if he had failed to inflict any damage. Upon his return to the carrier, he was met by joyous squadron mates.

But Borley had to admit to them in shame that he had not fired a single shot because his guns had not worked. "I later learned that in the excitement and confusion of my first aerial combat, I had forgotten to charge my guns!"[25]

As THE ACTION commenced, Al Slack looked down from his high-cover position. Emerging from the swarm of Zekes, he spotted a lone Judy, a carrier dive-bomber with red meatballs on each wing. His division leader, Symmes, had already plunged into the fight. Deciding the straggling Judy was a good target, Slack seized the opportunity. Diving into a right turn, he commenced a high-side run. The Judy began mild jinking maneuvers, but Slack hung tight and began firing. Ignoring the Zekes, he opened with all six .50s and landed bursts in its engine and wings. Smoke and flames belched from the dive-bomber.

"He was burning and smoking, but he wouldn't explode," Slack recalled. The Japanese pilot simply maintained a straight and level course as flames devoured his plane. Slack continued his pursuit, although his engine was struggling to allow him to keep up. "I bet I'd put a couple of hundred rounds in him before I had to break off," he recalled. Intent on finishing this victim, he had completely forgotten about the gaggle of Zekes. Although another pilot saw Slack's Judy head into a tight spin toward the ocean below, his focus on his prey was suddenly lost.[26]

A sharp explosion erupted somewhere behind Slack's head, followed quickly by a second bang. Glancing to his left, he saw metal from his left wing stub pulling back through the rivets. An unseen Zeke had hammered his Hellcat with two direct 20mm hits. Flipping his F6F to the right, Slack dived away but saw no attacking Zeke. When he found himself free from attack, his plane seemed airworthy. Slack looked back to the left, intent on rejoining the dogfight. Lieutenant Symmes was nowhere to be seen.[27]

Glancing back to his right, Slack spotted another F6F a couple of thousand feet lower in a tumbling scrap with two Zekes. Slack went into a downwind dive, pushing his airspeed so fast that he had time for only one quick burst at one of the fighters. He missed, and the Zeke pulled up into a tight loop. "I got on his tail, but I could never get my sights ahead of him," he remembered.

Slack's tracers were missing just astern of the Zeke's tail. After two fruitless loops, he was still unable to attain a good firing position. "I knew he was an experienced pilot, and he knew what our capabilities were, I guess," Slack recalled. "The third time I shot, he was getting farther away from me. I knew then what his game was: if I kept doing loops with him, it was going to be me. He'd be on the back of me." He would report only damage to one Zeke before he opted to dive for the deck to escape the scene.[28]

En route back to his carrier, he passed over light green circles on the deep blue water below. Most were the spreading slicks of downed Japanese planes. As he flew on, he encountered an empty white parachute floating slowly down from the clouds. With his own plane crippled, Slack soon joined on another single F6F and flew in company until they reached the task force.

By this point, the attack had been largely dispersed. Baynard Milton picked up a vector being given to intercept bogeys at lower altitude. He and Symmes took out after them, but they arrived too late to secure any further victories.

Milton's wingman, George Pigman, had become separated after his first two firing passes. He proceeded to attack a Judy, holding a long burst until the plane broke into flames and started down, crashing out of control. Pigman pulled up and almost into another Judy that was crossing over from behind. He poured slugs into its belly and port wing. The Judy started into a wingover but exploded at the top of it.

Minutes later, Pigman saw a third Judy a thousand feet below and nosed down to effect a high-side full-deflection run. His first bursts drew smoke. The Judy went into violent skids as Pigman recovered and then pressed his next run. From slightly above, he fired into its cockpit and wing roots until the Judy burst into flames from nose to tail. His third kill went over lazily into a wide turn into the ocean.

By this point the Japanese formation had been slashed and the attack was effectively broken up. Dave McCampbell set his sights on a lone Judy that had been leading the lower formation. Making a modified high-side run, he found that only his starboard guns would fire. After just a short burst, he was forced to make a violent skid and an early pullout. He charged his guns again twice. By now CAG's target had pushed over and gained high speed. He set into a stern chase.

"Bursts of my starboard guns alone, before all guns ceased to fire, caused him to burn and pull up into a high wing-over before plummeting into the sea," McCampbell related. Neither pilot nor gunner escaped before the plane disintegrated into the ocean. By the time of his last victory, McCampbell was within range of TF 38 guns, forcing him to the north. During this time, he witnessed a direct hit on the battleship *South Dakota*.

McCampbell circled the kill site, attempting to clear his gun stoppages without success. At that point he assumed all ammo had been expended. McCampbell then returned and orbited near *Essex*.

Among the last to return, on his own, was Al Slack. He was humbled to see his own *Essex* turn into the wind to collect him. After flying down the starboard side to obtain the green light for landing, he circled back into the groove. Lieutenant Roy Bruninghaus coached him in for a normal landing, his tailhook neatly snagging the first arresting cable. As Slack taxied up the deck, he saw sailors in the portside catwalk staring in astonishment. As the plane handlers helped him unbuckle from his harnesses, Slack finally understood their looks when he stepped out onto his wing. "In the fuselage behind my seat was a hole at least two to three feet in area," he recalled. "Twelve smaller holes surrounded it."[29]

Essex repair crews would haul Slack's F6F below to install large patches on his fuselage and paint over them. He was fortunate. He later decided that any pilot who managed to return to the carrier every time he was launched was certainly beating the odds. Out of seventy-five launches from his ship during his combat tour, he would prove lucky enough to require a water rescue only once.

Although VF-15 had knocked down a considerable portion of Raid II, the remainder of the intercept now fell on other fighter squadrons. Among them were several divisions from *Lexington*'s VF-16, including the Navy's leading ace still in the combat zone, Lieutenant (jg) Alex Vraciu. In eight minutes of dogfighting, Vraciu chased Judys all the way into the American warship flak zone. He became an "ace in a day" with one to spare by knocking down six Japanese planes. With his aerial victory count now at eighteen planes, Vraciu later remarked of his June 19 battle, "That was my payback for Pearl Harbor."[30]

Fighter teams from *Yorktown* and *Bataan* intercepted Raid II, but about twenty Japanese strikers fought their way through to attack Admiral Willis Lee's heavy warships. One bomb exploded near the battleship USS *Alabama*, while a damaged Jill caromed off USS *Indiana* without causing any serious damage. Only a half dozen Judys pressed farther on to reach Task Group 58.2, but most were brought down by AA fire. A small phosphorus bomb detonated above *Wasp*'s flight deck, killing one sailor and injuring a dozen. A pair of Judys bombed *Bunker Hill*, landing near misses close enough for casualties, but Marc Mitscher's carrier fleet had escaped without any serious damage.

By the time Dave McCampbell's victorious fighters made landings on *Essex* at 1226, the enemy's strike force had been decimated. His VF-15 pilots claimed 20.5 victories. All told, 162 American fighters had been sent to assault 119 enemy strikers. They claimed eighty victories, and AA fire had finished off at least half a dozen more. Only thirty-one Japanese pilots from Raid II managed to return to either Guam or Ozawa's CarDiv One flattops. In return, only four Hellcats had been lost, including that of VF-15's Red Rader.[31]

Four other VF-15 Hellcats had been shot up, but all would be repaired. Joe Power was sidelined for the balance of the Marianas fight with his leg wound, but his hiatus would be brief. The Hellcat garnering the most attention upon landing was that of Ensign Bud Plant. Sailors counted more than 150 holes in his plane, including bullets that had pierced his prop.

On *Lexington*, ace-in-a-day pilot Alex Vraciu glanced up at the bridge as his Hellcat taxied up the deck after landing. He flashed six fingers, indicating his number of kills. As soon as his F6F was chocked, a ship's pho-

Lt. (jg) Alexander Vraciu of Lexington's VF-16 holds up six fingers to indicate his number of kills on the morning of June 19, 1944. For the moment, he was the U.S. Navy's leading ace fighter pilot. U.S. NAVY

tographer had Vraciu repeat the victory gesture. Ordnancemen found that the VF-16 pilot had fired only 360 rounds, knocking down six opponents while shooting just an average of 10 rounds per gun per kill. The snapshot of Vraciu and his marksmanship feat was one for the record books.[32]

But the aerial combat on June 19 was still in its early stages.

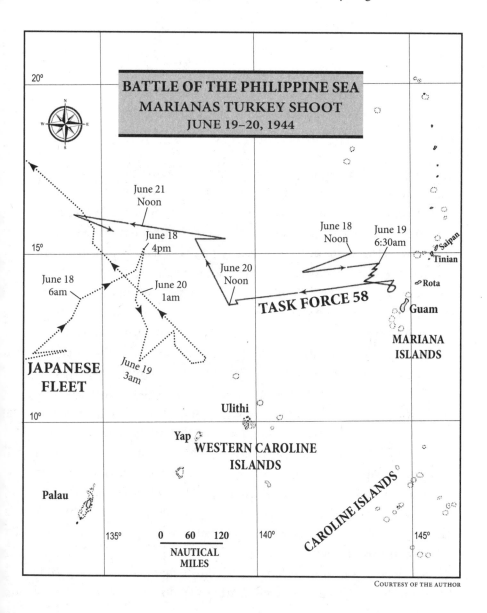

BATTLE OF THE PHILIPPINE SEA
MARIANAS TURKEY SHOOT
JUNE 19–20, 1944

EIGHT

A RESCUE AND A TRAP

June 19, 1944
Early Afternoon

John Barry's morning had been frustrating. He had participated in an uneventful early-morning CAP and returned hours later to refuel. When Dave McCampbell's divisions were scrambled late in the morning to intercept the latest Japanese raid, Barry had not been included. He manned a Hellcat on the hangar deck but remained on *Essex* when flight operations were shut down to button up for the potential enemy air strike.

He sat in the cockpit of his F6F for some time, cursing his luck. Soon the distant sky beyond the task force was painted with white contrails of dueling airplanes, black puffs of AA fire, and multicolored plumes of exploding cruiser, battleship, and destroyer shells. "You could see smoke trailing as Jap planes hit the water," Barry wrote in his diary that evening.[1]

The ship's talker had kept up running commentary on the battles. Barry listened as the distance narrowed for some of the incoming planes. At thirty miles, he began to worry, knowing that any surviving Japanese pilots would begin their high-speed runs within minutes. "I sweated out a lifetime sitting on the hangar deck, as it is one hell of a place to be when the ship is attacked," he noted. The thought occurred to him that any bullets from a strafing Japanese plane could easily penetrate the flight deck above. He was a sitting duck, but he preferred to be ready in case he needed to be scrambled to help.

Someone finally ordered Barry out of his fighter and off to safer confines. In the wardroom, he found another two dozen pilots from VF-15.

Their nervous grins told it all. They were excited that the task group was under enemy attack and eager to contribute. In between strikes, the VF-15 pilots often grabbed a quick sandwich from a little refrigerator that Commander McCampbell had had installed in their ready room; he kept it stocked with the aid of an *Essex* mess attendant.

When the call came around 1020 for four pilots to man planes, John Barry was among those who sprinted topside with Bert Morris to be catapulted. "I was out like a flash, anything to get out of that wardroom, which was hotter than Hades," Barry recalled.[2]

Morris, Barry, and their two wingmen spent the next four hours aimlessly circling the task group, praying for a productive vector. Satan's Playmates had been first to intercept each of the first two Japanese raids on June 19. But their good fortune ended during the next two assaults launched from Admiral Ozawa's carriers.

Lieutenant Morris's quartet was airborne at 1225 while *Essex* was in the process of landing the divisions that had battled Raid II. Task Group 58.4 radar sets then made first contact with bogeys about 110 miles out. Ozawa's Raid III comprised only forty-seven planes: forty Zekes and seven torpedo bombers. This time, *Hornet's* VF-2 was in position to make the first tallyho. After VF-2 was joined by VF-1 *Yorktown* fighters and a pair of VF-32 *Langley* F6Fs, Raid III was largely broken up by 1320. One Zero fighter-bomber made it close enough to unleash his bomb toward *Essex*, but it exploded six hundred yards wide of the mark. Mechanic Elmer Cordray was on the flight deck. The bomb's near miss "scared the living —— out of us," he recorded.[3]

Barry had been on CAP duty for three hours when the fourth Japanese air raid was detected at 1320. Ozawa's Raid IV had been launched beginning at 1100. It included eighty-four aircraft—the second-largest group of the day. Shortly after their launch, the U.S. submarine USS *Cavalla* (SS-244) found and attacked the carrier *Shokaku* at 1222. Four torpedoes ripped apart the former Pearl Harbor attacker. *Shokaku* hung on until 1500, when a bomb cooked off on her hangar deck and ignited lingering fuel vapors.

Shokaku settled by the bow and disappeared under the waves minutes later. Two-thirds of her crew perished: 1,263 men. But Admiral Ozawa's woes were not over. At 1532, another gasoline vapor explosion cooked off on the torpedo-damaged carrier *Taiho*, and she began to settle. The Japanese admiral and his staff were transferred to the cruiser *Haguro*, and *Taiho* went down that evening, taking 1,650 men with her.

Ozawa's Raid IV was only partially successful in locating Admiral Mitscher's U.S. carriers. Half the force broke off their search and headed for Guam and Rota to land and refuel. The small contingent that headed in to attack Task Force 58 was picked up by the carrier *Monterey*'s radar at 1320. Another hour would pass before the first enemy aircraft pressed in close enough to land near misses with their bombs against the carrier *Wasp*. A few planes from Raid IV were knocked down by *Wasp*'s VF-14, but the majority of the original force was soon found to be approaching the island airstrips for landing.

The sections under Lieutenants Morris and Barry were already entering the *Essex* landing circle by the time the first intercepts were made on Raid IV. In his diary that evening, Barry wrote in disgust that he had spent "four hours around the ship, not even sighting a darn Jap plane. I have been strictly out of phase."[4]

The equally luckless Raid IV planes heading to land at Rota and Guam were reported by fighter pilots in that vicinity, and Mitscher responded quickly. Throughout his task groups, he ordered fresh fighter sweeps out toward Guam, hoping to knock down any enemy strikes staging there. Other VF-15 pilots would enjoy more success than Barry had.

ENSIGN DUZ TWELVES was sweating it out in the VF-15 ready room. Around 1400, executive officer Jim Rigg received word from air command to ready three divisions of Hellcats for a sweep against Guam. After a quick briefing, he ordered his pilots to head for their planes at 1415.

Twelves scrambled up the ladder to the *Essex* flight deck and made his way to the ready F6Fs. He was disappointed to find that Lieutenant Commander Rigg had already manned his personal plane, adorned with the name *Lady La Rhea* in honor of his fiancée. Duz simply grabbed the next ready Hellcat and swung into the cockpit to buckle in. For this scramble, he would again be flying wing on Lieutenant Commander George Duncan. By 1423, Dave McCampbell's CAG division had roared off the flight deck, followed by the divisions of Duncan and Lieutenant John Collins—the latter having recovered from his bullet wound from the previous month.

As was often the case with scrambles, McCampbell's leading division was a mixed bag. Ensign Joe Power was wounded and in sick bay, and Bud Plant's F6F had been shot to hell on his previous hop. The air group commander took Ensign Roy Nall as his wingman, with his second section comprising Jim Rigg and Ensign Dave Johnson as his wingman. In the second division, Twelves tucked up neatly against Duncan's Grumman during the rendezvous. Formed closely on them was their second section of Lieutenants (jg) Bud Henning and Carl White.

Ensign Jim Duffy, normally wingman for John Strane, was included in this scramble. Like John Barry, he had spent part of his morning sitting in an armed Hellcat. Chucked in as second section leader for Lieutenant Collins for this flight, he was relieved to now have a fighting chance in the air.

McCampbell set a fast pace for Guam at 260 knots. Duz realized that his overeager CAG was hoping to collect more scalps this afternoon and was pushing their formation's speed to reach the kill zone. After a morning flight devoid of action, Twelves was also hungry for a dogfight. "We had missed out on everything while we were flying CAP," he recalled. "We didn't want to miss out again."[5]

McCampbell took his group to Angels 24, passing around Rota Island at high altitude before approaching Guam from the northeast. He gradually circled the latter twice, then began easing down to 12,000 feet. His division investigated an incoming flight of a dozen fighters, but they proved to be friendly. McCampbell's radio then crackled to life with a sharp warning: "Forty enemy planes circling Orote Field at Angels 3, some with wheels down."[6]

As the islands came into view, Twelves recognized each distinctive shape. He had never been there before, but he had diligently studied the available maps. Having committed them to memory, he now knew exactly where he was. His division was near Orote Field on Guam and was approaching Cabras Island, off the coast of Guam, when the action commenced.

The VF-15 divisions poured on the throttle and at 1515 had visual confirmation of the enemy aircraft. McCampbell tallyhoed many Japanese aircraft above Guam, all flying in small and scattered formations under low clouds. McCampbell moved in first against the leading two Zekes of a four-fighter formation. The CAG opened fire on one of the Zekes, which burned and exploded on his second run. His wingman, Nall, attacked the second of the leading Zekes and left it smoking.

McCampbell pulled out in the direction of two new Zekes that had begun diving and firing on him and Nall. "Since little speed remained for breakaway, attack was countered by pulling into them," McCampbell recalled. He and Nall took the fire of both Zekes in the process. Nall would emerge from the battle having flamed a Zeke that was seen to crash into the ocean. But his elevator was shot away and his plane was badly damaged. He and McCampbell eluded further attacks by retiring at full speed, during which they took defensive formation on each other.[7]

McCampbell's efforts to protect Nall proved to be one of the very few times the CAG employed the defensive Thach weave maneuver. Although VF-15 had practiced it during its early training period, McCampbell had largely done away with the tactic after two of his pilots had collided in March during maneuvers over Hawaii. In his mind, the Hellcat's superior performance negated the need for the Thach weave, which had benefited 1942 fighter pilots flying the older F4F Wildcat. But in this case, Nall was unable to maintain sufficient speed due to his damaged F6F.[8]

Straggling, Nall's F6F quickly became the center of attention of a pair of Zekes. McCampbell responded to the threat by scissoring back across and opening fire on the closest Zeke. It burst into flames and was seen to crash. This marked the seventh kill of June 19 for Dave McCampbell in just two flights.

The other Zeke split-S'ed and headed for Orote. McCampbell ordered Nall to head for base due to his plane damage. The *Essex* CAG then turned and struck out after the fleeing Zeke. He fired on it from dead astern. "He attempted to evade by completing the most beautiful slow-roll I have ever seen," said McCampbell. As the Zeke finished its roll, McCampbell opened with continuous fire. His opponent began to smoke without visible flame. The Zeke dived for the field, hoping to make an emergency landing. McCampbell made no effort to follow. As a lone F6F, he headed for the squadron's rendezvous point and later caught up with Roy Nall to shepherd him back to base.[9]

DURING THIS ACTION, the CAG's second section commenced its attacks over Apra Harbor at the same time as McCampbell and Nall. Squadron XO Jim Rigg poured lead into an Aichi D3A dive-bomber (code-named "Val") and sent it crashing into the water during his opening attack. He then found several Vals to his left, apparently ready to break up for a landing. They were flying in closed-up three-plane sections. As Rigg bore in, he saw many of his bullets hitting home in the Vals but then felt the thumps of enemy bullets slamming into his Hellcat. One of the Val rear gunners stitched his F6F in the belly tank and fuselage.

Flashing past this group of Vals, Rigg encountered another dive-bomber almost ahead of him at about five hundred feet. By this point, his guns were largely burned out and malfunctioning from his previous action. In order to score any hits, he pressed his attacks to point-blank range. Zooming in on the Val, he shot up its fuselage and wings. He then turned his attention to another Val that was in its landing approach on Orote Field. Although he did not notice any of his bullets hit, this dive-bomber abruptly nosed up on the field.

Rigg then pursued a third Val he found east of Apra Harbor at only three hundred feet. As he closed, he noted a few phosphorus streamers between it and his plane. He was forced to pull up sharply to avoid colliding with the Val. There was simply no remaining altitude to use for an escape dive below. Feeling quite alone in the mass of Vals, Rigg proceeded to the area north of the harbor. There he noticed two F6Fs at about 1,500 feet. Below them were more than a half dozen other planes circling. Assuming them to be Hellcats, Rigg headed to join up. He was soon surprised to see the circling planes were Zekes.

Rigg immediately went into low pitch, with full throttle and water injection on. At an altitude of only five hundred feet, he tore through their formation firing in a head-on run against one of the Zekes. As he shot at the plane, another Japanese fighter came in on his port side. Rigg felt numerous hits thumping into his Grumman. One slug hit his prop and created a tremendous vibration.

As Rigg hauled clear, he looked in his rearview mirror. The two F6Fs that had been above had diverted the attention of the remaining Zekes. Although he had made numerous attacks, VF-15's XO conservatively claimed only one Val destroyed, plus four Vals and one Zeke probably destroyed. He reduced his rpm to 1,700 and headed for the nearest carrier base. Rigg landed his badly shot-up F6F on *Enterprise*, where he spent the next several days having it repaired before flying back to *Essex*. His wingman, Dave Johnson, accounted for one Val destroyed and another probably damaged.

Flying as high cover at the start of this melee was the four-plane division headed by John Collins. They had been preparing for a strafing run on Guam when the action commenced. "All of a sudden, the radio opened up and I could tell there was something going on over the airfield," Duffy recalled.[10]

Duffy was puzzled to see that Collins remained unconcerned with the radio calls. Pulling up close to him, Duffy waggled his wings and exchanged hand signals with the division leader. He found that Collins had a malfunctioning radio, and acting lead was handed over to the ensign. Duffy turned toward the enemy airfield at full throttle and soon spotted a gaggle of Japanese planes stacked from the deck all the way up to 10,000 feet. *Hot damn! Looks like a bunch of buzzards circling over a kill*, he thought.[11]

From that point the action became general, and Duffy's second section was almost immediately left on its own. Lieutenant Collins and his wingman, Ensign Ken West, dived onto the circling planes. Collins nailed a Zeke from about five hundred feet and watched it plunge into the ocean, as witnessed by West. In the minutes that followed, Collins tangled with five other Zekes but claimed damage to only four of them. West fired short bursts at Japanese fighters that approached his division, and his own F6F collected 7.7mm and 20mm hits in the fray.

As Duffy and his wingman, Ensign Len Hamblin, reached the vicinity of the fight, Duffy noted that a Zeke would occasionally pop out of the big circle and then fight its way back in. He and Hamblin did not have long to wait for the next Zeke to pop free. They dived from 4,000 feet, but their first run failed to score lethal damage. Coming in full throttle on this first pass, Duffy utilized his altitude advantage. He had only a split second to fire and he could see that only some of his bullets impacted the Zeke's tail section. "As hard as I could pull, I couldn't get the hits forward on him," he recalled. Overrunning his opponent, Duffy reduced his speed and pulled up to regain altitude.[12]

I'm not going to make that mistake again, he thought.

Spotting another Zeke pulling out of formation, Duffy made a shallower dive. This Zeke was painted dark green with a touch of yellow and bright red meatballs on its wings. Duffy never backed off his throttle. Using his superior speed, he came in behind his second Japanese fighter. Firing a short burst, he was disappointed to again overrun his target. But as he flashed past, Duffy glanced down quickly at the Zeke's cockpit. "It was just a mass of flame," he recalled. His short burst had apparently struck the reserve fuel tank, located just below the pilot's cockpit. "It was a terrible way to die," he recalled. "I was hoping that maybe I had killed him, so he wouldn't have to burn to death."

Duffy snapped into a tight spin and went down to escape. His Zeke opponent never recovered, as his plane was seen to slam into the water in flames. On his section's final run, Ensign Hamblin spotted a Zeke going into a left turn to escape another F6F. Turning inside, he fired at close range and saw smoke pour from the Zeke. It turned over onto its back and spun into the drink. At that moment another Zeke zoomed in and began scoring. A 20mm shell perforated Hamblin's starboard wing and a 7.7mm round hit his engine. Hamblin and Duffy scissored out of the action without further damage.

Within ninety seconds, it was all over. The remaining Japanese planes had dispersed, and all was suddenly quiet again. Duffy was amazed. *All this intense fighting for a minute and a half, and then there's nothing!*

As the main action wound down, Dave McCampbell circled over Orote Field. From his vantage point, the *Essex* CAG counted about seventeen fires or oil slicks on the water in a radius of just one mile off Apra Harbor.

It had been a frenzied fight. McCampbell's attention soon turned to assisting a pair of fellow Hellcat fighters. They were attempting to prevent numerous Zekes from strafing a pair of helpless rescue floatplanes. For his part in the afternoon dogfights, McCampbell's *Minsi* F6F emerged with only minor battle damage. "I received six 7.7 holes in tail and wing," CAG recalled of his own plane.[13]

It was only upon his return to base that CAG McCampbell would learn his command fighter had likely been winged by one of his own young VF-15 pilots.

THE FLOATPLANES SPOTTED by McCampbell taxiing on the ocean surface far below had been launched by the cruiser USS *Montpelier* (CL-57). Operating about thirty miles out from Guam with other warships, the cruiser had received orders to conduct a rescue mission from Rear Admiral John Walter Reeves Jr., one of the carrier task group commanders. *Montpelier* responded at 1455 by launching a pair of Curtiss SOC Seagull single-engine scout observation seaplanes.

Launched by catapult, each Seagull was equipped with a single large pontoon to enable the aircraft to taxi on the ocean to retrieve downed airmen. Upon returning to its home battleship or cruiser, each SOC was normally retrieved by a ship's crane. The two *Montpelier* pilots fired off by cat shot this afternoon had been Lieutenants (jg) William H. Edmiston and Orris Clayton Boettcher.

Upon arriving about two miles north of Orote Point on Guam, Edmiston and Boettcher spotted a yellow life raft bobbing in the sea. In it was a dive-bomber crew from *Lexington*'s VB-16. The pilot, Lieutenant (jg) Gerald L. "Gerry" Marsh, was a twenty-five-year old Kentuckian who had been launched during the early Japanese air raids on June 19. As enemy planes approached his task group, Marsh's flight leader had taken his own initiative in leading his SBD Dauntlesses over to bomb Orote Field. Their unplanned strike commenced at 1330 against Japanese buildings, planes, and gun positions. During his dive, Marsh's SBD was hit in the engine, forcing him to make a water landing to the west of the town of Agana. He and his gunner, ARM2c W. L. Lindsey, scrambled into their raft uninjured and became spectators for the waves of carrier planes battling over Guam.

Other *Lexington* SBDs circled their downed comrades until word was received that *Montpelier* was sending in her rescue floatplanes. Edmiston and Boettcher reached the scene and spotted the downed airmen at 1528. The seas were rough, with large swells six to eight feet high, topped with whitecaps from a 16-knot wind. Although prospects were poor of taking off again, both planes landed to pick up Marsh and Lindsey. Boettcher soon radioed back to the ship that neither Seagull was able to get airborne in the rough seas.[14]

Each SOC zipped along the rough surface, cutting a thin white wake plainly visible to anyone airborne. *Lexington* airmen Lindsey and Marsh clung to a pontoon as their rescue pilots began motoring the twenty-five miles out toward *Montpelier*. But eager Zeke pilots soon spotted the helpless rescue planes and moved in for the kill.

ENSIGN DUZ TWELVES, still smarting from a luckless morning CAP, found plenty of action near Guam. McCampbell's two leading divisions were already embroiled in combat as George Duncan's third division approached Cabras Island. Duncan spotted two Zekes flying at higher altitude, and he signaled Bud Henning to attack with his second section of their division.

Henning and wingman Carl White combined to knock down a Japanese fighter. Henning then chased another Zeke toward the water, firing on it from such close range that, when it exploded, numerous parts from the enemy aircraft bounced off his F6F.

Lieutenant Commander Duncan, in the meantime, had intercepted a distress call on the combat frequency. Two SOC Seagull rescue seaplanes were in peril on the ocean surface just a thousand yards off Orote Point on Guam. Around 1550, a pair of Zekes had pounced on them and were making strafing runs. One of the pilots, Lieutenant (jg) Boettcher, was now shouting for help from any available carrier fighters. "I could hear the desperation in his voice," Twelves recalled.[15]

As Duncan and Twelves descended toward the besieged Seagulls on the water, the pair of Zekes dropped out of the cloud cover from above. "We jinked out of their line of fire and Duncan radioed me to go help the Seagulls while he tangled with the Zeros," said Twelves. Orote Point was eight miles away from his position, at least two minutes' time at his high speed. Duz rolled into a left turn, pushed his throttle to the stop, and took up a heading for the SOCs. "I leaned forward against the straps to urge a little more speed out of my airplane," he remembered. *If I'm going to do anything for the rescue planes, I have to get there quickly,* he thought. *They are just sitting ducks for those Zeros.*

As Twelves raced to the rescue, his division leader was fighting for his life against the other two Zekes that had appeared above them. "The action was hot and heavy," Duncan recalled. He maneuvered radically and made slashing attacks from above, behind, and head-on in a frenzied sixty seconds of jockeying his Hellcat. One of his opponents was hit in the engine and cockpit. The Zeke went into the drink in flames from a low altitude.[16]

While climbing on his pullout, Duncan nailed another Zeke in its wing roots and belly. As the Zeke exploded in front of him, he had to dodge the debris. He made head-on runs against three other fighters. He scored damaging hits on a Kawasaki Ki-61 Hien fighter (code-named "Tony") and two more Zekes, one of which headed for the beach, trailing smoke. John Collins witnessed it crash and burn, helping to verify Duncan's claims of three Zekes destroyed plus a Tony and two more Zekes damaged.

While protecting and aiding the retirement of the two floatplanes, Duncan joined the *Essex* CAG. McCampbell made several runs on the attacking Zekes, but he chose not to give lengthy pursuit to any of them. He sent radio dispatches back to *Lexington* that her planes were under attack but had survived and were taxiing toward the task group.

Ensign Twelves was coming up fast on Orote Point while Duncan was battling his Zekes. Below him, he could see brilliant white parachutes floating in the water. They belonged to the downed *Lexington* airmen whom the task force floatplanes had been sent to rescue. The little Seagulls taxied away from the beach, their pontoons churning a white wake behind them. The rescued aviators held on to the pontoons as the SOC pilots dragged them farther away from enemy gunfire from the beach. Small splashes ripped the ocean near them as a pair of Japanese Zekes made their strafing runs.

Twelves then caught sight of one of the Zekes. It was just ahead of him at lower altitude, its dark wings glinting in the sun. The Japanese pilot lined up to make another strafing run. A sinking feeling gripped Duz: *I'm not going to be able to get into firing position before he begins shooting at those guys. I'm just too far away.*[17]

DUZ WAS CRUISING at 4,000 feet when he first spotted the Zeke only a few hundred yards off the deck. But their paths were converging. He could see that the Zeke would cross his own course from the right, so Twelves pushed his F6F's nose down and went for the kill. He had already armed his six wing guns, so he placed his gunsight squarely on the Zeke. His airspeed indicator showed 360 knots as his Grumman plummeted from above. A quick glance showed no signs of the other Zeke, so Twelves lined up on his prey.

The Japanese pilot was already on his trigger; smoke tracers rose from the Zeke's 7.7mm guns. As bullets ripped into the water near the pair of Seagulls, Twelves saw the rescued men release their grips on the pontoons of one SOC and dive underwater. "The pilot of the Seagull gunned his engine and turned his aircraft in a circle to make it harder for the Zero to hit it," Twelves remembered. Small white splashes peppered the water all around the floatplane. In the next instant the water boiled with heavier splashes as the Zeke pilot began firing with his larger 20mm cannons.

As Twelves narrowed the distance in his dive, he saw the Zeke pilot stop firing as his Mitsubishi flashed directly over the top of the Seagulls. As the A6M2 started a shallow bank to the left, its pilot was clearly unaware that he was in the sights of a diving Hellcat. Twelves had set his guns to converge their fire at 1,200 feet, making a 45-degree deflection shot. Pulling a hard three g's to bring his .50-calibers to bear, Twelves put the enemy fighter in his marks. His gunsight was an illuminated reticle, consisting of central dots surrounded by three concentric rings. With the enemy now about five hundred yards away, Duz led his target slightly, putting the Zeke's nose just touching the second circle.[18]

The Zeke pilot spotted the incoming Hellcat at four hundred yards, and he tightened his bank. But it was too late. Twelves was on his trigger, unleashing a three-second burst of glowing tracers that curved toward the enemy fighter. "I saw that my lead was on the money," he remembered. He watched his bullets thump into the Zeke.

Although Hellcat gun cameras often failed to capture sufficient evidence for claims, Twelves was fortunate enough to return with interesting footage from this kill. His slugs were clearly seen to flame his Zeke opponent. As Duz continued to fire, another F6F suddenly swooped down on the Japanese fighter's tail. Caught in mid–firing stream, Duz could not abruptly end his firing fast enough to prevent his own slugs from tearing into the Hellcat. As events would later show, he had unwittingly winged his own CAG in the process of downing his quarry!

Dave McCampbell, hell-bent on slashing into every enemy fighter he could hit, had simply flown right through Twelves's firing line. Duz clearly recognized the distinctive markings of the CAG plane. Because of the confusing swirl of dogfights, McCampbell would record in his post-battle narrative only that he had collected six rounds in his tail and wing. McCampbell's Hellcat flashed past Twelves and disappeared just as quickly as it had appeared.[19]

By the end of his firing pass, Twelves swept over his winged Zeke. He quickly rolled his F6F to the left to get into another firing position. But his opponent was finished. The Zeke had descended to just two hundred feet above the waves and burst into flames.

Duz watched its nose pitch down, and within seconds the Zeke hit the ocean at a shallow angle. "It skipped and cartwheeled endlessly, leaving a brilliant trail of fire on the water," he recalled. Twelves bent his F6F around to check on the SOCs and instantly spotted the other Zeke at his 12 o'clock position. His second opponent was at about 5,000 feet, two miles out, and banking into a shallow turn to make a run on the Seagulls.

Postwar research and interviews conducted by historian Henry Sakaida determined that this opponent was twenty-four-year-old Warrant Officer Sadamu Komachi, who had graduated with the 49th Pilot Training Class in Japan in June 1940. Known as a daredevil pilot, Komachi stood slightly over six feet tall and had flown in the attack on Pearl Harbor from the carrier *Shokaku*. He had also participated in three 1942 carrier battles: Coral Sea, Eastern Solomons, and Santa Cruz.[20]

On June 19, Komachi was part of a fifteen-plane flight that departed

Truk for the long flight to Guam. He had been lining up to make his landing attempt at Orote when the *Essex* Hellcats struck.

Twelves's airspeed indicator showed nearly 340 knots, so he pulled up and traded the speed he had gained in his dive for more altitude. As his Hellcat leapt skyward, he was encouraged. *I still have time to hit this guy before he can fire on the Seagulls!*

Komachi was concentrating on his sitting ducks, continuing into a wide turn before making his approach on the SOCs. Twelves quickly decided that a depressed wingover would bring him in behind the diving Zeke for a high-side deflection shot from above and behind his opponent. "I flew it just like I saw it in my mind," he recalled. "The world turned upside down around me." Keeping his nose pointed just ahead of the Zeke as he turned, Duz found the Japanese plane slipped nicely into his gunsight.

He eased back on the throttle slightly to keep from overrunning the enemy plane and fired several short bursts while sliding into a stern position. Twelves saw debris coming off the Zeke as his bullets struck home. Heavy black smoke belched from the Mitsubishi's engine. The Zeke rolled to the right and spiraled into the sea, slamming hard against the waves. Twelves rightfully assumed he had killed his opponent, but he was mistaken.

Komachi later related that his Zeke was hit in the fuel tank underneath the pilot's seat. "The plane went up in a blast and into flame at once," he recalled. Because of his low altitude, Komachi was unable to parachute out. He switched off his engine and banked his plane to the left to make a water landing, hoping his turn would pull the flames away from his face. He needed to hit the water as quickly as possible. Without opening his eyes or breathing, he still felt the intense heat scalding him. "My face, hands and legs turned into like steak meat," he said. His plane slammed into the waves about three hundred meters offshore.[21]

Burned and bleeding heavily from his face, hands, and legs, Komachi struggled from his sinking Zeke. Grasping at plants and small trees growing in the shallow water, he pulled his body toward shore. Soldiers helped him to a local hospital, where he lay for days with his face completely covered in bandages. (Decades later, Henry Sakaida put Twelves in touch with Komachi, and the two opposing pilots exchanged friendly correspondence about their June 19 encounter.)

Wendell "Duz" Twelves receives the Navy Cross in 1945. On June 19, 1944, Twelves helped save the lives of four aviators who were being strafed by Japanese fighters.   VALERIE TWELVES GILLEN

After downing Komachi, Twelves had just started to look around for other aircraft when he found himself in a hail of 7.7mm smoke tracers. "They were streaking past my cockpit like a blizzard," he recalled. In his pursuit, he had failed to spot a third Zeke, which was now on his tail. Knowing that the 7.7mms would be followed by the Zeke's 20mm cannons, Duz acted instinctively. He rolled his F6F left into a six-g turn. But the enemy pilot had a bead on him. Duz felt the impact of 7.7mm bullets all over his Hellcat and realized he was in deep trouble.

Already buffeting on the edge of a high-speed stall, Twelves could not turn any harder. So he threw his plane to the right, then left again with all his strength. With no available cloud cover, he was in a tough spot. His only recourse was to employ wild jinking to dodge the red-hot tracers licking at his Grumman.

And then, just as quickly as his doom seemed to come upon him, the smoke tracers ceased. Twelves twisted his head around to get a fix on the Zeke. To his absolute delight, he saw another F6F firing on his opponent.

Duz righted his plane and quickly scanned around for more trouble. As he finally released his breath, he saw the third Zeke belching smoke and heading toward the ocean. As he crawled back toward altitude, his savior F6F—likely that of Duncan or McCampbell—was now gone. His own Hellcat sported bullet holes in the wing, fuselage, and tail section.

The whole incident had transpired in only about two minutes. Twelves finally spotted George Duncan far above him. The rest of the sky around him was empty of Zekes. He made a quick inventory of his situation. His gauges all read normal, despite the numerous bullet holes through his wings. *Thank you, Leroy Grumman,* he thought, *for that nice slab of armor plate behind my back and the self-sealing fuel tanks!*[22]

Twelves let down to check on the two *Montpelier* seaplanes. He was pleased to see that both were underway, although each had sustained damage. "I could see a lot of daylight through their wings and fuselage," he remembered. "Blue smoke from a damaged oil line was swirling in the prop wash of the lead Seagull." He knew their flying days were over but assumed they would be able to taxi on toward a lifeguard submarine. As he circled low, he could see pilot Marsh and radioman Lindsey now sitting on the wings of their savior SOCs.

"Everyone on and in the airplanes was waving and cheering," Duz recalled. "I felt like cheering myself." He rocked his wings in response. *I know just how they feel,* he thought. *I'd sure like to shake the hand of the pilot who just shot that last Zeke off my tail!*[23]

Over the radio, he heard a call for their division to rendezvous. "Roger," he replied. Within seconds he was pleased to also hear rogers from Henning and White. As the quartet effected their rendezvous near Guam, each pilot reported his results. Duncan said that he had downed three Zekes. Henning claimed two, and White reported one kill. *With my two, that makes eight Zekes,* Twelves thought. *Not bad for a bunch of beginners.*

Commander McCampbell's division joined the procession circling near the harbor. One by one, the other VF-15 Hellcats appeared. As Duz circled, he reflected on his good fortune. His own life had been saved by another pilot at the last second. For his part, he felt elated to have knocked down two Zekes and saved the lives of four helpless Americans. All the months of hard work he had put into sharpening his skills had finally paid off. He could only now say a silent prayer for the two floatplane pilots and their rescued aviators. But it was time to head for base and live to fight another day.

Wendell Twelves would not learn until the following day from the *Essex* CIC that the two Seagulls were successful. The SOC-1 piloted by Bill Edmiston had suffered engine damage from the strafing Zeke. Because of that damage and the rough seas, neither floatplane could take off again. So Edmiston and fellow pilot Orris Boettcher simply continued taxiing seaward toward their cruiser, *Montpelier*, about twenty-five miles distant. Fortunately, they did not have to go that far. Rear Admiral Reeves had sent the destroyers USS *Anthony* (DD-515) and USS *Braine* (DD-630) to the rescue. At 1824, *Braine* recovered pilots Edmiston and Gerry Marsh, while *Anthony* moved in to scoop up the other two aviators. The destroyers then finished off the battered Seagulls with gunfire and by 1910, Reeves had word that all four airmen were safe and en route back to their task group.

Ensign Twelves was relieved to find his Hellcat still in good enough shape for the return flight to *Essex*. They arrived at 1724, three hours after their hasty departure. As McCampbell's fighters awaited their turns to land, Twelves reflected on his mission. He was calm now, ready to refuel, rearm, and get back into battle again. "I was a whole lot smarter," he felt. "I'd be keeping a close eye on my tail from then on."[24]

After roughly a half hour of intense aerial combat near Guam, McCampbell's men had returned with all twelve F6Fs. Some sported battle damage, but his group turned in claims for fifteen kills and another six planes probably destroyed.

When McCampbell landed, VF-15 ordnanceman Elmer Cordray was afraid he and his comrades would be reamed out for his fighter's poor performance. "Just before he went out, we changed his gun barrels and did not get to time the port wing," he recalled. He met McCampbell as he climbed out of his plane and tried to apologize for not having the CAG's *Minsi* guns in perfect condition.[25]

"Leave them the way they are," McCampbell said, smiling. "They were perfect!"

The day's actions thus far gave VF-15 a claims tally of 59.5 shoot-downs and 10 probables. Although their claims proved to be a bit lofty, TF 58's fighter jockeys had knocked down dozens of Japanese planes and badly damaged nearly twenty more. By the time McCampbell's *Minsi* snagged an arresting wire on *Essex*'s flight deck, another batch of VF-15 pilots was on their way to further assault the enemy airdrome on Guam.

LIEUTENANT JOHN STRANE was in the ready room with skipper Jim Brewer. It was around 1645, and it had already been a long day. Awake since 0200, Strane had already made the long early-morning search flight in which he shot down two aircraft.

But action was brewing over Guam, and the Marianas Turkey Shoot—as the day would come to be known—was still raging in the skies. Word was flashed to Commander Brewer that McCampbell's flight and other fighter squadrons were in heated combat with enemy planes near the island. Two more VF-15 divisions were needed to scramble to meet a large incoming flight of Japanese planes heading for Guam. A makeshift combat team was organized from the ready pilots, and Strane was among those who raced up toward the flight deck.

He scrambled into his F6F and was first to launch at around 1658, followed by two other pilots not normally part of his division: Ensigns Swede Thompson and Bob "Rod" Johnson. Because of their haste to get airborne, the fourth plane that would have joined Strane's division was scratched. "At the time, I happened to be the senior of the seven, so I took off and took the lead," Strane recalled.[26]

In his rush, Strane failed to notice that skipper Brewer also raced topside to man one of the ready planes. There were plenty of young pilots eager for more action on June 19. Among them was Ensign Al Slack. Although he had claimed one kill earlier during Raid II, he felt he had not done his best. He weaved his way across the flight deck to reach the Hellcat of the skipper, who was just buckling up his harness and parachute.[27]

"Is there any way I can get scheduled again?" Slack asked.

"No, Slack. It's too late," Brewer told him before climbing into his plane.

Like Strane, Brewer found that he would not be flying with his normal wingman. As Dick Fowler reached his F6F, he was anguished to find that it had a blown tire. Fowler felt it was his job to follow the skipper on every mission, but Ensign Tom Tarr took off next in a spare Grumman to join on Brewer. Second section leader Ted Overton and Ensign Ed Mellon rounded out the flight of only seven F6Fs, leaving a frustrated Fowler to return to the ready room to wait out their results.

As the meager force made rendezvous above the fleet, Strane was surprised to see Brewer joining up. He handed over the lead to the skipper, who was annoyed with the lack of available planes. Dave McCampbell, having returned in company with Ensign Nall and the rest of his strike group, overheard his fighter leader calling to *Essex*.

"Is this all the planes I get for this flight?" Brewer asked.[28]

"Yeah, that's all we've got," replied the fighter director, John Connally.

"Charlie, there's lots of Japs over Guam, so when you go in, you'd better go in high and fast and stay that way," McCampbell advised over the radio.

By this point in the afternoon, *Essex* was steaming only seventy miles from Guam, making for a short flight in. "We were still climbing as we approached the island," Strane recalled. They clawed up toward 15,000 feet, where a heavy overcast was forming. Upon reaching the area above Orote Field, Brewer orbited his combat teams and began gradually letting down in altitude. There was no evidence of the inbound flight of Japanese planes.[29]

Then, at 1820, Strane tallyhoed a lone Judy. It was circling a few miles west of Guam at 5,000 feet, apparently intent on making a straight approach for the runway at Orote. The flight immediately headed in for the attack. Strane's division closed the distance first, his airspeed indicator showing 280 knots. Strane slowly gained a favorable position and opened with his first burst just as the Judy started an evasive turn to the north.

His first slugs created flames in the Yokosuka D4Y two-seat carrier-based dive-bomber. As the Judy turned to its right, Strane's second burst hit the engine, which immediately erupted in flames. The Japanese pilot pulled into a tight right turn, rolled onto its back, and slammed straight into the ground. "I could see a good ball of fire," Strane remembered. Returning toward the west side of the island, he headed for the squadron's designated rendezvous point alone. Strane's chase had been successful, but his six comrades had found trouble in the meantime.[30]

At 1825, Brewer called a tallyho on a large number of Zekes. At least four divisions of Japanese fighters had suddenly appeared, plunging down from 8,000 feet. Coming in from astern, they caught the Americans completely off guard. "All surviving pilots are of the firm belief the Japs sent in a Judy low over the field as a trap to draw down the F6Fs," wrote VF-15 ACIO Bob McReynolds. "If such were the case, the Japs were very successful, and the trap will always be remembered by this squadron."[31]

Out of defensive position and strung out, Brewer and the other five pilots still with him did their best. The skipper and his wingman, Tom Tarr, wheeled their Hellcats around sharply to counter the diving Zekes. Brewer was seen to hit the leader of the Japanese division that was diving into his F6Fs. Badly raked, the Zeke continued its plunge, plowing straight into the island in a massive ball of fire. Within a split second of Brewer's kill, another Zeke from the same division burst into flames and crashed, courtesy of lethal rounds of .50-caliber from Tarr. From that moment on, the other members of the flight lost any further positive sight of Commander Brewer and Ensign Tarr.

The skipper's second section, Ted Overton and wingman Ed Mellon, had also turned to meet the diving Zekes. But both F6Fs were hit by their enemy's first pass. Japanese 7.7mm slugs ripped through Overton's belly tank, causing it to ignite. The lieutenant immediately jettisoned the blazing cargo and fired head-on at other Zekes that were ripping through Brewer's division. His shots stitched the tanks of the leading Zeke in the next division. It flamed immediately and the Japanese fighter went into a spin from which it did not recover. Overton's port wing was hit by a 20mm that started a brief fire.

For several anxious minutes, Overton was separated from his wingman. Each F6F pilot was operating purely on the defensive. Mellon's Hellcat was also hit in the first enemy pass, forcing him to drop his belly tank as he worked to chase two Zeros off Overton's tail. He hit a third Zeke solidly in the engine and saw it spin into the drink, trailing smoke. During the next five minutes, Mellon was too busy firing at multiple planes to properly assess the damage he created. At any point when he saw an F6F attacking a Zeke, Mellon saw a Zeke chasing that Hellcat.

Reunited with his wingman after the first assault, Overton fired a long burst into the cockpit of a Zeke chasing another F6F. It rolled over and crashed into the water. More than five minutes into the melee, the odds were whittled down to better numbers, something closer to two Zekes for every Grumman. The remaining Japanese planes began making single attacks, which proved to be less aggressive.

Overton next fired head-on at an approaching fighter at his same level. The Zeke began smoking and dived under him. Although the Zeke was last seen out of control, Overton could not follow it visually to confirm its demise. Another Zeke was already in his sights. His burst entered the Zeke's fuselage. And then, almost instantly, Overton found the immediate skies clear of any other Zekes. Overton would claim two Zekes killed, one probable, and others possibly destroyed or damaged. In the closing minute of the fight, Ed Mellon sent rounds into the cockpit of a Zeke, which was seen to smoke, waver, and fall off without crashing.

Meanwhile, John Strane returned to the west side of the island, gaining altitude as he headed for the VF-15 rendezvous point. Two Zekes suddenly made runs on his F6F. He turned his plane into them but caught only a fleeting glimpse of their light gray camouflage in the gathering dusk. As Strane evaded these attackers, he witnessed the last of Overton's fight going on below.

Strane's second section leader, Swede Thompson, had initially pursued the lone Judy. Upon hearing the tallyho from Brewer's division, he and his wingman, Rod Johnson, had headed into the fight to assist the two surviving F6Fs flown by Overton and Mellon. Thompson shot up the cockpit and engine of one Zeke, which flamed and crashed. For his part, Johnson caused another Zeke to become engulfed in flames and crash. He was also credited with a probable on another Zeke, which was last seen smoking after Johnson's head-on run against him.

As the fight subsided, Overton called for a squadron rendezvous. It had been eight minutes of pure hell. Two other F6Fs, those of Mellon and Strane, soon joined up. It took several more minutes for the remaining VF-15 section, Thompson and Johnson, to appear. Minus radio communication, Overton signaled for them to join up. The five Hellcats circled the area in search of Brewer and Tarr.

Overton called for them over the radio, but there was no reply. One of their F6Fs had been seen to start into a wingover or a loop, but in its climb the Grumman shuddered, fell off, and did not recover. Lieutenant Strane also made unanswered calls. He saw neither dye markers on the water nor yellow life rafts as the sun set over the Marianas. Tarr and Brewer were simply gone. "I knew it was fruitless to stay any further because of darkness," Strane remembered. After he made a pass over the area and found nothing, it was time to depart.[32]

Low on fuel, Lieutenant Overton led the other four surviving F6Fs back toward base. They trapped around 1910, after sunset. For Strane, his day had started with a predawn launch and ended with a post-sunset landing. In between that time, he had accounted for three enemy planes downed during two missions. Charlie Brewer's flight had claimed eight Japanese kills and three probables, but they had paid dearly for them. Two of the returning Hellcats were shot up, and two pilots were missing in action, likely killed when their planes had impacted on the ocean.

JOHN BARRY, WHO had made two CAP flights on June 19, was dejected about not having contributed to the squadron's record-setting number of kills. But in the ready room that evening, he was sobered by the news that three of his comrades were gone: Brewer, Tarr, and Ensign Red Rader. Disappointment and frustration eventually played on his tired nerves. To Barry, some of the younger pilots were more involved in celebrating their aerial victories than in mourning their fallen comrades. "All some of the boys can think of is how many Jap planes were downed," he wrote in his diary.[33]

To be fair, June 19 was a fighter pilot's dream, not only for *Essex* and her Air Group Fifteen but for most of Admiral Mitscher's Task Force 58. Four Japanese air assaults had been turned away without serious numbers of casualties to personnel or shipping, and numerous other potential raiders had been successfully engaged over the enemy's island airfields.

"We knew it was going to be a long, hard day, and it was," recalled Duz Twelves. He was rightfully proud of having helped save the lives of four fellow airmen in the water near Guam. But he was troubled that evening to see the initial shoot-down tallies credited per pilot by Dave McCampbell.

It was clear that one of his Zekes had been claimed by the air group commander. Duz protested his case to his division leader, George Duncan, who in turn called a meeting with McCampbell. The commander was reluctant to give up one of his Zero kills, but he agreed to review the gun camera footage with Duncan and Twelves.[34]

The grainy footage clearly showed Twelves smoking the Zeke a split second before McCampbell's Hellcat entered the image, still carrying its drop tank. Several hits could be seen on the CAG fighter before it continued out of the frame. Yet McCampbell remained intent on taking at least half credit for the aerial victory.[35]

"How's about I split it with you?" he offered.

Twelves stared intently at his air group commander and said, "No, sir!"

McCampbell could see the determination in his young pilot's face. He could have pulled rank, but he opted for a peaceful remedy.

"Yeah, okay," McCampbell said, smiling. "It's yours."

The more sobering task for VF-15's pilots that evening lay in addressing the obvious. Their skipper, Commander Brewer, was gone. Their XO, Lieutenant Commander Jim Rigg, was marooned for at least the night on board *Enterprise*, where he had trapped in the shot-up F6F normally flown by Ensign Twelves. McCampbell addressed his pilots. For the moment, George Duncan—third in seniority when the day had started—was the senior VF-15 officer, and Bert Morris would continue to manage the flight schedules.

"The day our skipper didn't come back, it just about blew our squadron apart," recalled Twelves. "We just loved to have him as a fighter skipper."[36]

Upon returning to his four-man stateroom, Twelves jotted in his diary that things had "hit the fan just off Guam. We were under air attacks by Nips all day. My squadron got 67 planes." He, Dick Fowler, and Ralph Foltz had plenty to discuss. Among the three, they had shot down eight enemy planes. But their victories were bittersweet. The empty bunk of their fourth roommate, Ensign Red Rader, was sobering. "No one saw him go in," Twelves wrote in his little journal. "God bless him."[37]

Fowler was even more troubled by the loss of Commander Brewer. After numerous missions flying in tight formation on his skipper's wing, he was grief-stricken. A blown tire on his own Hellcat had put another young ensign in his place for the pre-dusk mission. The anguish and big question would linger with Fowler:

Could I have made a difference for Charlie if I had been there?

IN THE FINAL tally for the day, exuberant pilots and task force gunners turned in claims that exceeded four hundred enemy planes, with 380 Hellcat victories claimed. Aviation historian Barrett Tillman places total Japanese aircraft losses this day—including those that sank with *Taiho* and *Shokaku*—at 314. The final tally would long be debated, but Task Force 58 had scored an immense victory. It was the finest hour for the U.S. Navy's carrier fighter squadrons. In return, Mitscher's flattops had lost only thirty-one planes, including twenty-one Hellcats, although four of the latter were noncombat operational losses.[38]

On board *Lexington*, one VF-16 pilot, Lieutenant (jg) Zeigel "Ziggy" Neff, remarked that it had been "just like an old-time turkey shoot" back home in Missouri. His skipper shared the comment, and the air battles of June 19 would soon come to be known in history as the "Marianas Turkey Shoot."[39]

Fighting Fifteen claimed top honors for all TF 58 air groups, with a collective 68.5 kills. It was the most scored in one day by any American fighter squadron. Second-place honors went to *Lexington*'s VF-16, turning in claims for forty-six shoot-downs. And her squadron now sported the Navy's leading ace, Alex Vraciu, a young man who had been coached by LSO instructor Dave McCampbell the previous year in Florida.

Within Air Group Fifteen, Commander McCampbell led the scoring parade with seven victories on June 19 alone. George Carr had downed five enemy aircraft, making him the squadron's second "ace in a day." Thirty VF-15 pilots were credited with a half (shared) kill or more. Four pilots—Brewer, Dick Fowler, Ted Overton, and Bud Plant—had shot down four opponents. John Strane, Norm Berree, George Pigman, and George Duncan had each downed three.

By nightfall, Dashing Dave McCampbell's total wartime tally was nine. He was now in an elite group of U.S. Navy aces, in striking distance of surpassing some of them. The Navy's top ace as of the morning of June 19,

1944, was Lieutenant (jg) Ira Kepford of VF-17, who had sixteen kills to his credit while flying F4U Corsair fighters in the Solomons. Kepford was trailed by Lieutenant Commander Tom Blackburn (also from VF-17) and Lieutenant (jg) Don Runyon, each with eleven victories. Right behind these aces sat 1942 ace Lieutenant (jg) Stanley "Swede" Vejtasa with 10.25 kills, and Lieutenant (jg) Hamilton McWhorter, with ten.

But during the June 19 Marianas Turkey Shoot, he had been leap-frogged by Alex Vraciu. Vraciu had entered the morning with a dozen victories to his credit, but, by day's end, the twenty-five-year-old Indiana native had added six more kills, increasing the feather count in his war bonnet to eighteen.

One enemy victory away from attaining double-ace status, McCampbell found himself on the evening of June 19 in seventh place on the leaderboard in the U.S. Navy's ace race.

NINE

NIGHT FIGHTERS AND
THE NEW BOYS

June 20, 1944

T he weary VF-15 pilots, many jubilant over their Turkey Shoot victories, some mourning their three fallen pilots, were finally drifting off to sleep. But their brothers-in-arms, the *Essex* night fighter pilots, were just waking up.

In the first hour of June 20, Lieutenant Commander Bob Freeman and three of his VF(N)-77 night fighters were preparing for action in the ready room. Loosely associated with the daylight Hellcat jockeys of VF-15, Freeman's bat men were briefed on their mission. Admiral Pete Mitscher was still hunting Ozawa's carrier force. The epic aerial victories of June 19 were a thing of the past. The Bald Eagle wished to keep his enemy's airfields shut down on June 20, allowing his search planes the clear skies they needed to snoop out the Mobile Fleet.

Beginning at 0208, four F6Fs of VF(N)-77 were flung into the dark skies via hydraulic catapult launch. Freeman and his wingman, Ensign George Tarleton, were first off. They rendezvoused over the fleet in a star-filled sky with no moon. Their heckler mission was to suppress and destroy any Japanese aircraft over Orote Field on Guam, 144 miles away. Cat-shot off behind the first team was another, that of Lieutenant (jg) Jake Hogue and Ensign Ernie Roycraft, who were ordered to sweep the skies over Rota Island.

Freeman and Tarleton headed out, climbing to 6,000 feet. Visible on radar in *Essex's* CIC, they flew in close formation at a modest pace at 120 knots. Aviation experts at Pearl Harbor had installed exhaust flame damp-eners on their Hellcats, leaving them visible only out to two hundred feet. The Hellcats' wing guns had been fitted with flash hiders, helping to disguise their .50-calibers when they were fired. The biggest challenge for Freeman's pilots was the reflections of luminous switch buttons on their dashboards.

Each pilot utilized his AIA aerial radar set en route to check navigation against the landmasses of Saipan, Tinian, and Rota and to avoid friendly warships in the area. Hogue and Roycraft scouted Rota but found neither aerial resistance nor surface ships of opportunity to attack.

Freeman and Tarleton reached Guam around 0330. They found Orote Field darkened, but nearby Agana Field had runway lights on. The field appeared to be expecting the arrival of planes, they gathered from the blinker lights and blinker messages they observed. Using the blinker as a point of aim, they began a 45-degree strafing run on the field. Only light antiaircraft fire rose from a battery on the southwest corner of the field. By the time the teams pulled out of their dives at 0335, the runway lights had been extinguished. They orbited five miles east of the field, and in about ten minutes the runway lights came on again.

While preparing to make another run at 0350, Freeman saw a white light passing below them at 5,000 feet. Determining it to be a Japanese aircraft, he led Tarleton down in a high-side section run. Freeman triggered a short burst but lost visual sight of his wingman in the process. The startled enemy pilot immediately extinguished his lights and disappeared. Freeman opened up on the radio, ordering Tarleton to cover the east side of the airfield while he buzzed the west side.[1]

At 0410, Freeman spotted two blinking lights traveling across the traffic circle, seeming to effect a rendezvous. As he cut across the field to join on it, another plane behind the original target suddenly switched on its wing lights and an amber taillight. Freeman moved in closer on it and could see enough to distinguish a single-engine plane with fixed landing gear, apparently a Val dive-bomber. The target was hard to distinguish on his AIA set due to considerable land signal interference. "I didn't need the radar anyway since he had his lights on," Freeman recalled.[2]

He closed on the Val's port quarter as his opponent circled the field at 2,000 feet. Freeman opened fire with his four inboard .50-calibers from a mere hundred feet away. The sight of his bullets tearing into the dive-bomber's fuselage was startling enough to make Freeman chop his throttle. "It looked as if an electric arc welder had run from his nose to his tail, completely blanking him out in blue flames," he reported.[3]

A long orange flame was emitted from the Val for six seconds as the plane decelerated rapidly. Freeman dropped his flaps to remain behind his opponent. The Val continued in its slow turn to port, decreasing speed to 85 knots. Even with his throttle chopped, Freeman's Hellcat slid directly underneath the Val. His flaps checked his progress, allowing Freeman to finally open fire from dead astern. A half dozen three-second bursts caused the Japanese dive-bomber to enter a steep dive toward the ocean. Pulling out at a mere five hundred feet, Freeman had scored the morning's first victory.

George Tarleton was busy on the east side of the field. He climbed to 6,000 feet and spotted some running lights in the traffic circle.

"I'm going down," he called to Freeman.

"Roger," said his section leader. "I'm clear."

Sweeping over Agana Field at 120 knots, Tarleton slid in behind another Japanese plane just two hundred feet ahead of him. Employing his dive brakes, he triggered his first burst into the enemy's fuselage. Tarleton pulled up his nose and walked his next five-second burst into the Val's wings and belly. With his altimeter showing a mere hundred feet, he watched the dive-bomber slam into the sea. Closing his flaps, Tarleton picked up speed and swept in behind another pair of running lights. He dropped his flaps again, but still overshot his quarry.[4]

Almost instantly, he sighted the silhouette of another darkened plane about three hundred feet ahead. Two bursts caused this Val's pilot to roll over onto his back and drop his nose. "Just as I went under him, there was a big orange flash on my port wing that blinded me momentarily," recalled Tarleton, whose own prop was nicked by the Val's debris field. In just minutes, the VF(N)-77 Hellcats had jumped five Vals and knocked down three of them.

The *Essex* night fighters returned to base at 0558, just as the first red rays of sunlight were peeking over the horizon. The second day of the Battle of the Philippine Sea was underway.

"If the enemy had planned on staging planes through to this field that morning, he obviously was disappointed," said Tarleton.[5]

DUZ TWELVES MANAGED only two more hours of sleep than Freeman's bat men. He was roused from his stateroom at 0200, just as the VF(N)-77 Hellcats were being launched. Grabbing a cup of coffee, he headed for the ready room for a briefing.

CAG Dave McCampbell was there, having rested little during the overnight. With his fighter squadron skipper missing, he joined Lieutenant Commander George Duncan in briefing the early risers. Fighting Fifteen was running low on division leaders: Charlie Brewer, Jack Ivey, and Mel Roach had all perished in the past week. To top it off, the new fighter skipper, Jim Rigg, was temporarily marooned on *Enterprise* with his damaged F6F. Lieutenant John Barry had been elevated to take command of Ivey's division.

Flight scheduler Bert Morris reworked his daily plans to make up for the lost division leaders. To supplement the team, former RCAF pilot George Carr was tapped by Morris to help lead a division. Replacement pilots were sorely needed, but the mission at hand of stopping the Japanese fleet simply meant everyone must step up.

Task Force 58 was sending out small parties of bomber and fighter scout teams to search for the Japanese carriers to the west. The chance to hit Admiral Ozawa's carriers was almost more than Pete Mitscher could resist. The majority of his TF 58 headed west, hoping that search planes would find the quarry close enough to launch a long-range strike on the afternoon of June 20. To cover Saipan, Mitscher detached Rear Admiral Keene Harrill's TG 58.4 (*Essex*, *Cowpens*, and *Langley*) while he chased after the Mobile Fleet. While this took place, Air Group Fifteen would be used to knock down any remaining enemy aircraft over the Japanese-held fields on Guam and Rota.

At 0405, McCampbell led eighteen fighters in a predawn launch. "Black as hell," Twelves wrote in his diary. "Went off instruments on take-off." The next challenge came two hours later as his sweep approached the west coast of Guam. Around 0610, McCampbell's group encountered four Zekes just taking off from Orote Field. Although they were pursued, the enemy fighters quickly disappeared into cloud cover. The air group commander led his Hellcats on toward Rota Field at high altitude. At 14,000 feet and ten miles from the enemy field, Twelves had his engine sputter and suddenly cut out. Now piloting a lifeless bird, he wrestled with his Grumman as it rapidly descended.[6] He ran through a rapid checklist as he prepared for a water landing off enemy territory.

Luckily, Twelves's worries were erased when he finally managed to restart his engine 2,500 feet above the ocean. Meanwhile, after strafing the field at Rota, two of McCampbell's divisions shot up a medium-sized freighter offshore and left small fires burning on its decks.

As they were returning toward the ship along the east coast of Guam, they found four Zekes heading south, possibly the same four McCampbell's sweep had seen taking off earlier. Three escaped through the cloud cover, but Lieutenant Bert Morris was credited with probable destruction of one Zeke.

McCampbell's early-morning group returned to *Essex* intact around 0730. Air Group Fifteen was relieved from further flight duty as Rear Admiral Harrill's task group proceeded to fuel from fleet oilers. More important than oil for Air Group Fifteen during that time was the receipt of replacement aircraft and aviators. The nine rookie pilots received by VF-15 were sorely needed.

JACK CRAWFORD TAYLOR was eager for his new opportunity. It was finally time to join the big leagues—Task Force 58.

The tall, lean twenty-two-year-old ensign had spent the past two weeks in transit to the Marianas. After a quick breakfast on the morning of June 20, Taylor donned his flight gear and stood ready. He and other rookie ensigns had been notified that Admiral Mitscher's fleet carriers had suffered many pilot losses. Several fighter squadrons needed replacement F6Fs and pilots. Taylor was more than ready for the challenge.

Born to stockbroker Melburne Martling "Mel" Taylor and his wife, Dorothy Crawford Taylor, Jack entered the world on April 14, 1922. Raised in St. Louis, Missouri, Jack had taken an interest in cars and mechanics at an early age. After graduating from Clayton High School, he went through two semesters of college at Washington University but struggled as a student. Although he ran track, wrestled, and played some basketball during school, he never considered himself much of an athlete.[7]

On the day Pearl Harbor was attacked, he was on his way to pick up his girlfriend, Mary Ann MacCarthy, for a date. Two months later, having left college, Taylor decided he would join the service. *Well, I'm going to have to enter the military, so I might as well go where I want to go,* he thought. His first interest was to become an aviator, although he had never been in an airplane in his life.[8]

Jack applied for the U.S. Army and went before an Army Air Corps recruiter to take their test. He was crestfallen when they turned him down for having hay fever. "I went back home, and was depressed because I didn't know what to do," he recalled. When a friend suggested he try for naval aviation, Taylor jumped at the chance. This time, he successfully passed their entrance tests without being asked about any sinus congestion problems. He was accepted into the V-5 air cadet training program.

"We'll call you when we need you," Taylor was promised. While he waited, he took a job in a St. Louis machine shop and continued dating Mary Ann. Jack was finally called up for flight training in December 1942, a full year after the Pearl Harbor attack. He reported to a little base called Kratz Field in St. Louis, along with other new recruits. Jack's first flight was in a Piper Cub with an instructor who took him up several times. Additional training and ground school consumed the next week as Taylor anxiously awaited his chance to get behind the controls.[9]

One morning, he made another flight with his instructor. Upon returning to Kratz Field, the instructor climbed out of the cockpit and said, "Okay, take her up."

"By myself?" Taylor asked.

"Yeah."

So, he took the Cub up, flew around the field a few times, and landed. His first solo was a success.

*Two of the new pilots joining VF-15 on June 20 were Ensigns Jack Taylor
(left) and Dick McGraw, seen in Hawaii in 1944. After the war, Taylor
would go on to form Enterprise Rent-A-Car.* ENTERPRISE HOLDINGS

After additional preflight and flight training, Jack earned his golden
wings and was commissioned in December 1943.[10] Taylor then went to
Florida for advanced fighter training, where he got to know some of his
fellow students very well. Among his friends was Ensign Dick Davis, a
farm boy raised with six siblings near Tappahannock, Virginia. After his
father was killed in an automobile accident when Dick was only seven
years old, he and his four brothers and two sisters were raised on their
grandparents' farm while his mother worked as a nurse.

The oldest of the brothers, Dick was athletic. He excelled on the high
school football, basketball, and baseball teams. As a boy, he would sit on
the roof of his home and marvel at Army Air Corps planes flying to and
from nearby Langley Field. By age twelve, he had read a well-worn paper-
back called *Naval Aviator* numerous times. *These guys have gotta be the
best,* he thought. *I want to be a naval aviator.*[11]

After graduating high school in 1940, Davis enrolled at the College of
William and Mary in Williamsburg. In between classes, he worked in
the school's dining room to help pay his tuition. Unable to meet the

required two years of college needed to join the naval aviation program, Dick enlisted in the U.S. Navy in June 1941, hoping that would speed his efforts to reach flight school. But his first three months of service following boot camp proved to be in the role of an aviation mechanic for patrol squadron VP-74. It was not until Christmas 1942 that Davis finally received his orders for flight school.

UPON BEING QUALIFIED in carrier landings at NAS Glenview, Taylor and Davis were temporarily split up. Davis and dozens of other new pilots boarded trains for the cross-country trip to San Diego, where they were assigned to a Navy carrier aircraft service unit, CASU-5. Taylor and several other new pilots were instead assigned to fly new F6Fs from New York to the West Coast. From late March into early April, the new ensigns put in additional hours flying F4F Wildcats, making jeep carrier landings off the West Coast. Meanwhile, Dick Davis made his practice traps on April 3 on the carrier USS *Prince William* (CVE-31). Earning their certifications with him that day were five other pilots with whom he would later serve on *Essex*: Charlie Dorn, Herman Foshee, Paul Bugg, Merwin Frazelle, and Howard Green.

Weeks later, the new pool of pilots was loaded onto a jeep carrier at San Diego and shipped out to Hawaii. "At Barbers Point, they had formed a replacement pilot group of all types of pilots: fighters, bombers, torpedo bombers," Davis recalled. Flying both F4Fs and F6Fs, Davis, Taylor, and their comrades operated with training squadron VF-100 until their numbers were called. Their destiny in the Pacific theater finally came on the morning of June 7, 1944, when fourteen VF-100 pilots were ordered to board another jeep carrier, USS *Breton* (CVE-23).[12]

Taylor could scarcely imagine the luxury of soon making his landings on an *Essex*-class fleet carrier. Built on a former merchant ship hull, *Breton* displaced 7,800 tons and was only 495 feet in length, with a flight deck that stretched 440 feet. In comparison, the *Essex*-class flight decks were nearly double the length for takeoffs, at 862 feet.

Underway from Pearl Harbor on the afternoon of June 7, *Breton* conducted gunnery drills en route to Eniwetok in the Marshall Islands. She arrived on the morning of June 15, and the ship remained there through the next day to refuel and take on provisions. *Breton* was underway from Eniwetok before dawn on June 17, carrying replacement pilots and a load of spare planes—SB2Cs, TBMs, F6F-3s, and one SBD—for delivery to Task Force 58.

By 0630 on June 20, *Breton* was maneuvering to join with Whiskey Harrill's Task Group 58.4. Her replacement aircraft began launching via catapult at 0838 as two new F6F-3s were shot off to land on *Essex*. Several hours later, at 1231, *Breton* resumed firing more spare planes off her catapult. For her part, *Essex* would receive another five Hellcats, three SB2Cs, and two TBM Avengers. The new fighter pilots sent to *Essex's* VF-15 and VF(N)-77 outnumbered the F6Fs, so two pilots simply climbed into the rear seats of Helldivers being flown over. They circled the fleet for two hours until refueling was complete before making their landings at 1447.

For Dick Davis, it was his thirty-first carrier landing. "I had ten landings in SNJs, ten in F4Fs, and ten in the F6F before I made my eleventh landing in an F6F on the *Essex*," he recalled. The other eight new pilots reporting to VF-15 this day with Davis were Ensigns Taylor, Charlie Dorn, Howard Green, Herman Foshee, Larry Self, Merwin Frazelle, Dick McGraw, and Lieutenant (jg) Richard Wilbur Davis. Joining VB-15 were Lieutenants (jg) Earl Mallette and Loren Nelson, along with Ensign Kent Lee.[13]

One of the new pilots was Larry Self, with six years of naval service under his belt. A farm boy from Ardmore, Oklahoma, he rode his horse to school before enlisting in the Navy at age seventeen to escape the Great Depression. Rising from the enlisted ranks as an ordnance handler and rear gunner, Self eventually secured a position in flight school. Upon graduating, he was a chief petty officer, but four additional months of officer training school helped him earn his commission as ensign in 1942. Self would soon be assigned to help fill out George Duncan's division.[14]

As Jack Taylor entered his new ready room through clouds of bluish cigarette smoke, he found a salty-looking bunch of pilots in their khaki overalls. He and the other new boys were directed to Lieutenant Morris—seated in the first row of leather seats—to be added to the flight schedule. Taylor was a bit awestruck at first, realizing he was standing before Hollywood movie star Wayne Morris. *I'm in the big time now!* Taylor thought.[15]

But he and his comrades quickly learned that Morris was no different from them, a fellow pilot who now had his fair share of combat experience. He made a point that he did not want the new pilots talking about his movies or using his screen name. "Don't call me Wayne," he told Dick Davis. "Call me Bert."

The nine newbies were given details of what would be expected of them. Commander McCampbell would want to monitor their abilities—in landing, in taking off, and in flying proper formation. They could expect to begin mixing into routine CAP duties before they would join a strike group.

At the moment, nearly two dozen of their new squadron mates were out in harm's way, making strikes against the enemy's airfields. The newbies settled in, listening to radio updates to see how the rest of their new team would fare.

FOR JOHN BARRY, the afternoon fighter sweep on June 20 was a first. He was now a division leader, responsible for the performance of his four-plane combat team. Twenty Hellcats had launched from *Essex* at 1422, the sweep under charge of Lieutenant John Collins. Barry's plane and that of his wingman, Ensign Al Slack, were among those carrying five-hundred-pound bombs to crater enemy runways. Rear Admiral Harrill had ordered the fighter strike against Agana and Orote Airfields on Guam and against Rota, aimed to keep enemy air surprises away from his fleet.

Upon reaching Agana Field, Collins sent two divisions in to bomb the runway. Barry's division was first. Returning to their rendezvous site ten miles west of Orote Field, they were jumped by four Hamp fighters. Barry charged head-on toward one Hamp that was firing at the outermost F6Fs in the circle. He drove off the attacker and received credit for damaging its engine.[16]

When the Japanese attack commenced, three planes from Barry's division were just joining the rendezvous circle with five other VF-15 Hellcats of Collins's high-cover team. The Hamps bracketed the tail-end F6F flown by Ensign Joe Power, the longtime wingman for Barry. Power was last seen heading toward a cloud with a Hamp close on his tail. He did not return. The other Hamps also headed for the clouds, but Barry's new wing-man, Al Slack, closed on one at high speed. Slack landed shots in its cockpit and engine until his first kill spun vertically into the ocean.

Lieutenant (jg) George Carr, leading the intermediate cover division of VF-15, was unable to attain attack position before the Japanese fighters took cover in the clouds. After the Japanese scattered, Carr, Collins, and Barry led their divisions in searching for Ensign Power, without luck.

It was dusk by the time the nineteen surviving Hellcats trapped on board *Essex*. They had attained only one certain kill in exchange for the loss of Power. Other elements of Task Force 58 suffered even greater losses that evening. While Whiskey Harrill's task group was separated from Pete Mitscher's main body for refueling that day, an *Enterprise* search plane had finally located Admiral Ozawa's carrier force. Although at the extreme limit for his carrier-based planes to strike and return, Mitscher nonetheless had sent off 240 Hellcats, Avengers, and Helldivers that afternoon.

While fourteen were forced to abort for various reasons and return to their ships, the remainder of the group pressed on and attacked Ozawa's warships. *Wasp*'s air group found only a trio of Japanese tankers, damaging two so severely that they were later scuttled. Other TF 58 warplanes damaged the carriers *Zuikaku*, *Junyo*, and *Chiyoda* with bombs, and sank the carrier *Hiyo* with bomb and torpedo hits. Twenty American planes were downed by Japanese fighters and antiaircraft fire, but the ordeal of the survivors was far from complete.

In what was later dubbed the "mission after darkness," the carrier strike groups returned to TF 58 after sunset, dangerously low on fuel. In the confusion of darkness, pilots trapped on any flight deck they could find. Deck crashes ensued, and some planes were forced to land in the ocean as their fuel dwindled. At final tally, eighty-six planes failed to land that evening, although many airmen were recovered by task force vessels and search-and-rescue operations.

Ignoring the danger of lurking enemy submarines, Mitscher boldly passed the order "Turn on the lights." It was a move that his aviators would never forget. Flight decks were illuminated, lanterns and searchlights were switched on, and picket destroyers fired star shells.

The personnel losses could have been much worse in the closing act of the Battle of the Philippine Sea. The fact that Marc Mitscher was himself a brown shoe (a naval aviator) had spared many lives through his selfless action of turning on the lights.

For *Essex*, the loss of only one Hellcat and Ensign Power on June 20 was a lesser blow. But for VF-15, it was another devastating loss. Since May 19, the squadron had lost its skipper and eight other pilots killed. The nine new pilots received this day exactly matched the unit's total losses since entering the war zone, keeping the active pilot roster at forty-six. But because the squadron had a one-fifth casualty rate already, Jack Taylor wondered how kindly fate would treat the newbies of Satan's Playmates.

TEN

MOPPING UP IN THE MARIANAS

June 21, 1944

The Battle of the Philippine Sea was winding down. Ozawa's Mobile Fleet was limping away, while Mitscher's Task Force 58 carrier groups spent much of June 21 sorting out the confusion and losses endured by the previous evening's mission beyond darkness. Whiskey Harrill's task group remained active, continuing to pound enemy airfields throughout the day.

From *Essex*, VF(N)-77 repeated its predawn heckler tactics this day. Lieutenant (jg) Jake Hogue and his wingman were launched by catapult at 0229. They found little activity over Rota Island. Proceeding to Guam at 0400, Hogue's team made a strafing run on the only visible light on the island before turning for home. All was quiet over the Japanese fields. By the time Hogue trapped at 0545, just before sunrise, elements of VF-15 led by CAG Dave McCampbell had already departed on an early sweep to pound Agana Field again.

Additional F6F and SB2C search teams were sent out to scour the seas for any more evidence of the Japanese fleet. Ensign Duz Twelves, sent on a five-hundred-mile search mission with Ensign Calvin Platt of VB-15, helped locate a *Lexington* bomber crew downed during the previous evening's attack on the Japanese fleet. Once again, Twelves flew cover over downed comrades while he and Platt called in a destroyer to the rescue. Duz's fuel tanks were dangerously low by the time he finally made his forty-fifth carrier landing that afternoon.[1]

Commander McCampbell's sweep arrived over Agana Field at 0645 in bright sunlight, finding no aerial opponents. His Hellcats shot up Japanese gun positions, allowing the trailing bombers to crater the runways and lace revetments with hundred-pound incendiaries and fragmentation bombs. During the midday hour, Lieutenant Ted Overton led a second *Essex* sweep to escort bombers in to hit the Marpi Point airstrip on Saipan. Enemy gunners were more alert this time, and Ensign Bill Nolte was hit in his dive.

Ensign Spike Borley was among the fighter pilots making strafing runs and dropping depth charges on the field. He saw the SB2C go into a spin, briefly right itself, and then take another flak hit that sheared off part of the Helldiver's wing. The rear seat man, ARM2c William Lowe, was unable to escape. "I watched him try to get out, but the plane was spinning so badly with that wing gone that he couldn't," recalled Borley. Nolte's plane slammed into the ocean off the southeastern tip of the island, leaving only an oil slick on the surface.[2]

Returning to *Essex* at 1512 on June 22 was Lieutenant Commander Jim Rigg, the new VF-15 skipper. It was his squadron's off day for combat, affording Rigg the chance to catch up with his comrades on all that had happened since he had been forced to land his battle-damaged F6F on *Enterprise* on June 19 during the Turkey Shoot. Rigg quickly settled into his new command role and helped prepare his pilots for their next attacks, scheduled for the following morning.

June 23, 1944

Roused from his sleep at 0200, Lieutenant (jg) Jake Lundin moved with purpose. During the previous day's brief hiatus from action, his squadron had reorganized some of its divisions. New skipper Jim Rigg had nine fresh faces in the ready room. He and Bert Morris would slowly blend these young men into CAP rotations. One, Ensign Dick Davis, would even make his first combat flight this day.

As for Lundin, the former Royal Canadian Air Force pilot would make his combat debut as a division leader. *Essex* and other carriers had orders to conduct additional strikes against Guam to keep the enemy's aircraft at bay. Flying as Lundin's wingman would be Lieutenant (jg) Jim Bruce, another RCAF veteran. In the ready room, Commander Dave McCampbell gave a quick talk. He would be leading the morning sweep, accompanied by the divisions of Lundin and Lieutenant John Strane.

McCampbell's dozen pilots manned their F6Fs before dawn and were climbing into the sky by 0530. The CAG division led the sweep to 22,000 feet, circling to the east of Guam to approach from down sun. As McCampbell orbited the island in a right-hand turn, he saw about eight enemy planes warming up on the field. Two or three others, well camouflaged, were hidden among trees south of the runway and only observable due to the morning sun reflecting off their props turning over.

McCampbell decided to make an east–west strafing run to knock out the planes on the field, but before his F6Fs could get into strafing position, the Japanese planes were already lifting off. Painted in effective camouflage and using the bright sun to their advantage, they quickly disappeared. For the next fifteen minutes, there was no air opposition. During this time, McCampbell's men surveyed both Agana and Orote Fields. The fighter sweep had descended to Angels 15 when the first enemy aircraft, four Zekes in formation, were encountered approaching them on their same level.

VF-15 turned into them at 0700. The Zekes dived and formed a tight Lufbery circle about 2,000 feet below. Due to their own high speed, McCampbell's pilots were not able to immediately attack. For the moment, VF-15 circled the Japanese group, wary that the enemy was setting up a trap. The ambush that had cost the squadron its skipper and his wingman was fresh on everyone's mind. Each of the Japanese fighters below was painted in the usual green-brown scheme, sporting large red meatballs. After about two circles, and seeing no other approaching enemy planes, McCampbell sent in two divisions to attack.

Sure enough, just as the eight Grummans moved in, another six Zekes came swooping down from high above. McCampbell's division dived in first on the four circling Zekes, who were the bait. He made a rear run, cracking his flaps to stay on a Zeke's tail. His opponent pulled out of the Lufbery circle, smoking, and headed for Orote Field. The *Essex* CAG saw this Zeke explode in midair a short distance from the scene. "When I pulled off his tail, the air seemed full of them and I wondered how could four turn into eight or more so quickly," McCampbell related.[3]

First to kill, McCampbell had just reached double-ace status.

McCampbell pulled back into the fight and got onto another Zeke's tail as it finished an overhead run on a VF-15 Hellcat. The Japanese pilot pulled out and performed a semi–split S in an attempt to scissor into position on McCampbell. After three bursts, the CAG saw him burn and fall into the water below. During his last pass, Ensign Bud Plant had also latched onto the Zeke's tail and was firing at the same time.

McCampbell then singled out a Zeke 1,000 feet below him. "He headed south at full speed, but I was able to overtake him in two minutes using war emergency power," said Dave. His first long-range burst caused the Zeke to enter a wingover to the left. This allowed CAG to close and get in a good burst before he dived under him. Without using flaps, Dave tried to follow him around in a high wingover. Due to his own excessive speed, McCampbell swung wide, which enabled his opponent to pull back up under the F6F, although the Zeke was more than five hundred feet lower.

Still sporting his wing tank, McCampbell was suddenly at a disadvantage. "He was gaining on me in the wingover, so when I got to the top, I just Immelmanned out, and took off back to where the rest of my people were," he recalled. (Named after World War I German fighter ace Max Immelmann, the Immelmann turn is an aerobatic roll-off-the-top, fast-climbing maneuver that results in level flight in the opposite direction at a higher altitude.)[4]

The *Essex* CAG had a bit of a jump on his opponent, and he poured on the throttle. The Zeke stayed on his tail, but McCampbell was slowly gaining distance. As he neared Orote Peninsula on Guam, he opened up on his radio: "This is 99 Rebel. Anyone not doing anything, please come down and get this Jap off my tail!"

McCampbell offered that he would pass Orote Peninsula about one mile to the west at Angels 4. As he approached Orote, his radio calls drew the desired intercept. "I led him right into the mouths of two or three Hellcats that came down," McCampbell recalled.[5]

The other three planes of the CAG division scored. McCampbell's wingman, Roy Rushing, helped chase Zekes over Orote Field. Minutes later he spotted a single Zeke heading toward him. The pair commenced scissoring and went into climbing and diving turns. Rushing eventually got on his tail and got in a good burst. The Zeke burst into flames, went out of control, and crashed in the water.

Rushing then headed back for the main melee. He flew only a short time with McCampbell before both were locked in their own individual pursuits and evasive maneuvers. Rushing took after one of a pair of Zekes. He got in a good burst for three seconds. His Zeke was believed to have crashed but it was not observed, giving Rushing a probable.

In the melee, McCampbell's second section leader, Jack Symmes, and his wingman, Bud Plant, became separated while chasing a Zeke. Several other Zekes pounced on Plant, who teamed with McCampbell to down one of them as the Zeke turned into the large group.

Elsewhere, Symmes joined three other F6Fs chasing a lone Zeke full throttle. Unable to keep up, Symmes slowly fell about three hundred feet astern. Two Zekes started in on his tail. In the ensuing scrap, Symmes hit one in the cockpit. The Japanese pilot was seen to crash-land on the field, demolishing his plane in the process. The other Zeke tailed Symmes through the fight, but he was unable to get a lethal shot. After pulling out, Symmes was attacked by another Zeke, which made a half-hearted pass. Symmes got the upper hand on this one, starting a fire in its starboard wing root that sent the Zeke crashing into the water just off Orote Point.

After sharing a kill with Commander McCampbell and narrowly escaping other enemy fighters, Plant tallyhoed another Zeke down at 2,500 feet. The enemy chandelled and came toward Plant, firing at the F6F as he climbed. Once his opponent was in range, Plant held his firing trigger down solid. The two planes barely missed each other, with the Zeke just clearing over the top of the F6F. Plant's Zeke, as witnessed by two other pilots, burst into flames and crashed on the side of a hill. With 5.5 kills to his credit, Plant became VF-15's fifth official ace.

WHEN THE MELEE broke out, John Strane was flying high-cover duty with division mates Jim Duffy, Bob Stearns, and Warren Clark. Strane watched the leading divisions of McCampbell and Lundin pounce on the four cir-cling Zekes, only to be assaulted by six Zekes that dived from high above.

Strane's team immediately went after these surprise Zekes. On their first pass, Stearns and Strane each scored a kill. During the dogfighting, a diving Zeke raked the cockpit of Stearns, wounding him. He was last seen slumped over his control stick in a steep glide toward Orote Field. Clark managed a Zeke kill to avenge his fallen division mate, and Strane sent another Japanese fighter into the ocean off Orote Point after chasing the Zeke off Duffy's tail.

Lieutenant (jg) Lundin's division made the most of its assault on the circling Zekes but suffered more than the CAG division. Jake and wing-man Jim Bruce were first pounced on by a Zeke making an overhead run. In his first pass, the Japanese pilot scored hits on Bruce's engine, which immediately began belching black smoke. Lundin saw his buddy stand up in the cockpit and bail out of his lifeless Hellcat.

Bruce was seen by Lundin to drift down in his parachute and drop into the ocean. During his descent, Bruce's life raft was seen by both Lundin and McCampbell to fall from his parachute harness. During the swirling

Left to right: *Ensigns Swede Thompson and Warren Clark and Lieutenant (jg) Jim Bruce in Hawaii, March 1944. Bruce was killed in action on June 23, 1944.* Doyle Bare collection, courtesy of Rita Bare

dogfights, neither pilot was thereafter able to ascertain Bruce's exact location in the ocean. Radio calls were made for a task force rescue vessel to look for Bruce, but he was never located.

Pausing only long enough to see his companion drifting down toward the water, Lundin began climbing back for fighting altitude. On his way up, he encountered a Zeke slightly below and gave a long burst. When last seen, the Zeke was smoking and heading down in a steep, straight dive toward the water. Lundin could only claim this as a probable, for his attention was instantly drawn to another Zeke above him. Jake fired a long burst until he stalled out, but the range was a little too great.

Lundin's second section leader, Bob Stime, dived in to help CAG McCampbell, who was being pursued by a Zeke. Stime nailed one Zeke in the engine and cockpit, leaving it smoking and heading for the water. Stime then maneuvered against a second Zeke, hit its engine, and watched the fighter crash into the side of a cliff, burning.

Stime's wingman, Ensign George Pigman, found a Zeke ahead of him and above. He pulled up, but the Zeke climbed away. Pigman fired just out of range, and the Zeke rolled over on his back, did a double roll, and split-S'ed out. As he was diving away, Pigman hit the Zeke in the fuselage and Stime also fired at him. Pigman got on his tail and fired long bursts that set the plane on fire. As Pigman pulled up, he and Stime saw the Zeke hit the ground and explode.

HAVING LOST HIS own pursuer, McCampbell arrived back at the melee point, but the air was clear of enemy planes. The main battle had raged nearly thirty minutes a half mile west of Orote Field. He called for a rendezvous at the point where a friendly parachute had been seen. Circling for about ten minutes, he collected seven of his F6Fs and returned to base. When he reached *Essex*, Dave found three other F6Fs—the remnants of Jake Lundin's division—already in the landing pattern. Due to communication problems, they had not heard his rendezvous order and had gone to the original rendezvous point.

The sweep had been successful in knocking down eleven enemy planes and claiming at least three other probables. But two pilots, Bob Stearns and Jim Bruce, had been lost. Since the start of its war cruise on *Essex*, VF-15 had now lost one-quarter of its original pilots. Three of the Hellcats that returned sported battle damage. One had been raked by 7.7mm fire that pierced its prop, engine, fuselage, cockpit, wings, elevator, stabilizer, fin, and rudder.

The losses were bittersweet. Dave McCampbell had attained double-ace status over Guam, and Strane and Plant had each reached five kills. Satan's Playmates now sported six aces: McCampbell, Strane, Plant, Charlie Brewer, George Carr, and Jack Symmes.

McCAMPBELL'S TEN SURVIVING Hellcats were waiting to land as *Essex* turned into the wind and launched her first mixed attack group at 0834 on June 23. Lieutenant Ted Overton led eleven fighters, a dozen Helldivers, and eight Avengers on strafing-and-bombing runs on Tinian. The *Essex* group returned without loss, although one VT-15 rear gunner suffered broken bones in his left foot when his Avenger was hit by shrapnel in its bomb bay and tunnel area.

Prior to the return of Overton's strike, *Essex* launched another deck-load strike at 1155. Led by new VF-15 executive officer George Duncan, the Hellcats under his charge again found no enemy opposition in the air. Duncan's fighters made strafing runs on parked aircraft and ground installations on Orote Field on Guam ahead of the *Essex* dive-bombers and torpedo bombers. A fourth *Essex* strike group, launched at 1444 just ahead of the return of Duncan's force, did encounter aerial resistance.

New VF-15 skipper Jim Rigg led this flight. En route to Orote Field, he stacked his three divisions to cover their eighteen SB2Cs and TBMs from enemy attack. There was no sign of enemy planes until the first of VB-15's Helldivers pushed over into their dives on parked aircraft south of the runway. At that moment, four olive-colored Zekes dived out of the scattered cloud cover and attempted a pass on the Helldivers.

Weaving above the bombers, Lieutenant Bert Morris and his division were in the best position to intercept the attackers. Utilizing a 4,000-foot altitude advantage, Morris made three swift firing passes until his Zeke opponent slammed into the ocean and disintegrated. The two pilots in

Morris's second section, Lieutenant (jg) George Carr and Ensign Norm Berree, each destroyed another Zeke.

Morris and Carr, with wingmen Ken Flinn and Berree, joined up over the *Essex* Helldivers and covered their retirement to the rendezvous site. After they had started their return to base, a lone Zero made a threatening run. All four members of Morris's division went after him. The VF pilots reported this pilot to be "the grand-daddy of all stunt pilots." The Zeke flew on its back from fifty to a hundred feet above the ocean. He managed to outmaneuver all four VF planes, performing "every stunt in (and some not in) the books," wrote ACIO Bob McReynolds. This Zeke was one of the few that managed to escape VF-15 completely unharmed.[6]

The *Essex* air group was assigned to continue pounding Guam the following day, June 24. Dave McCampbell led the first strike group off at 0527, covering the bombers until they completed their runs on Orote Field and a nearby fuel dump. Torpedo Fifteen slammed a 7,000-ton freighter in Apra Harbor with bombs and rockets.

Before returning to the carrier, McCampbell's nineteen fighters found a Japanese navy landing barge loaded with about four dozen soldiers clad in khaki. When their strafing runs were complete, the vessel was burning furiously, with no survivors in sight.

McCampbell's men queued up in the landing circle shortly after *Essex* launched her second strike group at 0829. Jim Rigg's nine Hellcats found no enemy planes to tangle with, instead expending many of their bullets on another landing barge that was left dead in the water. The only aircraft loss for Air Group Fifteen was the Helldiver flown by Lieutenant (jg) Jim Barnitz. He limped back to base with a smoking engine struck by AA fire. Although forced to make a water landing near the task force, Barnitz and his gunner were quickly recovered by a destroyer.

George Duncan led the four VF-15 divisions tasked with guarding the third *Essex* strike group. In addition to pounding Orote Field's runway, some of the bombers expended their ordnance against a small freighter in Apra Harbor. The fourth and final *Essex* strike of the day was escorted in by Jim Rigg. Two of his divisions covered the bombers as they struck Orote Field again. A third division comprised two photo Hellcats, each flying with a protective wingman.

Ensign Art Singer made vertical sorties over Rota Island with his photo F6F, taking obliques of the Rota village beach. He was suddenly approached by four Zekes, flying in pairs. The Zekes split, with one section keeping in a port turn. They overran Singer, and one Zeke ended up dead ahead of his F6F and filling Singer's sights. Singer pulled up and fired, getting hits in his wing roots, and the Zeke exploded.

The second Zeke section split to Singer's right in a climbing wingover. He turned to meet them with his nose up so sharp that his F6F nearly stalled. He fired head-on at the leading Zeke, hitting its engine and wing root. The plane flamed immediately, fell off on its starboard wing, and slammed into the water.

Singer ducked his nose, using full throttle plus war emergency power as he retired on the deck toward base. During the second head-on run, Singer was wounded, with multiple abrasions to his face from 7.7mm and 20mm hits taken in his cockpit and wing.

On June 25, *Essex* launched a single strike group to hit Orote Field again. The only aircraft Lieutenant Commander Rigg and his pilots encountered were wrecks parked along the runways on Guam. Bombs, bullets, and rockets were expended on aircraft dispersal areas, fuel tanks, and a small freighter in the harbor. Rigg was pleased that all of his flock returned, and the following afternoon he received two new replacement pilots from the escort carrier USS *Copahee* (CVE-12). These rookie ensigns were Johnny Brex from Ohio and Minor Craig from Pinckneyville, Illinois. Each was new to the fleet and raring to go.[7]

Craig was a country boy who had been nicknamed "Dusty" during flight training. After graduating high school in 1939, Craig utilized President Roosevelt's Work Progress Administration (WPA) project to learn the trade of welding. When America entered World War II, Craig and a buddy left their Mississippi River metal construction project and rode his motorcycle up to St. Louis to enlist. Craig struggled with some of his bookwork, but he proved to be a natural behind the controls of his various training aircraft. Although a Christian, Dusty understood what was expected of him. During his aviation schooling, he wrote a letter to his mom, explaining his situation: "They are training me to be a killer and a killer I will be, because I will have to be to give freedom and peace to the next generation. That is the price we have to pay. We got a war to win, and we will win it with the help of God."[8]

More than once, Dusty nearly washed out of flight training due to the demerits he collected. "One morning, I dropped down and touched my wheels on a freight train," he recalled. "An instructor had done that with me once." That stunt, and another incident of flying inverted over the base airfield at NAS Corpus Christi, landed Craig before Rear Admiral Alfred Montgomery, who commanded the local naval air training program.[9]

"We need pilots, but we don't need no damned fool pilots!" Montgomery snapped.

The admiral gave Craig another chance, seeing how the young pilot was just weeks away from being shipped to the war zone. Securing his wings and ensign commission, Craig moved on to NAS Pensacola and then was sent to VF-100 in Hawaii as he got closer to deployment.

The arrival of Brex and Craig on board *Essex* was less than spectacular. Ensign Al Slack was topside in Vulture's Row to watch the rookies land. Slack saw LSO Roy Bruninghaus wave off both ensigns for approaching too high and too fast. Their second landing attempts also ended in wave-offs. Slack later heard it reported that Captain Ofstie became exasperated with their poor performance. "If they don't make it this next time, shoot them down," he joked.[10]

In fairness, landing on *Essex* was a first for Craig. "I'd made a lot of simulated carrier landings, but I'd never made a carrier landing," he recalled. "I took a wave-off six times, and the seventh time I got aboard." He made a point of seeking out landing signal officer Bruninghaus to learn how to fix his mistakes. He was told he had been either too high, too fast, or too tight on another plane each time he made his approach into the groove. "I never had trouble after that," Craig recalled.[11]

Amused by the frustrations shared both on the bridge and on the flight deck, Slack headed for the flight deck after the new Hellcat pilots had successfully trapped. Near the island superstructure, he extended a hand and a warm grin to welcome the two heavyset young men before him. "I'd been out there two or three months, and I felt pretty old-hand at the time," Slack recalled. Brex and Craig certainly appreciated the gesture after their stressful first landings, and the trio soon became close friends.

In addition to VF-15 receiving new pilots, some of the squadron's other pilots took the chance to shuffle staterooms. John Collins and John Barry moved two decks higher to another two-man stateroom. With the loss of roommate Red Rader, Duz Twelves, Dick Fowler, and Jigs Foltz welcomed their buddy Jim Duffy to move into their stateroom 271 on the second deck.

DAYBREAK OF JUNE 27 found *Essex* and her task group operating only 155 miles from Saipan. The former Japanese-held Aslito Airfield had been seized by U.S. Marines on June 18, just days after they had stormed ashore. The first plane to land on the newly captured airstrip was actually a Zero that had been damaged in dogfights with Navy planes that afternoon. His plane ablaze as he came to a stop, Petty Officer Hari Tsubu of the 261st Air Group jumped out and was promptly apprehended. On June 22, twenty-five P-47 Thunderbolts from the 318th Air Group's 19th Fighter Squadron were catapulted off the escort carrier USS *Natoma Bay* (CVE-62) and landed at Aslito. Within two days other planes joined and swelled the squadron to seventy-three P-47s.[12]

Vice Admiral John McCain, on board *Essex* on June 27, decided that Saipan was secure enough for him to make a short visit to the island. At 1007, *Essex* launched one Avenger from VT-15 piloted by Lieutenant Commander VeeGee Lambert. He flew with ARM2c Thurman Sutcliffe as his radioman, with McCain going along in the bombardier's seat. Lambert's TBF was escorted by Lieutenant Commander Jim Rigg and Lieutenant Bert Morris, making them the first Task Force 58 planes to land on Aslito Field. They returned from Saipan at 1530 without incident, all sporting new enemy memorabilia. "Sutcliffe brought back a few souvenirs from what the Japs once held in their possession," VF-15 mechanic Elmer Cordray logged in his diary.[13]

That afternoon, Dave McCampbell led a strike against the runway, barracks, and fuel storage area on Rota Island. The task group took on fuel during the day, and *Essex* took the chance to exchange movies with one of the destroyers. Among the films received was *Kid Galahad*, in which Wayne Morris had a starring role. During his time with VF-15, Morris had gone to great lengths to make sure he was called Bert. He wanted no special attention, so the arrival of one of his films was embarrassing to him.

In the wardroom, *Kid Galahad* was screened numerous times over the ensuing days. "He hid in his room all during the show," Duz Twelves recalled. "He wouldn't let anybody come in." Morris's attempts to pay off a steward to "lose" the film were in vain. McCampbell found that his nephew-in-law took the teasing in stride, but he eventually became tired of it. Seeking out the air officer, Dave McDonald, Morris complained that he had had enough of seeing himself on-screen whenever he entered the wardroom. "Please get something else," he begged. Morris was pleased when *Kid Galahad* was eventually replaced with a new film.[14]

Air Group Fifteen continued with attacks on Pagan Island on June 28, destroying buildings and firing rockets into three small boats in the harbor. The relentless bombing attacks were quickly depleting the *Essex* ordnance arsenal. John Barry flew CAP duty this day, helping to break in some of the newer VF-15 pilots. "We do not have very many bombs left," he wrote in his diary. "We all are ready to go back to Eniwetok for a few days. Since we have had no air opposition lately, flying has lost its stimulus."[15]

The *Essex* fighter squadron handled CAP duty over the fleet the next two days. Although VB-15 planes made a strike on Rota Island on June 29, they were escorted by fighters from *Cowpens* and *Langley*. The only noteworthy flight this day for *Essex* Hellcats involved an early-morning special delivery to Saipan. At 0525, CAG Dave McCampbell was launched with a wingman to deliver photo intelligence taken by VF-15 photo Hellcats to the ground troops. Although not the first from AG-15 to land on Aslito Field, McCampbell believed he was one of the first to land once the airstrip was sufficiently patched up.[16]

But enough battle debris still littered the airstrip that he was faced with a new problem. "It still had a lot of shrapnel on it, because the Japs were up in the mountains," McCampbell recalled. "They were still shooting down there on it." Some of this metallic debris pierced one of the tires on his command F6F, *The Minsi*, when it came time to return to the ship. "I had no strain getting in, but when I started to take off, I suddenly got a flat tire while I was taxiing out," he later related.[17]

Well, this is going to pose a problem, he thought. *But I guess it's not too much unless the other one goes flat.* The *Essex* CAG lifted off mainly on his one good wheel. Landing back on his carrier with one flat tire created a new challenge, but McCampbell managed to do so without serious mishap.

A different situation had developed during his absence. Rear Admiral Whiskey Harrill, long considered by his fellow task group commanders to shy away from combat, had begun complaining about stomach pains. When his senior surgeon suggested the admiral might be suffering from appendicitis, Captain Ofstie reportedly recommended that the appendix be removed. Some, including McCampbell, believed the operation was really a chance to remove a cautious admiral from the path of progress for *Essex.* In any event, the surgery took place and Harrill would spend days recovering in a special senior officers' room in sick bay. On June 29, a temporary replacement TG 58.4 commander, Rear Admiral Wilder D. Baker, was received on board.[18]

During this period, Air Group Fifteen's involvement with island strikes was limited to night heckler raids. Bob Freeman, skipper of VF(N)-77, and a wingman arrived over Rota Island at 2000 on June 29. Twenty minutes of searching their radar scopes showed no enemy aircraft aloft, so Freeman's team proceeded to make strafing runs on lights, airfield revetments, building areas, and Rota Village.

Combat duties were largely curtailed for VF-15 as the *Essex* task group operated west of the Marianas for the next several days. Lieutenant (jg) Jake Hogue and another VF(N)-77 bat man launched at 0230 on July 1 for another heckler raid over Rota. Finding no airborne Japanese aircraft, they strafed Rota Village and dropped 350-pound depth bombs on a nearby sugar mill. Satan's Playmates found no enemy opponents during the day on July 1 but suffered the loss of yet another pilot.

Ensigns Wayne Dowlen and William Catterton—the latter hailing from Fort Worth, Texas—were newly received in VF-15. Assigned to this flight as his first mission, Catterton spun into the drink at 1500 as he was attempting to land after his CAP duty. His F6F plowed into the waves just aft of *Essex.* Catterton's head slammed into his instrument panel, shattering his jaw in three places and knocking out four teeth. "He was lucky to get out alive," John Barry noted in his diary. Plane guard destroyer USS *Lang* (DD-399) moved in quickly, retrieving the bloodied ensign. Catterton was transferred back to *Essex* within the hour, but his face required extensive surgery. He was transferred to a base hospital days later, his tenure with VF-15 having lasted less than a week.[19]

Skipper Jim Rigg led three divisions of VF-15 on a final strike against Rota Island on July 3. His Hellcats covered VB-15 and VT-15 strikers on bombing-and-strafing runs, all aircraft returning without loss. With that, Task Group 58.4 eased away from the Marianas for a run to the new fleet base in the Marshalls to take on provisions after a month at sea in support of the Saipan landings.

During the task force's run toward the Marshalls, the *Essex* wardroom was served a rare Fourth of July feast, complete with turkey, peas, asparagus, cranberry sauce, rolls, and pumpkin pie à la mode, plus distributed cigarettes and cigars. As noted in his letter that day to Olive, Lieutenant Barry was well aware of such wartime luxuries. "I never would have celebrated in such a manner if I were in civilian life."[20]

ELEVEN

MINSI II

July 6, 1944
Eniwetok Atoll, Marshall Islands Chain

For Duz Twelves, Eniwetok was still a diamond in the rough. As *Essex* and her task group entered the harbor entrance, he took in his first glimpse of the former Japanese outpost. Small islands and thin strips of land dotted with patches of green shrubbery and white sand rose no more than five meters above the ocean at any given point. A series of islets formed a circle fifty miles in circumference around a deep blue lagoon.

Eniwetok Atoll, seized from the Japanese in February, was the latest advance refuge for the U.S. Pacific Fleet. Twelves and fellow pilots standing topside saw only crude island terrain ravaged by naval bombardment, with splintered palm trees and blackened stumps. Centrally located 2,370 nautical miles southwest of Hawaii and 2,300 nautical miles southeast of Japan, Eniwetok was the newest anchorage for Task Force 58 as it continued to stage raids in the Marianas and prepared for future operations in the Philippines.

John Barry was more moved by the fresh fruit and bags of mail from home unloaded on *Essex* soon after she dropped anchor. He received twenty-two letters from Olive after a month of no correspondence. For the next five days, VF-15's pilots enjoyed some rare downtime ashore at the new facilities. Rum, bourbon, and beer were in good supply at the local O Club, and the crystal-clear waters invited afternoon swims and sunbathing.

For his part, Dave McCampbell found time to make only one trip ashore at Eniwetok. In his incoming mail, he found letters from back home. "I was courting two girlfriends at the time," he recalled, as his correspondence included letters from both Mary "Minsi" Wiener and Jill Heliker. His second CAG fighter had been nicknamed *The Minsi* in honor of Mary, but McCampbell soon christened a third Hellcat with the name *Minsi II.*[1]

McCampbell's Minsi II *Hellcat undergoing maintenance on the* Essex *flight deck while anchored at Saipan on July 30, 1944.*
NATIONAL ARCHIVES, 80-G-373647

The switch was due largely to a new batch of Grumman F6F-5 Hellcat variants that Air Group Fifteen received during this stay at Eniwetok. These were tested ashore and later flown back onto *Essex* on July 12 by McCampbell and other pilots, including Barry and Duz Twelves. Skipper Jim Rigg was pleased to find that the new "dash-5" fighters sported an R-2800-10W engine with a water-injection system, making them faster than the previous F6F-3s. The F6F-5 also had a flat armored-glass front panel versus the curved plexiglass panel of the previous model, and included strengthened rear fuselage and tail units.

The newer F6F-5s had a distinctive overall gloss sea-blue finish, as opposed to the tricolor scheme on the F6F-3s, which had a sea-blue upper surface mixed with intermediate blue-and-white lower surfaces. Gunnery officer Ted Overton put his assistant gunnery officers, Jack Symmes and Al Slack, in charge of bore sighting all guns on each plane, old and new. Chief Aviation Ordnanceman Frank "Skip" Harris and two of his men, Elmer Cordray and Wilbert Jones, rigged up a bore sight template on July 6 as *Essex* entered port. Climbing about on Hellcat wings on the flight deck in broiling heat proved to be a four-day chore on just the existing squadron aircraft.[2]

Essex was underway from Eniwetok on the afternoon of July 14. Whiskey Harrill, who had recovered from his appendectomy, had been reassigned and the temporary Task Group 58.4 commander had been replaced by Rear Admiral Gerald Francis "Gerry" Bogan, who had first trained as a naval aviator in 1925. Bogan's flagship was *Essex*, and she put to sea this day in company with the light carriers *Langley* and *Princeton*, four cruisers, and eight destroyers. The first operation for his new task group was continued suppression of Japanese aerial threats from Guam in the Marianas.

VF-15 pilots at a beer bash on Eniwetok, July 1944. Standing, left to right: *Bud Plant, Dick McGraw, Ed Mellon, George Carr, Roy Rushing, and George Pigman. Kneeling*, left to right: *unknown, Rod Johnson, Al Slack, and Jake Lundin.*

By the morning of July 18, *Essex* was roughly sixty miles southeast of Guam as flight operations commenced at 0745. Commander McCampbell's *Minsi II* was first off, his fighters assigned to protect twenty-three VB-15 Helldivers and VT-15 Avengers. His F6F pilots went in first, strafing the town of Agat and dropping depth bombs on gun installations and buildings. Skipper Jim Rigg led the second Guam strike to continue the pasting of enemy installations. Throughout the day, photo Hellcat pilots Art Singer, Ralph Foltz, and Roy Nall documented the results of the *Essex* strikes. By day's end, George Duncan and McCampbell had each led additional strikes to hit gun positions, bridges, and storage dumps. The air group's sole loss was an Avenger hit by antiaircraft fire whose crew was recovered by a task force destroyer.

On July 19, Jim Rigg, Bert Morris, and Ted Overton alternately commanded the fighter contingent of four strikes made against Guam. In the absence of enemy fighters, Air Group Fifteen had its way in pounding camouflaged enemy troop concentrations, buildings, and gun positions. Duz Twelves found the area so tame that he playfully zoomed over Guam at low altitude after making his strafing runs. "Flat-hatted over entire southern area," he wrote in his journal that evening. Commander McCampbell escorted two Avengers over to Saipan to deliver mail and pick up several bags for the *Essex* crew.[3]

Essex warplanes pounded Guam again on July 20 with another five strikes. The only loss was the Helldiver piloted by Lieutenant Niles Siebert, whose left wing broke off during his dive. Siebert's SB2C plunged to the ground in flames, with no survivors. Allied troops stormed ashore on Guam on July 21, supported by three Air Group Fifteen missions. Duz Twelves watched the first waves of 56,000 Marine and Army troops grinding onto the beaches in their amtraks as he strafed ahead of them to knock out enemy strongpoints. From his vantage point, he deemed the day's work to be "very successful."[4]

The following day was consumed with refueling TG 58.4 carriers and destroyers, but the *Essex* air group was back in action on July 23 to support Marine landings on Tinian Island. Three missions resulted in only two plane losses this day. Lieutenant (jg) Cliff Jordan of VB-15 was forced to make a water landing after his low-flying Helldiver suffered damage from bomb fragments. He and his gunner were recovered by an American destroyer minelayer.[5]

The second plane loss on July 23 was the F6F-3 flown by Ensign Al Slack. He had completed his strike on Guam and was making his final turn for a landing approach on *Essex* when his fuel tank suddenly cut out.

VF-15 squadron photo of officers taken on July 10, 1944.
Front row, left to right: *Ens. Ken Flinn, Lt. (jg) Rod Johnson, Ens. Bud Plant, Lt. (jg) Bob Stime, Lt. (jg) Norm Berree, Lt. (jg) Warren Clark, Ens. Duz Twelves, Lt. (jg) Dick Fowler, Ens. Dave Johnson, Ens. George Pigman, Ens. Jim Duffy, and Ens. Al Slack.*
Second row, left to right: *Lt. Richard Davis, Lt. John Strane, Lt. Bert Morris, Lt. George Crittenden, Lt. Bob McReynolds, Lt. Cdr. Jim Rigg, Lt. Cdr. George Duncan, Lt. Joe O'Brien, Lt. Ted Overton, Lt. (jg) John Hoffman, and Lt. (jg) Carl White.*
Third row, left to right: *Lt. (jg) Glenn Mellon, Lt. (jg) Doyle Bare, Lt. (jg) Royce Nall, Lt. (jg) Roy Rushing, Lt. John Symmes, Lt. George Carr, Lt. Jake Lundin, Lt. (jg) Duke Henning, Lt. (jg) Swede Thompson, Lt. (jg) Art Singer, and Lt. (jg) Ken West.*
Fourth row, left to right: *Ens. Jack Taylor, Ens. Wayne Dowlen, Ens. Merwin Frazelle, Ens. Herman Foshee, Ens. Minor Craig, Ens. Johnny Brex, Ens. Charles Dorn, Ens. Dick Davis, Ens. Clarence Borley, Ens. Howard Green, Ens. Len Hamblin, Ens. Dick McGraw, and Ens. Larry Self.* Doyle Bare collection, courtesy of Rita Bare

With no power at a mere three hundred feet, Slack made a hasty water landing astern of the carrier. As his fighter impacted the water, Slack hit his face on the gunsight hard enough to kill the nerves in his front teeth. He struggled to free himself from his parachute gear as his Hellcat sank under the waves, pulling him down with it. Slack believed he was meeting his end as he finally kicked free and pulled for the surface, choking on salt water. By the time he managed to inflate his life raft, the plane guard destroyer USS *Thatcher* (DD-514) was fast approaching. On *Thatcher*'s first pass, Slack feared he would be sucked under the destroyer's massive stern into her propellers.[6]

The Hellcat pilot was too exhausted to climb the Jacob's ladder dropped over the side for him. *Thatcher* sailors shouted to Slack to cling to the rope ladder as they hauled him up the tin can's slick side. After being checked over by the destroyer's medical officer, Slack was allowed to retire to an officer's bunk to catch some rest.

But the tossing and pitching of a small warship in rough seas made for fitful sleep as *Thatcher*'s bow dived into each trough. "I sunk into the bed, and when it got to the top of the pitch, I rose completely off the bed," Slack said. "It did that a few minutes, and I had all the destroyer duty I wanted." He was pleased to be returned to *Essex* within hours when *Thatcher* went alongside the carrier to deliver mail.[7]

Essex CONTINUED TO supply aerial support on July 24 for the Tinian landings taking place that morning. Dave McCampbell led eighteen other fighters off at 0529, with orders to strafe and bomb White Beach 2 as the Second Marine Division stormed the shores.

Duz Twelves was flying in the vicinity of the battleship USS *Colorado* (BB-45), operating about 3,200 yards directly west of the island. Japanese artillerymen firing a 150mm gun hit the battlewagon at 0740. Over the next ten minutes, *Colorado* was hit twenty-one more times in the starboard side of the ship, the forecastle, and the CIC. Fires raged for more than a half hour and the battleship sustained 43 men killed and 198 wounded. "She burned fiercely for a while but put out fires and steamed out of range," Twelves recalled. "Quite a sight."[8]

Lieutenant John Barry, leading one of the early VF-15 divisions, was gravely concerned by the sight of the burning *Colorado*. He worried for the safety of his brother, William "Budd" Barry, who was serving on the battleship. Days would pass before Barry had confirmation that Budd had escaped injury on the burning warship. Loaded with either a 350-pound depth bomb or a half dozen hundred-pound general purpose (GP) bombs, McCampbell's fighters worked over enemy gun positions in the cliffs on Tinian before returning to base.

Jim Rigg led the second Tinian strike on July 24. His eleven fighters were again loaded with a mix of GP bombloads and depth bombs to pound gun positions in the jagged island cliffs. During one of his strafing runs, Ensign Dusty Craig had a piece of shrapnel pierce the cylinder wall of his engine. Oil spread across his windshield, which he wiped with his glove. Engine trouble forced him to land on Isley Field on Saipan. As Craig

Ensign Minor "Dusty" Craig was forced to make an emergency landing on Saipan on July 24.
MARSHA CRAIG KUHNERT

taxied to a halt, a Marine hopped onto his wing and motioned to him to get out of the plane, as enemy AA guns were still active in the area. "Later, they found a cylinder part and repaired my plane," Craig recalled. After a brief visit on Saipan, Craig was able to make the return flight to *Essex*.[9]

Rigg and the remainder of his flight began landing on *Essex* around 1045. Ensign Dave Johnson was in the cross leg of his landing approach when LSO Roy Bruninghaus waved him off because his landing gear had not dropped. Johnson added throttle, but his engine apparently cut out. His wheels-up F6F rolled over onto its back and slammed into the ocean nose down. Horrified onlookers did not see the pilot emerge from his sinking Hellcat. The destroyer USS *Charles Ausburne* (DD-570) was sent to recover him, but Johnson was not found.

The loss of Johnson was particularly hard on Duz Twelves. Since his early training days, he had grown particularly close to Johnson, Red

Rader, and Jimmy Wakefield. In his diary that evening, Twelves somberly recorded that all three of his VF-15 buddies had been lost in a ten-month period.[10]

Three more *Essex* air strikes were launched against Tinian and Guam that day, led by Duncan, Rigg, and McCampbell. Two planes from the fourth strike failed to return. En route to the target area, Ensign Larry Self's F6F started leaking oil. His engine began to overheat, and Self was ordered to make an emergency landing on Saipan's Isley Field with his wingman, Red Bird Clark.

When Self reached the airstrip, his oil leak created other problems. Unable to lower his landing gear, he was forced to make a belly landing on the runway,

Ensign Dave Johnson, in March 1944, was lost on July 24. DOYLE BARE COLLECTION, COURTESY OF RITA BARE

effectively wiping out his Hellcat. There, Self spent time with the local pilots, until another badly wounded F6F pilot from another carrier landed. Once the plane was refueled, Self and Clark flew out and found their fleet, landing on board *Essex* at 1417.[11]

The deck crews and the officers on the bridge noted that Self's Hellcat lacked the distinctive white band on its tail. It instead had a white triangle with a black ball in the middle. Self was ordered to the bridge, where he was confronted by the new task group commander, Rear Admiral Bogan.

"What ship are you from?" Bogan asked.

"The USS *Essex*, sir," said Self. He then quickly explained his landing on Isley Field and borrowing the wounded man's plane.

"Glad to have you back aboard, son," said Bogan.

Essex airedales moved Ensign Self's borrowed F6F to the hangar deck, where they painted over the ball-and-triangle symbols and added the proper VF-15 white stripe. After reporting into the ready room, Self soon retired to his stateroom to clean up. There he was shocked to find a sailor boxing up all his personal gear to ship home, as he had been reported missing in action. "I stopped that crap," Self recalled.[12]

THE FOLLOWING DAY, July 25, *Essex* sent her dive-bombers to hit Guam again, but VF-15 remained on task force CAP duty. John Barry spent the balmy tropical afternoon sunbathing on the flight deck, hoping to gain a deep base tan in case he was ever forced down at sea. Writing to Olive that evening, Barry mused that he had now been away from her for five months of their ten-months-old marriage. "It is hard to believe that in approximately two months I shall be a father," Barry wrote.[13]

The *Essex* air group flew additional strikes against Guam and Rota Island the following day. The carrier made a brief stop in Saipan Harbor on July 28 to replenish its bomb supply from an ammunition ship. From the flight deck, Elmer Cordray borrowed Dave McCampbell's binoculars to watch dive-bombers pounding nearby Tinian Island. "Everything torn to hell," he wrote. George Duncan hopped a ride on a VT-15 TBM that flew into Saipan ahead of the ship. He carried with him a bottle of Scotch that he delivered to his younger brother, who was serving with the Marines on Saipan. It was a brief but happy reunion. His brother chided him for being a fool, flying fighters through enemy flak over Japanese-held islands. "I see you down here, and I'd rather be up in the airplane!" Duncan replied.[14]

The following day, Commander McCampbell's aviators were back in business, conducting two strikes on Guam in support of the troops still fighting to seize control of the island. For the next eleven days *Essex* operated in the vicinity of Guam, launching deckload strikes and fighter sweeps to bomb and strafe troop concentrations, supply dumps, buildings, and enemy roadways. On July 31, Lieutenant Carl White and Ensign Roy Nall landed on Guam, marking the first American planes to land on the newly captured airstrip since the Marines invaded that island.[15]

Air Group Fifteen flew as many as three support missions per day in addition to maintaining regular CAPs over the task group. The air support was crucial to the ground troops, as progress was sometimes measured only in yards on the bloodiest days. On August 7, *Essex* skipper Ralph Ofstie was decorated with a Silver Star, promoted to admiral, and transferred. "Our captain was the best that I have encountered," wrote John Barry. "Everyone aboard ship shall regret his departure, as he was well liked by everyone." That afternoon, *Essex* received a replacement, forty-nine-year-old Captain Carlos Wilhelm Wieber—a Virginian and 1917 Naval Academy graduate who had previously commanded the escort carrier USS *Sangamon* (CVE-26).

The following morning, Jim Rigg and Lieutenant Barry took their divisions up for another troop support mission over Guam. They returned in the late morning without loss after strafing and bombing ravines where Japanese troops were concentrated. "We had the worst lunch imaginable today, fried spam, rice, and asparagus," Barry wrote. "If it had not been the fact that I missed breakfast, I would have skipped my lunch."[16]

The only highlight of the day for Barry was that a Navy photographer captured an image of his *Olive* Hellcat seconds after trapping. He was just taxiing forward with his belly tank beneath, immediately after his tail-hook had been removed from the arresting cable. He sent a copy of the photo to Olive, adding a note: "The man in that plane loves the girl for whom the plane is named."

Barry's combat hop over Guam on August 8 was the last such mission for VF-15. Routine CAP duties remained during the next two days, but word soon made the rounds that *Essex* and her task group were due to return to Eniwetok to reprovision and rest their air groups. Barry's diary entry for August 10 summed up the feelings of his fellow pilots. "We all are glad to leave, as we were doing nothing but routine CAP and air support flights against Guam."[17]

The weeks of island support missions had been flown primarily by the more seasoned VF-15 pilots. McCampbell and Rigg spent those weeks breaking in new pilots like Jack Taylor with CAP duty. The newbies could not complain about missing out on enemy dogfights. Satan's Playmates had gone nearly six weeks without a single aerial kill. Rest in Eniwetok was certainly anticipated, but the more aggressive fighter pilots were left yearning for more real action.

As *Essex* headed for port, Commander McCampbell took the chance to begin writing up a lengthy report on Air Group Fifteen's combat actions during the period of July 18 through August 8. In it, he noted that the lack of proper target maps with grids had increased the difficulties of effective bombing of camouflaged enemy positions. Damage assessment was difficult at best, causing his pilots to feel "as though they were not accomplishing very much."[18]

McCampbell wrote that although his recent batch of eleven replacement pilots each had at least 350 hours of flight time, most were not yet deemed ready to engage in actual aerial combat. One pilot had forgotten to charge his guns before making an intercept. Another rookie pilot had signaled for an emergency landing, reporting that he had only ten gallons of fuel remaining. "It turned out that he had exhausted nearly all his gas, except 150 gallons in his belly tank which he knew nothing about," McCampbell wrote.[19]

McCampbell further recommended future replacement pilots should be trained together as a combat team and they should be sent to fleet carriers as complete replacement divisions. "There is little or no advantage to be gained in acquiring only one replacement pilot at a time," he added. Dashing Dave was already working on a new plan to create a team of fighter-bombers within VF-15. The time in port would offer him the perfect chance to develop this group.[20]

His fighter pilots desired shore leave, but they wondered what would happen next. "Scuttlebutt is going berserk," Barry wrote on August 11. *Essex* and her task group entered Eniwetok Atoll on the morning of August 13. Although mail was delivered on board, the carrier was anchored too far out for boats to ferry the troops ashore. Many pilots would spend the next week marooned on board their carrier. Even worse, the newly promoted *Essex* XO, Dave McDonald, proved to be a stickler for protocol. Barry was disturbed that McDonald demanded an 0815 muster on the hangar deck each day. "All of the aviators are screaming, as we usually sleep till nine-thirty or ten while in port," he wrote to Olive.[21]

Satan's Playmates grew restless sitting in Eniwetok Harbor. A short distance away, thousands of other sailors enjoyed liberty on the white sand beaches and in the officers' club. Dejected, Barry wrote on August 18, "The thought of a beer while sunning is pure unadulterated torture."[22]

Commander Dave McCampbell in the cockpit of his *Minsi III* Hellcat, on board *Essex* in early October 1944. Note the stickers for twenty-one aerial victories as of this date. NATIONAL ARCHIVES, 80-G-K-2179

McCampbell's second F6F was painted with the nickname *The Minsi* in honor of his girlfriend. That plane is seen here warming up on the deck of *Essex* in June 1944. NATIONAL ARCHIVES

Catapult launch of an F6F Hellcat of VF-15 from the hangar deck of USS *Hornet* on February 25, 1944. NATIONAL ARCHIVES, 80-G-367107

Due to many aircraft crashes, Air Group Fifteen was not in the good graces of *Hornet*'s skipper, Captain Miles Browning. At left, *Hornet* deck crews help a Helldiver pilot from his VB-15 SB2C, which split in half upon crash-landing on January 7, 1944.
NATIONAL ARCHIVES,
80-G-367068

This VF-15 Hellcat shut down flight operations for forty-five minutes after dropping its landing gear into *Hornet*'s portside catwalk on January 19, 1944.
NATIONAL ARCHIVES,
80-G-367099

A group of VF-15 pilots poses atop Mount Haleakalā on Maui in March 1944. Rear (*l-r*): Doyle Bare and Dave Johnson. Front (*l-r*): Jack Ivey and George "Red" Rader. DOYLE BARE COLLECTION, COURTESY OF RITA BARE

Air Group Fifteen was cast ashore in Hawaii for more training in early 1944. Dave McCampbell was promoted to air group commander, and Commander Charlie Brewer (*above*), seen in Hawaii in March 1944, became skipper of VF-15. DOYLE BARE COLLECTION, COURTESY OF RITA BARE

Fighting Fifteen finally found a home on the carrier *Essex* (CV-9), seen under way and heavily loaded with aircraft in 1943. NATIONAL ARCHIVES, 80-G-68097

The first strike for Air Group Fifteen was against Marcus Island on May 19, 1944. Smoke rises from burning buildings. US NAVY, NARA

The remains of David McCampbell's *Monsoon Maiden* Hellcat on May 19 before it was pushed overboard. Note the explosive hit in the fuselage, which caused a loss of his hydraulics and rudder control, and seared the lower fuselage before McCampbell jettisoned his belly tank. US NAVY, NARA

Hellcat No. 32 of VF-15, minus half its port tail, piloted by Ensign George "Red" Rader, back on *Essex* after the Marcus Island strike on May 20. US NAVY, NARA

The *Essex* flight deck crew scrambles to help Lieutenant John Collins from his Hellcat, damaged by AA fire. He has just crash-landed after an attack on Wake Island on May 23, 1944. NATIONAL ARCHIVES, 80-G-373617

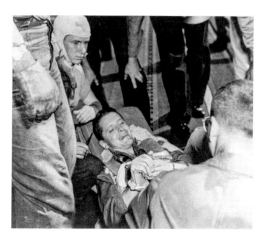

Collins, seriously wounded, on a stretcher after being removed from his F6F. NATIONAL ARCHIVES, 80-G-373619

A Japanese freighter burns after Air Group Fifteen attacks on June 12, 1944. US NAVY, NARA

With 68.5 enemy planes downed in one day, VF-15 took top honors on June 19, 1944, during what became known as the Marianas Turkey Shoot. Sailors on board the cruiser *Birmingham* watch fighter plane contrails mark the sky above Carrier Task Force 58. NATIONAL ARCHIVES, 80-G-248549

Some of the top-scoring *Essex* fighter pilots of the June 19 Turkey Shoot pose before the VF-15 battle flag scoreboard. *Left to right*: Lieutenant Commander Jim Rigg (the new VF-15 skipper), Commander Dave McCampbell (seven kills on June 19), Ensign Dick Fowler, Ensign George Carr, and Ensign Claude "Bud" Plant. NMWWIIA

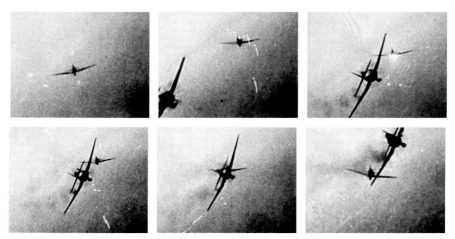

Aerial victories were often determined by gun camera footage when the Hellcats returned to the carrier. In this dramatic series taken from the plane of Ensign Duz Twelves, he is firing on a Japanese Zeke fighter in the upper left. *Top center*: CAG Dave McCampbell zips in behind the Zeke while Twelves continues to fire. *Top right*: Zeke begins to burn from hits by Twelves. *Lower left and center*: McCampbell's F6F takes hits as Twelves continues to fire. *Lower right*: Both the Zeke and CAG Hellcat are smoking by the time Twelves ceases his firing. Van Twelves

VF-15 photo pilot Art Singer returns from combat with a bullet hole through the upper corner of his windshield. US Navy, via Jon Abbott

Publicity photo taken of VF-15 ace pilot Lieutenant Bert Morris in his F6F in November 1944. Prior to the war, he was better known as Hollywood movie star Wayne Morris. National Archives, 80-290680

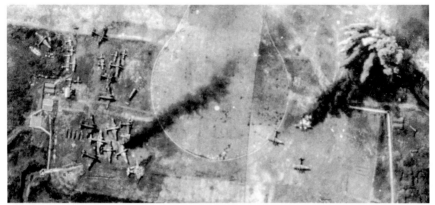

June 15 air strikes against an Iwo Jima airfield; photo taken by Ensign Art Singer of VF-15. Note the exploding bombs and large group of planes at lower center. US Navy, NARA

Japanese shipping under *Essex* attack at Mindanao Harbor on September 9, 1944. US Navy, NARA

McCampbell's *Minsi III* after landing on *Essex* on October 22, 1944, during the Battle of Leyte Gulf. It sports nineteen Japanese rising sun "kills" below his cockpit. National Archives

Pilots in the VF-15 ready room during the Battle of Leyte Gulf, posing as they study a map regarding the position of a Japanese fleet. *Left to right*: Lieutenant John Collins, Lieutenant Commander Valdemar "VeeGee" Lambert (skipper of VT-15), and Lieutenant (jg) Art Singer. NATIONAL ARCHIVES, 80-G258192

A VF-15 Hellcat in flight in early 1944. Note the white horizontal stripe on the top of the tail fin and rudder, belly drop tank, and the two-tone color scheme. US NAVY

Flinn, seen with his Japanese Army captors. He did not survive as a POW. KATIE RASDORF

Ensign Ken Flinn, credited with five kills, was shot down on October 13, 1944, and captured.
DOYLE BARE COLLECTION, COURTESY OF RITA BARE

Japanese carrier *Zuiho* is still under way during the October 25, 1944, attacks but is burning heavily from bomb hits from *Essex* pilots. Note the flight deck camouflage pattern. NHHC, NH 95471

Carrier *Zuiho* sinking after carrier attacks off Cape Engaño, as photographed by a *Franklin* plane late in the attacks. Air Group Fifteen and VF-15 scored bomb hits on *Zuiho*. National Archives, 80-G-272552

Japanese carrier *Zuikaku* maneuvering while under attack on October 25. NHHC, NH 95785

Japanese *Ise* class battleship under attack on October 25, with smoke rising from her antiaircraft guns. Several VF-15 pilots were credited with direct bomb hits. NHHC, NH 63440

Successful VF-15 division photographed in October 1944 after their strike on Formosa. *Left to right*: Lieutenant (jg) Doyle Bare, Lieutenant Bert Morris, Ensign Ken Flinn, and Ensign Dick Davis. Flinn was shot down and captured soon after this photo.
Doyle Bare collection, courtesy of Rita Bare

Lieutenant (jg) Duz Twelves makes a spectacular crash-landing in his F6F on *Essex* on November 13, 1944, and is helped from his plane. These photos were taken by war correspondent Joe Rosenthal, who later received the Pulitzer Prize for his iconic 1945 Iwo Jima flag-raising photo. VAN TWELVES

VF-15 ace buddies Jake Lundin (6.5 kills) and George Carr (11.5 kills) on the flight deck in 1944. WALTER LUNDIN COLLECTION, NATIONAL MUSEUM OF WORLD WAR II AVIATION

Lieutenant Commander Jim Rigg (11 kills) became the VF-15 executive officer during the war cruise. DOYLE BARE COLLECTION, COURTESY OF RITA BARE

Badly shot up, and with only one set of landing gear operational, the Hellcat of Baynard Milton drops onto the deck of *Essex* on November 13, 1944. These motion picture stills show Milton's wheel shearing off as his props chew into the flight deck. US NAVY

CAG-15 Dave McCampbell (with chart) confers with command staff on the bridge of *Essex*. He had just returned from leading a raid on Manila, on November 13, 1944. NATIONAL ARCHIVES, 80-G-258656

This photo was taken by Ensign Ralph Foltz of VF-15 on November 11, 1944, over Ormoc Bay, Leyte. In the background, two Japanese transports are under bombing attacks by *Essex* planes, while the damaged destroyer *Wakatsuki* maneuvers at high speed in the foreground. US NAVY

Japanese cruiser *Nachi* burning as she dodges *Essex* bombs on November 5, 1944, in Manila Bay. NATIONAL ARCHIVES, 80-G-287019

VF-15 aces seen on board USS *Essex*, November 1944, at the end of their tour, beneath McCampbell's *Minsi III* Hellcat. Front row *(l-r)*: Roy Nall, John Symmes, George Duncan, Bert Morris, James Rigg, John Strane, Ted Overton, Dick Fowler, George Carr, Walter Lundin, Norm Berree, David McCampbell, Charles Milton, Roy Rushing, and George Pigman. Rear *(l-r)*: Robert Fash, Art Singer, Wendell Twelves, Larry Self, Ralph Foltz, Jim Duffy, Wally Johnson, Albert Slack, and James Bare. Not pictured are three VF-15 aces lost in action and Al Borley, rescued by a submarine but still at sea. NAVAL HISTORY AND HERITAGE COMMAND, NH 106328

Publicity photo of Commander McCampbell with thirty-four flags on the fuselage of his *Minsi III* Hellcat, with long-time plane captain Chet Owens. US NAVY

President Franklin D. Roosevelt looks on as David McCampbell is pinned with his Medal of Honor by his mother in the White House on January 10, 1945. In the background are his sister, Frances Stewart, and Admiral Ernest J. King. DAVID P. MCCAMPBELL

TWELVE

FIGHTER-BOMBERS

August 19, 1944
Eniwetok Atoll

Kent Lee was among the first Air Group Fifteen pilots to find a way to get ashore. But his exodus came with a price.

Twenty-one-year-old Lee was born on a farm in Florence County, South Carolina, that had been family land since the 1700s. Like other rural kids in the region, he helped with the cotton and tobacco crops when he was not in school. In the summer of 1939, Kent had just enough money, sixty cents, to afford a ride in a Ford Trimotor airplane at the county fair. Noisy and bumpy during takeoff, Lee's first flight lasted all of ten minutes above Florence. But he was hooked. *Someday, I will fly on my own*, he thought.[1]

He graduated high school in June 1940 in a class of seventeen. After one year at Clemson College, he enlisted in the U.S. Navy that August, a scrawny five-foot-nine teenager weighing only 133 pounds. Following boot camp, he was sent to aviation machinist's mate school at NAS Norfolk and spent the next year working on aircraft at NAS Miami before applying for aviation cadet training. He received his golden wings and was commissioned as an ensign on August 7, 1943, at NAS Kingsville with 235 flight hours.[2]

On June 20, 1944, the second day of the Marianas Turkey Shoot, Ensign Lee and Lieutenants (jg) Loren Nelson and Earl Mallette had flown onto *Essex* with three replacement Helldivers. The trio experienced the same breaking-in period that Jack Taylor, Dick Davis, and the other new VF-15 replacement pilots had experienced.

Lieutenant Commander Jim Mini put his rookies through a training program in July, but he was quicker to put Lee, Nelson, and Mallette on combat flights than Jim Rigg had been with his newbie fighter pilots. In early August, Lee was finally assigned to participate with VB-15 in some of the strikes on Guam, Tinian, and Saipan, and he made seven combat flights. "The night before the first flights, I was always very nervous and didn't sleep very well," he admitted. "Once we manned the airplanes, revved up the engines and were ready to go, it was all business."[3]

Lee considered the SB2C to be a "dog" of a dive-bomber. He made strafing runs on shore installations and was part of a six-plane division to attack a Japanese freighter one day. "Not one hit," Lee recalled. "But that was sort of standard for the SB2C. Not a very good dive-bomber." He was still mastering the Helldiver when *Essex* dropped anchor in Eniwetok. That was where Ensign Lee seized the chance to jump into a different aircraft. Dave McCampbell's Air Group Fifteen was ahead of the curve in August 1944 in organizing a mini–VBF unit within VF-15.

McCampbell wanted to train a small group of pilots to fly the F6F Hellcat as a versatile fighter-bomber. The normal complement of planes on *Essex* had been three dozen fighters and thirty dive-bombers. But the need for fighter protection was stronger than the need for bombers. By month's end, *Essex* would be cutting back VB-15 to twenty-five SB2Cs and VF-15 would be increasing to forty-nine F6Fs. By the beginning of 1945, fleet carriers would begin operating with both a traditional VF squadron and a separate fighter-bomber outfit, designated as VBF.

While anchored in Eniwetok, Jim Mini called his dive-bomber pilots together in the ready room for a briefing. Nine volunteers were needed to make the switch to fighters. Lee was one of only six pilots who raised his hand to volunteer. *I've seen what flying a dive-bomber is like*, Lee thought. *I'd like to try a fighter plane. Maybe I'll get myself a Japanese plane.*[4]

The other five volunteers had each been with VB-15 since the start of the cruise. Lieutenant (jg) Bill Anderson from Pennsylvania had been a flight instructor before entering the Navy. Lieutenants (jg) Monchie "Monk" Gunter from Florida, Homer Voorhest from New York, and John

Van Altena from Wisconsin had been with VB-15 since its early formation period. The last of the six volunteers was another ensign, Tom Hoey from Daytona Beach; he had attended the Stevens Institute of Technology before entering flight training.

With only six volunteers, Lieutenant Commander Mini was forced to select three more VB-15 pilots to make the switch to fighter-bombers. Senior among the trio he picked was Lieutenant Henry "Dutch" Kramer from Nebraska. Kramer was a VB-15 original officer who had flown twenty-one combat missions. The other two were less experienced ensigns. Henry Gaver, a married West Virginian, had been with the bombing squadron only since April.

Wilbur Deming had completed two years at Brown University on scholarship before entering flight training. He and two of his siblings had been born in India, where their father served as a missionary until 1934. Upon returning to the United States, Deming and his family settled in Washington, Connecticut, where his father took over the local Congregational church. Despite being a preacher's son, Deming proved to be a hellion in the skies.[5]

During his stateside training with the new Air Group Fifteen, Ensign Deming was known to be a hotshot. Once, while ferrying a plane to Bradley Field near Hartford, he had buzzed his father's church on a Sunday morning, a maneuver that did not go over well with local authorities. Lieutenant (jg) Scott Matthews and other VB-15 pilots soon gave Wilbur the nickname "Wild Bill."

On August 19, Kent Lee, Deming, and the other seven volunteers and draftees were ordered to grab some gear to head ashore for training. They climbed down rope ladders to a motor launch bobbing in the waves alongside Essex and endured a 2.5-hour ride to the distant docks on Eniwetok. The VF-15 XO, Lieutenant Commander George Duncan, and Lieutenant Ted Overton were in charge of training this new bunch. Accompanying them to help service the training planes ashore were three VF-15 enlisted mechanics: AMM1c Chet Owens, ART1c Warren Stafford, and AOM1c Elmer Cordray. "We slept in a tent and on army cots," Cordray wrote in his diary. "Chow was mostly canned goods. Water was very scarce."[6]

Duncan and Overton led their new fighter-bomber pilots through the basics of flying the Hellcat. Lee's total flight time on Eniwetok would amount to only a dozen flights and two field carrier landing practice sessions. In the evenings, the group enjoyed a few drinks at the local officers' club. With his tent pitched near the beach, Lee was able to swim almost daily.[7]

John Barry, stuck on board *Essex* for more than a week, was among the VF-15 officers to finally make the long whaleboat ride to Eniwetok. He had spent days reading, playing bridge, and even cutting down a 40mm casing into a brass ashtray to alleviate his boredom. Ashore, he ran into numerous old friends from his flight training days and was able to get in three beers before it was time to catch a speedier return launch with four fellow pilots. "We managed to ride back in an Admiral's boat, which was making 25 knots all the way back to our ship," he wrote.[8]

Duz Twelves was another who made it ashore to enjoy the officers' club beverages and time on the beach. His only downfall was missing the last launch back to *Essex*. He was punished with five days under hack aboard ship, but he missed no action.[9]

On August 25, *Essex* moved closer to the beach, allowing hundreds more men to make their way ashore for liberty. After two weeks of rest and recreation, the fun came to an end as *Essex* made ready for sea again on August 28. She was underway the next morning, part of a new task group, with a new admiral flying his flag on board. Fifth Fleet commander Vice Admiral Ray Spruance had been relieved on August 24 by Vice Admiral Bill "Bull" Halsey, commander of the U.S. Third Fleet. Overnight, Task Force 58 was redesignated as Task Force 38. *Essex* was now part of Task Group 38.3, which included the carriers *Lexington* and *Princeton*, four battleships, and their escorting destroyers.

New to *Essex* on August 15 was Commander Stanley Carter Strong as the air officer, as Commander Dave McDonald fleeted up to XO of *Essex*. Designated a naval aviator in 1931, Strong was operations officer of NAS Jacksonville from January 1942 to December 1943, so McCampbell was familiar with him from his own days as a Florida instructor.

During this interim, McCampbell made good on a promise to his regular plane captain, AMM1c Ed Carroll, by signing orders for him to enter flight training. Carroll's replacement was Chet Owens, the young man from Alabama who had once survived the depth charge blast at Norfolk.

Owens proved to be equally efficient, and he would remain as the CAG plane captain for the rest of the war cruise. "I would wax his plane each night and it gave him 10 knots more speed," Owens recalled. Like his predecessor, he made sure that McCampbell's plane always had a fresh pack of cigarettes near the custom-installed ashtray. Aside from *Minsi II* on its sides, McCampbell's command fighter also began sporting miniature Japanese "Rising Sun" flags to denote each of his aerial kills.[10]

The new commander of TG 38.3 was Rear Admiral Frederick Carl "Ted" Sherman, who had been skipper of the first carrier, *Lexington*, when she was lost in the 1942 Coral Sea carrier battle. Admiral Halsey's first plan of action in charge of TF 38 was to stage a series of carrier raids into the western Carolines, the Palaus, and the Philippines. The invasion of the Palau Islands had been set for September 15, and it was time for Air Group Fifteen to return to war.

August 29, 1944

Ted Sherman's TG 38.3 was well clear of Eniwetok when *Essex's* shore-based planes were launched for their mother ship. Among those coming aboard were the nine new F6F fighter-bombers under the supervision of senior pilot Lieutenant Dutch Kramer. Each new VF-15 pilot was required to make four landings to become carrier qualified in the Hellcat. "That was the extent of our [carrier] training," Kent Lee recalled.[11]

When Lee and his comrades made their way to the fighter ready room, they felt like newbies all over again. Lieutenant Commander Rigg and the original VF-15 pilots had already taken in nearly a dozen replacement fighter pilots in late June, including Dick Davis and Jack Taylor, who were still slowly working their way into combat flights. Now the blended *Essex* fighter squadron included nine new former VB-15 pilots.

"We weren't especially greeted with open arms by the fighter pilots," new fighter-bomber pilot Bill Anderson recalled. "We were doing some of their job and for a while we got nothing but CAPs." Ensign Lee was equally turned off by their rather cold reception. "We got absolutely no indoctrination and no training," he recalled. Dutch Kramer took it upon himself to conduct his own little training sessions with his new fighter-bomber pilots. When the time came to make combat strikes, the fighter-bombers would fly as a four-plane division. They were a special part of VF-15, though still somewhat distant cousins.[12]

Before heading to sea, Commander McCampbell had taken the liberty of securing yet another new F6F-5 for his personal CAG fighter. His previous *Minsi II* Hellcat had proven to be a "dud" in his mind. At altitude, the plane failed to deliver full power at times. While in port, he had mechanics tear down the engine and replace its entire electrical system, but he was still dissatisfied with its performance. After commandeering a new F6F, he had plane captain Chet Owens and VF-15 mechanics thoroughly check it out. It proved to be mechanically fit and McCampbell liked its performance. Owens and the squadron's painter added *Minsi III* under the sides of the cockpit. *Minsi III* would serve as the official CAG plane for the remainder of the tour.[13]

As Air Group Fifteen headed back for the combat zone, McCampbell was under new orders. His task group's new commander, Admiral Ted Sherman, congratulated McCampbell on his fine record as a fighter pilot, but he issued an ultimatum. As air group commander, Dave's job was not to engage every Japanese aircraft he could find. McCampbell was responsible for the success of his entire air group, and he was to act as a strike coordinator for the missions he led. "Zero fever" would no longer be tolerated. He should only defend himself if attacked or engage enemy planes only where necessary to defend other planes of his squadrons.[14]

McCampbell swallowed his pride and hid his resentment behind a poker face.

"Aye, aye, sir," he replied.

Two days out from Eniwetok, Captain Wieber passed the word that *Essex* would soon be crossing the equator. He granted permission for a "line-crossing" ceremony to initiate the "pollywogs," who had never crossed 0 degrees latitude, an imaginary line midway between the earth's north and south poles. Since the eighteenth century, various naval vessels had conducted initiations of the virgin pollywogs into seasoned "shellbacks" with various hazing rituals sanctioned as a boost to morale. But for the men making their first line crossing, these age-old rites were anything but morale boosters.

Ensign Jack Taylor was among the many pilots who received an official subpoena on August 31 from the "Royal High Court of the Realm of Neptune." The charges filed against Taylor were that he, "a qualified flyer of kites, has been reported by the Royal Domain for flat-hatting over the Royal Waves in an attempt to peek on the virtuous Royal Mermaids." He and hundreds of other officers and sailors began their initiation with a head shaving from the Royal Barber. "It is the first time in my life that I have been bald-headed," John Barry wrote to Olive.[15]

At 0926 on September 1, *Essex* officially crossed the equator. All of the subpoenaed and freshly shaven polliwogs were gathered on the flight deck for their initiation. Taylor, Dowlen, Barry, and others were first forced to run a gauntlet three-quarters the length of the flight deck. "I was beaten with canvas sacks of cloth," recalled Barry. "Some of the sacks contained boards and after three blows on the head, I was almost knocked out."[16]

At the end of the gauntlet, Barry and others were forced to kneel on an electrical plate. This was followed by drinking nasty concoctions and paying their debts by kissing the belly of the Royal Baby, a fat sailor whose hairy navel had been smeared with grease. "Hostilities began. Everyone practically scalped. Fanny is pretty sore," Ensign Duz Twelves jotted in his diary that evening. "Three fourths of the officer personnel have the most grotesque haircuts you have ever seen," Barry wrote. "Poor Joe O'Brien was the color of a rainbow when they finished with him."[17]

Each bruised and battered new shellback was issued a signed card from the "Ancient Order of the Deep Domain of Neptunus Rex" confirming his proper initiation. The new initiates of VF-15 were relieved that *Essex* had more days en route to the Palaus for their smarting rears to recover. Aside from the line-crossing hazing, Duz Twelves and seven of his fellow comrades found reason to celebrate their promotions to lieutenant (junior grade).

FIRST ATTACKS ON PALAU

September 6, 1944

Noon on September 6 found *Essex* 170 miles away from the Palau Islands as her air group prepared for its first combat mission in a month. Commander McCampbell, still smarting from the no-fight orders issued him by Admiral Sherman, was to act as target coordinator for the group.

The most eager pilot in the ready room was Jack Taylor. Since his arrival as a replacement pilot on the second day of the Marianas Turkey Shoot, he had yet to fly any mission more dangerous than routine task force CAPs. His adrenaline was pumping when Lieutenant Bert Morris's flight schedule listed Taylor on the strike roster. "Here I am a boot ensign on a new combat carrier. My first flight was assigned to fly with David McCampbell," he recalled.[18]

The newly christened *Minsi III* was first off the flight deck at 1259. Hot on McCampbell's heels was Taylor, who retracted his wheels and closed on the group commander's F6F. The first *Essex* strike against Palau included fifteen fighters and one photo Hellcat, all joining formation with fighter sweep groups launched from *Lexington*, USS *Intrepid* (CV-11), and USS *Bunker Hill* (CV-17). "We all were very nervous as we were not sure of the number of Japs that would rise to meet us," Lieutenant Barry confided in his diary. With bad weather, Barry found it more challenging to remain vigilant for other planes that were diving and climbing from attacks.[19]

Taylor was even more nervous. He knew of McCampbell's disdain for stragglers, so he was overly careful to hold tight to the CAG's wing. After a one-hour flight, VF-15 was over the Palau chain, which had first been hit by U.S. carrier strikes in late March 1944. Their targets were a pair of Japanese airfields on Ngesebus Island and nearby Babelthuap Island, both located in the southern end of the chain. Once McCampbell determined there were no enemy aircraft airborne, he led his divisions down for strafing runs on the airstrips, their aircraft revetments, and troop bivouac areas.

Taylor was tucked in tight alongside the CAG Hellcat when he saw McCampbell waggle his wings. The lead F6F then rolled over and commenced a steep dive down toward the enemy airfield. "He must have put the throttle to the firewall, because I was trying to stay on his wing," Taylor recalled. The leading Hellcats roared in low over the island. Small trees and jungle greenery flashed past at alarming speed until McCampbell opened up with his six .50s. Taylor could not be certain if the CAG was testing the abilities of his young wingman or if he simply flew that aggressively at all times.[20]

"He scared the hell out of me, but I stayed with him," Taylor recalled. "But it took some doing." McCampbell noted that the heavier antiaircraft guns were firing phosphorus shells. After working over the airfields and their adjacent areas, his division and that of John Barry strafed several barges they found just off Babelthuap Island. Their return flight was shorter, as *Essex* had narrowed the range in their absence. Taylor was greatly relieved to survive his first island strike and fly to the satisfaction of his air group commander. *My training must have worked*, he thought.

The following day, September 7, saw six missions against the Palau Islands for Satan's Playmates. With *Essex* operating within seventy miles of Palau, the flights were much shorter than usual. The first fighter sweep, led by Jim Rigg, shot up several landing barges, sinking one, and destroyed four Japanese trucks ashore. Duz Twelves buzzed the island at low altitude, strafing one ammunition dump that blew up and burned furiously for hours. George Duncan, escorting the day's first deckload strike, returned with his flock intact after strafing AA positions and a radio direction finder station on the island of Peleliu.

The next two strikes were led by McCampbell and George Duncan to continue working over Peleliu. For VF-15, it marked the first time the squadron's Hellcats were loaded with napalm bombs that were released at low altitude on four heavy AA gun emplacements. McCampbell returned to the air at 1224, leading the fifth *Essex* flight of the day. Fourteen of his F6Fs carried five-hundred-pound bombs to blast previously damaged enemy aircraft and plane revetments. Antiaircraft fire was more intense on this mission, and two Hellcats were damaged by enemy fire. The pilot flying the photo F6F, Art Singer, was forced to return his damaged plane to base without having taken any photos. He landed on one of the light carriers, where he would remain for two days until his engine was overhauled.

Skipper Rigg led the final afternoon strike against Peleliu, taking in eight fighters to drop bombs on gun positions and a radio station. His squadron returned without loss, although John Barry—making his second combat mission of the day—observed a Hellcat from another squadron flopping down into the sea. "Tail surfaces must have given away in his dive," Barry surmised.[21]

ON SEPTEMBER 8, Commander McCampbell sent his new fighter-bomber pilots into combat for the first time.

The CAG division was first off at 0645, carrying five-hundred-pound bombs to destroy enemy installations on Peleliu and Babelthuap Islands. Two of the new VBF pilots, Lieutenants (jg) Monk Gunter and Homer "Red" Voorhest, were credited with blasting apart small buildings north of the airdrome with their quarter-tonners. Ensign Al Slack, flying wing on division leader George Crittenden, was credited with a direct hit on an ammunition dump. It exploded in spectacular fashion, with smoke rising 5,000 feet above the island.

Other pilots concentrated on AA positions, a radio station, and various buildings. From George Duncan's division, Ed Mellon and Duz Twelves created a large explosion when their bombs struck a building. Jack Symmes demolished a storage warehouse at the island's bauxite plant, and Larry Self's bomb started a tremendous fire in a building in the state of Ngatpang.

Things were not nearly as smooth for the second *Essex* fighter sweep against the Palaus. The sweep was the first Hellcat combat mission for Ensign Kent Lee, and it was one he would not forget. Launched with four VF-15 divisions at 1043, Lee was flying wing on Lieutenant Dutch Kramer, the senior officer among the nine new fighter-bomber pilots. As skipper Jim Rigg led the Hellcats in their approach toward Peleliu and Angaur Island, Lee could see fires and heavy black smoke rising from the damage inflicted by the morning's first sweep.

Kramer's four F6Fs, each loaded with a five-hundred-pound bomb, were assigned to attack thickly wooded areas near the planned landing beaches on southwestern Peleliu. The thicket was believed to contain pillboxes, although heavy weather made good target assessment nearly impossible. As Kramer led his division in to bomb and strafe, his F6F was struck in the right wheel well by an AA burst. After pulling out of his own attack run, Lee called to Kramer over the radio: "You're on fire, Dutch!"[22]

Another of their division mates, Ensign Henry Gaver, saw fire spreading to Kramer's port wing as he tailed the two leading F6Fs. Kramer jettisoned his belly tank, but the fire continued to spread through his wing until it began consuming his cockpit and fuselage.

"Get out!" Lee shouted over the radio.

Kramer pulled up above 1,000 feet and opened his hood as if preparing to bail out. At that moment he apparently lost control, as his Grumman did a wingover and went into a spin. Kramer's F6F was engulfed in flames as it struck the deep waters off the shore of Peleliu and sank from sight. Former dive-bomber pilot Dutch Kramer's first combat flight in a Hellcat was his last.

In addition to Kramer, Air Group Fifteen suffered the loss of two VT-15 TBMs. Both were struck by AA fire while bombing Peleliu. Lieutenant (jg) Walter Harper made an excellent water landing, and he and his two crewmen were later recovered by the lifeguard submarine USS *Grouper* (SS-214). Lieutenant Charles Webb, injured, was forced to jump from his blazing Avenger, although his two enlisted men did not escape. Webb was also rescued from his life raft by the busy *Grouper* crew.

During her lifeguard work, *Grouper* was provided aerial cover by a pair of VF-15 ensigns, Bud Plant and Len Hamblin. Launched at 1045, they had only a sixty-mile flight to reach the submarine. Each Hellcat pilot circled the downed airmen they discovered and made zooms down toward the surface above the life rafts to bring in *Grouper*. Upon being relieved of lifeguard duty, Plant and Hamblin strafed enemy vehicles and antiaircraft positions on Malakal Island.

The VF-15 duo next pressed on to make strafing attacks on AA positions on Babelthuap and Koror. But in the process, Ensign Hamblin's F6F was hit by AA fire, and he crashed into the ocean. Bud Plant circled the area of Hamblin's crash until he ran dangerously low on fuel and was forced to return to base. Hamblin, a popular twenty-four-year-old squadron veteran from Wyoming who had joined in April, was never found.

With two pilots lost on September 8, the results of the Palau strikes this day appeared questionable to some. John Barry, for one, tried to remain upbeat despite such losses. His focus was on the impending birth of his first child. On September 4, he wrote to his wife, Olive, "It is amazing that I shall be a father in three weeks." Knowing the delay time in his correspondence reaching North Carolina, he began writing from that day forward with questions about how their baby was doing.

During the evening of September 8, he admitted to his diary that heavy opposition was expected on the next day's flights. *Essex* and her Task Group 38.3 were scheduled to conduct strikes on Mindanao Island in the southern region of the Philippines archipelago. "Everyone is nervous as hell, as we do not even have a decent map of the place."

THIRTEEN

TRIUMPHS AND TRAGEDIES
OFF MINDANAO

September 9, 1944

Reveille came at 0350 for forty-eight pilots and twenty-eight enlisted aviators of Air Group Fifteen. By 0420, the men were sipping coffee and shoveling down a quick breakfast. By 0450, all seventy-six aviators had reported to their respective ready rooms, where final briefings were offered.

In the VF-15 room, Dave McCampbell, skipper Jim Rigg, and intelligence officer Bob McReynolds offered what they could in terms of expectations for the day. Satan's Playmates had piled up nearly a hundred aerial kills in a matter of weeks by late June. But the Hellcat squadron was now in a severe drought. It was approaching three months since Art Singer had scored the unit's last kill on June 24.

Mindanao Island was the great unknown. "We were to make a reconnaissance and take action where we ran into it," recalled McCampbell. "We had so little information even about where airfields were. I was supposed to hit approximately six airfields, and most of them weren't even on our charts."[1]

McCampbell planned to lead the first fighter sweep. He spent several minutes briefing the divisions that would fly with him. He wanted one division to attack each airfield, while another remained above to properly count enemy planes on the ground and gather intelligence on the unknown fields. But with so many potential airfields, the briefing process was very confusing, even to the CAG. He finally wrapped up the talk with his sweep divisions by saying, "I can't describe the targets that we're going to hit. Just follow me."[2]

Flight quarters sounded at 0510, and the pilots scrambled to the flight deck to inspect their planes. McCampbell's sweep—sixteen F6Fs split into four divisions—was first to launch for the northern Mindanao airfields. Each pilot knew little more than the six names they had been given: Del Monte, Lumbia, Cagayan, Gingoog, Butuan, and Berobe airfields.

Essex next launched a full strike group. Jim Rigg had eleven fighters to escort a dozen VB-15 Helldivers and eight VT-15 Avengers to destroy aircraft and installations on northern Mindanao. By 0555, forty-seven Air Group Fifteen strikers had cleared the deck and were proceeding on the 176-mile trek toward the enemy airdromes.

For the first time in nearly three months, enemy planes were encountered. The first bandit was tallyhoed at 0715, as the multi-squadron strike force reached northeastern Mindanao. It was an olive drab "Topsy"—a twin-engine Mitsubishi Ki-57 transport aircraft—with red meatballs. The first two divisions to gain altitude advantage over this airplane were those of Rigg and Lieutenant Bert Morris.

Rigg and his wingman, Lieutenant Richard Davis (different from Ensign Dick Davis), made the first firing runs from above. They passed over the Topsy and recovered on the opposite side, with many hits scored in its fuselage and right wing. The transport plane was already smoking as Morris swung in to make a high-side run. His .50-calibers ripped through the Topsy's starboard wing tank, causing the aircraft to burst into flames and spin off to the left. No parachutes were seen before the plane crashed. Morris received credit for the kill, with damage credit due to Rigg and Davis.

In the absence of other aerial targets, the VF-15 divisions led by Rigg alternated in covering the SB2Cs and TBMs on their attack runs. The Hellcats went in first, strafing targets found on the Lumbia and Cagayan airfields. They claimed three aircraft destroyed and four others damaged. In nearby Macajalar harbor, one division found a fifty-ton merchant vessel and made strafing runs that left it burning from stem to stern. Jim Mini's dive-bombers and Lieutenant Charles Sorenson's torpedo bombers landed their bombs on parked aircraft, fuel dumps, and various buildings.

Once their attacks were complete, the *Essex* squadrons made their rendezvous and headed back for base. En route, they happened upon a large Japanese shipping convoy off Bislig Bay that consisted of roughly three dozen camouflaged coastal freighters, smaller luggers, and fishing trawlers, all heavily loaded.

Commander Rigg ordered seven of his eleven Hellcats to continue on toward *Essex* as shepherds for the Helldivers and Avengers. He remained over the convoy with his wingman, Richard Davis; Bert Morris; and Morris's wingman, Ken Flinn. The quartet made numerous strafing runs at low altitude, shooting up the smaller vessels until each F6F was nearly depleted of bullets. By the time they finished, Rigg believed they had sunk four small ships, and left another in sinking condition. Three others were burning fiercely, and many others were trailing oil slicks from their damage. Before turning back for the task group, Rigg shared the contact report over the radio for other carrier planes to finish off.

DAVE MCCAMPBELL'S FOUR-DIVISION fighter sweep had been equally blessed with both aerial opponents and shipping targets. Their first tallyho had come at 0700 as the flight was passing over the Del Monte area at Angels 7.

Ensign Bud Plant alertly spotted two Val dive-bombers five miles distant off the northeast coast of Mindanao. Within minutes he had scored two kills. At 0730, over the Del Monte area, Lieutenant (jg) Baynard Milton and his wingman, Ensign George Pigman, tallyhoed a Topsy twin-engine transport plane and shared the kill. When no other aerial resistance was found, McCampbell proceeded with assigning his division, and those of Lieutenants Barry, Ted Overton, and George Crittenden, to strafe planes on the various northern Mindanao airfields. His Hellcats caught the enemy completely off guard, without time to get airborne. "They had people running out of the planes while we were strafing them," he recalled.[3]

The *Essex* F6Fs worked over the six airfields until their CAG was assured that none of the planes posed any danger of lifting off. Two divisions found a trio of trawlers or luggers in Gingseg (Ginseng) Bay. Repeated strafing runs left one of them burning and dead in the water. McCampbell then turned his attention to the Japanese convoy that had been previously attacked by Jim Rigg's team.

When McCampbell's four divisions arrived over the force, he counted about thirty-four coastal freighters, luggers, and trawlers. Three vessels already in sinking condition were bypassed; Dave assigned his combat teams to hit those still fully operational. Commander McCampbell and wingman Roy Rushing made runs on two small ships that they left burning and sinking. Crittenden and Bob Stime left two more ships gutted; they were later seen to sink. Another five ships attacked by Jake Lundin, Dick McGraw, Baynard Milton, George Pigman, and Al Slack were damaged and set afire.

The net result of the furious series of strafing attacks was three small ships exploding and sinking. Two others were left in sinking condition, and an additional two were burning fiercely and gutted, later seen to be sunk by other aircraft. More than a dozen other vessels were set ablaze or left trailing oil slicks. McCampbell's sixteen Hellcat pilots had severely wrecked the convoy.

Lieutenant Barry's section had made multiple runs on one of the larger freighters. But his zeal for annihilating this enemy force proved costly.

Ensign Al Slack was just lining up for his own run on one of the larger ships. Glancing to his left, he spotted a VF-15 comrade coming in low to attack the same vessel. It was Barry. Slack pulled off to the right and made a strafing run on a smaller ship while Barry zoomed across the larger one to rake its upper structures. The larger ship was already burning from numerous previous runs, and Barry's tracers apparently cooked off an ammunition supply or a battery of depth charges.

Before Barry's plane had cleared the freighter, it exploded violently with a towering ball of fire. Squadron mates saw the shock wave rip the tail section off Barry's plane. Recovering from his own run on the other vessel, Slack witnessed the plume rising toward the clouds. He saw Barry's F6F "tumbling straight forward, end over end. I watched until it hit the water."[4]

Division leader Ted Overton witnessed the explosion. He later wrote a somber letter to Barry's wife, Olive. "His target blew up, and he went right

Lieutenant John Barry's Hellcat No. 7, painted with his wife's name, Olive, just after landing on August 7, 1944. The arresting cable is still recoiling on the deck aft of his plane. Barry was killed in action a month after this photo was taken.   JOHN BARRY III

in," wrote Overton. "There just wasn't a chance for him to get out, and please believe me, it was terribly quick." Overton promised that Johnnie was looking down from heaven on his wife and young son. "He was one of the best, and always did a wonderful job. He always fought with all he had, and I'm terribly proud to have fought with him." Fighting Fifteen skipper Jim Rigg wrote to Olive: "His passing is keenly felt by all of us and is a distinct loss to the squadron."[5]

McCampbell rendezvoused his planes at the conclusion of the convoy strike and headed for home. His pilots had scored VF-15's first aerial kills in nearly three months and had decimated the Japanese convoy. But their successes had come at the cost of Lieutenant Barry, yet another seasoned division leader killed in action.

Back home in North Carolina, Olive Barry continued writing to her husband that day and in the days to follow. John's return letters usually arrived in batches, and they had been written daily. But there would be no more. "In your last letter, you told me it would be probably a couple of weeks before any mail came through," she wrote on September 10. At 0810 on October 2, she gave birth to the couple's son and wrote that day to John that "he looks exactly like you."[6]

Carrying out the couple's plan, she named him John Edmund Barry III, in honor of a daring father he would never have the chance to meet.

THE BALANCE OF September 9 saw repeated *Essex* air strikes against Mindanao. Lieutenant Commander George Duncan escorted the next strike. With wingman Bud Henning and his second section of Duz Twelves and Larry Self, Duncan led strafing attacks on three different vessels. Off Cagayan Light, they gutted an armed escort vessel and left it blazing and sinking.

Duncan's division next shot up a small freighter loaded with cargo and about forty soldiers. After numerous strafing runs, they left it blazing, sinking, and with no visible survivors. Finally, Duncan's division shot up and sank a large landing barge loaded with about 150 uniformed troops. "It was a first-class massacre," Twelves wrote in his diary that night.[7]

During the midday hour, Dave McCampbell led *Essex*'s third strike to Surigao on northern Mindanao, his fighters escorting Air Group Fifteen's bombers and torpedo planes in for attack runs on Japanese shipping. Lieutenant (jg) Red Voorhest, leading in a fighter-bomber division, ripped a large hole in a 4,000-ton freighter with his bomb. Close behind, Baynard Milton and wingman George Pigman attacked the same ship with skip bombing attacks. Pigman's bomb was a near miss, but Milton's five-hundred-pound bomb skipped into the midships section of the freighter. Left burning and listing, this freighter was seen to sink the following day.

Toward the tail end of the convoy strike, around 1445, George Crittenden and wingman Rod Johnson combined to down a lone Mitsubishi Ki-46 reconnaissance plane (code-named "Dinah") about fifteen miles off Cantilan Point. It exploded so violently that Critt had to pull up sharply to avoid flaming debris and flames.

A final *Essex* strike with ten Helldivers and five VT-15 Avengers was launched at 1400, under charge of Lieutenant Commander Jim Mini. Skipper Jim Rigg escorted the flight with fifteen F6Fs. Finding no aerial resistance, Rigg left six fighters to help strafe and bomb the Surigao airfield and its adjacent buildings.

The other nine Hellcats joined the Helldivers and Avengers in plastering the Japanese ships in the vicinity. Sweeping over the bays, the divisions of Rigg and Ted Overton located three landing barges underway, strafing and sinking them. Lieutenant (jg) Swede Thompson and Ensign Dick Fowler each landed bomb hits on a small coastal freighter, leaving it burning and abandoned. Rigg, Overton, Lieutenant Richard Davis, George Carr, and Herman Foshee combined to sink or disable six small coastal luggers near Surigao.

Just west of these vessels, Lieutenant John Strane led his division against a pair of trawlers. His strafing, and that of Jim Duffy, Jigs Foltz, and Charlie Dorn, stopped one dead in the water, and left the other burning and gutted. Two of the fighter-bombers, those of Monk Gunter and Tom Hoey, landed their bombs close alongside the stern of another small escort vessel, blowing off enough of its hull to later cause it to sink.

Mini's strikers returned to the task group just as dusk was falling. His force was intact, but one flak-damaged Helldiver was forced to make a water landing near a destroyer, where its crew was quickly recovered. Summing up the day's final strike, Lieutenant Commander Rigg stated, "Results were good, with substantial damage to the enemy."[8]

September 10

Rear Admiral Ted Sherman kept his task group on the offensive the following morning. Further strikes against northern Mindanao had been ordered, and *Essex* was heading into the wind at 0600 to launch her first strike group. But one-quarter of the Hellcats dispatched on this fighter sweep would fail to return.

Arriving over the target area at 0715 in good visibility, Rigg led his fighters down to strafe the Del Monte, Lumbia, and Cagayan airfields. Ensign Herman Foshee's F6F was hit in the engine by a 20mm round during his dive. He recovered, and division leader Ted Overton escorted him out to sea in hopes of reaching a duty lifeguard submarine. Foshee made it out over the ocean before his engine failed. He splashed down with a good wheels-up, flaps-down landing in the ocean and scrambled into his life raft.

Lieutenant Overton radioed the submarine USS *Bashaw* (SS-241) that an *Essex* fighter was down in the ocean. By 0820, *Bashaw* lookouts had Overton's Hellcat in sight. A half hour later, *Bashaw*'s crew spotted the downed aviator, and a topside crew hauled him on board. Foshee would ride out the next weeks on *Bashaw* until she returned to Seeadler Harbor on September 29 and transferred him ashore. In early October, the lucky ensign would make his way back to VF-15.[9]

At 0730, minutes after Foshee's plane was hit, Lieutenant Commander Rigg tallyhoed an enemy plane in the Del Monte area of northern Mindanao. It was a mottled dark green Irving, an IJN twin-engine Nakajima J1N1 Gekko reconnaissance plane carrying a pair of bombs. George Carr was first to make the intercept. As his division approached, Carr noted the Japanese pilot waggle its wings. Quickly deducing the Hellcats were not friendly, the Irving commenced evasion with a dive and very shallow turns.

Carr remained locked on his opponent, placing bursts that walked from astern into its engines. During the encounter, the Irving jettisoned two black bombs. It was difficult to immolate, requiring many bursts, but it eventually did catch fire and crash. While turning and twisting to intercept this plane, two VF-15 pilots from Rigg's division died tragically. The wingmen of the first and second sections, Lieutenant Davis and Ensign Howard Green, lost sight of each other and collided in midair. Green's F6F burst into flames and crashed to the ground. Davis's cockpit area was completely demolished and his engine was knocked free of the remainder of the plane.

Rigg had lost two pilots and three F6Fs in a quarter hour. After completing their strafing runs, Rigg and his remaining ten F6Fs were over Macajalar Bay when Rigg tallyhoed another bandit at 0845 at low altitude. It was a dark green Dinah with horizontal white stripes and two wing tanks. Having lost Davis and Green, Rigg now only had his second section leader, Carr, whose plane was suffering from direct AA hits in its prop, ring cowl, and engine. Rigg called on Lieutenant John Strane's division to help with bracketing.

On Rigg's first pass, the Dinah turned into him and escaped with only a few hits that drew smoke from its starboard engine. Other planes made passes, but Rigg was quickly back on track. On his third firing pass from astern, he blew pieces off the left engine and set it alight. The Dinah rolled into an almost vertical turn at only two hundred feet altitude and cartwheeled into the sea.

George Duncan had led the first main strike group off the deck minutes behind Rigg's early sweep. His fighters and their bombers struck buildings and warehouses on Mindanao without loss. Lieutenant (jg) Bud Henning tallyhoed a Dinah with red meatballs at 0820 over the west end of Macajalar Bay. Art Singer, flying a photo Hellcat, closed and set the Dinah's starboard motor aflame. Singer's further bursts raked the plane, and it was seen to crash-land in the ocean.

Dave McCampbell led the next Mindanao strike off at 0834. Lieutenant Bert Morris took two divisions of the fighters in with divisions of VB-15 and VT-15 to hit a pair of enemy airfields. At Cagayan Field, Morris's division made repeated strafing runs, which created heavy smoke billowing thousands of feet skyward from more than five dozen exploded fuel drums. Morris and wingman Ken Flinn also left a warehouse burning before their division proceeded to shoot up two trawlers and two barges.

At Lambia Field, Lieutenant John Van Altena led his VF-15 fighter-bomber division in ahead of their bombers. Monk Gunter exploded three fuel drums along the airstrip's southern side. Ensigns Tom Hoey and Henry Gaver blasted more fuel drums with their strafing, leaving the strip obscured by roiling black smoke.

Commander McCampbell's division did a recon flight over Surigao while Art Singer photographed the entire area for intelligence. McCampbell's flight found nothing better to strafe than previously wrecked shipping before turning for home.

In two days, his fighter squadron had suffered the loss of four planes and three good pilots. The need for replacement pilots was becoming a regular business for Satan's Playmates.

FOURTEEN

"A BUNCH OF HORNETS"

September 11, 1944
Near Mindanao

D uz Twelves was glad September 11 was an off day for most of the air group. The air group's flight doc, Lieutenant Paul Maness, grounded him due to a bad cold. High-altitude flying did not pair well with congestion.

Essex and her task group were in the process of refueling about three hundred miles east of Mindanao. Aviation mechanic Elmer Cordray had the dreaded duty of working with Lieutenant (jg) Bob Hoffman to itemize the personal effects of Lieutenant Barry and the other three missing pilots. The fueling process also provided the opportunity for the task force carriers to take on replacement aircraft and pilots, courtesy of the escort carriers USS *Nassau* (CVE-16) and USS *Steamer Bay* (CVE-87).

Fighting Fifteen took on seven new pilots. Ensign Paul Bugg arrived with a new F6F-5 from *Nassau*, while the others came from *Steamer Bay*: Lieutenant (jg) Robert Paul Fash and Ensigns Don Gonya, Jerome Lathrop, Earl Lewis, Jim Mooney, and Howard Smith. The only seasoned pilots were twenty-three-year-old Illinois native Bob Fash and Ensign Smith from Portland, Oregon. Both pilots had flown with VF-50 through July 11, but *Bataan*'s forward elevator permanently failed the following day. Fash and Smith were among several VF-50 pilots put into a replacement pool in mid-August after they requested to keep flying with another squadron.

Smith had no prior kills with VF-50's "Devil Cats," but Fash had downed three Japanese planes on June 24 during the Philippine Sea battles. With thirty-seven combat missions, a DFC, and three Air Medals, Fash was pulled into the division of skipper Jim Rigg.[1]

The other five were green rookies who would be slowly broken in with various divisions. Jim Mooney, born in Anderson, Indiana, in 1921, had had an interest in flying from an early age. As a youngster, his first flight had been with his father and famed World War I ace Eddie Rickenbacker, who took the Mooneys up in an old Fokker Tri-Motor plane as part of his role as general manager of Fokker Aircraft.[2]

Mooney earned his private pilot's license at age sixteen and his naval aviator's golden wings by October 1943. He had since flown escort missions from Espiritu Santo, New Hebrides, before being sent back to NAS Barbers Point in Hawaii for fighter training. He was more than ready for action when he and the other ensigns were loaded onto the escort carriers *Nassau* and *Steamer Bay* in August. "By the time I had my first combat mission, I had well over a thousand hours of flight time," Mooney recalled.[3]

With her newbies received and fueling complete by late afternoon, *Essex* steamed through the Sulu Sea. Task Force 38 had orders to soften up target areas in the central Philippines, with first strikes scheduled for the following day.

September 12, 1944

The VF-15 ready room was abuzz with excitement over the first chance to hit enemy airfields in the Visayas archipelago. Intelligence officer Bob McReynolds pored over maps of the Japanese air bases and laid out plans with Bert Morris. Division leaders gathered around McReynolds for his briefing. Eighteen teams flying all thirty-six serviceable F6Fs were directed to hit eighteen out of twenty known fields.[4]

"Who's going to get the other two fields?" asked Baynard Milton.

"Well, the people that make out the best and don't have anti-aircraft or any trouble on the first two fields can go over and take the last two fields," said McReynolds.

George Duncan's division and that of skipper Jim Rigg launched first at 0800. Their eight F6Fs were part of a fighter sweep over Cebu and Mactan Islands in the Visayan chain. Coordinator of the sweep was *Lexington* fighter squadron skipper, Theodore Hugh "Pedro" Winters, leading eight Hellcats of VF-19.

The weather was poor, but Admiral Mitscher had brought his carriers in so close to the targets that a massive sweep was deemed unnecessary. Approaching the target area, Commander Winters ordered the two *Essex* divisions to investigate the airdrome while his group provided cover. Diving through the thin overcast, Rigg's eight F6Fs came out over the Cebu airfield. "It looked more like a commercial airport than a military base, with its white and glass operations tower and a couple of aluminum DC-3 types parked nearby," recalled Winters.[5]

Rigg and Duncan led their divisions down on a heavily packed field. Numerous aircraft, mainly fighters, were staggered along the runway on the aprons and taxiways. All appeared to be gassed and in ready condition. Three quick strafing runs destroyed most of them or put them out of action. Enemy AA fire progressed from moderate to intense but was not accurate.

As the *Lexington* group pushed over to attack, Rigg noticed enemy aircraft taking off from Opon Airfield on Mactan Island, less than five miles away. VF-15 headed there, and the two divisions were immediately swept into intense action around 0930. Numerous Japanese aircraft were already airborne, with many more continually taking off and coming in from other airfields. Rigg spotted two Zekes taking off from Opon and destroyed one of them as it reached only a hundred feet of altitude. Even with the other eight *Lexington* VF to assist, Rigg wished he had more F6Fs to further the slaughter.[6]

Pedro Winters's *Lexington* fighters had a field day. "It was like a family of minks in a henhouse," he recalled. "I was able to get two taxiing, and one on takeoff run, and one just airborne with wheels and flaps still down (that one counted)." Winters then caught another plane wheeling back toward the airstrip, and blasted it into two pieces.[7]

Commander Rigg next encountered two Tojos flying in formation that suddenly appeared in front of him, climbing. In quick succession, he flamed one Tojo and then sent a Zeke into the water of Cebu's harbor. His fourth victim was another Zeke, whose after section was shot away before the rest of the fighter burst into flames. "A beautiful sight," Rigg recalled.[8]

Having downed four planes, Rigg headed back to Cebu airfield and caught another Zeke taking off. It flew low, jinking through buildings and treetops. Rigg made a stern pass and watched the Zeke pilot glide to a flaming crash landing in the water. He joined the ranks of three other Satan's Playmates pilots who had previously entered the ace-in-a-day ring of honor.

Rigg then joined with two *Lexington* F6Fs to work over another Zeke at low altitude. "The Zeke's flying ability was excellent and maneuverability admittedly superior," Rigg recalled. He and the *Lexington* VF could never land more than a few hits no matter how hard they tried to match the Japanese pilot's turns. After about ten minutes of pursuit, they finally lost the Zeke. By this point, the main task force strike group launched behind them was commencing its attacks.

Rigg's wingman, Ensign Johnny Brex, had become separated immediately after their first pass on the two Zekes taking off from Opon Field. Brex ended up in a head-on run against one. His shots caused it to smoke and drop into the water. Brex then made a run on a Zeke taxiing across the runway, damaging it enough that it went down on one wing and was put out of commission.

Bud Plant, second section leader for Rigg, was seen to destroy at least one Zeke shortly after it launched from Cebu. Plant remained in radio communication with his skipper through the fight. Halfway through the fifty-minute battle, Plant called, "Someone get him off my tail!"[9]

Rigg looked down and saw a Zeke chasing an F6F. Two or three VFs at higher altitude dived in to help Plant, but Rigg could do little more than fire some distant shots. The enemy aircraft departed, but Rigg soon saw the F6F below him with a fire in its port wing stub. The Hellcat burst into flames and crashed just south of Opon Airfield. With his last recorded kill, Claude Plant had increased his final tally to 8.5 victories. "They got me, Skipper!" was his last transmission before he was seen to bail out.

Plant drifted down near the Japanese airstrip, where he was quickly captured. Fate was not kind to Plant, as his captors were enraged that their airstrip and dozens of aircraft had just been wiped out. Other VF-15 pilots would learn after the war that Ensign Plant was executed soon after being taken prisoner.

Ensign Rod Johnson downed three fighters just as they lifted off from the field and his section leader, George Carr, knocked a Tojo and a Zeke into the water. Carr and Larry Self then shared a kill by shooting another Nakajima Ki-43 Hayabusa fighter (code-named "Oscar") off Johnson's tail. Rejoining on his section leader, Bud Henning, Self flamed another Zeke that was heading toward him. Self pulled up hard as Henning slid underneath, toward the flaming Zeke. There was an immediate massive explosion; the concussion forced Self's F6F violently upward. Self whipped around and saw parts of the aircraft falling. Smoke spun toward the ground, and Henning was never seen again, apparently having collided with the wounded Zeke.

Lieutenant (jg) William "Bud" Henning in the cockpit of his Little Duchess *F6F at Maui in March 1944. Henning was killed in action on September 12.*

George Duncan, leading VF-15's second division, was on his own almost instantly when the fight commenced. His second section leader, Henning, had been downed, and his two remaining combat team members were embroiled in their own fights. Duncan placed a radio call to Commander McCampbell, who was leading in the main strike group. He then dived down on Cebu Field, where Japanese aircraft were lifting off "like a bunch of hornets."[10]

Duncan's first victim was a Zeke that he blazed as it struggled off Cebu field up to eight hundred feet. A short time later, over Opon Field, he nailed another freshly launched Zeke that crashed in flames at the end of the runway. The Satan's Playmates' XO next encountered a Zeke over Mactan Island. His slugs created a heavy smoke trail. Although the Zeke spiraled down, Duncan did not witness it crash, giving him only a probable kill on his third fighter.

The massive air battle between the Japanese planes and the *Essex* and *Lexington* fighters lasted fifty minutes. By 1020, Rigg and Duncan collected their remaining fighters and served as supporting cover for a new round of fighters.

The *Essex* fighters claimed at least eighteen planes destroyed on the ground and many others damaged. Against aerial opponents, they had downed at least seventeen planes. From *Lexington*'s Air Group Nineteen, Pedro Winters had destroyed three fighters, and Lieutenant Albert Seckel had knocked down four. Winters's eight *Lexington* fighters had tallied fourteen kills. "Total score of 31 to two was disappointing, considering the value of these men," he recalled.[11]

The two downed pilots were both VF-15 veterans. The loss of Henning and Plant on September 12 ran the total to seven pilots killed from the squadron in just five days. In addition, Ensign Hamblin was riding out the month on a lifeguard submarine. The *Essex* fighter squadron would need to begin mixing in more of its newer pilots sooner than CAG McCampbell preferred.

Rigg and Duncan led their four surviving division mates back toward the carrier. It was time to pass the fight to the Johnny-come-latelies.

DAVE MCCAMPBELL REACHED the scene at 1015 while the Duncan and Rigg divisions were still duking it out. His flight, launched at 0800, included fifteen fighters: one "Photo Joe" Hellcat piloted by Art Singer; thirteen Hellcats equipped with five-hundred-pound bombs; and his own F6F-5 command fighter, *Minsi III*.

This flight marked a first for the *Essex* CAG. The new F6F-5 Hellcat model had three stub pylons under each wing, for a total of six. Each rail could carry a single 12.7cm (5-inch) unguided high-velocity aircraft rocket. The HVARs had only completed their testing phase in June 1944. Each rocket was fitted with a Mark 4 general-purpose warhead holding 7.6 pounds of TNT or a Mark 2 antipersonnel warhead with 2 pounds of explosive. While VT-15's Avengers had been using these rockets for months, McCampbell's squadron had yet to test them. Prior to the strike, McCampbell sought the advice of the torpedo squadron commander, VeeGee Lambert. "I didn't know anything about them, but he had found them quite useful, and I figured that I would, too," McCampbell recalled.[12]

Once airborne, McCampbell's division rendezvoused with the traditional VF divisions of Bert Morris and John Collins and the fighter-bomber division of Lieutenant John Van Altena. They were tasked with safeguarding eleven VB-15 Helldivers and eight VT-15 Avengers in to attack Cebu and Mactan Islands. Commander McCampbell was overall strike coordinator for his *Essex* group, three dozen *Lexington* warplanes, and another dozen *Langley* fighters and Avengers.

Thirty miles out from the ship at 0900, McCampbell sighted a plane three miles away. He at first assumed it to be a friendly plane returning from the Cebu attacks. But division mate Roy Rushing soon reported, "Bogey, nine o'clock, down."

McCampbell immediately nosed over to investigate. "It was realized that, although he was in range of ship's radar, it would be impossible to pick him out from among the large groups of friendly aircraft in the area." During the short chase, the bogey proved to be a mottled olive drab Dinah with red meatballs. After one burst of about fifteen rounds, McCampbell created fire in its wing root. It nosed over and crashed into the sea in a ball of flaming wreckage.

McCampbell and Rushing then hurried back to rejoin their strike group, assuming a high-cover position. Upon reaching Cebu around 0945, McCampbell found the area still in the middle of a considerable melee. While the attack group was parceled out to hit targets, the CAG division remained on high cover. His team was immediately caught up in the fight.

They bounced a pair of Zekes that pulled up into a high wingover as the Hellcats approached. McCampbell flamed the first one with a long burst that sent the Zeke diving straight into the bay. His wingman, Ensign Dick McGraw, knocked the second Japanese fighter into the bay.

McCampbell's second section, led by Roy Rushing, intercepted other Zekes. He doggedly pursued one, although his own engine began cutting out at full power. In repeated runs, Rushing finally shot the Zeke into the water. Minutes later McCampbell sighted a lone Zeke at lower altitude that was climbing to attack his division. "I rolled over on him, getting a long burst from overhead to tail position," McCampbell related. The Zeke burst into flames and spun into the ocean, marking Dave's third kill of the morning.[13]

Six other planes from McCampbell's group engaged enemy planes upon arriving over the harbor. Three pilots jettisoned their bombs to take on and destroy three Zekes. Van Altena's fighter-bomber division plowed into a group of Zekes that was closing in on the *Essex* torpedo planes. Van Altena and wingman Henry Gaver each scored a kill, and their second section leader, Monk Gunter, shot a third Zeke into the harbor. Gunter's wingman, Tom Hoey, returned to the airfield to drop his bomb, and flamed a parked plane in a revetment with his strafing.

Art Singer, while making a photo run over Opon Field, destroyed a Mitsubishi J2M2 Raiden fighter (code-named "Jack") that had just lifted off the strip. While these pilots battled the aerial bandits, Lieutenants John Collins and Bert Morris led their divisions down to attack harbor shipping. Three pilots straddled a 3,500-ton freighter with their bombs before Bob Stime landed a direct hit amidships. The merchantman broke out in intense fires, and aerial photography later showed that it sank. Collins's bomb slammed into the forecastle deck of a small freighter, passed through, and exploded alongside, leaving the ship listing badly and deemed to be sinking.

The *Essex* Hellcats swarmed over various ships. The divisions of Collins and Morris strafed and sank a PC-1-class subchaser and a fifty-foot armed aircraft barge. Having downed three planes, McCampbell finally led his division down to join the attacks on the shipping. He made a strafing-and-rocket attack on a medium freighter in the harbor. Two of his rockets hit short of the target. After that, he headed for the rendezvous point. Upon arrival, he spotted two F6Fs with a Jack on their tails.

McCampbell and Rushing dived in to attack, and their hits caused the Jack to break off its attack with its engine smoking. "As he pulled up and away, I was able to stay on his tail and fired two rockets," said McCampbell. Dave learned that firing the five-inch HVARs at an aerial target was ineffective while twisting and jinking. He then let loose with his .50-calibers. The Japanese pilot dived for the water as if finished but leveled off low instead of crashing. McCampbell dived down and gave chase, finally able to overtake him at full water-injected power. As he opened fire, the Jack burst into flames inside the cockpit and pulled up into a loop that ended up in the water. McCampbell was one kill shy of attaining ace-in-a-day status again.[14]

The strike group then rendezvoused and headed for the ship, having lost only the Avenger of Ensign Thomas Carl Maxwell Jr. His TBM was believed to have been shot down by AA fire over the target area, and its three aviators were not recovered.

THE FRANTIC RADIO calls of aerial action over Cebu spurred Rear Admiral Ted Sherman to launch more strike groups. At 1058, two hours after the departure of McCampbell's first strike force, Lieutenant Ted Overton departed with another three dozen planes. Following the lead of his CAG, Overton launched in an F6F-5 equipped with six of the new five-inch rockets under his wings. His four VF-15 divisions flew in company with a *Lexington* strike group until they reached Cebu Harbor in the Visayas.

After covering the bombers in to make runs on dock facilities and petroleum stores, the F6Fs still retaining bombs turned their attention to various harbor shipping targets. Overton slammed two of his rockets into a small freighter. John Strane and his wingman, Jim Duffy, started fires with direct hits on oil storage facilities and thereafter turned to strafing various ships. Ensign Dick Davis left a small subchaser dead in the water with his direct bomb hit.

By the time Air Group Fifteen's attacks were completed, smoke was rising to 10,000 feet from the island and its air base. There were no aerial engagements for VF-15 on this strike and no plane losses. A final *Essex* strike group, led again by Dave McCampbell, moved in over southern Negros Island at 1515 to mop up on what remained. Once again *Minsi III* had been loaded with a half dozen HVARs. The remainder of his four divisions of F6Fs carried either five-hundred-pound GP bombs or seven smaller one-hundred-pound GPs.

Bob Stime and wingman Johnny Brex swept over Dumaguete Airfield, leveling an aviation building and a shed hangar with their bombs. Twenty-two Oscars and Zekes were found lined up in one group on the airfield with three more on the other side of the field. The entire group was bombed and strafed by VT-15 planes, leaving them destroyed or heavily damaged. The rest of McCampbell's fighters pounced on various shipping targets in company with their dive-bomber and torpedo plane charges.

McCampbell and Roy Rushing dived on a pair of speeding torpedo boats, firing their wing guns and four HVARs launched from *Minsi III*. The rockets failed to stop the small motorboats, but repeated strafing runs ended with both boats exploding and sinking. McCampbell fired his last two rockets at a small freighter but claimed only near misses. Roy Nall wrecked another torpedo boat, and George Pigman's bomb forced another sinking small ship to beach itself on the northeast coast of Siquijor Island. Larry Self and Dusty Craig left another small vessel burning after two bomb hits. Baynard Milton and his new wingman, Merwin Frazelle, strafed two AKs (freighters) and left them burning fiercely. One of Milton's second section pilots, Ed Mellon, damaged a 500-ton vessel with a near miss.

The strike group reached *Essex* at dusk, low on fuel after a furious four-hour mission but jubilant with the havoc they had wreaked. By day's end on September 12, George Duncan, Jim Rigg, and Art Singer had each attained ace status, bringing VF-15's squadron total to nine aces.

September 13, 1944

Ensign Dick Davis was eager to get his crack at dogfighting. Having joined VF-15 in late June with Jack Taylor and other rookie ensigns, Davis had only been in one scrap in his three months with the unit. Now regularly flying with Lieutenant Bert Morris's division, he had an obvious advantage. "He was our flight officer. If he wanted to duck anything, he could certainly drop himself off," Davis recalled. But Morris was eager to get a taste of the combat over the Visayas on September 13.

Morris and Davis were among the dozen pilots firing up their Pratt & Whitneys at daybreak. Their division was to be included on a sweep with a dozen VF-19 *Lexington* Hellcats led by CAG Dave McCampbell and XO George Duncan's divisions. Ensign Duz Twelves was sufficiently recovered from his head cold to lead Duncan's second section. Johnny Brex had flown wing on Duncan the past two days, but Twelves was not about to miss out on this one.

Outbound for Cebu by 0630, the *Essex* and *Lexington* groups made a quick sweep of the area. Seeing no opposition, McCampbell released the VF-19 bunch to cover their incoming *Lexington* strike force. The *Essex* CAG led his own dozen F6Fs on to Bacolod in northern Negros to sweep that area and cover their own incoming main strike group. Heavy weather forced McCampbell to drop to 6,000 feet to be able to observe the field. He saw about twenty planes parked in revetted or camouflaged positions. One Betty bomber was in the process of taking off at 0730, with a second one ready to follow. There was no time to waste.

McCampbell and Roy Rushing pushed over, followed by their second section, Lieutenant (jg) Jake Lundin and Dick McGraw. The first big bomber was already airborne by the time they reached the Negros airdrome. The Japanese pilot kept his big plane low on the water, making the task difficult for the F6Fs pilots approaching at high speed. "The Betty was bracketed by sections and all members of my combat team made from two to three runs," McCampbell recalled. Lundin, firing from a high-side position, destroyed the Betty's port engine. He was joined by George Duncan, who poured a long burst into the bomber's starboard engine, wing root, and cockpit. The Betty burst into flames and hit the water in a slight gliding turn to the left. Duncan and Lundin were each credited with a half kill on the day's first victory.[15]

The second Betty made it only a mile from the field before Duncan closed on it from directly behind. Only a hundred feet above the water, he set fire to both engines with his bullets, sending the bomber toward the ocean. The Betty hit in a flat glide, bounced back into the air, and exploded violently. Duncan's Hellcat was passing directly overhead, and the ensuing blast lifted his F6F about five hundred feet into the air.

Lundin then spotted a lone Oscar above him approaching on the tails of four F6Fs. Lundin pulled up and fired into its fuselage and engine, setting it on fire. The pilot made no attempt to escape, having been caught by surprise. His plane crashed in flames.

Duncan's wingman, Johnny Brex, had a much more difficult experience. Shortly after departing *Essex*, he noticed that his radio was out. He followed Duncan through the two attacks on the Bettys, but his engine was hit by a burst that slowed his speed. Brex remained determined and made two strafing runs over the field despite his crippled engine. He started a small fire on the field and damaged a single-engine fighter that was taxiing down the apron.

After his sweeps, Brex rejoined on Duncan and flew up close to his division leader. His attempts to hand-signal Duncan about his failing engine were not seen, as two Oscars suddenly swept in on them. Duncan got on the tail of one and shot it down. Brex turned in toward the other Oscar and opened with a burst so far out of range that it had no effect. Checking his fire, he closed to less than three hundred feet, firing until the Japanese fighter pushed into an almost vertical dive straight into the ocean.

Brex then climbed to rejoin Duncan, but his engine was suddenly hit by a stream of small-caliber tracers from his port quarter. In a fleeting glance, he saw that an Oscar had scored the hits on his F6F. Roy Rushing quickly dropped in to assist. Rushing had scored damaging hits

Ensign John Brex, in April 1944. After being downed on Negros Island on September 13, 1944, Brex avoided capture for weeks, thanks to island natives. Walter Lundin collection, National Museum of World War II Aviation

on the Mitsubishi Ki-21 heavy bombers ("Sallys") downed by Lundin and Duncan, and had downed an Oscar before spotting Brex in trouble. Rushing maneuvered in as the Oscars attacked Brex and caught one that pulled up in front of him. Holding his trigger for a four-second burst, he created smoke in one Oscar's wing root and watched with satisfaction as the plane spun into the ocean.

Rushing then saw Brex's plane below him smoking badly, its windshield smeared with oil. He dropped down to cover his squadron mate as Brex proceeded across the island at 2,000 feet. Making 120 knots, he hoped to reach the west coast of Negros. Brex's prop eventually ran away from him at 3,500 rpm and windmilled to a stop. He found his electrical and manual flap controls to be inoperative, and had no time to use his hand pump. His lifeless Hellcat began dropping downward.

Brex dropped his seat, braced himself, and made a good landing in a clearing between native huts. His F6F plowed forward smoothly until a stump snagged his fuselage and brought the aircraft to an abrupt halt. The force of the impact snapped off one of his shoulder straps, injuring Brex's face as he slammed forward into his controls. Rushing circled long enough to see Brex climb out of the cockpit and wave to him. Rushing dropped his first aid kit before proceeding back to the fleet in company with a group of *Wasp* planes.

Almost immediately after climbing out of his crashed plane, Brex was surrounded by natives who raced from their huts. They approached his Hellcat brandishing spears and rifles. With his hair closely cropped from his equator initiation two weeks prior, Brex was mistaken for a Japanese. He had short crow-black hair, black eyebrows, and a dark tan. His face was further obscured by blood pouring from a gash in his head where it had slammed into his gunsight during the crash landing. As the natives trained their rifles on him, he shouted, "American! American!" That and his American dog tags helped him convince the locals he was not the enemy. The natives dressed his wounds and took Brex into their care.[16]

The Negros Islanders stripped Brex's Hellcat of worthwhile goods, burned the plane, and took care of him for the next seven weeks. During the next day's *Essex* strikes against Japanese airfields on Negros Island, including Fabrica Airfield, Jim Rigg and George Carr flew cover for the Helldiver of VB-15's Lieutenant John Brodhead Jr., who dropped a waterproof container in a pilot chute close to Brex's burned-up Hellcat. Included in the survival supplies were instructions for the safeguarding of Ensign Brex written in English, Spanish, and Tagalog.

Sufficiently recovered by October 22, Brex was moved south on mules and water buffalo by native scouts until they reached a coastwatcher's contact point. He remained there from November 6 until radio contact was finally made with the 5th Fighter Command.

Nine more days would pass until a "Dumbo" rescue seaplane was dispatched from Morotai Island to retrieve the VF-15 ensign. On November 17, Captain Clarence L. Solander's weary Dumbo crew finally deposited Brex, along with two other downed aviators, at the Morotai air base.[17]

Days later, the survivors were flown to Manus Island to await transportation back to their units. Although Johnny Brex was thrilled to have survived his harrowing journey, it would be a full 2.5 months before he was finally reunited with his VF-15 squadron mates.

WHILE BREX WAS being surrounded by local people, the remainder of Duncan and Bert Morris's divisions made continuous strafing runs on the field. Clawing back to 8,000 feet, Morris caught sight of a lone Zeke making a firing pass on four F6Fs. He saw the Zeke "start to run like hell," but his slight altitude advantage allowed Morris to stay with the enemy fighter. Following his opponent in a wide diving spiral, he fired until the Zeke exploded into pieces at 4,000 feet.[18]

Lieutenant Commander Duncan had lost his wingman in the fight. Having knocked down a Nakajima Ki-27 fighter (code-named "Nate") and an Oscar, and with credit for one Betty and a shared kill on another, he was still primed for the fight. He scored damaging hits on another Oscar. But as he closed on another Nate just a hundred feet above the waves, he found that his ammunition had been depleted. "I pulled right up behind him just to give him one quick torpedo and then shove off," Duncan recalled. "When I pressed the trigger, nothing."[19]

Duncan charged his guns and pulled the trigger once more. Again nothing. Out of bullets, the VF-15 Exec could do nothing more than maneuver to keep himself out of harm's way before returning to the rendezvous site. Pulling alongside a junior pilot, he signaled that he was giving him the lead. But by the time the pair prepared to head back into the fray, Commander McCampbell signaled that the fight was over. It was time to turn for home.

Duncan's second section of Duz Twelves and wingman Larry Self had enjoyed a field day in the meantime. Having completed his strafing runs, Twelves climbed with Duncan's division to engage a group of Nates. These planes were small open-cockpit monoplanes—officially Imperial Japanese Army Air Service fighters. Although slow and lightly armed, the Nates were highly maneuverable, likely used by the Japanese for advanced training. As one opponent attempted an overhead run on him, Duz did a wingover and was able to land hits on the Nate. As the enemy plane started to spiral, Twelves power-spun behind him, firing solidly into the Nate until it rolled over and plunged straight into the water.[20]

Returning to altitude, Twelves chased another Nate into a cloud, firing short bursts. By the time the two emerged from the cumulus bank, the Nate caught fire, went out of control, and slammed into a hill. On his back at 3,000 feet, Duz almost collided with another Nate. His bursts drew smoke from the Japanese plane's engine. His opponent was badly damaged and did a wingover into a cloud. Twelves could claim only a probable on this plane, as his attention was immediately diverted to a Nate slashing in against his wingman, Self.

Twelves was quicker on the draw, landing .50-caliber slugs that caused this Nate to explode in midair after only one solid burst. But he had no time to bask in the glory of his third certain kill of the morning. Tracers were suddenly zipping past his tail from yet another Japanese fighter that had latched onto him. Some thirty holes were punched in his Hellcat, knocking out his hydraulic system. Duz believed the Grumman's armor plating saved his life this day. Dodging into a nearby cloud bank, he lost this latest Nate as his own wingman brought it under attack.

Self had already downed two Nates on his own in a series of attacks while Twelves was racking up his kills. He then came to the aid of Twelves by jumping onto the tail of the Nate that had shot up Duz's F6F. The Japanese pilot spotted Self and tried to evade, but the VF-15 pilot shattered the Nate's cockpit with a solid burst. Although his third victim did not catch fire, Self watched the enemy aircraft slam into the ground southeast of Bacolod Field.

DICK DAVIS FOUND himself the tail-end Charlie of the action. He was flying wing on James Doyle Bare in Lieutenant Morris's second section. Ahead of him, planes were swirling about, dropping like flies from the clouds. Davis worried momentarily that everything would be shot down before he entered the dogfights.[21]

Ensign Ken Flinn, flying wing on Morris, flamed the first Nate his section engaged. As he pulled up over the fighter, he observed its pilot slumped over the controls seconds before the Japanese monoplane entered a "graveyard spiral from 6,000 feet." An unseen Zeke fighter made a firing pass on the Morris division, then fled as the four F6Fs swung onto him. Flinn and Morris struggled to catch up, but their altitude advantage gave them just enough edge. A sharp burst from Morris's six .50s caused the Zeke to explode.[22]

While the division recovered from this action and rejoined, another Nate monoplane was tallyhoed. Bare and Davis raced ahead to intercept, but the nimble Nakajima abruptly wheeled about. Flashing toward them head-on, the skillful Japanese pilot dodged both Hellcats. Morris snapped off a quick head-on shot as Flinn banked hard left to pursue the Nate. Firing several bursts from astern, Flinn knocked pieces off the Nakajima's starboard engine cowl as its pilot started a sharp left turn. Flinn had to chop his throttle to avoid overrunning his prey. His last burst flamed the Nate, causing the Japanese pilot to attempt to bail out as his monoplane plummeted through the clouds.

Dick Davis spotted another Nate starting to pull in behind an F6F. He turned into it, pulled within range, and fired a long burst from full deflection to 5 o'clock down. The Nate was badly hit, a long black cloud of smoke belching from its engine. The pilot continued in a downward spiral. But

Davis had no time to follow his victim toward the water to guarantee a victory. His job was to remain on Doyle Bare's wing. He was later dejected to be credited with only a probable kill.

Morris regrouped his division and began the return to base. Near Fabrica Airfield, they tallyhoed another lone Nate flying just above a layer of clouds. The enemy pilot swung back toward the four Hellcats, pulling his nose up toward Bare and Davis, who began a head-on run toward the Nakajima. As the Nate flashed past beneath them, Bare pulled up into a sharp wingover. Morris and Flinn made firing runs, but the enemy pilot was "maneuvering beautifully, making sharp turns to throw Flinn off." As the Nate made a sharp nose-down turn to escape into the clouds, Bare swung in behind it and opened fire. His tracers walked right into the monoplane's fuselage, causing it to burst into flames and then explode.[23]

Davis was pleased that his entire division returned to *Essex* intact, having claimed four kills and a probable. Still wearing their leather helmets and sweat-stained flight gear, the jubilant Morris division was photographed with wide grins upon reaching the VF-15 ready room.

AIR GROUP COMMANDER Dave McCampbell came close to being downed on this mission. He had remained at high cover while the divisions of Duncan and Morris made the first attacks. His teams then made repeated strafing runs on the airfield until just before the attack made by the next incoming strike group. The sweep Hellcats had climbed to about 7,000 feet and were a little north of the field when the first tallyho was made by a bomber pilot.

McCampbell immediately led his fighters to the area. One of the Oscars sighted the approaching Americans and turned into them briefly before pulling out to the right. McCampbell rolled over onto him and got in a long burst. The Oscar's right wing burst into flames and he spiraled into the drink.

McCampbell, Rushing, Lundin, and McGraw began climbing. As they reached 8,000 feet, two Nates were sighted ahead. "We turned towards them and continued to climb until they rolled over on us," said McCampbell. As the first one dived down, Dave followed it and got in a short burst as he started his pullout, adding another as the Nate turned to the left. It started burning in the right wing root and crashed into the bay.

The second Nate was attacked by Jake Lundin and Ensign McGraw. Another F6F joined in the melee, firing bursts that caused the Japanese pilot to employ a split S maneuver. McGraw stitched the Nate with slugs until it finally shuddered and spiraled into the ocean.

Minutes later, McCampbell was joined by McGraw and they made a run on a lone Nate. He was easily overtaken and CAG sent him crashing into the ocean out of control in flames. McCampbell then called for a rendezvous of his Hellcats ten miles south of Bacolod Airfield.

"While waiting for my flight to rendezvous, I was attacked from above by a lone Nate, which I did not see until too late to counter," said McCampbell. After one pass, CAG was able to get behind his opponent but could not fire because of the Nate's excess speed carrying him out of range. McCampbell dropped his belly tank, shifted to low blower and water injection, and tried to climb with him. His opponent was gaining altitude and distance when he suddenly rolled over to make an overhead run on the CAG plane. Dave did a split S and dived away into a cloud to escape.[24]

When CAG returned to the rendezvous area at 10,000 feet, five Nates were circling 2,000 feet above him. Although he was alone, he felt confident. He tailed in behind them and had almost climbed to their level when the leading Nate spotted his F6F and turned toward McCampbell. Dave simply held his course and violently rocked his wings, hoping to confuse the enemy that he was friendly. The Nate soon made another turn toward Dave, who again waggled his wings.

"He wasn't fooled this time," said Dave. "The whole outfit tailed in behind me as I pushed over." As he dived, he spotted five F6Fs below him, so he attempted to pull the enemy formation down into their range. "The melee was on and it seemed that flaming planes were falling all around," he added. McCampbell managed a long burst on one of the Nates, which dived off, smoking, into the clouds.

A short while later, after his team "got smart," they made a rendezvous and climbed to 12,000 feet. With time and gas running short, McCampbell called off any further action and ordered his planes to return to base.

By the time the surviving eleven pilots from the divisions of McCampbell, Duncan, and Morris made it back to *Essex*, they proudly claimed nineteen enemy aircraft destroyed on the ground by their strafing. Another ten enemy aircraft had been knocked down in aerial combat, with two more probable claims.

THE FIRST *ESSEX* strike group arrived over northern Negros as McCampbell's sweep was heavily engaged in its fighting. Lieutenant Ted Overton led two fighter divisions off at 0604, although one F6F was scratched as a dud. Six of the seven Hellcats carried full loads of HVARs, which were used to fire into parked planes on the airfield.

Many of the junior pilots were introduced to HVARs awkwardly. Before he left, CAG McCampbell had given a briefing on their proper use, based on his limited experience thus far with the five-inch rockets.

"Gentlemen, today we are going to use rockets," McCampbell announced. He then handed each pilot a mimeographed sheet on the proper use and firing of an HVAR. After allowing them a moment to read over the standard procedures, the CAG continued. "If you follow exactly what the piece of paper says, then you will hit what you aim at, guaranteed."[25]

Ensign Jim Duffy did not question this. "If the CAG said it was going to work, then by God, it would work, or there would be hell to pay!"

Twenty-seven five-inch rockets were fired into a trio of twin-engine bombers. Overton, Dick Fowler, and Wayne Dowlen were credited with destroying the whole group. After rendezvous, the strike skirted northwest Negros. On their return to base, the group was jumped by a number of Oscars and Zekes. The Hellcat pilots fought viciously to protect their bombers and torpedo planes. A few bursts from the guns of Lieutenant John Strane quickly sent one Zeke diving into the ground in flames.

The *Essex* dive-bombers maintained a tight formation as a group of Zekes attacked from their rear. The VB rear gunners threw out enough lead to claim one kill. Strane's division turned toward the enemy in bracket formation and he opened fire on three Zekes. Two broke off, but the third Zeke kept firing at Strane as they approached each other head-on. Pieces of the Zeke's wing started coming off and its engine was hit.

The Zeke pressed over Strane, who ducked out of the way. The Zeke continued down, out of control, and crashed. As Strane recovered, three Zekes got on his tail, but they were driven off by Ted Overton.

Strane's wingman, Jim Duffy, pulled out of an overhead pass to find an Oscar making a head-on run against him. He pulled up, firing bursts into the Oscar's engine and port wing tank, causing it to burst into flames. Duffy stalled out at the top of his zoom but watched the Oscar continue down until it crashed into the ocean. In further action, he landed bursts on two more Oscars but did not see them burn.

Overton's wingman, Dick Fowler, chased an Oscar off the tail of some *Essex* dive-bombers but soon found that the Oscar had managed to slide onto his own tail. Fowler led his opponent into the path of another F6F, which shot it down. Fowler in turn then shot a second Oscar off the tail of his savior pilot. Minutes later, Fowler downed another Oscar and scored a probable against a third opponent. The final tally for Overton's flight was eight planes destroyed plus a probable and others damaged.

By the time *Essex* launched her third strike group for Negros Island at 0855, VF-15 was stretched thin. Escorting the sixteen bombers were three divisions under skipper Jim Rigg. Some thirty-one Hellcats were now aloft between the three morning launches.

Finding no enemy aircraft aloft to tangle with, Rigg led his fighters in ahead of the bombers to strafe planes on Saravia Field. They counted fifteen destroyed, plus others likely wrecked that simply did not burn. But enemy AA fire took a toll on the Helldivers. Lieutenant Philip Eugene Golden's SB2C was hit and slammed into the ground in flames. The VB-15 crew of Lieutenant Richard Glass and his gunner, AMM2c George A. Duncan, were credited with flaming a pair of Bettys with their strafing. But return fire claimed the life of Duncan. His lifeless body slumped over his machine guns as they continued to fire. One VB-15 division was detached to escort Glass and his crippled bomber back to base in hopes of saving his gunner's life. But when they landed at 1225, medics found that Duncan had been killed instantly.

Rigg moved his flight on to Fabrica Airfield, where they blasted apart more parked planes. Lieutenant (jg) Jack Symmes, tasked with investigating other nearby airfields, found feverish construction work underway at

San Pablo Field on Leyte. Symmes dived in, leading Warren Clark, Bob Stime, and Dusty Craig. As they shot up field trucks and bulldozers, the pilots saw the remaining Japanese operators running for their lives to take cover.

Three additional afternoon strikes from *Essex* returned without loss. George Duncan's flight destroyed twenty-one aircraft on the ground. "I got a Sally bomber on the ground," Duz Twelves logged in his diary that evening.

By day's end of September 13, Twelves, Rushing, Self, and Fowler had reached ace status, making a baker's dozen total of ace pilots now in VF-15. Commander McCampbell had raised his personal victory score to 17.5 kills. In the U.S. Navy's ace race, the *Essex* CAG had climbed past VF-17's Ira Kepford. Dashing Dave now sat in second place, trailing only his former *Lexington* Hellcat student, Alex Vraciu.

FIFTEEN

FIRST STRIKES IN THE PHILIPPINES

AIR STRIKES ON MANILA

September 21, 1944

Four days of heavy carrier strikes in the southern Philippines had destroyed most of the effective Japanese aircraft in the region for the time being. Admiral Bull Halsey reported the area to no longer be a worthwhile target, and Allied leaders began making plans to bypass strikes on Mindanao Island. The scheduled invasion of Leyte would be advanced to late October.

As the invasion of Palau commenced, Ted Sherman's task group spent two days refueling. Task Group 38 was next charged with staging raids on Manila, the capital of the Philippines, and other parts of Luzon Island, as the fulfillment of Douglas MacArthur's promise to return to the Philippines moved closer. This would mark the first return of American carrier forces since Manila had been bombed by the Japanese in December 1941. The scuttlebutt about *Essex* was that the carrier would be heading back to the States for an overhaul after this next big operation.

On the morning of September 21, air strikes on Manila commenced, with sweeps over Clark Field and Nichols Field on Luzon. It was an all-hands-on-deck day, with four strike groups and four CAPs on Bert Morris's schedule. By dusk, fifty-two fighter pilots would be launched, many at least twice, including most of the newer pilots. Art Singer, Jigs Foltz, and Roy Nall would rotate flying "Photo Joe" duty through the day to document the effects of each strike.

At 0805, Commander McCampbell led the first strike group toward

Manila. Loaded with rockets, the Hellcats went in first against Nichols and Las Piñas Fields to knock out targets of opportunity. The CAG division and those of George Duncan, Bert Morris, and Baynard Milton left an administration building, a large hangar, and a barracks building in flames.

The second *Essex* strike group, launched at 0900, included twenty-eight Avengers and Helldivers and the sixteen VF-15 fighters. At Nichols Field, the divisions of Jimmy Rigg, Ted Overton, John Strane, and George Crittenden strafed and dropped eleven 350-pound depth bombs among the estimated seventy-five parked enemy planes they found. Dozens of aircraft were wrecked on the field by the time Rigg turned his strike force back for their carrier.

Dave McCampbell returned to the air after lunch with a third *Essex* strike group. His *Minsi III* was loaded with rockets, while the other eleven Hellcats carried depth bombs. In company with three dozen *Lexington* warplanes, the *Essex* CAG led an attack on a Japanese convoy reported off west of Luzon, near Salvador Island. Named MATA-27, the convoy had gotten underway from Manila at 0800 for Cebu in the Philippines. It consisted of two freighters, several tankers, an auxiliary troop transport, the minelayer *Enoshima*, a destroyer, and four coast defense warships. MATA-27 was first attacked around 1030 by other TF 38 warplanes that managed to sink an auxiliary transport. A second strike thirty minutes later left a tanker blazing and abandoned. McCampbell counted only seven ships present when his *Essex* force arrived overhead at 1515; some of the coast defense warships had remained behind to rescue survivors from the first two strikes.[1]

The divisions of Jack Symmes and John Van Altena attacked one of the escorting destroyers with repeated strafing runs and five depth bombs. Lieutenant (jg) Monk Gunter, flying tail-end Charlie for the fighter-bomber division, was credited with a direct hit dubbed "the most outstanding result for the VFs" in VF-15's action report. Follow-up strikes couldn't locate the badly damaged destroyer, and it was presumed to have sunk.[2]

McCampbell and Symmes led their divisions down on a smaller freighter, strafing and dropping two depth bombs. McCampbell fired all four of his five-inch rockets and claimed damaging hits. The ship was left smoking and heavily damaged. Van Altena's division strafed another destroyer escort and dropped two more depth bombs near it. Bombing Squadron Fifteen and VT-15 planes worked over another of the larger Japanese tankers, leaving it dead in the water and sinking.

By the conclusion of this attack, the *Essex* and *Lexington* strikers had severely damaged several warships and had the tankers *Yuki Maru* and *Shichiyo Maru* and the cargo ship *Nansei Maru* in sinking condition. But the sad fate of Japanese convoy MATA-27 was not complete. A fourth *Essex* and *Lexington* strike group arrived over the battered force at 1600. For Jack Taylor, Jim Duffy, and nine other pilots, it was their first combat flight carrying five-inch rockets. Each had their CAG's mimeographed instruction sheet and had absorbed all they could. It was now time to put his knowledge to the test.

Jim Rigg, John Strane, and Ted Overton split their divisions up to make strafing-and-rocket attacks on a 3,000-ton merchant ship and two of the coast defense warships, believed by the pilots to be smaller destroyer escorts. Duffy executed a 30-degree dive, put a small lead on his intended target area, and fired off all his rockets when his Hellcat reached 3,000 feet. "Streams of fire raced toward the ship below as the rockets stayed true," he recalled. He watched with satisfaction as his HVARs penetrated the merchantman's hull. Lieutenant Frank West, leading six Helldivers down on the large freighter *Surakaruta Maru*, claimed a trio of 1,000-pound bomb hits. One of VT-15's Avenger pilots added another, lighter bomb hit, and it was enough to finish off the ship. "The ship began to glow red-hot," recalled Duffy. "The fire inside the ship must have been hellish, as the hull began to burn and melt."[3]

By the time the attack was over, *Surakaruta Maru* was under the waves. The *Essex* warplanes claimed two small luggers sunk and another merchant ship probably sunk. One of the escorting warships, *CD-5*, was set afire and heavily damaged. This coast defense vessel later exploded and sank. "The sea was full of burning Japanese ships, compliments of VF-15's rockets' red glare!" Duffy recalled.[4]

On September 22, Task Force 38's pounding of Luzon continued. Air Group Fifteen committed thirty-five planes to the first strike group, launched at 0625. Dave McCampbell's command division remained on high cover at Angels 12 over Manila Bay while he sent in the divisions of Lieutenants Morris, Collins, and Van Altena. Their first strafing runs at 0745 were against targets in and around Nichols Field. Morris and fighter-bomber pilot Bill Anderson exploded two large fuel tanks with their HVARs. Heavy columns of black smoke billowed thousands of feet into the sky as smaller explosions continued to rock the area.

Fighting Fifteen then attacked shipping within the harbor. Doyle Bare scored two HVAR hits on a small freighter, leaving it ablaze. Not to be outdone, Morris led two divisions of fighters down on a submarine that his wingman, Dick Davis, spotted docked in the harbor's inner basin. Accompanied by photo Hellcat pilot Art Singer, Morris led Davis, Bare, and Ken Flinn in from 15,000 feet to make a rocket attack on the I-boat. "We were supposed to fire the rockets between 1,000 and 1,500 feet to be effective," Davis recalled. "Just as I passed through 2,000 feet, Bert yelled that there were barrage balloons."[5]

For Davis, there was nothing more to do than salvo his rockets and weave past the balloons. Of the sixteen rockets fired by VF-15 pilots, Morris and Singer were credited with the best marksmanship. Eight of their HVARs slammed the I-boat, and the submarine was later photographed out from its pier, heavily damaged and gushing fuel oil into the harbor.

McCampbell's division was still on high cover at 0800 when he tally-hoed a twin-engine aircraft heading south at about 20,000 feet. They gave chase, climbing to Angels 18 during the next ten minutes. They were unable to close the distance until the Dinah suddenly reversed course. Another five minutes utilizing water injection power boost allowed McCampbell and wingman Roy Rushing to attain position astern for their first shots.

After the fifteen-minute chase, McCampbell was ready to close the deal. He suddenly remembered that his *Minsi III* was carrying six five-inch HVARs. *Well*, he thought, *this is as good a time as any to see if my rockets are any good in the air.*[6]

Pulling onto the rear of his prey, he let go with two rockets. It was his second attempt to hit an aerial opponent with HVARs within a week. "One rocket hit his starboard stabilizer and knocked off the outboard one-third, although it did not explode," McCampbell reported. The Dinah be-gan fishtailing and making shallow turns, and one of the crewmen was seen to bail out with a parachute. Failing to down his quarry with the HVARs, McCampbell resorted to traditional techniques. "I gave him one short burst in the starboard engine and wing root, causing him to burst into flames and go into a left spin," he reported. The Dinah's right wing panel tore off and the right engine broke away from the plane, with the flaming components crashing about ten miles south of Manila Bay.[7]

A second *Essex* strike escorted by Jim Rigg's fighters damaged more enemy shipping. In the only aerial engagement, George Crittenden was credited with a probable kill.

On September 24, a massive TG 38.3 strike was launched against ship-ping in the Calamian Group in the Philippines. John Strane took two di-visions of VF-15 to cover a dozen VB-15 Helldivers, all flying in company with strike planes from *Langley, Princeton,* and *Lexington.* Near Coron Bay off Busuanga Island, Strane's group made repeated strafing runs on Japanese freighters, but their SB2C companions managed only near misses with their half-ton bombs. The outbound flight of 350 miles and the lengthy return was a record strike distance covered by Air Group Fifteen, but all planes returned safely after 5.6 hours in the air.

Dave McCampbell led four rocket-armed VF-15 divisions off the deck right behind the first morning strike group. His force hit shipping and shore installations at Cebu Harbor and Mactan Island. His Hellcats, Avengers, and Helldivers worked over a variety of smaller ships, sinking one small freighter with bombs and rockets. Two other small vessels ex-ploded and sank after absorbing numerous F6F rockets. Four more vessels were left dead in the water, and another in sinking condition.

As these assaults were wrapping up around 0840, McCampbell tally-hoed two Mitsubishi F1Ms (code-named "Pete") taking off from the harbor. With his division, he pushed over from 12,000 feet, then dived through the clouds and rained down to 2,000 feet. The Petes headed south in close for-mation at a mere five hundred feet. Closing from astern, McCampbell shot up the inboard Pete while Roy Rushing took on the other. Both floatplanes started to smoke and break away from each other in a 180-degree turn back toward the harbor, dropping their depth charges as they fled.

McCampbell and Roy Nall fired simultaneously into the inboard Pete, which flamed and crashed. Rushing got on the tail of his Mitsubishi F1M and a two-second burst between the engine and cockpit caused it to flame and crash into the water.

With this half kill, Dave McCampbell had finally tied Lieutenant Alex Vraciu for first place in the U.S. Navy with nineteen victories.

ESSEX CONTINUED TO work the Cebu area, launching another three strike groups on September 24. Without aerial opposition, Satan's Playmates demolished wharves, oil tank farms, and small luggers in the harbor. The squadron's only loss came during the day's third mission, as Ensign Henry Gaver of the fighter-bomber unit sank a 100-ton lugger with his 350-pound depth bomb. His Hellcat was struck by antiaircraft fire over the harbor, and he notified section leader John Van Altena that he was making a forced water landing. As Gaver settled to within a few feet of the waves, his wing suddenly dipped into the ocean. His F6F somersaulted across the surface, bursting into flames.

The AA fire was intense as George Duncan led in the fourth *Essex* strike against Mactan Island. Strafing ahead of the bombers, Ensign Duz Twelves worked to dodge the enemy gunners. "AA bore-sighted us," he wrote in his diary that evening. "Had to dive to treetop level to keep from being hit." The flight returned without loss, after the fighters put the rest of their bullets and rockets into smaller luggers and barges in the harbor.[8]

Bert Morris closed out the day with an eight-plane fighter sweep from *Essex* over the Visayas in company with *Princeton* and *Langley* F6Fs. Near Panay Island, the Hellcats strafed and burned several small luggers. Air Group Fifteen's softening of the area was concluded with the September 24 strikes. Ted Sherman's task group retired toward the Palaus the following day, launching only a single combat air patrol from *Essex*. Commander McCampbell used the downtime this day to consolidate his fighter forces.

Since the start of the *Essex* war cruise, a six-plane night fighter detachment from VF(N)-77 had operated within the air group. Having received no replacement radar-equipped Hellcats, the unit was down to only four flyable planes by September 25. Their skipper, Mark Freeman, was detached for other duty. His four remaining VF(N)-77 pilots—Jake Hogue, Sam Lundquist, Ernie Roycraft, and George Tarleton—were simply absorbed into Lieutenant Commander Rigg's VF-15 by September 24 to help fill vacancies within divisions.

Essex refueled the following day and stopped in the Palaus on September 27 to load more bombs and ammunition. Sherman's task group remained in the area for the next few days without action before moving into Ulithi Atoll in the Caroline Islands on October 2 to take on supplies for the ship. Recently seized from the Japanese, Ulithi—a thousand miles from the nearest Japanese air base—was now the Navy's principal anchorage in the western Pacific. After long weeks of aerial combat, the fighter pilots were eager to get ashore. The first day in port, Jim Rigg and George Duncan found that there were no launches to haul their pilots to the island. Rigg paid a visit to *Essex* executive officer Dave McDonald and secured permission to break out a bottle of Four Roses they had previously purchased. "We decided there wasn't going to be a liberty boat, so we went on down to our cabin and uncorked the bottle," Duncan recalled.[9]

The next morning Commander McDonald arranged for a liberty boat and made sure that Air Group Fifteen pilots and rear gunners were the first to go ashore. "We had a real evening on that beach," Duncan said. "All of us [got] crocked."[10]

Essex remained through the next day, giving her aviators a short time to enjoy some warm beer and Spam sandwiches on the beach. The following evening, TG 38.3 pulled out of the anchorage to ride out an approaching storm. Duz Twelves wrote that his carrier spent "all day and night riding out a hurricane, one of the worst I have ever seen."[11]

Essex returned to Ulithi late on October 5, and remained until the following night, preparing for TF 38's next engagement. This time, the target areas was in the Ryukyus, a lengthy island chain stretching from a hundred miles north of Formosa to a hundred miles south of Kyushu, the southernmost home island of Japan. Pete Mitscher's Third Fleet was venturing into strange waters; little was known about the key Japanese air base on the big island of Okinawa.

The food stores on board *Essex* were running thin by this point, as little quality food had been obtained at Ulithi. Ensign Spike Borley found the wardroom was down to dehydrated eggs, canned beets, canned asparagus, and canned meat. "There are only so many ways to cook Spam," Borley recalled. "Most of us were at the point where the only reason we were eating was to avoid hunger pangs."[12]

By evening on October 9, Borley and his fellow pilots had reason to shelve their grumblings over the poor food quality. Commander McCampbell and Jim Rigg held briefings on what was expected the following day. Task Force 38 picked up speed for the final run-in toward the following morning's launch point. In a matter of hours, their Hellcat jockeys would be part of the first U.S. carrier air strikes on Okinawa.

SIXTEEN

"A REAL CRAP SHOOT"

October 10, 1944
200 Miles off Okinawa

Ted Sherman was aware of the ace race within the U.S. Navy. On board Sherman's flagship, *Essex*, Commander Dave McCampbell had nineteen aerial victories. Although his CAG was now tied with Lieutenant Alex Vraciu, Rear Admiral Sherman had no interest in Dashing Dave moving into the lead spot.

As his task group approached the Nansei Shoto, the Ryukyu Island chain, Sherman pulled McCampbell aside to advise him. His job was to coordinate the air strikes over Okinawa and Kume Shima. He was not to be hotshotting, chasing after Japanese planes. McCampbell was to leave that business to his trained Hellcat jockeys.

When the first *Essex* fighter sweep was launched at 0543 on October 10, McCampbell was strike coordinator for his task group's aircraft. During his five-hour flight with wingman Roy Rushing, Dave would make no intercepts. At 0650, they arrived over Okinawa's main harbor after a two-hundred-mile flight. McCampbell and Rushing strafed and fired rockets at the merchant ships they found. Two HVARs were seen to explode in a 4,000-ton freighter, and their bullets apparently hit depth charges stored on the stern of another merchant ship whose afterdeck exploded violently.

Launched directly behind the CAG section, the first large *Essex* sweep reached Okinawa at the same time. Jim Rigg and his fighters strafed numerous twin-engine bombers and a fuel truck parked on Yontan Airfield.

The skipper salvoed his four rockets into parked planes. By the completion of multiple runs, VF-15 claimed at least a dozen fueled bombers destroyed, many of which exploded when strafed. No aerial combatants were found, and few enemy planes were discovered on nearby Yontan South Airfield or at Kume Shima.

The first full deckload strike from *Essex*, escorted by George Duncan and four VF-15 divisions, arrived next. It worked over barracks and installations at Yontan Airfield and wrecked a hundred-foot lugger with rockets. Fighting Fifteen had no airborne Japanese opponents until 0830, when the next *Essex* and *Lexington* composite strike arrived over Okinawa. Four VF-15 divisions were led by Lieutenant Bert Morris.

McCampbell sent VB-15 skipper Jim Mini's Helldivers against three freighters in the harbor near Nago Bay. Their 1,000-pound bombs achieved only one direct hit on a previously beached minelayer. Torpedo 15's Avengers sank a pair of fuel barges with their five-hundred-pounders. Morris's fighter division, each F6F toting a quarter-ton bomb, was more successful.

Ensign George Pigman, who scored 8.5 aerial victories with VF-15, sank a Japanese freighter with his bomb hit on October 10, 1944. He is seen here after making the 12,000th landing on USS Essex *on July 30.*

NATIONAL ARCHIVES, 80-G-373646

Taking on an 8,000-ton freighter, Morris and Ken Flinn employed skip bombing techniques to lob their bombs into the merchantman's sides. Morris's five-hundred-pounder erupted alongside the ship, but Flinn's bomb skipped across the waves and exploded forward of the freighter's superstructure. Baynard Milton and his wingman, George Pigman, made standard dives, and Pigman's bomb—released at a mere 1,500 feet—was a direct hit. The ship's bow began settling immediately, and aerial photos would later show it to have sunk. Photo pilot Roy Nall led another division against a trio of smaller warships. The bombs of Swede Thompson and Jim Mooney were credited with destroying these subchasers.

As VF-15 completed its shipping attacks and made rendezvous, a tallyho was called. A few miles to the south, enemy fighters were spotted lifting off from Yontan Airfield. In a swirling series of dogfights, the squadron shot down eight planes and damaged two others. Firing from only three hundred feet above the water, Morris sent a Tony cartwheeling into the sea near Zampa Misaki. Flinn made firing runs on another Tony all the way back to the airfield, and he splashed it just as the Japanese pilot was lowering his wheels to make an emergency landing.

Milton shot up a Tony as it launched, sending it flaming into a nearby thicket of trees. Pigman chased a fourth Tony back to the airstrip, landing hits in its cockpit and wing roots. The Japanese fighter slammed into the runway with its wheels still up, then cartwheeled across the ground as it splintered into pieces. In the process of destroying this plane, Pigman became the fourteenth member of VF-15 to reach ace status.

Ensign Spike Borley was an acting division leader this day after Lieutenant Strane had been unable to launch. Borley led his quartet into battle against five Zekes and Oscars they encountered while approaching Yontan Airfield. In two firing runs, Borley hammered a Zeke into the ocean. Ensign Merwin Frazelle flamed an Oscar, while Lieutenant (jg) Norm Berree claimed another Oscar and a Nate, both shot down at low altitude. Roy Nall claimed damage to another Nate and Oscar in the quick battle.

The next two *Essex* deckload strikes wrecked parked aircraft, buildings, and ammunition dumps on Okinawa. Art Singer and Jigs Foltz, flying photo F6Fs on the day's last mission, documented the strikes with numerous clear images. At 1400, while approaching Ie Shima, an island near Okinawa, Singer spotted seven Japanese aircraft, mainly Yokosuka P1Y Ginga Fighter bombers (code-named "Frances," shortened to "Fran" by the U.S. aviators), approaching. Singer dived down on the airfield and exploded two Frans trying to land. He then pursued a Sally bomber all the way back to the airfield. His bullets caused the bomber to slam into the runway, its landing gear folding up as its prop chewed into the runway. Singer was later frustrated to only receive credit for a probable on that kill. Down to only three operational wing guns, Singer climbed for altitude and soon shot down another Fran. Already an ace, Art Singer had pushed his overall score to eight kills.

By day's end, Task Force 38 fighters claimed about a hundred aerial victories, with half this score going to TG 38.3's *Essex* and *Lexington* squadrons. Yontan Airfield had been severely pounded, and shipping around Okinawa had taken a beating, with at least four ships sunk and dozens of other vessels damaged. Mitscher's carriers had lost five pilots, four airmen, and twenty-one planes. From Air Group Fifteen, two rear gunners had been wounded by AA fire, including ARM2c Charles Rowland of VB-15. His left arm was so badly mangled by flak that *Essex* doctors were forced to remove it.[1]

Ted Sherman's task group refueled in the East China Sea on October 11 upon heading south from the Ryukyus. Commander McCampbell's air group had been tasked with hitting another unfamiliar target, the island of Formosa, the following morning.

October 12, 1944

Dave McCampbell was up early, smoking a cigarette with his morning coffee. He skipped his preflight paperwork to head down to the fighter ready room. Intelligence officer Bob McReynolds was giving a briefing on Formosa, including the enemy forces, their aircraft, the number of anti-aircraft guns expected, and the terrain. McCampbell listened as his ACIO detailed potential dangers for any pilot forced to bail out over Formosa. "We could expect to encounter many types of poisonous snakes," he recalled.[2]

Spike Borley was more worried about Japanese fighters than snakes. The best intelligence of Formosa that McReynolds had came from U.S. submarine periscope photos. Borley was alarmed when his ACIO stated that the island held as many as twenty-four Japanese airfields that could contain more than three hundred aircraft.[3]

For Task Group 38.3's morning strikes, McCampbell would serve as strike coordinator. His place in the afternoon would be taken by Commander Ted "Pedro" Winters, the new CAG for *Lexington*'s Air Group Nineteen. Commander Karl Jung, the former *Lexington* CAG, had suffered badly burned hands when his belly tank erupted into flames upon making a water landing after a strike on September 12. Being the previous Hellcat squadron skipper, Winters followed the thinking of McCampbell. He continued flying an F6F-5 in his new role, whereas many air group commanders more commonly flew Avengers.

Knowing the first strike on unfamiliar Formosa was a big deal for Task Force 38 commander Pete Mitscher, Winters eased up to flag plot on the *Lexington*'s bridge to confer with the admiral.

"Since I will be coordinating the attacks on targets in the afternoon, it would be a good thing to go in with the early sweep to familiarize myself with the area," Winters offered.

Mitscher concurred. Winters was authorized to fly with the first *Lexington* fighter sweep as an observer. He felt smug and excited, even if he did harbor a certain jealousy for the leading ace role that his *Essex* equal, McCampbell, held. *McCampbell can go after all the planes he wants*, thought Winters. *But if I'm included on this free ride, I might just get the chance to shoot down another plane if it presents itself.*[4]

With four kills to his credit, the new *Lexington* CAG had secret hopes of becoming an ace. The flight to Formosa would be 158 miles, and the first planes were turning up their engines before 0600. The sea was running strong, and the deck was not illuminated as the pilots mounted their Hellcats. "It was dark as midnight," Spike Borley recalled. "We were going to have to go on instruments as soon as we were off the ship, then rendezvous in the darkness to go in and hit a target we knew nothing about. It felt like a real crap shoot to me."[5]

Essex and *Lexington* each contributed sixteen F6Fs to the early sweep. Skipper Jim Rigg's division was accompanied by those of George Duncan, John Van Altena, and Baynard Milton. Commander McCampbell's coordinator division brought VF-15's total to twenty Hellcats. His team would remain over Formosa until the first two follow-up strike groups had also reached the area. Fighting Fifteen had been assigned the western side of Formosa, with the port of Kaohsiung and the Pescadores Islands as its target areas.

Twenty minutes out from the ship, Lieutenant (jg) Norm Berree reported that his fuel pump was failing. Leaking oil was splattering his windscreen, and his aileron controls had become jammed. His division leader, Milton, acknowledged the trouble and the pair wheeled about to return to the ship. Milton's second section leader, Ensign George Pigman, pressed on with the fighter group with only Borley remaining on his wing. Borley really wanted to find a mechanical fault with his Hellcat No. 24. "But unfortunately, everything was working perfectly."[6]

The fourteen remaining fighters under Rigg trailed McCampbell's CAG division slightly. By 0645, the skies had brightened enough to show rough seas below the low cloud level. A storm was brewing as Air Group Fifteen approached the western coast of Formosa. On the island, Admiral Soemu Toyoda, chief of the Imperial Japanese Navy's general staff, had intelligence that an American carrier strike was likely. As the Task Force 38 fighters approached, Toyoda had more than two hundred fighters airborne or in the process of taking off.

Another massive air battle was in the making.

AT 0700, JIM Rigg tallyhoed the first bandits. His four divisions were between the islands of Kagi and Taichu at 19,000 feet. Many Japanese aircraft were spotted above, at Angels 23. Fighting Fifteen climbed to intercept.

Rigg damaged a Zeke on his first pass, and his wingman, Bob Fash, polished off the cripple. Continuing in the fray, Rigg dropped his belly tank before making passes on other opponents. He claimed damage to another Zeke and two Tojo fighters. He later scissored back and forth with another Zeke, firing until he dropped it in flames. Fash followed with another kill, a Tojo seen to spiral toward the ocean without recovering.

George Carr chased a Tojo down to 12,000 feet with Bill Deming. As Carr locked onto the fighter's tail, the Tojo pilot dropped his landing gear in hopes of making the Hellcat overshoot. But Carr nailed its engine and saw it crash and burn. Now at lower altitude, Carr and Deming spotted three Tojos mixing it up with an F6F division at 6,000 feet. As Carr descended, one Tojo pulled up into a spin. Carr and a *Lexington* VF-19 pilot combined to share a half kill on one of the Tojos. Deming nailed another in its engine, causing its pilot to flip the plane on its back in an inverted spin until it crashed.

George Duncan's division was at Angels 19 when he spotted a Tojo at 10 o'clock, slightly below his altitude. As he pushed into a head-on run, the Tojo turned to meet him. Both pilots held their courses, firing, until Duncan had to pull up violently to avoid being rammed. The Tojo burst into flames as he slid under the Hellcat to its demise. With this, Duncan had reached 10.5 kills, making him a double ace.

Duncan's wingman was Ensign Paul Bugg, a rookie pilot who had been with VF-15 for only a month. As his division bracketed a Tojo from astern, the Japanese pilot turned toward Bugg, who swung around with the enemy fighter. As they descended a thousand feet, Bugg fired almost continually until the Tojo burst into flames. The Japanese pilot bailed out, but his parachute failed to blossom as his plane plowed into the ocean.

Jack Taylor, flying high cover, was attacked from above by many Zekes. His section leader downed one of the attackers. Seconds later Taylor spotted a pair of Tojos making runs on an F6F below him at Angels 15. He made an overhead pass with another VF-15 pilot, scoring hits. Taylor's bullets apparently struck the Japanese pilot, as the plane was seen to crash without even a plume of smoke after losing control.

Taylor climbed back up to 20,000 feet and next spotted three Tojos flying in formation far below. Pushing into another overhead pass, Taylor flamed a Tojo that was seen to crash, giving him two solid kills. His greatest pride came after the mission when George Carr offered, "Nice flying, Taylor!"[7]

Duz Twelves, second section leader for Duncan's division, was approached by a Zeke flying head-on toward him. The enemy fighter was at Angels 18, slightly above Twelves. Other F6Fs were apparently already firing on this Zeke, as Duz saw his opponent making evasive maneuvers. But the Japanese pilot had Lieutenant (jg) Twelves in his sights, and he opened fire first.

Japanese 7.7mm bullets ripped through the *Lady La Rhea*. One bullet struck Duz's oil tank. Another punched through his plotting board in the cockpit. Other bullets pierced his propeller, wings, ailerons, fuselage, elevators, stabilizer, vertical fin, and rudder and even knocked the cylinder head temperature gauge completely out of the instrument panel. "I gave a call on the radio that we were being attacked," Twelves recalled. "He went screaming by, and all I got was a quick glance."[8]

As the Japanese pilot completed his dive, he suddenly pulled his A6M up right in front of Twelves. This maneuver put Duz in the "saddle position." With a slight deflection shot, he opened up with all six .50s. The Zeke immediately burst into flames and its pilot was seen to bail out.

Although his Hellcat was badly damaged, Twelves remained in the action zone. He later encountered a Jack at 18,000 feet. It began maneuvering and weaving to come in out of the sun, doggedly pressing its attack. The Jack outclimbed the F6F-3, having no trouble keeping altitude advantage. Twelves's combat team stayed in formation, and when the Jack started to recover below, Twelves got in good bursts. He hit its engine and cockpit, creating heavy smoke before it went out of control and crashed—Twelves's second kill of the mission.

SPIKE BORLEY ENTERED the fight near Formosa with only his section leader, George Pigman. Prior to this mission, Borley's lone aerial victory had been notched only two days prior. As the action commenced, Pigman and Borley were at 17,000 feet and climbing. A group of Tojos suddenly plunged down on the *Essex* F6Fs. Pigman latched onto the tail of one of the retreating fighters. Two of his bursts shot the enemy fighter's entire empennage off, and the Tojo pilot bailed out.

Returning to formation, Pigman next made an overhead run on a Zeke, which exploded in front of him as he pulled up sharply. Minutes later Pigman put two bursts into another Zeke, causing large pieces of the plane to break loose. The Zeke was last seen smoking, but "Porkchop" was so wrapped up in other combat he could not follow it to its demise, leaving it only as a probable.

During this time, Ensign Borley made the most of his opportunities. "I did not get into any dogfights, but rather I was able to see and hit four different airplanes without engaging in a fight," he remembered. Borley's first kill came against a Tojo he spotted about 3,000 feet below him. Borley made a high-side run and opened fire about 1,500 feet away. His bullets stitched the Tojo's cockpit and wings and it started smoking badly. Small bursts of flames belched from its cowling before the Tojo went into a 45-degree dive into the ocean.

One kill. Borley's wartime total had doubled.

Recovering at about 14,000 feet, he spotted a Zeke at 12 o'clock on an opposite course. It was below him, so he commenced an overhead run. His lead proved to be too far, so he adjusted his fire on the next burst and the Zeke flew into his tracers. It caught fire in the engine and went into a lazy spiral, exploding when it crashed.

Two kills for the day now.

Borley then joined with several other F6Fs. They soon sighted Oscars dead ahead about five hundred feet below them, on an opposite course. Spike increased his power setting and closed to about 2,000 feet from one of the enemy planes. His opponent was starting a left turn and appeared to look back just as Borley opened fire. The Oscar pilot immediately rolled his plane over and bailed out, leaving his fighter to crash pilotless into the sea.

Three kills for the day.

Ensign Clarence "Spike" Borley attained ace status on October 12 with four kills, but was forced to ditch his Hellcat in the ocean. He would spend days adrift in his life raft. U.S. NAVY

Having dropped to 7,000 feet, Borley spotted another Oscar. It was at 2 o'clock, flying toward land, making about 200 knots. He turned, gunned his throttle to attain 240 knots, and closed the gap. The Oscar pilot spotted the F6F and started to dive. Borley increased his speed to 280 knots and opened fire when the range narrowed to eight hundred feet. His bullets hit both sides of the engine. Spike then fanned his rudder, wiggling his F6F to spray bullets all over the Oscar.

As Borley overtook the fighter, he saw that it was burning in the engine and starboard wing root. The inside of the Japanese cockpit was a sea of flames. The Oscar continued in a steady dive and crashed on the ground, exploding upon impact.

With four kills for the day, Spike Borley was VF-15's newest ace pilot.

DURING THIS TIME, John Van Altena's fighter-bombers tangled with a group of Zekes and Tojos over Formosa. Monk Gunter flamed two Zekes, Tom Hoey destroyed a Tojo, and Van Altena chalked up two Tojo kills of his own.

The aerial action began to wind down. All fourteen of skipper Rigg's Hellcats had survived, although Duz Twelves was piloting a flying wreck. Rendezvousing his troops, Rigg led them to the Keishu Airdrome. They found numerous enemy aircraft on the ground, some single-engine fighters turning up to get airborne and twin-engine bombers in revetments in pairs and trios. Fighting Fifteen made numerous strafing runs, creating fires in at least a dozen of the Japanese fighters and a half dozen bombers. Although soldiers began lighting smoke pots, the rising black clouds did little to affect visibility. A far greater concern proved to be the accuracy of Japanese antiaircraft gunners.

Lieutenant (jg) Van Altena's F6F was hit by AA fire in the engine during one of his runs. He nursed his crippled Hellcat only far enough along to safely ditch offshore. His wingman, Ensign Charlie Dorn, circled his division leader's life raft and began making radio calls to the duty lifeguard submarine, Lieutenant Commander Robert Ward's USS *Sailfish* (SS-192).

The good luck of twenty-year-old Spike Borley also ended over Keishu Airfield. As Borley pulled out of one of his strafing runs over Formosa, 2,000 feet above the island, an antiaircraft shell, estimated to be of 40mm size, slammed his F6F. His cockpit filled with smoke, and he was aware of a sharp pain in his left leg from shrapnel. His cockpit smelled like burning rubber.

Borley's belly tank caught fire, and he struggled to jettison it. He feared his plane might explode at any second. Finally, the tank dropped. But then his engine suddenly seized up and quit. The revolutions of his prop caused considerable vibration. Borley turned his fuel off, pulled the mixture back to idle cutoff, and switched off the mags. In his last radio call to wingman George Pigman, Spike reported that he had downed two enemy fighters.

Borley was making about 300 knots when hit. His only hope was to reach the open ocean before his powerless Hellcat dropped onto the enemy island. His plane finally stalled out over the coast at about 90 knots at thirty feet of altitude. It hit hard, broke up, and sank in mere seconds. By the time Borley struggled free from his cockpit, the F6F was already submerged. He sputtered to the surface in time to see its tail going under the waves.

Afraid of being spotted by Japanese planes, Borley removed his parachute harness to avoid being pulled down and ditched his life raft. Partially inflating his Mae West life jacket, he bobbed in the chop while air strikes continued a short distance away. Pigman buzzed his position but was soon forced to move on. "Shrapnel from all the antiaircraft guns ashore was coming down all around me like a hail storm," Borley recalled. "I didn't know it at the time, but I was also in the middle of a minefield."[9]

With two of his Hellcats downed, Jim Rigg collected the balance of his flock and headed for their task group. Charlie Dorn remained over the life raft of Van Altena, circling his position until he was certain his division leader was properly reported. But the ensign was critically low on fuel. About twenty miles out from *Essex*, Dorn's fuel gave out, and he made a water landing.

Several F6Fs circled Dorn as long as they could. Once word was received that a task force destroyer was underway to effect a rescue, they were forced to move out. But Dorn's life raft was never found. Rigg's sweep returned to base having scored well, but three precious F6Fs had been lost. One pilot was not recovered, and the lives of two other VF-15 veterans— now bobbing in rafts near Formosa—remained in jeopardy.

Aside from these losses, the early *Essex-Lexington* sweep had been very effective. For its part, VF-19 claimed 27 kills and VF-15 added another 22.5 kills. Commander Pedro Winters, the *Lexington* CAG flying as an observer with VF-19, shot down two Zekes and reached ace status with six kills now to his credit. Winters's command F6F, named *Hangar Lilly*, returned with forty-seven holes and was pushed overboard.

DAVE MCCAMPBELL'S DIVISION was the only early *Essex* VF group to remain over Formosa. As strike coordinator, he circled until the first mixed-squadron strike group arrived at the target area at 0745.

Flying with warplanes from *Lexington* and *Langley*, the *Essex* bunch numbered eight Hellcats, ten dive-bombers, and eight torpedo planes. Ted Overton led the two VF-15 divisions, most armed with five-inch rockets. They found the skies over the enemy island void of Japanese opponents. The *Essex* group was assigned to hit Kobi Field, but heavy fog made its location a challenge. The approach was made over mountains. Low stratus clouds just after sunrise caused bothersome glare, but the pilots saw more than they expected on Formosa. Whereas intelligence had briefed them on as many as four enemy airfields, they saw approximately fifteen airstrips. Kobi Airfield was located with some difficulty, but it was loaded with twin-engine medium bombers, mostly in revetments.

Wary of enemy interception, Overton allowed his fighters only one strafing pass ahead of the bombers. Air Group Fifteen wrecked hangars and buildings on the south side of the airfield, and VF-15 claimed at least a dozen aircraft wrecked on the ground.

Three VF-15 pilots had been launched at dawn for long search missions off the east coast of Formosa, each in company with a VB-15 Helldiver. At 0813, fighter-bomber pilot Kent Lee's team was 150 miles out from *Essex* on their first search leg. A 1,000 feet above the wave tops, Lee tallyhoed a large twin-engine bomber up at Angels 4. He hand-signaled to his Helldiver companion, Lieutenant (jg) Dave Hall, and said, "Let's catch that Betty."[10]

Hall and Lee turned to give chase at more than 170 knots. Lee pulled ahead of Hall, chased the Betty through a cloud bank, and opened up with his guns on the bomber's right side. "I let all six go, and hit him in the starboard wing root," said Lee. The large bomber hit the waves with a big flash of fire, followed by black smoke. Lee and Hall circled the wreckage once before resuming their search. "The adrenaline was flowing freely," Lee recalled of his first kill as a new fighter pilot. His former VB-15 buddy Hall was just as excited.[11]

Ensign Merwin Frazelle, flying some distance away with a different *Essex* search team, spotted a Nell around 0940. A single burst from Frazelle's guns caused the Nell to shudder violently, nose over, and burst into flames just before it crashed into the ocean.

—————

SPIKE BORLEY COULD see the air strikes continuing against Formosa. Forced into the ocean an hour earlier, he was drifting in his Mae West life jacket, having discarded his life raft shortly after his Hellcat sank. Soon he realized that the prevailing currents had carried him to within two miles of the beach.

Fearing capture by the Japanese, Borley began swimming. *The farther from shore I can get, the better my odds of being rescued*, he reasoned. When he paused a short while later, he was alarmed to see a sampan underway from the nearby harbor moving toward him. For a while, it stayed some distance away. He assumed that Chinese fishermen were on board, but Borley knew that they would likely take the chance to retrieve an American aviator to please the Japanese who occupied the area.

About an hour after first spotting them, Borley saw the sampan drawing closer to him. In hopes of reducing his profile, the ensign released some air from his Mae West. Minutes later the sampan got to within ten yards of his position. Borley pulled his .38 revolver from his vest, wondering if exposure to salt water had already ruined it.

But his weapon fired. His first shot knocked one man out of the boat. He fired three more times, and a second man also fell overboard. "I don't know whether I hit him or not, but it sure tipped him overboard and he capsized the boat as he went over," Borley recalled. Borley saw no more movement, and the little sailing vessel posed no further threat to him.[12]

Throughout the day, several other small craft made attempts to head out toward him. He continued swimming hard to put more distance between him and the shore. Fortunately, the Japanese searching for American survivors remained close to shore, and he was not spotted. Sometime around midmorning a Hellcat spotted him. It circled twice, acknowledging his waving by dipping its wings.

Okay, I've been spotted, he thought. *A floatplane or lifeguard submarine will come for me soon.*

As the morning hours moved toward midday, Borley and John Van Altena each bobbed in the ocean, miles from Formosa. Both pilots hoped a lifeguard vessel would reach them before the Japanese did.

HIGH ABOVE THE downed aviators, CAG Dave McCampbell was still flying as strike coordinator over Formosa at 1000 hours when the second *Essex* strike group arrived. Launched nearly two hours prior, it consisted of eleven fighters, ten dive-bombers, and eight Avengers. Lieutenant George Crittenden headed the VF-15 contingent, with most of his F6Fs carrying a five-hundred-pound bomb each.

Near the Pescadores Islands, McCampbell had spotted Japanese ships. He directed some of the fighters to make strafing runs on a nearby airfield, but the majority of the TG 38.3 warplanes from *Essex*, *Lexington*, and *Langley* were ordered to attack the shipping targets. Crittenden, Jack Symmes, and Swede Thompson claimed a bomb hit on one small freighter. Two near misses near the stern and multiple strafing runs left the merchantman dead in the water. Symmes and his wingman, Bob Stime, made passes on another freighter and a small patrol craft.

Air Group Fifteen's squadrons believed they left several small vessels destroyed, along with two merchant ships sunk and several minesweepers and destroyer escorts damaged. Ed Mellon was credited with a damaging bomb hit on a warship, leaving it down by the stern, trailing oil. As the attacks wrapped up, Lieutenant Commander VeeGee Lambert called for his TBMs to return to the south over one of the islands.

But the Air Group Fifteen planes were caught in heavy Japanese antiaircraft cross fire as they retired. The Avenger flown by Ensign Houston Ray Copeland was struck in the engine, and three of his cylinders were blown off. Copeland's crippled Avenger remained airborne only as far as the southern tip of Formosa before he was forced to make a water landing. He and his two enlisted men—ARM2c Russell J. Bradley and AMM2c William C. Poppel—scrambled into the ocean as the remainder of their air group turned for home.

Lieutenants (jg) Symmes and Ed Mellon remained behind to circle their downed comrades. Symmes circled low and dropped his own life raft, which Copeland and his TBM crew climbed into. But they were quickly spotted by the crew of a nearby small Japanese merchant ship, and it changed course to capture them. Symmes made multiple strafing runs, causing the small vessel to burst into flames and begin sinking. Leaving Mellon to circle the downed VT-15 aviators, Symmes flew out to sea until he made visual and radio contact with the U.S. lifeguard submarine.

Symmes returned to the area of Copeland's life raft and made firing passes on another enemy surface craft. By the time he and Mellon finally headed for base, they were desperately low on fuel. The VF-15 pilots were forced to pancake (quickly land) on the nearest CVL to refuel before returning to *Essex*.

THE EFFORTS OF Jack Symmes proved to be lifesaving. His radio calls for help were acknowledged by Bob Ward's USS *Sailfish*. His crew had been the first U.S. submariners to successfully sink a Japanese aircraft carrier, *Chuyo*, in December 1943, but their work this day was focused on recovering TF 38 aviators.

Bill Dillon, a young radioman and radar operator serving on *Sailfish*, was tasked with monitoring the lifeguard radio waves off Formosa. "Everyone on the circuit was talking at the same time," Dillon later related. "It was difficult to know who was in trouble and who was not. The one in trouble had to shout louder than the rest." While Dillon communicated with the carrier pilots, Ward put a rescue party topside as *Sailfish* raced to save lives.[13]

Beginning at 1235, *Sailfish* pulled her first two aviators on board, a VB-20 Helldiver crew from *Enterprise*. Twenty minutes later, Ward's men saved a VF-14 *Wasp* Hellcat pilot before receiving the frantic calls from Symmes from the *Essex* fighter squadron. At 1314, *Sailfish* eased up alongside the life raft containing Copeland, Bradley, and Poppel. Within forty minutes, the busy submarine crew had also recovered a downed VB-20 Helldiver crew. Bob Ward's gunners fought off Japanese vessels that threatened their work. By late afternoon they had pulled aboard another *Wasp* Hellcat pilot and a downed VB-14 *Wasp* Helldiver crew.

By 1435, *Sailfish* had successfully saved six pilots and five enlisted aviators from Task Force 38. Commander Ward and radioman Dillon continued to receive frantic calls about another downed *Essex* fighter pilot. But his position was at least twenty miles distant from *Sailfish*. Ward duly remained surfaced and proceeded toward that position through the night, hoping the VF-15 aviator could be saved the following morning.

THE THIRD *ESSEX* strike force to work over Formosa arrived while *Sailfish* was engaged in making her rescues. George Duncan, leading the fighter group, found no Japanese planes to fight. His Hellcats strafed and fired rockets at buildings and planes parked near Rokko Airfield No. 1 on Formosa after their primary objective was found to be socked in by weather.

By 1400, *Essex* had sent forth its final strike group. Skipper Jim Rigg had four F6F divisions to cover their bombers, with *Lexington* CAG Pedro Winters serving as strike coordinator. Roy Nall circled in his photo Hellcat, capturing images of the attacks. Rigg and his divisions dropped five-hundred-pound bombs and strafed parked planes on Nikosho Airfield. "These aircraft were old biplanes either used for training or reconnaissance," Rigg reported. "A few appeared to be dummies and did not burn."[14]

Commander Winter then directed his pilots and those from *Essex* to attack small merchant ships and a cluster of fishing trawlers just offshore. Several were left burning and dead in the water. By about 1600 the TG 38.3 strikers were ordered to rendezvous and head back for their carriers.

More than two miles off the coast of Formosa, Ensign Spike Borley was still riding the swells in his bright yellow Mae West. The Japanese were aware of his presence. In the afternoon a Japanese patrol boat had ventured out of the harbor in his direction, but it was turned back by a division of strafing Hellcats. Hoping to catch their attention, Borley popped his dye marker container, allowing the chemical contents to stain the water around him.

It worked. The Hellcat division leader circled low and dropped his landing gear to cut his speed. The pilot opened his canopy and tossed down his own life raft. Borley swam to it, inflated the raft, and climbed inside. By the time the reddish tints of sunset began dipping below the horizon, the carrier planes had long since departed. Borley set to his oars and began paddling farther out to sea.

Separated by about twenty miles, VF-15's Ensign Borley and Lieutenant (jg) Van Altena each faced a lonely evening at sea near Formosa.

SEVENTEEN

SILENT SERVICE SURVIVORS

October 13, 1944
Off Formosa

Jim Rigg and fifteen of his pilots were roused from their staterooms during the early hours of October 13. Pulling khaki coverall flight suits over their uniforms, the VF-15 aviators downed coffee and a quick breakfast before heading to their ready room.

During the briefing, Commander Rigg reminded his men that three of their comrades had been lost the previous day near Formosa. All were seen to make safe water landings, two near the enemy island and one closer to the task group. Hope remained for someone spotting them again, but for the moment ACIO Bob McReynolds proceeded with the briefing on the main mission at hand. Coupled with a similar force from *Lexington*, *Essex* was to launch a predawn fighter sweep over northwestern Formosa to investigate other enemy airfields; that sweep would be coupled with a similar force from *Lexington*.

By 0515, Rigg and his sweep were making rendezvous above the carriers before daybreak. Two hours later they found such a heavy haze over Formosa that he moved them on to another target, and they found fair visibility over the airfield at Taien. Multiple strafing runs were made on twin-engine bombers, but their failure to burn indicated that alert Japanese ground crews had degassed the planes overnight. Three Oscars were tallyhoed, but in each case the enemy pilots chose to flee for cloud cover rather than fight.

Ted Sherman waited until nearly 0830 to send off his first deckload strikes from *Essex*, *Lexington*, and *Princeton*. Commander McCampbell took three divisions to cover the bombers, whose objective was to hit shipping and installations at the Ansan Naval Base in the Pescadores Islands. The 150-mile journey was completed by 1000, whereupon McCampbell remained aloft to direct the efforts of his planes through the prevailing poor weather conditions.

Lieutenants Bert Morris and John Collins led their divisions down to bomb a graving dock at the naval base. Damage assessment was difficult to ascertain in the poor visibility, although one VF-15 pilot's five-hundred-pound bomb was listed as a near miss. Collins and his wingman skip bombed their weapons toward a small destroyer escort and followed through with strafing runs. The VB-15 pilots bombed installations at Ansan, destroying a number of buildings. But the Helldiver piloted by Lieutenant (jg) Earl Mallette was hit by AA fire and was seen to make a forced landing close offshore. Neither Mallette nor his gunner survived.

SPIKE BORLEY WAS still drifting off Formosa on the morning of October 13. Shortly after daybreak, he heard engines and saw the *Lexington-Essex* fighter sweep pass above him. His overnight rowing had done little good. "Now the current was working against me, carrying me along the coast," he recalled.[1] Ensign Borley held out hope that a lifeguard submarine or a Dumbo flying boat would soon appear. But the morning hours passed quietly for him.

Miles from his location, luck was in store for one of his squadron mates, fighter-bomber division leader John Van Altena.

Commander Bob Ward's submarine *Sailfish* had remained on the surface through the night, chewing up the miles toward the last reported position of the downed *Essex* fighter pilot. Radioman Bill Dillon and his gang eagerly monitored the fighter circuit, and by 0929 they had word from a Task Force 38 warplane that a rubber boat had been spotted to the north. *Sailfish* raced for the location and had Van Altena's yellow raft in sight within fifteen minutes. Ward's rescue party moved out on deck, and torpedoman Ray Bunt, an expert swimmer and former lifeguard captain, went over the side to help the VF-15 pilot onto his submarine.

Skipper Ward, observing the procedure from the bridge, was amused.

He saw that Lieutenant (jg) Van Altena had carefully tied his knife, compass, and other survival gear to the raft to avoid losing them. He had set sail for China and was seen to be casually smoking his pipe as *Sailfish* nudged alongside his raft. But Van Altena's cool composure crumbled as he was escorted up to the bridge to meet the sub skipper who had dared to stay surfaced to rescue him. "He was still dry, with pipe in hand, and he had been in the boat for a day or two," Ward recalled. "He broke down and cried."[2]

Helped below, Van Altena was treated for skin exposure by the *Sailfish* pharmacist's mate. His war cruise on *Essex* was over, and he was now resigned to a bunk for the near future until his salvage vessel could find a port to off-load him in. Van Altena was warmly greeted by three fellow Air Group Fifteen survivors, Houston Copeland's Avenger crew, who had been rescued by *Sailfish* the previous day off Formosa.

ESSEX SENT TWO more strike groups against Formosa. The first, launched at 0932, had a special task. Four of the Avengers carried Mark 13 aerial torpedoes to be used to bust a concrete dam near some power plants northeast of Lake Jitsugetsutan.

Due to foul weather, the combined *Essex-Lexington* force missed the big lake and instead found a smaller lake a short distance away. But the torpedoes did not have sufficient runs to properly arm. Two hit the dam and failed to explode. Jack Symmes and two wingmen dropped their depth bombs on the dam but achieved only questionable results. After bombing and strafing other facilities in the area, the luckless flight headed for home.

Hours later, a final *Essex* fighter sweep was ordered to reconnoiter Miyako Shima and Ishigaki Shima in the southern Nansei Shoto chain near Okinawa. George Duncan led the flight of ten VF-15 Hellcats in company with a division of F6Fs from *USS Cabot* (CVL-28).

Ensign Dick Davis eagerly climbed into his Hellcat at 1300. He was flying in Bert Morris's division, in company with the second section of Lieutenant (jg) Doyle Bare and Ensign Ken Flinn. "We were supposed to go up and find out where the Japanese were hiding their airplanes," Davis recalled. "They were always getting more airplanes from somewhere, and we figured they were using these islands as a staging place."[3]

Around 1445, Duncan's flight arrived over Miyako Shima, about two hundred miles east of Formosa. His fighters strafed parked aircraft but they were apparently degassed, as they failed to burn. In the process of their runs, Duncan and Morris's pilots observed several previously unreported airfields nearby. One was an X-shaped airdrome with good facilities and many revetments. Located about two miles southwest of Riarara, this field had considerable construction work underway.

Japanese workmen scattered as Hellcats roared in to strafe their vehicles. "Got a jeep and one cow," Duz Twelves wrote in his diary. Other F6Fs blasted trucks and fuel drums. The *Essex* flight worked over two other airfields before moving to Ishigaki Shima, where two airfields were found along the southern coast of the island. Several small boats were strafed off the coast, but nearby Iriomote Shima could not be attacked, as it was "closed in" by heavy weather.

The VF-15 pilots returned to the more important fields on Miyako Shima to continue shooting up the bases. "Then we got sloppy," recalled Davis. "We were strafing around, and while we were doing that, the Japanese boys finally managed to get to their guns." Several F6Fs were struck by 13.7-caliber bullets and antiaircraft fragments. "I got shot up real good," said Davis. "They shot off my aileron and most of my right horizontal stabilizer."[4]

Davis feared he might have to make a forced landing. He slowed his airspeed and fought to gain control of his fighter. "I need a little help," he called over the radio. "Will someone come over and get on my wing and help me back?"

A few minutes later he was joined by Bert Morris and Doyle Bare. But Bare's wingman, Ken Flinn, was missing. During one of his strafing runs over Miyako, Japanese gunners bore-sighted his F6F and hit it solidly. Flinn began losing altitude immediately and headed for the coast. He barely made it offshore before his Hellcat skipped into the shallow water within sight of the airfield he had been attacking. The water there was only about six feet deep. Flinn scrambled out onto his wing and waved to his comrades.

Morris reported Ensign Flinn's coordinates, but he was heartbroken by the reply from Task Force 38. Rescue operations were not feasible, as sea conditions were too rough to attempt a floatplane rescue off the Japanese island. "The possibility of escaping capture as POW was virtually out of the question," Duncan later reported.[5]

Davis, still struggling to control his own crippled F6F, made another circle above his division mate with Morris and Bare. "We had to leave because we were running low on fuel, and it was starting to get dark," he recalled. "We didn't feel very good, because everybody liked Flinn." En route back to the task group, Davis had to slow his Hellcat to about 90 knots due to the loss of an aileron. It was after 1700 when he finally made the cut and landed on his own carrier.

Ken Flinn was Fighting Fifteen's only loss of the day. As expected, he was surrounded by Japanese soldiers soon after his fellow fighter pilots were forced to head for home. A sizable man, Flinn was photographed in his flight khakis standing alongside his smaller-sized enemy captors. Interrogated for some time, he was later moved to mainland Japan, to the secret interrogation camp called Ofuna. Treatment for captured American aviators and submariners was particularly brutal, and Ensign Flinn suffered greatly during the next nine months of captivity.

As Task Force 38 recovered its strike groups at twilight on October 13, Japanese aircraft launched from Formosa moved in. In Vice Admiral John McCain's TG 38.1, the heavy cruiser USS *Canberra* (CA-70) suffered twenty-three sailors killed from a torpedo hit from a Jill. *Canberra* lost power and had to be taken under tow by another cruiser. Task force gunners and CAP pilots downed many Betty bombers, but another torpedo bomber slipped in close enough to launch a torpedo at the carrier USS *Franklin* (CV-13).

The "war fish" passed under *Franklin*'s fantail, and AA fire set the Jill afire. The Japanese pilot dived toward the carrier and slammed into the flight deck, causing only minor topside damage before the wreckage slid off into the sea. Duz Twelves and other pilots who watched from the *Essex* catwalk saw a spectacular fireworks show and countless red tracers.

Twelves was pleased to see two enemy aircraft tumble from the sky in flames.[6]

Chet Owens, plane captain for Dave McCampbell, was in the shower when the torpedo attack commenced on his task group. Hearing the battle stations gong, he raced to a nearby porthole across from the shower. "I stood there, naked, looking out at four approaching Japanese torpedo planes," Owens recalled. He braced himself for a torpedo hit, but their drops did not impact *Essex*. When Commander McCampbell landed back on board, Owens joked with him, "If you can't protect me any better than that, you'll have to put up with a smelly plane captain the rest of our combat tour!"[7]

Admiral Halsey had planned to retire from the Formosa area after the day's strikes, but the crippled *Canberra* changed things. His staff ordered a limited number of carrier air strikes again for the following morning, plus a healthy umbrella of Hellcat cover to fend off a repeat performance of Japanese aerial assaults on his flattops. In addition, the Army Air Force sent a raid of 109 B-29 bombers from Chinese airfields to help plaster the Takao, Formosa, area.[8]

Daybreak on October 14 found Spike Borley of VF-15 still adrift in his life raft. The previous afternoon he had inventoried his emergency supplies and decided to use as little of his can of water as possible. To pass the time, he utilized his fishing line from his survival kit, trailing it over the side of his yellow raft. But the fish did not cooperate. His stomach ached with hunger by the following morning, but his spirits were still high.

Although the seas were growing stronger, Borley had slept well overnight due to sheer exhaustion. He had been carried farther away from shore by the prevailing currents, out into the China Sea. He was pleased to see Army B-29s moving over him to hit Formosa during the day, but their extreme altitude negated any chance of him being spotted. The winds increased that afternoon and the seas became heavy. By the end of his third day adrift, Borley worried that a storm was brewing.[9]

Miles from his position, Dave McCampbell had led the early-morning *Essex* strike force against Formosa on October 14. His Hellcats made strafing-and-rocket runs against several airfields, destroying parked planes. But enemy aerial opposition was not encountered. Admiral Toyoda had chosen to send his available strike planes out against Halsey's carriers again.

Fighters from other TF 38 carriers intercepted various bandits throughout the morning while the crippled cruiser *Canberra* was being towed away from Formosa. From *Essex*, Lieutenant John Strane was launched at 0841 with a dozen VF-15 Hellcats for task force CAP duty. Shortly before 1100, Strane's divisions were vectored to intercept a bogey seen on radar to be approaching fast.

It proved to be an Oscar fighter, low on the water and under pursuit by a division of VF-19 fighters from *Lexington*. "Being the one to spot him and the one to give him tally-ho gave me the privilege of shooting at him first," recalled Ensign Jim Mooney. He turned inside his division mates and maneuvered onto the Oscar's tail. At 2,300 rpm and making 250 knots, he opened up with his four inboard guns at only fifty feet altitude. The Oscar flamed and glided steadily down until it hit the ocean. "He met his ancestors in a real hurry," Mooney recalled.[10]

The only other action for VF-15 on October 14 came that afternoon. Lieutenant (jg) Baynard Milton and nine other pilots launched around 1230, each pair of Hellcats coupled with a VB-15 Helldiver crew to conduct searches over three-hundred-mile sectors. Three of the teams found nothing of interest, but two groups encountered Japanese bandits.

First to spot prey, at 1411, was the team of Lieutenant (jg) Norm Berree, wingman Dusty Craig, and dive-bomber pilot Lieutenant (jg) Scott Matthews. They tallyhoed a lone Judy at 2,000 feet and gave chase. Closing from astern, Berree and Craig combined firing to knock the mottled brown plane in the water. Fifteen minutes later the team spotted a Fran on a converging course at their same altitude. As the Fran entered a circle, Berree and Craig turned inside. Berree's guns failed to fire but Craig scored damaging hits on its engine. Matthews also opened fire, getting 20mm hits. Smoking in both engines, the Fran headed west. Although making 250 knots, the F6Fs could not keep up. It disappeared, leaving a trail of smoke in its wake. "He went into the clouds smoking," recalled Craig. "I probably got him, but I didn't get credit for him."[11]

Around the same time, another *Essex* search trio tallyhoed a lone Judy, apparently on anti-submarine patrol, about two hundred feet above the waves. Gunning their throttles, Lieutenant (jg) Milton and Ensign George Pigman left their VB-15 companion, Lieutenant (jg) Don McCutcheon, behind for the moment. Milton and Pigman each landed hits until the smoking Judy was seen to crash into the ocean.

In a repeat performance of the previous evening, Formosa-based Japanese aircraft assaulted Halsey's carriers near dusk. Frans attacked Admiral McCain's task group, and the cruiser USS *Houston* (CL-81) was rendered powerless by a torpedo hit in her starboard side. The cruiser USS *Boston* (CA-69) took *Houston* under tow, leaving Bull Halsey with the agonizing decision of scuttling two of his cruisers or using some of TF 38's carriers to cover their salvage attempts. Three cruisers and eight destroyers, officially designated Task Force 30.3, were detached to tow the crippled ships and became known as "CripDiv 1."[12]

Admiral Toyoda's Formosa-based aircraft continued to harass CripDiv 1, with the largest strike effort coming in the early afternoon of October 15. Fortunately, Halsey had detached the light carriers *Cowpens* and *Cabot* toward the area in company with six supporting warships. Their Hellcat squadrons claimed more than forty raiders shot down, but one Fran delivered a second torpedo hit to the cruiser *Houston*. A jubilant Radio Tokyo put out enough propaganda reports that it was evident the Japanese believed CripDiv 1 to be the last floating remnants of Task Force 38. Admiral Halsey therefore detached Ted Sherman's TG 38.3 carriers to move between his crippled cruisers and Japan, hoping to use the newly renamed "BaitDiv 1" as a lure to bring out heavy warships from the Japanese fleet.[13]

SPIKE BORLEY WAS growing weaker. He had no knowledge of the chess match playing out at sea between the crippled American warships and Toyoda's air force. His fight was now against Mother Nature and the China Sea.

His raft was riding large swells, believed by Borley to be the outer fringes of a typhoon. He was unable to sleep, fearing his boat would capsize. That night his raft did flip over in the rough seas. Although his gear had been lashed down, Borley lost his can of water, his extra dye markers, his sailcloth, and other supplies by the time he managed to right his little boat. "All I had left was my rubber boat and my gun and my knife," he recalled.[14]

Throughout the night, he rode out the worst of the storm. He was knocked out of the raft several times but managed to climb back in each time. His little yellow boat rose high on the swells, sometimes battered by another wave coming from the other side. "I went through the eye of the typhoon that night, thirty minutes of calm and then into the wind and waves on the other side," he later stated. The storm carried him into the middle of the Formosa Strait, somewhere between Formosa and the mainland of China.[15]

By October 15—his fourth day adrift—Borley was starving. He was suddenly startled by a small flying fish that landed right in his boat. Deciding to give it a try, he pulled off the winged fins and attempted to eat the raw fish. "I took one bite and that was about as far as I could go," said Borley. "I wasn't that hungry yet."[16]

As the storm's intensity ebbed, the VF-15 ensign managed a little rest the following night. By the morning of October 16, Borley was beginning to hallucinate from the effects of dehydration, hunger, ingested salt water, and lack of sleep. He feared being captured by a Japanese ship, and at one point his confused mind almost got the better of him. "In the middle of these hallucinations, I took out my gun and decided to kill myself," he remembered. "I put the gun to my head, and then thought that it had been in the water and might misfire."[17]

Borley lowered his .38 to the water and squeezed the trigger to test-fire his weapon. It worked. The sound of the shot brought him back to reality, and he decided not to commit suicide.

By afternoon of his fifth day at sea, Borley sighted a dark shape on the horizon. As it slowly approached, he assumed it might be a Japanese I-boat. He pulled out his .38 again, put it in his right hand, and clutched his hunting knife in his left hand. But his luck had finally changed. The approaching vessel was the submarine USS *Sawfish* (SS-276), which was patrolling on lifeguard duty near Formosa for an afternoon B-29 strike on the island.[18]

At 1425 on October 16, *Sawfish*'s starboard lookout spotted a man in a one-person rubber boat. Commander Alan Banister changed course and approached. "We could not determine whether he was a Nip or one of our own," Banister wrote. "He was very dark, with a short haircut that made him look very much like a Nip. He did not show very much enthusiasm as we approached." The dark-skinned man was clutching a knife in one hand and a pistol in the other. Banister sent his gunner's mate up on the bow with a carbine trained on Borley.[19]

Borley was greatly relieved to hear an American voice command, "Put down that gun!"

He tossed down his .38 and weakly raised his arms. But skipper Banister remained unconvinced whether the man was Japanese or American. Borley's hair, shaved off during the recent equator-crossing ceremonies on *Essex*, had still not grown out. "His face was badly sunburned and swollen, but his equipment appeared to be good U.S.," Banister logged. Although a rope ladder was draped over *Sawfish*'s side, Borley was too weak to move after 4.5 days in his cramped raft.

He was helped on board by a pair of sailors who then destroyed his yellow boat with a knife. "I croaked I was American, and pulled out my dog tags," Borley recalled. Commander Banister had him taken below for treatment by *Sawfish*'s pharmacist's mate for his severe sunburn and dehydration.

Banister's boat sent word that evening of Ensign Borley's rescue. For the time being, the new ace was now a submarine passenger, resigned to riding out the war patrol until *Sawfish* could off-load him.

Several days later, on the afternoon of October 23, *Sawfish* attacked a Japanese merchant ship convoy, and four torpedo explosions were heard as Banister took her deep.[20] Japanese escorts raced in to deliver a depth charge attack during the next half hour. For the veteran submariners, the explosions were not considered very close. But the jarring of the submerged vessel and the sound of enemy screws churning overhead while he lay sweating in silence were terrifying for Spike Borley. "I was sure I was finally going to die after surviving being shot down and a typhoon," he recalled.[21]

Banister returned to the surface three hours later and set off in pursuit of the convoy. *Sawfish* fired her last five torpedoes and was rewarded with another depth charging. *Sawfish* and other submarines in the area were called upon by Vice Admiral Charles Lockwood on October 26 to scour the seas for aviators downed during heavy fighting in Leyte Gulf the previous afternoon. During the next several days they found only floating debris and oil patches. On October 29, Ensign Borley was called to the bridge to help identify a distant raft with binoculars, but it was empty.

Sawfish and the submarine USS *Drum* (SS-228) headed toward Majuro that evening to refuel. Borley, sufficiently recovered from his sunburn and shrapnel wounds, was up and about, ready to contribute to standing watches in the control room. "Our aviator guest was back to battery and full of fight, so put him on the Junior Officer watch list," Banister noted in his patrol report.[22]

After more than three weeks of submarine life, Borley was happy to finally see land again on November 8 when *Sawfish* entered Majuro Harbor. John Van Altena, rescued three days prior to Borley, spent less time in the Silent Service than his comrade. Due to radio equipment breakdowns, Bob Ward's *Sailfish* was forced to proceed to newly captured Saipan Harbor for repairs. Van Altena went ashore with the other eleven rescued aviators. Although his journey back to *Essex*, and that of Spike Borley, would take many more weeks, the VF-15 pilots had plenty of submarine stories ready to share with their squadron mates.

EIGHTEEN

"LOOKS LIKE I'VE SHOT MY BOLT"

October 16, 1944

The last great carrier battle of World War II was brewing.

The Formosa strikes were complete, and Rear Admiral Ted Sherman's TG 38.3 was helping to clear the area. Fighting Fifteen flew CAP duty over the crippled cruisers *Houston* and *Canberra* on October 16 but saw no enemy attacks. Over the next two days, CripDiv 1 inched toward safety at Ulithi, while Admiral Bull Halsey began his planning for direct support of the next major Allied initiative, the occupation of Leyte in the Philippines.

The following day, Sherman sent scout groups out to search for the Japanese fleet, but their efforts were in vain. On a more positive note, Duz Twelves logged on October 19: "Received word that Borley has been rescued by a sub." Twelves flew a three-hundred-mile search the following day, sighting only a Japanese submarine that crash-dived before he and his VB-15 companion could attack.[1]

Operations in the Philippines were centered around Halsey's Third Fleet, with Vice Admiral Pete Mitscher's TF 38 as its main component. On October 20, as American troops began landing on Leyte, Ted Sherman's TG 38.3 made rendezvous with Rear Admiral Gerry Bogan's TG 38.2 off Luzon. Their directive was to intercept any naval forces sent to interrupt the Leyte landings, while two other Task Force 38 groups—those of John McCain and Ralph E. Davison—stood by off Leyte to support the efforts of light carrier groups protecting the ground offensive.

McCain's and Davison's carrier air groups were assigned to make strikes on Japanese airfields on Cebu, Negros, Panay, and northern Mindanao. Expecting his enemy to make attacks on the invasion ships off Leyte, Halsey planned to help keep the air clear over Luzon by dispatching Sherman's and Bogan's planes against airfields in the Visayas. American submarines were patrolling the Philippines area, but the Japanese Mobile Fleet had yet to show itself. For the time being, Air Group Fifteen was briefed for another round of island strikes set for the following morning.

The ace race was still a hot topic among the fleet. As of October 10, Major Dick Bong had increased his kill record to thirty victories for the Army Air Corps. Meanwhile, Commander Dave McCampbell's tally still rested at nineteen kills, but the impending Leyte Gulf action afforded him the chance to finally draw closer to Bong.

Weeks had passed since McCampbell's last victory, and he was becoming disgusted with his lack of action. During his spare time, he continued to write to both Minsi Wiener and Jill Heliker. In one of his October letters to Jill, the *Essex* CAG confided, "I'm beginning to think I'll never see a Jap plane again. It looks like I've shot my bolt."[2]

October 21, 1944

Still under orders from Rear Admiral Sherman not to actively engage enemy aircraft unless he was absolutely required to do so to defend his fellow pilots, McCampbell was first off the deck minutes before 0600. His eleven Hellcats, armed only with bullets, were to make a sweep over Mindoro Island and the northern Visayas ahead of the first *Essex* strike mission.

He led his divisions toward San Jose Field, with only scattered clouds dotting the horizon at 8,000 feet. Flying above this cover at Angels 10, McCampbell spotted a Japanese freighter swinging at anchor near the northern tip of Romblon Island. He duly relayed the contact back to his trailing strike group and continued on to snoop out San Jose Field. The island's air facilities appeared to be nonoperational. McCampbell continued toward Tablas Island, where an enemy airfield was reported to be in operation.

At 0730, while scouring this area, the CAG division was jumped by a

pair of Nate fighters. Since this was clearly a case of self-defense, Mc-
Campbell had no second thoughts. He and his wingman, Roy Rushing,
immediately placed the leading Nate under fire. Damaging hits were
scored in both wings and fuselage, but the Nate did not burn until Mc-
Campbell followed him through a split S and finished him up from the
"saddle" position. He flamed and crashed in the water. Rushing got in
damaging bursts to the second Nate, leaving it smoking as it fled the scene.

McCampbell next tallyhoed a Dinah above his division. Explaining to
the admiral later whether this target was attacked purely in self-defense
never crossed Dashing Dave's mind: a twelve-minute tail chase ensued.
Only after the speedy plane made a series of zooms was the CAG division
able to close the distance and altitude on him. With his belly tank, Dashing Dave was still able to make 260 knots, his superior F6F-5 slowly pulling away from Rushing's F6F-3. One long burst from McCampbell started
both engines smoking and created fires in the right wing and fuselage.
"He nosed over in a steep glide and about 25 seconds later exploded in a
sheet of flame," CAG related. Three seconds before the explosion, a parachute blossomed out and the occupant was seen to land about fifteen miles
from the nearest land.[3]

With these two kills, Dave McCampbell's score had reached twenty-
one victories. He also now held the honor of becoming the U.S. Navy's
first fighter pilot to become a quadruple ace.

WHILE MCCAMPBELL AND Rushing engaged these aircraft near Tablas,
CAG sent his second and third combat teams on to conduct their scheduled sweep at San Jose Field. There, Lieutenant George Crittenden and his
wingman, Texan Al Slack, tallyhoed a Sally. Critt winged both engines
with his first pass, but the Japanese plane headed for the clouds as Critt
was forced to switch fuel tanks during the fight. Slack followed through,
blasting its wing roots. The Mitsubishi heavy bomber headed for the ocean
in flames. Back on *Essex*, Slack would rightfully claim half credit for the
kill, although he would later wish he had given full credit to his section
leader. (Crittenden would end the war with 4.5 kills, just a half kill shy of
becoming an ace.)[4]

Slack then tallyhoed a Nate at about 10,000 feet and sent it flaming into the sea within minutes. Ensign Dusty Craig, flying the tail-end Charlie position for the combat team, then looked over and spotted a Dinah going under him on an opposite course.

"Bogey, six o'clock down!" Craig called.[5]

"Go get it!" Crittenden radioed.

Craig pulled off to give chase, charging his guns as he swept in. "I pulled the trigger and I hit him solid," he remembered. His first bursts set the Dinah's port engine on fire. Craig closed, and his next burst caused the Dinah to turn over and plunge toward the water, where it exploded fifty feet before hitting.

McCampbell regrouped his divisions and extended their search to include other reported airfields. The airfield at Bulan, on southern Luzon, proved to be the only one in full operation. During their return, the group strafed the freighter they had bypassed early in the mission and called attention to it for the first main strike group to finish off.

The main TG 38.3 strike force departed minutes behind McCampbell's sweep. Led by skipper Jim Rigg, the four VF-15 divisions strafed Legaspi Airfield in the Visayas, shooting up parked aircraft. Only two aerial combatants were encountered: a mottled brown Dinah downed by a *Lexington* Hellcat and another Dinah attacked by VF-15's Ensign Howard Smith.

The *Essex* dive-bombers worked over several freighters, claiming one as sunk. Before returning to base, Rigg led his F6Fs on strafing runs against the anchored freighter reported off Romblon Island by the CAG sweep. Twenty HVAR hits from fifty-eight rockets salvoed left the 3,000-ton merchant vessel burning heavily and in sinking condition.

Launching at 0924, George Duncan led four VF-15 divisions to attack Japanese airfields at Naga on southern Luzon. No aircraft were seen, but heavy doses of strafing and bombs were applied to revetments and barracks. Duz Twelves burned one parked aircraft on Legaspi Airfield and unloaded his five-hundred-pound bomb on a large warehouse found at his third target area. After additional fighter sweeps over other nearby islands, Rigg collected his combat teams and headed for base. Three Air Group Fifteen planes sported fresh bullet damage, but the group returned intact.

THE TOKYO STAFF of Admiral Soemu Toyoda, commander in chief of the Imperial Japanese Combined Fleet, were the architects of "Operation Sho-Go." Although an act of desperation at this point in the Pacific War, the operation was intended to stop the American advance toward the Japanese home islands. Defense of key island chains like the Ryukyus, and even key home islands like Kyushu, were given operational names. The defense of the Philippines, now under invasion by American troops, was designated "Sho-1."

Toyoda's Sho-1 plan called for the Combined Fleet to engage the U.S. Navy in a decisive showdown. A Northern Force, under Vice Admiral Jisaburo Ozawa, was underway, with plans to draw Admiral Halsey's Third Fleet up north into battle. With Task Force 38's carriers thus engaged, other Japanese naval forces could surround and annihilate the amphibious fleet and its fire support ships in Leyte Gulf. Vice Admiral Takeo Kurita's First Striking Force wielded formidable firepower. The newer battleships *Yamato* and *Musashi* moved in company with five older battleships, eleven heavy cruisers, two light cruisers, and nineteen destroyers.

Such a vast number of enemy warships advancing toward Leyte Gulf could hardly have been missed. But search flights from *Essex* and other carriers failed to locate Ozawa's carriers or Kurita's battleships during their long-ranging recon missions on October 23. The task of snooping out Toyoda's Sho-1 combatants fell to a scouting line of American submarines positioned near the Philippines.

First to contact Kurita's warships near the southern entrance to the Palawan Passage that morning were the submarines USS *Darter* (SS-227) and USS *Dace* (SS-247). After sending off radio contact reports, they attacked around 0630. *Darter* unleashed all ten of her bow and stern torpedoes, hitting the cruisers *Atago* and *Takao*. Admiral Kurita and his staff were rescued before his flagship, *Atago*, went down at 0653. *Takao* was left dead in the water, while *Dace* torpedoed and sank the cruiser *Maya*. Further attacks on Kurita's fleet became impossible during the overnight hours, when *Darter* ran solidly aground on a reef in the passage. *Dace* moved in to rescue the stranded *Darter* crew, putting both submarines out of further action. But, by knocking out three heavy cruisers and reporting Admiral Kurita's fleet, *Darter* and *Dace* had given Admiral Halsey the upper hand in preparing to meet the Combined Fleet in the Sibuyan Sea.

By noon on October 23, John McCain's TG 38.1 was en route to Ulithi to be rearmed and refueled. Ted Sherman's TG 38.3, Gerry Bogan's TG 38.2, and Ralph Davison's TG 38.4 were operating about 260 miles northeast of Samar. There was little activity on board *Essex* as she awaited results from her search teams. But the *Essex* aviators had heard scuttlebutt of the Japanese Combined Fleet approaching. During the overnight hours, the three Task Force 38 carrier groups approached their respective positions to launch dawn searches.

October 24 would be one of the biggest days in VF-15 history. Sherman's carriers would cover the west coast of Luzon, while Davison operated to the southward near Leyte Gulf and Bogan's carriers moved in close to San Bernardino Strait. The *Essex* flight deck was abuzz with activity long before dawn.

Commander McCampbell, under orders from Admiral Sherman to leave fighter sweeps to VF-15, remained on board ship while Jim Rigg led the morning mission to Manila Bay and nearby airfields. Near Cavite Point, Satan's Playmates made a mess of anchored enemy shipping. John Strane, Tom Hoey, and John Collins were credited with causing significant damage from their five-hundred-pound bombs. Rigg's fighter sweep found no aerial bandits, so they expended much of their brass on strafing a *Nagara*-class cruiser and destroyer found heading out of Manila Bay.

THE FIRST *ESSEX* fighters to engage enemy aircraft were those launched right behind Lieutenant Commander Rigg's sweep. Coupled with pairs of VB-15 Helldivers, fighter teams under George Duncan and Jack Symmes departed at dawn for long-range flights to snoop out the Combined Fleet near southwestern Luzon and the South China Sea approaches.

First to make contact at 0730 near Manila Bay was the team headed by Lieutenant (jg) Symmes. His group of four F6Fs and four SB2Cs was on its outbound leg, just north of Balesin Island. Ensign Jerry Lathrop, one of VF-15's new rookie pilots, tallyhoed a lone Jill and jettisoned his bomb. He and his section leader, Symmes, maneuvered for a stern bracket. Lathrop bored in, firing until the Jill burst into flames, did a wingover, and dived into the ocean.

About an hour later, on the cross leg of their search, Symmes found a trio of Japanese planes flying at low altitude between Cabra and Lubang Islands. The Japanese planes immediately broke up. With Lathrop on his wing, Symmes called to his second section—Lieutenants (jg) Ed Mellon and Bob Stime—to go after two fleeing Betty bombers. The third plane, an Irving fighter, was already turning in to challenge the American snooper team.

Still toting his five-hundred-pound bomb, Symmes could not match the turn of the Japanese fighter. He pickled (released) his bomb and shouted a warning to Lathrop. Minus his ordnance, Symmes was finally able to close the distance as the Irving dived violently to starboard in hopes of escaping. The Irving had reversed into a hard left turn before a one-second burst from Symmes's gun flamed its port engine and sent the agile fighter into the ocean almost vertically.

This kill marked 5.5 victories in Fighting Fifteen for Jack Symmes, making him one of only four U.S. Navy pilots to achieve ace status in two different aircraft: the F4F Wildcat in 1943 and the F6F Hellcat in 1944.[6]

Mellon and Stime each pursued one of the Betty bombers and finished them both off. Symmes then led his team over Manila Bay. Near Luzon, they found a damaged Japanese heavy cruiser, possibly *Darter*'s torpedo victim, *Takao*. The entire division made strafing runs. Mellon, who had not dumped his bomb while chasing his Betty, landed his quarter-tonner within ten feet of the cruiser's hull amidships.

Lieutenant Commander Duncan's team of fighters and Helldivers in the north made their first contact at 0950. Lieutenant (jg) Bob Fash spotted a Kawasaki Ki-48 light bomber (code-named "Lily") circling Malvar North Field at only five hundred feet. Fash reported his tallyho, slid in behind the Lily, and caused it to crash after flaming an engine and wing tank.

Between two small islands southwest of Luzon, Duncan's team found a Japanese light cruiser of the 5,200-ton *Nagara* class making 20 knots. Lieutenant Frank West's four Helldivers carried no payloads on this search, but the VB-15 crews flew cover for Duncan's four Hellcats to attack. "The AA fire was intense, and I called the other three guys and told them to glide-bomb, not to get down so low," Duncan recalled. Three of their bombs were near misses but Duncan scored a damaging direct hit with his skip bombing efforts. Its screws apparently damaged, the cruiser was last seen making only slow speed and spewing oil.[7]

On the return leg of the search, Duncan's eight-plane team passed north of Malvar North Field. Ensign Larry Self, flying just below the cloud cover, spotted a pair of Zekes launching from the field. Self notified Duncan, and together they went after the fighters. Self hit his Zeke's cockpit, causing it to ground-loop off the runway to port. It nosed up, broke off its port wing, and burst into flames. Self kept shooting as the pilot tried to climb out.

Duncan made a high-side run on the other Zeke and nailed its engine with slugs. Aflame, the Zeke was only three hundred feet above the airfield when the pilot made a desperate attempt to bail out. His parachute was just starting to blossom as the aviator hit the ground. His pilotless fighter continued in a right gliding turn until it slammed into the ground.

The search groups would not land on *Essex* until 1130, 5.5 hours after launching. They had damaged two warships and shot down four planes. By that time the group was in a hectic state; Japanese strike planes were already inbound for Task Force 38. The Sho plan called for maximum attacks on the American warships on the morning of October 24. In preparation, hundreds of attack aircraft had been ferried down from Formosa the previous day to air bases scattered around the Philippines.[8]

Carrier strikes had kept the Japanese air groups pinned down. Efforts to pinpoint the carriers of Admiral Halsey's Third Fleet had been unsuccessful for days. Flying boats and dawn scouts were sent out during the night of October 23, and they found a large force of U.S. ships about 250 miles off Manila. Admiral Shigeru Fukudome responded by launching his first wave of strike planes before dawn on October 24. Foul weather turned back the first strike force, but additional strike groups began taking to the skies at 0630.[9]

Within two hours, Japanese strike groups were approaching three of Halsey's four carrier task groups. The first telltale blips began showing on

Task Group 38.3's radar scopes at 0750. They indicated that three attack waves of at least fifty enemy planes each were heading toward Ted Sherman's four carriers, spaced about fifteen miles apart.[10]

For the moment, planned deckload strikes—prepared to launch against the Japanese Mobile Fleet when solid sighting reports were in hand—had to be scrapped. Task force defense was paramount. On *Essex*, *Lexington*, *Princeton*, and *Langley*, loudspeakers called for flight quarters. All available fighters were to be launched at once.

NINETEEN

"I WAS READY TO GO"

October 24, 1944
0800

Ll fighter pilots, man your planes!"

The announcement on *Essex* was electrifying. Topside, the deck had been spotted with additional Helldivers, Avengers, and Hellcats for a strike group against the Japanese airfields and shipping in Manila Harbor. But now radar screens in the CIC high in the island structure showed an incoming enemy air strike. At 0758 the "Hey, Rube" call was issued by radio to the fighter sweep over Manila.

Commander Dave McCampbell's *Minsi III* command Hellcat had already been loaded onto a catapult by his plane captain, Chet Owens. Deck crews were working to fuel his F6F when word was passed to scrub the main strike group. Dive-bombers and torpedo planes were hustled out of the way to clear space for two divisions of fighters to be launched. McCampbell was aware of his orders to avoid direct fighter missions, but he prepared nonetheless, strapping on his pistol, parachute harness, and life jacket in the ready room.

McCampbell placed a call to the bridge to speak to the *Essex* air officer, Commander Stan Strong. Knowing there were only two divisions of fighters serviceable, he asked Strong if he wanted him to lead the group into battle since *Minsi III* was already spotted. Strong said, "Yes, the group commander is to go."[1]

Within a minute, as McCampbell was still adjusting his buckles, the fighter pilots were ordered to man their planes. Then a surprising follow-up announcement crackled over the loudspeakers.

"The group commander is not, repeat not, to go!"

Although dejected, he was not completely surprised by the harsh orders. Ted Sherman had made it clear that he was not to be a hotshot fighter pilot. With his carrier and others suddenly at risk of attack by Japanese dive-bombers and torpedo planes, Admiral Sherman was content to let his four Hellcat squadrons intercept this latest threat. McCampbell turned to take his seat in the ready room as eight other VF-15 pilots snatched up their leather helmets and chartboards, then raced toward the flight deck.

As bombers were hustled below and the available Hellcats were positioned for launch, the *Essex* loudspeakers came to life again.

"Now hear this!" a sailor announced. "Air group commander is to fly. Repeat, affirmative. Air group commander is to go."[2]

McCampbell never quite figured out how the orders were changed, but he believed that air officer Stan Strong had intervened on his behalf with Captain Wieber.

Plane handlers already in the process of moving McCampbell's dark blue Hellcat toward the aircraft elevator quickly positioned it back on the hydraulic catapult. He trotted onto the flight deck, where plane captain Owens helped him onto the wing. On the fuselage under his wing, *Minsi III* was now painted with twenty-one "Rising Sun" Japanese flags in recognition of his aerial victories. But his command fighter was ill-prepared for this fight. The *Essex* airedales had completed the fueling of McCampbell's belly tank, but his two wing tanks had been only partially filled before the flight deck was buttoned up. With only 275 gallons of fuel, he would be at great risk if aerial combat forced him to jettison his belly tank.

But Dashing Dave signaled to the sailors topside that he was good for launch. "I waved the gasoline detail away, and told them I was ready to go," he recalled.[3]

Only seven total Hellcats were considered flyable. Behind *Minsi III*, six other pilots were strapping themselves into the rest of them. They would make standard departures, as opposed to the CAG being cat-shot off the bow. Filling out his command division were wingman Roy Rushing and the second section of Jake Lundin and his wingman, Ensign Dick Mc-Graw.

By 0807 the hydraulic launch had fired *Minsi III* into the air. As he clawed for altitude, Dave charged his guns and prepared for immediate action. Seconds behind him, Rushing was cleared for his launch and his Hellcat sped down the deck. The launch of his second section was not nearly as smooth.

"The weather was heavy, rain and clouds almost to the water," Lieutenant (jg) Lundin recalled. As he and McGraw strapped into their fighters, Lundin noted with dismay that his F6F had been marked in chalk with FLYABLE DUD. This meant it was technically flyable but in need of an overhaul. Seeing McCampbell and Rushing already disappearing into the foul weather above, Lundin had no choice. He and McGraw raced toward the point where the squadron would normally rendezvous above the fleet. But McCampbell and Rushing were hell-bent on meeting the Japanese. They had simply continued toward the incoming bandits.[4]

With only three more serviceable Hellcats spotted on deck, *Essex* could not even launch two full CAP divisions for her own defense. Twenty-seven other VF-15 fighters were out on search-and-sweep missions. The final three pilots to launch on this scramble were Lieutenant George Crittenden and two wingmen, Lieutenant (jg) Ken West and Lieutenant (jg) Al Slack.

BY 0821, COMMANDER McCampbell had climbed to 6,000 feet. He took up station over Task Group 38.3, awaiting further direction while the other half dozen fighters attempted to join up on him. The *Essex* fighters would operate under the guidance of their FDO, Lieutenant John Connally, positioned in their carrier's CIC.

Connally began issuing orders. His first vector was to intercept bandits thirty-eight miles from the ship on a course of 300 degrees. Blips were soon dotting the radar scopes. Minutes later Connally called for another vector: 360 degrees, distance twenty-five miles. Calmly smoking a cigarette and sweeping the horizon with his binoculars, McCampbell was ready to strike.

At 0833 he first spotted a large group of enemy planes. They were dead ahead, at 12 o'clock, stacked in layers both above and below the altitude of the *Essex* Hellcats. For a moment McCampbell pondered whether they might have been part of a returning Task Force 38 morning sweep. But seconds later their distinctive outlines and colors betrayed them as Japanese aircraft.

McCampbell opened up on his radio with a contact report. His seven fighters were in position to intercept an estimated sixty "rats, hawks, and fish." The *Essex* CAG and wingman Roy Rushing immediately climbed for altitude. At the same time, they saw the Japanese formation begin to reverse course, causing some of their divisions and sections to become strung out.[5]

McCampbell made a hasty call to Lieutenant Crittenden's second combat team.

"Attack the bomber stragglers from the rear. Roy and I will work them over from the top down."

In the hasty launch and incomplete rendezvous procedure, the seven *Essex* Hellcats would commence their assault in an abnormal manner. McCampbell's lead section went high, leaving Crittenden's three-plane division to enter the fight ahead of the straggling CAG second section of Lundin and McGraw. Their attacks were near simultaneous, although the two groups were widely distanced from each other. Their dual thrust into the Japanese force caused the bombers and torpedo planes to dive down through the overcast in an evasive attempt to escape.

Rushing and McCampbell continued to climb toward Angels 25 to hit the high-cover rats. Upon reaching that altitude, they both dropped their wing tanks and moved in to fight, making their first run on a section of three Zekes about 5,000 feet below them. Each pilot knocked one down. CAG's victim burned immediately, while Rushing's Zeke smoked and broke into flames at about 18,000 feet.

Using their high speed to regain altitude, they took their time and then commenced their second run against a group of several Zekes. Each pilot downed another fighter, both of which were seen to smoke and burst into flames. Repeating these tactics, McCampbell and Rushing zoomed up, regained altitude, and carefully selected their next targets: a group of three

Oscars. This time Rushing could only claim one fighter damaged, as his Oscar was last seen with a badly smoking engine. There simply was no time to follow it down. McCampbell's Oscar was a kill, seen to fall in flames, running CAG's score to three kills in just minutes.

The CAG section pulled back up again and commenced a fourth run. This time Rushing did not have as much altitude as on the previous runs. McCampbell continued down to the right in pursuit of an Oscar. Rushing pulled to the left after yet another Oscar. It managed to get above them. Rushing started firing with a 75-degree deflection shot, slipping back to about 45 degrees, before he saw it explode and burn. Rushing ducked as the wreckage from his third confirmed kill flew past his F6F.

Turning to the right, Rushing rejoined the CAG. By this time the enemy's high cover had started orbiting in a giant Lufbery circle. It was too well organized to penetrate, so McCampbell and Rushing climbed back up to 23,000 feet. Both lit cigarettes and smoked to calm their nerves while anxiously awaiting their next chance. At high altitude, this was a risky maneuver, as the pilots had to breathe through oxygen masks. "It was a little difficult, but we did it," McCampbell admitted. "Periodically, you pull the mask away, take a puff on the cigarette, and then put your mask back on."[6]

GEORGE CRITTENDEN'S FIVE Hellcats were making their bullets count during these same moments. Below the high-cover fighters, Critt counted at least thirty Japanese bombers and fighters, stacked from about 16,000 to 18,000 feet altitude.

As he led his Hellcats in, the enemy planes went into a protective Lufbery circle. Crittenden made multiple runs upon the leading formation. On his second run, he flamed the leading Val with only two short bursts. On his third and fourth passes, Crittenden caused a Val to begin smoking and finally burst into flames before it crashed. At this point the Japanese formation was in full disarray. Planes began dropping their wing tanks and their bombloads, and some began diving away. Critt shot at several on their way down, but he developed gun trouble. He only claimed one additional Val as damaged.

Critt witnessed what appeared to be aerial phosphorus bursts from some of the Japanese planes, as well as numerous parachutes in the air. As he looked up from his last run, a Tony was making a high-side run on him. As he turned into it, a long burst of 12.7mm and 20mm rounds winked past his plane. Scissoring with the Tony, Critt managed to slide in behind it and open up. Only one gun would fire, but he saw pieces flying off the Tony's fuselage and wings. It rolled over, smoking, and dived straight down. As Crittenden did not follow his target, he was credited with a probable.

Ken West damaged a Zeke on his first pass against the large formation. He broke off when three enemy fighters closed on his starboard beam. After rejoining Crittenden's team, West got in a good tail shot on a second Zeke and saw it explode just as the pilot attempted to exit his cockpit. Another "rat" made a low-level attack on West that he escaped only by diving away with water injection emergency power.

Al Slack, the third member of Critt's division, did not claim any kills in the opening minutes of the battle as he worked to help protect his division mates. But the second CAG section, separated from McCampbell's main group, had drawn blood. As the mass of enemy planes appeared through broken cloud cover, Jake Lundin spotted a large group of Val dive-bombers in a loose V formation with two divisions of Zekes covering them.

Having climbed to Angels 25, Lundin and wingman Dick McGraw had not yet been observed by the Japanese pilots.

"The Val leader is mine," Lundin called to McGraw. "You take his wingman on the right."[7]

Lundin rolled over and caught the leading dive-bomber pilot off guard. His first bursts caused the Val to begin smoking and heading down. At 16,000 feet, the Val burst into flames. Neither passenger was seen to deplane before it crashed. McGraw's Val target also burst into flames and crashed. As Lundin and his wingman were working to regain altitude, Jake spotted a lone Zeke passing in front of him. The Japanese fighter, loaded with wing tanks and a bomb, appeared to be heading for home. Jake made a high stern run as McGraw covered him. Lundin's first burst caused it to flame, and its bombload exploded as it hit the water.

As the section pulled up, there were four or five Zekes on their tails.

Lundin and McGraw had lost altitude and speed advantage. Under heavy enemy cross fire, the Hellcat pilots were in a tight spot. "Turning left, right or going up would have made us sitting ducks," Lundin recalled. He and McGraw thus pushed over into sharp dives for the cumulus below and applied full throttle.[8]

Lieutenant (jg) Walter "Jake" Lundin, a former Royal Canadian Air Force pilot, in his F6F, August 1944. On the morning of October 24, 1944, Lundin was one of seven VF-15 pilots who combined to down twenty-five Japanese aircraft in a single mission. WALTER LUNDIN COLLECTION, NATIONAL MUSEUM OF WORLD WAR II AVIATION

The pair zipped through the cloud cover. Emerging from the bottom of the bank, Lundin and McGraw made 180-degree turns and went back up through the clouds to meet the Zekes head-on. Not a plane was in sight. Their attackers had moved on to fight other F6Fs or had dived for the deck to clear the area. In any event, Lundin and McGraw had no further enemy contact.

MCCAMPBELL AND RUSHING had time to finish their cigarettes as the Japanese planes continued circling. Eventually the enemy appeared to indecisively start on a course for Manila.

It was time for the CAG section to attack again.

McCampbell and Rushing started their fifth attack runs. They made a high-side pass, sucking into a stern shot on a section of three Zekes. With short bursts, each pilot flamed a Zeke and watched it drop. Rushing's score now stood at four kills and one damaged fighter, while Commander Mc-Campbell attained ace-in-a-day status for the second time on Air Group Fifteen's combat tour.

McCampbell pulled the pencil from his chartboard and made five marks on his instrument panel to note the kills.

Shortly after, Al Slack joined the men. The trio continued their chase of the Japanese formation, selecting larger groups. In their next attack, they started down on a group of five or six scattered singles on the right side of the formation. Each pilot selected his own Zeke. Rushing fired from close up on the tail of an unsuspecting fighter. The Zeke exploded in midair as Rushing pulled up to miss the debris.

With this victory, Rushing joined the ranks of VF-15's elite ace-in-a-day group.

During this same pass, Slack downed his Zeke by firing from close range on its tail until it burst into flames at its wing root. McCampbell had taken on another plane. His hits created a trail of smoke, but the enemy pilot banked and disappeared. Not witnessing this one crash, the *Essex* CAG could claim only a probable.

As he pulled up, McCampbell found that he had lost Rushing and Slack during this last chase. A minute later he noted the silhouette of another plane closing on his rear.

Momentarily concerned an enemy fighter was preparing for a run on him, McCampbell poured on the throttle and surged ahead. Glancing back in his rearview mirror, he called over the radio, "This is Rebel Leader. Roy, waggle your wings."[9]

Seeing the wings of the closing fighter move up and down, McCampbell relaxed. At around 20,000 feet, he was rejoined by Rushing and Slack. Selecting another group of six Zekes, they commenced an attack from the rear. Coming down on them from out of the sun, each of the VF-15 trio again selected an opponent. Slack's second victim of the day was seen to fall, as was McCampbell's sixth kill of the morning. Rushing's Zeke began smoking but was not seen to crash, leaving him with only a probable claim.

Next, McCampbell pushed over on a Hamp while Rushing and Slack weaved over him. They both witnessed CAG's bullets hit until the Hamp spiraled and went in. Dave was now up to seven kills, matching his best-ever one-day total—although that one had been accomplished in two hops.

The trio rejoined and pulled up for altitude yet again. McCampbell had made eight attacks against the formation, and Rushing had made six. They commenced another assault from about 20,000 feet, between the sun and the big circle of bogeys. The three pilots split up: Rushing followed an Oscar into a 180-degree turn, firing but observing no hits. He broke off his attack and turned back in hopes of again rejoining his comrades. Meanwhile, the CAG had claimed another probable and hit the rear of a section leader of Zekes, causing the plane to burn and its pilot to bail out.

The trio regrouped, and once they had favorable altitude again, they pressed in against four Zekes. For McCampbell, it was his tenth attack pass. McCampbell and Rushing were first into the fray, and each shot down another plane. Slack's Zeke turned over onto its back, flamed, and dived straight into the ocean. The kill count now stood at eight for McCampbell and four for Slack.

Slack, on McCampbell's port wing, got a good run on a lone Oscar while the other two pilots weaved. Sneaking up from astern level, his bursts caused the Oscar to begin smoking badly and lose control. The Oscar nearly recovered once but then entered a progressive spin from which the Hellcat pilots did not believe he could survive. Slack pulled up to rejoin the CAG section and did not see his victim crash, leaving him with only probable credit. On that pass, Slack had exhausted his ammunition. He informed McCampbell that he was out of bullets, and was ordered back to base.

Rushing reported that he was low on ammunition.

"Roy, I've got a little left," McCampbell radioed. "Do you want to stay up here and watch, or go down on each pass with me?"[10]

"Oh, no, I'll go down with you," Rushing replied.

McCampbell closed on the tail of a Hamp fighter as they neared the coast of Luzon. As he pulled the trigger, he felt his guns begin to fail.

But he continued to fire, and at least some of his guns fired enough to stitch the Hamp. Its fuel tanks erupted in flames. The enemy plane rolled over and began a dive toward the ocean with black smoke streaming behind.

It marked McCampbell's ninth certain kill, plus his two probables. But his guns had seized up, putting an end to his fight. He snugged up against his wingman, content to offer any support he could. With his ammunition running low, Rushing made one final attack against the tail of a Hamp. Going conservative with his remaining .50-caliber ammunition, Roy closed to a mere eight hundred feet before opening with a two-second burst.

He was right on the money: the Hamp erupted in flames and spun into the drink. It was the sixth kill for Rushing, but he was now down to only a hundred remaining bullets. It was time to call off the fight. By this time the CAG section had chased the Japanese formation well over Luzon.

Down to about 12,000 feet, McCampbell and Rushing assessed their situation. Each had very nearly exhausted their ammunition. The fuel gauges on *Minsi III* were alarmingly low. "I saw I'd emptied one main tank," McCampbell remembered. He estimated that he had only forty-five gallons left, just enough to return to the fleet in conservative fashion. Rushing had plenty of fuel, but he slowed to 130 knots to keep wing on his air group commander.[11]

They reached Task Force 38.3 around 1030 but were given a rude reception. He and Rushing overflew *Hornet*, the carrier aboard which his Air Group Fifteen had once served. McCampbell recognized her camouflage paint scheme but was shocked to suddenly find his pair of Hellcats taken under fire from five-inch gunners below. Weaving to avoid the friendly fire, an angry McCampbell opened up on his radio as he spotted an incoming fighter division moving his way.

"For Christ's sake, call off the dogs! We're friendlies, trying to get back to the *Essex!*"[12]

McCampbell and Rushing tried to move into the landing pattern, but *Essex* reported they would have to wait: air operations were in progress. At 1031, McCampbell announced that he was down to twenty minutes of fuel. He was directed to pancake on another flight deck. *Lexington*'s flight deck was also full, but the light carrier *Langley* made space by launching several Avengers.

Seeing *Langley*'s deck finally clear, McCampbell dropped into the groove on the carrier. Her LSO waved off the *Essex* CAG, as plane handlers were still moving aircraft about on deck. "I made a quick turnaround, came back again, and he gave me the cut," McCampbell recalled. Touching down at 1038, he felt *Minsi III* jerk to a halt as his hook engaged one of the cables. "When I tried to come out of the landing gear, I gave it near full gun, and the engine conked out on me," he remembered. "I ran out of gas on deck. They had to push me out of the landing area." He had returned with five of his wing guns emptied and only two bullets remaining in his sixth gun.[13]

Roy Rushing was in only slightly better shape. He landed on *Essex* with twenty gallons of fuel and one hundred bullets remaining. Each of their F6Fs had only superficial damage, caused by passing through the debris fields of exploding enemy aircraft. Other pilots from the historic scramble— Crittenden, Slack, Lundin, McGraw, and West—were finally able to begin landing on *Essex* at 1116 after her flight deck had been cleared.

As Jake Lundin approached, he saw only three carriers in his task group; he had expected to find four. "I looked back on the track the task force was coming from, and in the distance saw a carrier burning," he recalled. "It turned out to be the *Princeton*." Lundin would often wonder if one of the planes his group had attacked had managed to slip through and wreak this havoc on *Princeton*.[14]

All told, the seven scrambled *Essex* fighters had downed twenty-five enemy aircraft, listed four as probably destroyed, and damaged a half dozen more. (See the chart on the following page.)

"My claim of nine planes destroyed includes only those that were seen by my wingman and myself to flame or explode," McCampbell summarized. "Numerous others were seen with engine smoking and diving away, two of which were spinning apparently out of control toward the water, and are claimed as probables." McCampbell added, "It was not until we had destroyed five planes and business was beginning to get good that I decided to keep a box score by marking on my instrument panel with a pencil."[15]

Pilot on 10/24/44 intercept	Kills	Prob.	Damaged
Cdr. David McCampbell	9	2	-
Lt. (jg) Roy Rushing	6	-	3
Lt. (jg) Albert Slack	4	1	-
Lt. George Crittenden	2	1	2
Lt. (jg) Walter Lundin	2	-	-
Lt. (jg) Kenneth West	1	-	1
Ens. Richard McGraw	1	-	-
Totals	25	4	6

McCampbell dropped down to the *Langley* fighter ready room while airedales fueled and armed his *Minsi III* Hellcat. He was enjoying a sandwich and a glass of milk when Commander Malcolm Wordell, the VF-44 skipper, appeared. His *Langley* fighters had knocked down a dozen Japanese planes, and Wordell was well pleased with his own two kills.

"Dave, how many did you get today?" Wordell asked.[16]

Although somewhat embarrassed, McCampbell replied, "Well, I think I got eleven, with a couple of probables thrown in there. You'll have to wait and talk to Roy Rushing."

His statement was matter-of-fact, but the *Essex* CAG noted how stunning his claim was to Wordell. "That took the wind out of his sails," he remembered.

McCampbell remained on *Langley* for an hour and a half while his *Minsi III* was being serviced. At 1216, he was launched from the light carrier and was finally able to land on *Essex* shortly after 1400.[17]

McCampbell reported to the bridge to see Rear Admiral Sherman. Although his air officer and Captain Wieber had given McCampbell the "go" to launch that morning, they had done so against Sherman's wishes. "Sherman ate me out for taking part in the scramble," Dave remembered. He was somewhat relieved when one of Sherman's staffers, Commander Charles R. Brown, remarked, "Well, Admiral, we were sent out here to kill Japs, and that's exactly what Commander McCampbell did."[18]

McCampbell later figured that Brown's input might have softened up the admiral a bit, as Sherman eventually participated in the paperwork process of recommending McCampbell for the Medal of Honor.

With nine confirmed kills in a single sortie, McCampbell had set a record for American and Allied fighter pilots. For the moment at least, Dashing Dave had equaled Army Air Forces major Dick Bong with thirty kills. After ninety-five minutes of dogfights on October 24, the *Essex* CAG was in a tie for the ace of aces title.

TWENTY

BATTLE OF THE SIBUYAN SEA

October 24, 1944
0920

J ohn Strane heard plenty of excited voices on the fighter circuit as he approached Task Group 38.3. It was 0915, and he was among the nineteen Hellcat pilots returning from the early sweep led by Jim Rigg. Dave McCampbell's seven F6Fs and dozens of Hellcats from other fighter squadrons were still busy intercepting the incoming Japanese raids.

Lexington's VF-19, scrambled during the same rush as McCampbell's team, was credited with 11.5 kills. Operating near *Essex*, the light carrier *Princeton* had three divisions of her VF-27, nicknamed the "Hell Cats," on CAP duty even before the scramble was ordered. Four VF-27 pilots achieved ace-in-a-day status on October 24, but it would be their last day flying from their beloved carrier.

At 0938, a lone Judy dive-bomber plunged through the clouds over TG 38.3 and released a bomb. It smashed through *Princeton*'s flight deck, where fires began spreading. For the moment, flight operations were curtailed on *Princeton* while damage control parties struggled to contain the blazes. Lieutenant Carl Brown's Hellcat had been badly shot up in his dogfights with Zekes, but two other task group carriers, *Lexington* and *Langley*, refused to land the VF-27 division leader because his tailhook would not extend, preventing his plane from safely snagging an arresting wire. Brown was preparing for a water landing when *Essex* FDO John Connally radioed, "Hatchet 7, if you'll land immediately, we'll take you."[1]

Other *Princeton* fighters landed on *Essex* as the fight to save their ship went downhill during the day. A series of internal explosions rocked *Princeton* and sealed her fate. By late afternoon the carrier was burning out of control and would be abandoned and later scuttled. Rear Admiral Sherman was happy to take on the *Princeton* F6F orphans, but he was not amused with the eyeballs and shark mouth decals on each VF-27 Hellcat. He ordered *Essex* airedales to haul them to the hangar deck to remove the decals and paint over the other graphics.[2]

The VF-15 morning sweep fighters were rearmed and fueled for further use as needed. Four Hellcat divisions were split between two needs: escorting a strike group and replenishing the duty CAP. Japanese admiral Kurita's Center Force, a collection of heavy warships, had been spotted by search planes that morning, compelling Admiral Bull Halsey to order strike groups out from Task Force 38. *Intrepid* and *Cabot* aircraft from TG 38.2, closest to the scene, were launched first against this armada. They arrived overhead around 1018 and commenced their attacks.

Kurita's First Mobile Striking Force included the super-battleships *Yamato* and *Musashi*, the smaller battleships *Nagato*, *Kongo*, and *Haruna*, and nearly two dozen cruisers and destroyers. *Musashi* endured one torpedo hit, a 1,000-pound bomb hit, and damaging near misses from this American strike force. A second *Intrepid* strike force made attacks on Kurita's force shortly after noon, scoring two direct bomb hits and three more torpedo hits. Following these attacks, Kurita's force slowed to 22 knots so the wounded *Musashi* could keep pace. Her woes were just beginning.[3]

By late morning, Dave McCampbell's VF-15 had fended off the early Japanese carrier strikes against TF 38. Rear Admiral Ted Sherman then committed his own assault groups from TG 38.3. From *Essex* and *Lexington*, warplanes began leaping off their decks at 1050, winging toward the world's largest battlewagons. From Air Group Fifteen, skipper Jim Rigg launched with two divisions of Satan's Playmates, his eight Hellcats tasked with shepherding Jim Mini's dozen Helldivers and sixteen Avengers led by VT-15 skipper VeeGee Lambert.

Once the strike force had departed, *Essex* launched two replacement CAP divisions at 1105. During the ninety minutes that AG-15's assault group was approaching Kurita's force, the divisions of Bert Morris and John Collins would have their own opportunities to add to VF-15's already impressive scorecard for the day.

AFTERNOON INTERCEPTS

October 24

At 1245, the first indications of an approaching Japanese air strike appeared as green blips on the radar sets of Task Force 38 warships. Dave McCampbell, the hero of the morning intercepts, proved to be in the wrong position to catch this raid. That task fell upon some of his VF-15 comrades.

The divisions of Morris and Collins spent their first hour orbiting the task force at 8,000 feet near the crippled *Princeton* with no indications of Japanese bandit trouble. When the FDOs began directing Hellcats out to greet the enemy air raid, the division of Lieutenant Collins was ordered to maintain its orbit above the *Princeton* rescue efforts.

Meanwhile, Lieutenant Morris received the nod to take action. With wingmen Doyle Bare and Duz Twelves, Hollywood star Morris was vectored toward the first bogey at 1250. Climbing to Angels 20 as they headed out on a course of 30 degrees, the Morris trio had clear weather and good visibility. At 1300 they easily tallyhoed bogeys about thirty miles away. The Japanese strike force appeared to consist of thirty fighters, dive-bombers, and torpedo planes. The rats, all Zekes, had already formed a Lufbery circle at about 16,000 feet. As the *Essex* Hellcats approached, one Japanese bomber division dived for the deck and fled the scene.

The Zekes that remained were more than ready to fight. Twelves and his companions later reported them to be the most aggressive enemy fighter pilots they had encountered since the June 19 Marianas Turkey Shoot. "They flew excellent formation, kept good sections, and traded head-on shots," intelligence officer Bob McReynolds wrote in the after-action report. "They evidently were part of the No. 1 Team."[4]

Lieutenant (jg) Bare made a series of daring solo attacks and downed two Zekes before rejoining his division.

For his part, Morris made his first high-side attack on the leader of a two-plane section of Zekes. He saw four bursts go into it before the fighter flamed and crashed. Morris then made a steep climb back up above the overcast to rejoin his wingman.

On this first strike, Morris's wingman, Duz Twelves, had attacked a Jill that he caught straggling from the larger formation. Making a tail run from 20,000 feet, he closed fast and gave a long burst, which produced enormous flames. The Jill exploded, bouncing Twelves's Hellcat some 300 feet up in the air.

Lieutenant (jg) Doyle Bare, in his Satan's Playmates flight jacket in Hawaii in March 1944, was credited with two kills at Leyte Gulf on October 24.

DOYLE BARE COLLECTION, COURTESY OF RITA BARE

Two Zekes began a run against Twelves, so he used full power to join up on Morris at altitude. Using their altitude advantage, Morris and Twelves dropped down on other Zekes. Morris missed on his first pass, and the enemy fighters began shooting. He tried to turn inside the Zekes, but his plane was hit by numerous rounds. Looking over his left shoulder, Morris saw the winking fire of the incoming Zeke. Discouraged, Morris ducked into a cloud. He made a 360-degree turn on instruments and came out above the two Zekes.

Morris made a pass at the stern Zeke, and his slugs caused it to burst into flames. But a couple of 20mm rounds in his own engine were causing trouble. His cockpit was full of smoke and his hydraulic system was shot out, so Morris continued in his dive and departed. "He hit my plane with his cannons, so I decided I'd better get home," Morris recalled.[5]

In the meantime, Duz had hit a Zeke on one run in the engine in a head-on pass as he came down. As he was recovering, he pulled up onto another Zeke. He gave it a burst and evidently hit the pilot, as the Zeke went out of control and spun in. Duz had now killed one Jill and two

Zekes. Twelves then made three more runs into the Lufbery circle the Zekes were trying to maintain. On his last run, a damaged oil line gave way, covering his windshield with oil. Another F6F led Twelves back to base and into the landing circle.

Next to intercept this afternoon Japanese raid was the division of John Collins, which had been left to help safeguard the crippled *Princeton*. In the course of an hour, his four F6Fs were issued occasional vectors that resulted in three kills. Lieutenant (jg) Red Voorhest was first to score, dropping a Judy after two firing passes. Ensign Rod Johnson finished off a Val dive-bomber. Fighter-bomber pilot Bill Anderson closed out the action by nailing a Fran only 2,000 feet above the wave tops as it headed toward the American carrier fleet.

Although their CAG's combat air patrol team was scoreless, John Strane's division had better luck. Flying high cover at Angels 18, Strane tallyhoed his first bogey shortly before his team was due to return to base. He spotted a lone Zeke at 5,500 feet, just outside the TF 38 screen. Utilizing his altitude advantage, Strane slipped in unseen behind the enemy fighter and opened fire at eight hundred feet. Parts of the Zeke's wing and its stabilizer flew off. Strane pulled off his attack at a mere hundred feet altitude. The Zeke pilot parachuted out and one of the task force destroyers was sent to pick him up.

Once the afternoon raid action began tailing off about 1430, *Essex* retrieved her four CAP divisions. They had again succeeded in saving their carrier from any direct enemy damage. A short time after trapping back on his own flight deck, Dashing Dave learned that his AG-15 comrades had been productive against the Japanese battleship force.

BATTLESHIP STRIKE

Ensign Jack Taylor was beginning to wonder if they would ever find the Japanese fleet. For two hours he had been hugging the wing of Lieutenant (jg) George Carr, his division leader. Two other air groups had already assaulted Admiral Kurita's Center Force battleships, but Task Group 38.3's strike force had yet to lay eyes on the mighty dreadnoughts.

The collective group included eighty-five planes from *Essex, Lexington,* and *Langley.* With Dave McCampbell airborne on CAP duty, strike coordinator honors for this flight fell to Commander Pedro Winters, the *Lexington* CAG. From the start, he was frustrated. Prior to departing ship, he had argued with the *Lexington* air officer about the weapons loaded on his Avengers and Helldivers.

Kurita's warship force included the world's largest battleships and numerous heavy cruisers, all heavily armored. Winters strongly recommended AP bombs to be loaded in his SB2Cs instead of the usual instantaneous high-explosive bombs and rockets used against enemy airfields. He also wanted aerial torpedoes loaded in his TBMs; they were the proper weapons for torpedo bombers to hit the heavy warships with. Tempers flared, but the *Lexington* skipper backed up his air officer. Too much time would be wasted switching out all the ordnance loads. "We took off before lunch on a bear hunt, loaded for quail," Winters later wrote.[6]

The VF-15 divisions of Carr and skipper Jim Rigg were armed with five-hundred-pound bombs and carried belly tanks for the 250-mile flight. The two air groups became separated while circumnavigating a front fifty miles from base but were able to rejoin later. When they reached the target area, it was covered with broken overcast from 4,500 to 6,500 feet, preventing long-range visuals. The Japanese fleet was not where it was expected to be found.

Rigg dispatched Lieutenant (jg) Baynard Milton and his wingman to search for the fleet to the south. Lieutenant John David Bridgers, heading one of VB-15's two divisions, was pleased to hear his buddy Milton soon open up on the radio with "Jesus Christ, the whole Jap fleet is down there!"[7]

Coached in by Milton's section, Pedro Winters began assembling his various squadrons for attack around 1330. The massive *Musashi* had already been slowed by torpedo and bomb hits, reducing Kurita's advance speed to 22 knots. But *Musashi* still possessed fearsome gun power as the third TF 38 strikers approached. She was firing 460mm shells, 155mm shells, 127mm shells, and countless 25mm AA rounds.

Winters assigned the western group of ships to the *Essex* group. Commander Jim Mini led his first division of VB-15 against the battlewagon *Nagato* and claimed three bomb hits. Lieutenant Robert Cosgrove, leading four VT-15 TBFs against *Nagato* at 1345, witnessed explosions as they retired and claimed torpedo hits, although the high-speed maneuvering of this Japanese battleship spared her from damage from this *Essex* group.[8]

Lieutenant Bridgers led his second division of VB-15 beyond the western group and lined up over the damaged *Musashi*. Around 1331, George Carr and Jack Taylor of VF-15 made their approach at 13,000 feet, ahead of Bridgers's five SB2Cs. The big battleship's guns were tossing out frightening bursts. Taylor marveled at the multicolored bursts: pink, green, orange. He was surprised at the variety of colors but realized later that each ship's gunners needed to spot their own efforts. "When I made my run, I tried to get as vertical as I could," Taylor recalled.[9]

He reasoned that coming almost straight down would make him more difficult to hit. Carr had ordered his section to retain their five-hundred-pound bombs for another target. Upon completing his strafing run, Taylor pulled out low on the water, jinking through the AA bursts until he could rejoin on Carr. Taylor was content with having survived. Therefore, he was not pleased with the words radioed to him from Carr: "We gotta go back in."

Against his better wishes, Taylor followed Carr in for more attacks against other ships. They continued strafing *Musashi* until the torpedo plane attacks were complete. Taylor survived without a scratch on his Hellcat but considered it to have been one of his scariest missions. "I thought I was going to get my ass shot off," he remembered.

Three VB-15 pilots claimed 1,000-pound bomb hits. The explosions of gun batteries and near misses confused the pilots, as *Musashi*'s crew claimed only near misses from this first *Essex* strike. Still, shrapnel from these bombs played havoc among the exposed 25mm AA gun crews.

Torpedo Fifteen's divisions split to attack different warships, the mighty *Musashi* and a *Kongo*-class battleship. Two VT-15 Avengers were shot down, although two of the aviators would later be recovered. Lieutenant Commander Lambert's torpedo bomber crews claimed five torpedo hits. During this period, *Musashi* did suffer four more torpedo hits, including one in her starboard side near her main forward gun turret that created massive flooding.[10]

Jim Rigg led his VF-15 division on strafing-and-bombing runs on

Noshiro. They claimed near misses with their quarter-ton bombs. Another section of Satan's Playmates, led by Baynard Milton, strafed a *Kuma*-class cruiser, claiming one near miss with their two bombs. Photo Hellcat pilot Art Singer dodged about the massive enemy warship fleet, taking aerial photos of the attacks made by *Essex*, *Lexington*, and *Langley* warplanes. As Air Group Fifteen's bombing and torpedo runs continued, Carr and Rigg led their Hellcats on additional strafing runs on enemy destroyers to help suppress the AA fire. During the TG 38.3 attacks, the other super-battleship, *Yamato*, collected two bomb hits at 1350 that damaged her port bow.[11]

Jack Taylor was greatly relieved when the *Essex* group was finally ordered to collect at its designated rendezvous point, far beyond Kurita's warships. Multicolored AA bursts continued to dot the sky until the *Essex* force was formed up about fifteen miles beyond the task force. No heavy warships were knocked out directly as a result of TG 38.3's strikes, but strike coordinator Pedro Winters was pleased with the efforts of his airmen. "Nobody seemed to be sinking or burning, but we did shake them up a bit," he remembered. Winters was still smarting that *Lexington*'s high command had not allowed his planes to be loaded with torpedoes or armor-piercing bombs.[12]

Retiring through the gauntlet of intense AA fire took its toll on Air Group Fifteen. Two VT-15 Avengers were downed, and three VF-15 Hellcats collected minor flak damage. Jim Mini's Helldiver suffered the greatest damage. His SB2C collected a Japanese shell that wrecked his elevator control, magnetic compass, and tailhook. Escorted by Lieutenant (jg) Loren Nelson, the VB-15 skipper was ultimately unable to land when he reached *Essex*. He set his Helldiver down near the task group, whereupon the destroyer USS *Cotten* (DD-669) rescued Mini and his rear seat man.

By the time the VF-15 divisions of Carr and Rigg trapped on the *Essex* flight deck around 1515, they learned that a second assault force from TG 38.3 had already been sent out to continue the attacks on *Musashi*, *Yamato*, and the rest of the Japanese fleet.

LIEUTENANT (JG) DUZ Twelves was eager to make his first strike on a capital warship force. His squadron had missed attacking the Japanese carriers in the Battle of the Philippine Sea in June, but today was another story. In the ready room he had listened to the radio chatter of pilots assaulting Admiral Kurita's battlewagons.

Shortly before 1300, the call came for pilots to man their planes. A second *Essex* strike group was being sent out before the first group had even started their dives on the *Musashi* force. When Duz reached his F6F, *Lady La Rhea*, he found it loaded with a five-hundred-pound bomb and fully fueled. His division, that of Lieutenant Commander George Duncan, and that of Lieutenant (jg) Swede Thompson would be escorting in a dozen Helldivers under Lieutenant Roger Noyes. The VB-15 SB2Cs were packing lethal 1,000-pound AP bombs. Lambert's VT-15 had flung nearly its full complement into the previous strike, so this group departed without Avengers.

The inbound flight would be 180 miles. By 1420, strike leader Duncan and his second section leader, Twelves, had the Japanese warships in sight. They were greeted by a heavy barrage of AA fire rising from battleships, cruisers, and destroyers whose twisting white wakes churned the blue surface far below.

From 13,000 feet, Duncan directed his group to attack various targets. The much-abused *Musashi* was trailing astern of the main force, so Swede Thompson's division was sent against her sister battlewagon, *Yamato*, along with both VB-15 divisions. Duncan's division moved on to make bombing-and-strafing runs on the battleship *Nagato*. The previous *Essex* strike group had already cleared the area after its attacks had commenced forty minutes prior.

Duncan and Twelves led their wingmen down on *Nagato*. Their six wing guns chattered all the way, sending .50-caliber shells stitching into gun crews until the pilots reached their drop points. The seconds leading up to the release of their five-hundred-pounders seemed like days. The firepower from the battleships was as awesome to behold as it was deadly. Duncan noted that some of the larger shells were timed to burst like a Fourth of July explosion, spraying shrapnel in front of the diving American planes. One erupted dead ahead of his division. "I've never seen such a burst," Duncan recalled. "It they had waited another five to ten seconds, it would have put our whole flight in ashes."[13]

The fearsome explosions unnerved Duncan's wingman, Larry Self. He was certain this would be his last attack. Black puffs erupted all about his Hellcat, which was rocked mightily by their concussions. Duncan had ordered his pilot to hold their dives to 3,000 feet, but Self was terrified as several shells exploded directly ahead of him.[14]

I'm going to catch up to them, Self thought. *I'm going to hit one of these shells dead center!*

Still 6,000 feet above his target, he admittedly "chickened out." Self pickled his bomb and pulled out of his dive early, hoping to save his own skin. He had no idea where it landed. Although Duncan and Twelves maintained their dives to the proper release point, their quarter-ton bombs merely dented *Nagato*'s sides as they exploded within twenty feet of the racing battleship.

By 1430, Thompson's four F6Fs were in their dives on one of the two super-battleships. Swede's five-hundred-pounder was credited as a direct hit amidships, just aft of *Yamato*'s bridge structure. Wild Bill Deming, who considered his dive through the antiaircraft fire to be a real "rush," planted a second small bomb amidships, near the battleship's No. 3 turret. Lieutenant (jg) Al Slack, the second section leader, was worried about saving his own hide. "It looked like a Christmas tree," he recalled. "I had never seen guns firing from a ship like that." Slack decided to release a little higher than normal and make his escape run through the gauntlet of hellfire.[15]

Slack and wingman Dusty Craig landed near misses off *Yamato*'s port quarter. Craig poured .50-caliber bullets into the battleship all the way down, hoping to take out some of the enemy's gunners. He questioned whether any of his shots could even penetrate the steel fortress that was the thickly armored *Yamato*.[16]

Diving in right behind the VF-15 division were all twelve of Roger Noyes's dive-bombers. Lieutenant (jg) Conrad Crellin's Helldiver was directly hit by a shell in its dive, and the plane slammed into the ocean with no survivors. Noyes and his surviving pilots triumphantly claimed seven direct hits with their thousand-pounders, although their claims were overly optimistic. Still, *Yamato* was heavily damaged by their attack. One VB-15 bomb penetrated the battleship's anchor deck, exploding below the waterline with enough force to hole her bow. Two more thousand-pounders hit near the No. 1 turret, blowing a hole above the waterline. Regardless of how many bombs were direct hits, *Yamato* took in 3,000 tons of seawater and was listing 5 degrees as the *Essex* planes departed.[17]

Duncan's combat team then made strafing runs on the cruiser *Noshiro*, and both Thompson's and Duncan's divisions proceeded to make additional strafing runs on various destroyers. Ashamed of his abort over *Nagato*, Larry Self eased some of his frustrations by pumping slugs into one of the destroyers before he headed for the rendezvous point. Minus one dive-bomber, Duncan turned his flight back for base. By 1616, a little more than three hours after launching, the group was settling into the groove.

THE POUNDING OF Kurita's warships was not over.

At 1455, sixty-nine aircraft from *Enterprise* and *Franklin* commenced the fifth strike on the Japanese fleet. Nine VB-20 Helldivers planted four 1,000-pound semi-armor-piercing bombs into *Musashi* while VT-20's Avengers scored three torpedo hits on the battleship. *Musashi* was left smoking heavily, settling by the bow, and able to maintain only a 13-knot speed. A half hour later, Kurita's fleet was under its sixth air attack, with seventy-five planes from *Intrepid*, *Franklin*, and *Cabot* circling overhead.

Musashi absorbed numerous bomb hits from VB-13 Helldivers from *Franklin* and VB-18 SB2Cs from *Intrepid*. A dozen TBFs and TBMs from these two carriers put the finishing touches on the battleship, thumping her sides with two dud torpedoes and nine that exploded. By the completion of the attack, 259 carrier aircraft had worked over the Center Force. *Musashi* was still somehow moving despite having been punctured by nineteen torpedo hits, seventeen bomb hits, and at least twenty near misses. But damage control efforts proved futile, and the crew was ordered to abandon ship hours later. The Japanese admiral on board retired to his cabin and apparently went down with *Musashi* when she slid under the waves at 1936.[18]

On board *Essex* that evening, Lieutenant Bob McReynolds and his administrative staff were tireless in assessing all the day's action reports. Dave McCampbell's morning CAP scramble had been one for the record books. And the afternoon assaults on the *Musashi* force had capped off a glorious day for Task Force 38. For his part, McCampbell spent the evening catching up on events with Roy Rushing and Bert Morris. Their bull session lasted into the early-morning hours. The *Essex* CAG did not finally drift off to sleep until nearly 0200 on October 25.[19]

Larry Self was one of the few pilots not enjoying the celebrations. In his poststrike assessment with the ACIO, he admitted to his own meek bombing efforts against his battleship target. McReynolds, who was something of a father figure to his younger pilots, did his best to console the VF-15 pilot, telling him not to worry about it. There would be other chances.[20]

Still, Self had doubts about himself as he retired to his stateroom in Boys' Country and crawled into his bunk.

"All night long, I was wide awake," he recalled. "I felt so bad."

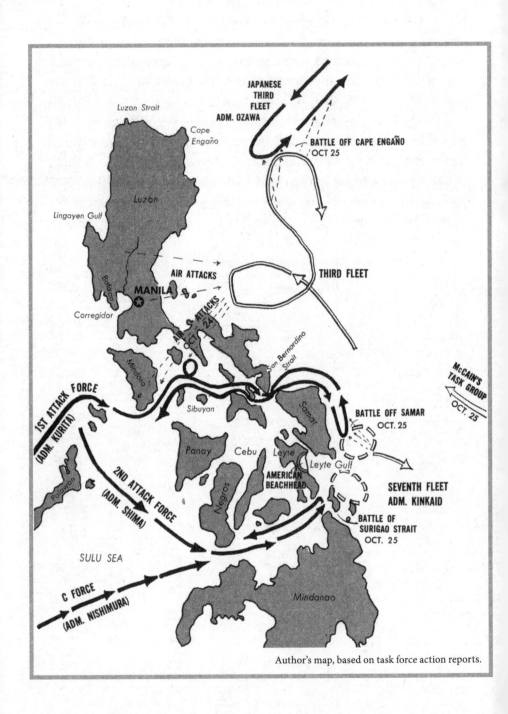

Author's map, based on task force action reports.

TWENTY-ONE

CARRIER STRIKES OFF CAPE ENGAÑO

October 25, 1944

Admiral Bull Halsey had carrier fever.

On the late afternoon of October 24, word had finally reached his staff of Vice Admiral Ozawa's Northern Force flattops. Contact reports placed four Japanese aircraft carriers, two light cruisers, and about five destroyers roughly 150 miles north of Cape Engaño on Luzon. His TF 38 carriers had pounded Kurita's battleship force throughout the day, and he no longer considered them to be a big threat. Halsey considered it "childish" to guard San Bernardino Strait through the night, so he ordered Pete Mitscher's fleet carriers to steam north that night to strike the enemy carriers after dawn on October 25.[1]

Overnight, Rear Admiral Gerry Bogan's TG 38.2 and Rear Admiral Ralph Davison's TG 38.4 raced north at 25 knots to join with Rear Admiral Ted Sherman's TG 38.3 to attack Ozawa. This was just the trap that Admiral Toyoda had devised, using his carriers as bait to lure Halsey into striking them. Shortly after *Musashi* slipped beneath the waves that evening, Toyoda sent word to Admiral Kurita. His force was to reverse course in the Sibuyan Sea and race back toward the San Bernardino Strait. Halsey mistakenly assumed the ships were decimated, certainly not strong enough to pose a serious threat to the escort carrier groups he left in that vicinity. Halsey had committed a blunder, and Kurita would make him pay.

On board his flagship, the battleship USS *New Jersey* (BB-62), Halsey was intent on wiping out Ozawa's group of carriers and prime warships. His sixty-five ships steamed at 16 knots into the early hours of October 25, leaving empty ocean and skies around Kurita's capital warships. Meanwhile, the light carrier USS *Independence* (CVL-22) launched a search group that reported two large forces of Japanese ships about a hundred miles to the north.

In the meantime, strike planes were readied on the decks of the three carrier task groups moving toward Ozawa's Northern Force. Vice Admiral Mitscher had four *Essex*-class fleet carriers, the older *Enterprise*, five light carriers, six battleships, two heavy cruisers, six light cruisers, and forty-one destroyers. Mitscher passed the word for his carriers to prepare deckloads of strike planes for dawn and to send out early searches and CAP teams.

On board *Essex*, Dave McCampbell was just drifting off to sleep. He had stayed up chatting with Roy Rushing and Bert Morris long past midnight. "I had hardly gotten in the bunk, when about 2 o'clock in the morning, one of the staff officers called me and told me that I was to lead a flight," McCampbell recalled.[2]

Weary from lack of rest, McCampbell turned to coffee and cigarettes to recharge his system. He decided to let his normal wingman, Rushing, catch up on his rest. Then he headed down to the ready room to harness up for another day in the saddle. There were enemy carriers within the reach of Task Force 38, and he was not about to miss out on that.

Ozawa's four carriers were steaming about 205 miles east by north of Cape Engaño at around 0230 on October 25. Although search planes pegged them in the proper direction, an error in transmission led Pete Mitscher to believe his opponent was about 120 miles closer to him than their actual distance. He ordered dawn searches from his flagship, *Lexington*, while his other carriers held their strike groups until after 0530. With or without any further clarifying reports, the Bald Eagle was poised to strike at Ozawa.[3]

Flight operations commenced on *Essex* around 0545. Lieutenant John Collins took his bombless four-plane division up to serve on task group CAP duty. Behind them, Commander McCampbell followed with an additional fourteen VF-15 Hellcats to cover fifteen VB-15 Helldivers and a dozen VT-15 Avengers loaded with Mark 13 aerial torpedoes. From *Lexington* and *Langley*, another sixty-one warplanes were launched, some ordered out on search sectors. McCampbell's main strike body was vectored out to a point fifty miles north of *Essex*. They were directed to orbit there at Angels 12 and effect a rendezvous with the *Langley* and *Lexington* strikers. Once a new solid contact report was received on Ozawa's carriers, the first TG 38.3 assault group would be ordered forward.

Essex FDO John Connally radioed the CAP team under Lieutenant Collins, sending them on a high-speed recon search to the north toward the last known positions of the Japanese carriers. As they reached the end of their cross leg at 0710, Lieutenant (jg) Red Voorhest spotted enemy ships below. He hand-signaled to division leader Collins, and their four F6Fs slipped closer to reconnoiter the force.

Collins and his team soon saw the distinctive shapes of Japanese carriers slicing white wakes through the blue sea below. Collins opened up on the radio, sending in a contact report. His group then climbed back to altitude, keeping the force in sight. His combat team flew CAP over Ozawa's carrier force, where they remained unmolested and continued to circle while awaiting the arrival of the first strike group.

The report from Collins and Voorhest was just what McCampbell wanted. Their advance orbit position was a mere fifty miles farther. After an hour of mindless circling ahead of Task Force 38, Dashing Dave collected his three carrier air groups and bent on the throttle toward Ozawa's fleet. By 0800, McCampbell announced, "I have the fleet in sight."[4]

By his best count, there were seventeen warships: one fleet carrier, three light carriers, two battleships, four cruisers, and six destroyers. As McCampbell's force began their approaches and confirmed the precise location of Ozawa's carriers, Mitscher scurried to launch follow-up strike groups.

COLLINS'S REPORT WAS fairly accurate in terms of total ships present. Vice Admiral Ozawa's Northern Force included the 32,000-ton fleet carrier *Zuikaku*, the 11,000-ton light carrier *Zuiho*, and the 15,300-ton carriers *Chitose* and *Chiyoda*. They were in company with the 39,805-ton sisters

Hyuga and *Ise*, a pair of converted battleship-carriers whose after gun mounts had been replaced in 1943 with a hangar deck and a short flight deck aft from which scout planes could be catapulted. Ozawa also had the light cruisers *Isuzu*, *Oyodo*, and *Tama* and eight destroyers: *Maki*, *Kiri*, *Akizuki*, *Hatsuzuki*, *Wakatsuki*, *Kuwa*, *Sugi*, and *Shimotsuki*.

At 0555, *Zuikaku* had launched four Nakajima B6N Jill torpedo bombers for a search mission. Fifteen minutes later she dispatched six planes to fly to Nichols Field to join other aircraft of her squadron that had flown to the Philippines the previous day. At 0717, about the time that John Collins and his VF-15 division first located Ozawa's carriers, *Zuikaku* launched four Mitsubishi A6M5 Zeke fighters for task force CAP duty. All was quiet for the next hour, until *Zuikaku*'s radar team announced enemy planes at 0804.[5]

The American warplanes were closing fast, so *Zuikaku* turned into the wind and launched her last nine planes, all fighters. The ship's company was called to battle stations and a large naval ensign was raised on her signal mast as a battle flag. Making 24 knots, the last surviving Japanese fleet carrier to have launched warplanes against Pearl Harbor on December 7, 1941, was ready to meet her fate.

Voorhest, Collins, and their VF-15 wingmen continued to orbit Ozawa's fleet, sending further clarification reports to their task force as a communications relay team. From high altitude at a point just midway between Mitscher's fleet and Ozawa's carriers, they would coordinate messages back to the U.S. fleet until their fuel supply became low. The second VF-15 section, night fighters Lieutenant (jg) Jake Hogue and Ensign Ernie Roycraft, similarly remained near the Japanese fleet and would later help to coach in a second strike group.

Strike coordinator Dave McCampbell fanned out his TG 38.3 planes during their twenty-minute approach before final push-overs. Sections of dive-bombers, torpedo bombers, and Hellcats slid into their proper attack positions.

Trailing just behind the CAG-15 division were three other combat teams from Satan's Playmates, led by Lieutenants Bert Morris, John Strane, and Jack Symmes. Ensign Dick Davis, flying wing on Morris, was in awe of the multicolored barrage of shell bursts beginning to paint the skies around the approaching American warplanes. "They put up a blanket of AA that I had never seen before and have never seen since," Davis recalled. "It was almost impossible to drop a golf ball through there and have it hit the bottom." He saw shell bursts of every color in the spectrum, "like the Fourth of July." Silently, he figured, *Well, this is it for me. I've had a pretty good life.*[6]

For his own *Essex* strikers, McCampbell selected one of the light carriers. *Chitose* was deployed on the starboard quarter of the disposition, and she was pulling out of the formation to begin launching aircraft. McCampbell opened up on the radio, calling to Lieutenant Jig Bridgers, leader of the fourteen VB-15 Helldivers, to attack *Chitose*.[7]

Bridgers waited only long enough for his VT-15 comrades to reach their desired attack position before he signaled his divisions to push over. Approaching from the southwest, Lieutenant Commander VeeGee Lambert split his flight so they could make their attacks in the "hammer-and-anvil" style from either side of the disposition.

All fourteen of Bridgers's SB2Cs made dives, although only twelve dropped their bombs on *Chitose*. They were deadly. Direct hits were credited to Bridgers and six other pilots. The pounding of *Chitose* was so complete that McCampbell made a hasty call to divert the remainder of his strike force. The light carrier was burning furiously, obviously out of action. He ordered Lambert to shift his eleven Avengers to the *Ise*-class converted battleship that was steaming close to *Chitose*. Lambert called back, alerting McCampbell that most of his "torpeckers" (Avenger torpedo planes) were already committed to their runs on *Chitose*.[8]

VT-15 aircrews were certain of at least two torpedo hits. The exact number of bombs and torpedoes striking *Chitose* may never be known, but Japanese reports show that she was ripped open on her port side near the No. 1 aircraft elevator. Due to massive hull ruptures, her boiler rooms flooded, and *Chitose* took on a dangerous 27-degree list. Swift damage control efforts soon lessened the list, allowing the carrier to remain underway. By 0855 her forward starboard engine room flooded, slowing her speed to 14 knots. By 0925 her port after engine room flooded, and *Chitose* went dead in the water. As her list continued to increase, Rear Admiral Chiaki Matsuda on *Hyuga* was forced to abandon efforts to take the crippled carrier in tow. At 0937, *Chitose* rolled over on her port side and nosed under quickly. Captain Yoshiyuki Kishi and 903 officers and men went down with the first carrier lost from Ozawa's fleet.[9]

AIR GROUP FIFTEEN's Helldivers and Avengers had knocked out *Chitose* with their loads. But three other Japanese flattops and plenty of other targets remained.

Following Commander McCampbell's orders, three other VT-15 TBMs did switch targets and claimed heavy damage to the converted battleship-carrier *Ise*. Lieutenant Charles Sorenson and his wingman shifted their focus to the light carrier *Zuiho* and claimed at least one torpedo hit on her.[10]

Two other VT-15 Avengers claimed a torpedo hit just forward of amidships on the light carrier *Chiyoda*. Pleased with the devastation being handed out by his Helldivers and Avengers, strike coordinator McCampbell remained high to coach in the *Lexington* and *Langley* warplanes. His other three divisions—under Bert Morris, Jack Symmes, and John Strane—were each loaded with five-hundred-pound bombs. "We peeled off, and Bert was first," wingman Dick Davis recalled.[11]

Ten of VF-15's Hellcats made dives on *Zuiho*. As Lieutenant Morris led his division down, Davis tried to ignore the shell burst concussions that were rocking his plane. His Hellcat was trimmed perfectly as he plunged into his near-vertical dive. The flight deck of the twisting carrier was growing larger and larger in his sights. Davis was well below 3,000 feet when he finally toggled his bomb and roared right down *Zuiho*'s flight deck. "I think if I'd have looked over, I would have looked the captain right in the eyes!" he recalled.[12]

Davis cleared the carrier by zooming out right over the deck, just above the wave tops. "I figured I had got a hit because it was a good run," Davis recalled. But he never looked back. His complete focus was on zigging and zagging through the AA fire to save his own neck. Giant pillars of water rose up all around him as warships fired into the waves, hoping to knock down American planes with the geysers that the shell eruptions created. Just behind him, second section leader Doyle Bare witnessed Davis's bomb landing nearly amidships on *Zuiho*'s flight deck near the port side.[13]

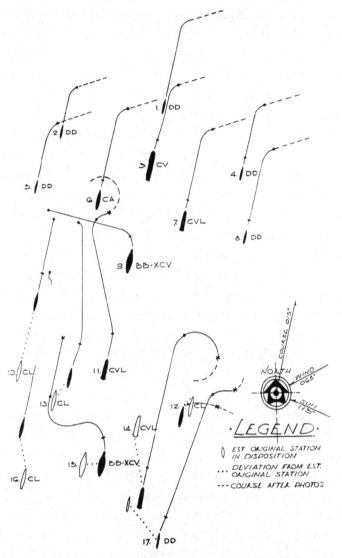

Forward group: carrier Zuikaku, *light carrier* Zuiho, *light cruisers* Oyodo *and* Tama, *destroyers* Akizuki, Hatsuzuki, *and* Wakatsuki, *with converted battleship-carrier* Ise *trailing. Admiral Ozawa's carrier force as originally encountered by VF-15 in its first strike off Cape Engaño on October 25, 1944, during the Battle of Leyte Gulf. Modified from a sketch included in the VF-15 action report. Per research of Anthony Tully for his "Combined Fleet" website, the trailing carrier force included the light carriers* Chitose *and* Chiyoda, *the light cruiser* Isuzu, *the converted battleship-carrier* Hyuga, *and the destroyers* Shimotsuki, Maki, Kiri, Kuwa, *and* Sugi. Courtesy of the author

John Strane's division followed on the heels of the Morris combat team. Jim Duffy remained focused on *Zuiho*'s flight deck as he plunged down. Dive-bombers from other carriers and the fighters ahead of him had already released numerous bombs. "I saw three bombs burst on the deck, so somebody had really plastered it good," he recalled. Duffy strafed all the way down, and he pulled out right on the deck. He figured the other elements of Strane's division must have pulled out sooner, as he found himself all alone, weaving through heavy explosions of antiaircraft fire.[14]

Behind him, Jack Symmes was credited with a direct hit on the flight deck amidships near the starboard side. His wingman, Ed Mellon, landed another two-thirds of the way aft. All told, VF-15 claimed three direct hits and seven near misses that exploded close alongside *Zuiho*'s hull.

Ted Sherman's words for the Navy's top ace must have sunk in. McCampbell and his wingman did not make dives but instead jettisoned their bombs to remain on high cover. They let other pilots handle the small number of Japanese fighters airborne that were encountered. Although the majority of VF-15 had assaulted the light carrier *Zuiho*, one *Essex* fighter pilot scored a near miss off a Japanese cruiser, while another strafed and just missed a destroyer with his bomb.

Task Force 38.3's attack on Admiral Ozawa's decoy force—referred to by Admiral Mitscher's staff as Strike No. 1 of the day—lasted about thirty minutes. Some 212 aircraft from seven carriers participated in the opening attack on the Japanese force. According to Japanese reports, all four carriers were at least damaged by this first strike. The *Essex* group had rendered the carrier *Chitose* useless and had damaged *Zuiho*. At 0835, *Zuiho* took three near misses off her stern and one direct five-hundred-pound-bomb hit on the aft section of her flight deck. The ship lost steering temporarily, but her fires had been extinguished and her steering corrected by 0855 as the last American planes were completing their attacks.[15]

Aircraft from *Langley, Lexington, San Jacinto*, and USS *Belleau Wood* (CVL-24) had contributed their fair share of damage to Ozawa's warships. The flagship *Zuikaku* had taken three direct bomb hits and one torpedo, which caused her to temporarily take on a 29.5-degree port list until her damage control teams could shore things up. The light cruiser *Tama* was hit by a *Belleau Wood* or *San Jacinto* Mark 13 torpedo in her No. 2 boiler room, leaving her crippled for the moment. An hour later she was underway and retiring from the main combat scene.

One of Ozawa's destroyers was less fortunate. Two *Lexington* VT-19 pilots made their runs on *Akizuki*. Lieutenant (jg) James Sipprell's torpedo hit at 0842 and created an immense explosion in *Akizuki*'s forward engine room. From a large hole, clouds of superheated white boiler steam rocketed skyward, partially obscuring the destroyer. Minutes after being struck, *Akizuki* broke in two and sank, carrying down more than half her crew.[16]

The light cruiser *Oyodo* suffered near misses and one direct hit that damaged her boiler room. The battleship-carrier *Hyuga* was rocked by multiple near misses that ruptured her hull and allowed in enough water to temporarily create a 5-degree list. The other converted battleship-carrier, *Ise*, was not hit directly but suffered some damage from near misses.[17]

By 0856 the first American attack was complete and the squadrons were making their rendezvous. The division of Lieutenant Collins remained in the vicinity, and Dave McCampbell's section remained on station to await the next group. But before heading for base, the *Essex* strikers ran afoul of a determined Japanese combat air patrol.

JOHN STRANE PULLED away from the carrier fleet, hoping to regroup his division. His wingman, Jim Duffy, had become separated but Strane still had his second section, Lieutenants (jg) Ken White and Jigs Foltz, the latter flying one of the two photo F6Fs.

Strane suddenly spotted enemy fighters that had not been seen before the *Essex* attacks on the Ozawa force. Prior to their arrival, *Zuikaku* had cleared her decks of fighters, and several others had apparently been launched by other carriers. At 10 o'clock a half dozen Zekes at 9,000 feet were moving toward the *Essex* dive-bombers below them. Strane signaled to his division mates and began climbing for altitude.

"I looked up and saw two Zeros to our right, and two Zeros to our left," Jim Duffy recalled. "Unfortunately, we were the targets!" Before he could even radio a warning to division leader Strane, Duffy saw that two of the

Zekes were going to pass under his section. He rolled right to get off a shot at them, but he wasn't fast enough.[18]

Lieutenant Strane waited until the Zekes commenced their run on the Helldivers below. On his first contact, he flamed a Zeke as it was pulling off from his attack. Strane saw this plane crash in the water, along with two other splashes. As he recovered, he spotted wingman Duffy recovering from his first unsuccessful pass on a Zeke. Strane saw that two other Zekes had slid in behind Duffy and were beginning to fire on his F6F.

Duffy noted one Zeke so tight on his tail, he felt he could have hit the plane by tossing a rock out of his cockpit. He turned as hard as he could, but the Japanese fighter kept turning inside of him. The Zeke's first shots zipped by just ahead of Duffy's Hellcat. He quickly reversed his F6F, but the Japanese pilot hung tight on him. Again tracers zipped by, just ahead of his cockpit. *If I keep this up, maybe that son-of-a-bitch will run out of ammo!* he thought.[19]

Duffy continued to turn and weave, hoping to shake his opponent amid the deadly AA fire from the warships far below. "I went across the whole Jap disposition," he recalled. *Where the hell is John?* he wondered as he jinked and dodged Zeke bullets. On his next turn, Duffy pulled so hard that his plane stalled out. His Hellcat was then raked by machine-gun fire. "It sounded like someone was banging on the plane with a sledgehammer," he recalled.[20]

He was uninjured, but his F6F's tail section, wings, and fuselage were laced with 7.7mm bullet holes. "Turning with the Zero was going to get me killed, so I pushed the Hellcat over into a dive," Duffy remembered. Unknown to him, John Strane was right behind the two Zekes chasing Duffy. He dived in sharply, firing short bursts into each. Both Zekes were set aflame and were seen to slam into the ocean. Strane saw Duffy recovering to the left ahead as the Zekes fell. For his part, Duffy had no idea where his division leader had appeared from, but he had been saved.

Later, when Duffy and Strane had the chance to discuss this mission on board *Essex*, Strane congratulated his wingman on their newfound tactic.

"From now on, you'll be the bait, and I'll shoot them off your tail," Strane announced.[21]

"It took me a while to find humor in that," Duffy recalled.

By this point in the battle, Strane had lost all sight of Duffy. Strane swept the horizon, hoping to catch a glimpse of his second section of White and Foltz. They were nowhere to be found. Strane did spot more Zekes jockeying about, attempting to attack the U.S. warplanes. Although flying solo, he turned into the closest one and fired a short burst. The Zeke burst into flames, but Strane was unable to follow it to its demise to claim a certain kill. His attention was diverted by bullets hitting his own F6F from another Zeke firing from ahead.

Strane tried to roll over to get in a shot but could not quite make it before the Zeke had flown directly in front and over him. His power then failed and his F6F started smoking and flaming badly abaft the engine. With his plane burning, another Zeke hit his port side many times, and his instrument panel broke loose. The VF-15 division leader had downed three Zekes and likely killed a fourth, but his fight was now over.

He considered trying to put the fire out in his cockpit so he could ditch, but it was beyond control. Strane prepared to bail out after giving his position over the radio, which was luckily undamaged. From 8,000 feet, his Hellcat was steadily losing altitude. "I tried to live by the law that I had been taught: 'take it easy and relax,'" he recalled. Strane unbuckled his straps, slid back his canopy, and stood to bail out. As he tried to step into the slipstream, a piece of his equipment was snagged on the arm that locked his canopy.[22]

Strane struggled free, only to get snagged a second time. Panic began to set in. "The six solenoids were burning, and all six guns were going off," he recalled. "Before I got out, I was down to 2,500 feet and I was not relaxed."

As he plunged over the side of his lifeless F6F, Strane noted two Zekes still circling above him. He waited as long as possible before pulling his rip cord a few seconds later. It was almost too late. As the fabric ballooned up, he jerked up and swung only once before he hit the ocean. He swallowed considerable salt water in the process of getting untangled. Once he popped his life raft and scrambled into it, he puked out the salt water. Overhead, the two Japanese fighters continued to circle for several minutes.

Lieutenant John Strane (center) was rescued by a destroyer after being shot down at Leyte Gulf. He is seen enjoying beers at the base club on Eniwetok Island in June 1944 with Dick McGraw (left) and Al Slack.

DOYLE BARE COLLECTION, COURTESY OF RITA BARE

Strane feared the worst. He had read, and heard from others, that Zeke pilots were known to strafe downed aviators. But he was greatly relieved when this did not happen. "They came down, made a pass over me, rocked their wings, and left," he recalled.

The remaining VF-15 pilots were impressed with the ability of the Japanese pilots this day. Two miles south of their disposition, other Zekes were congregating. Several of the Satan's Playmates pilots reported the Japanese pilots to be performing many stunts, such as slow rolls and split S's, in hopes of baiting in the Hellcats. The *Essex* VF instead chose to shepherd their SB2Cs and Avengers through the rendezvous until the Japanese began swooping down to attack.

Strane's second section leader, Ken White, had been turning and climbing above the *Essex* dive-bombers when he was jumped. Three Zekes were commencing an attack run on the SB2Cs. White pulled up sharply, and in two slashing attacks he knocked two Zekes into the ocean.

Jigs Foltz was in the division rendezvous when the Japanese fighters attacked from above. He turned sharply toward the first and almost spun out. He narrowly managed to ward off the Zeke and continued around. Foltz then spun out on top of another enemy fighter, which he fired at with three vigorous bursts. The Zeke fell off in a semi-spin in flames and crashed. Throughout the action, Foltz's rpm went to 2,900 and his engine detonated badly, resulting in his loss of power.

Art Singer, flying the other *Essex* photo Hellcat, also tangled with the Zekes. After his division, led by Jack Symmes, pulled out of the smoke belching from the Japanese warships, Singer turned toward the *Essex* rendezvous area. As he climbed, he spotted six Zekes straight ahead. Two were level with him and four were slightly above. He attacked the nearest of the two level ones from the starboard side. The Zeke flamed from the engine back to the cockpit on one short burst and crashed. Singer then claimed another Zeke probable.

In the meantime, Dick Davis had dropped his belly tank while clearing the fleet's AA fire at high speed. He suddenly spotted a group of Zekes starting to work over another Hellcat. Davis fired rounds into one of the Japanese fighters and saw smoke billow from it before he turned sharply to continue his defense of the other pilot. "I was almost in a stall, trying to get around and get on his tail," Davis later stated. The other pilot, Singer, was unaware of his own danger until tracers suddenly zipped by just below his wings. He tried a snap right turn, thinking the enemy could not keep up with his estimated speed of 270 knots. But the Zeke did.[23]

Davis noticed Singer employing his flaps to abruptly check his speed. Only as Davis closed on the other F6F was he able to see the three-inch white stripe painted on his stabilizer and realize he was defending a fellow *Essex* fighter pilot.

As Singer recovered and began to nose over, another Zeke came up from below, ahead and to his right. Singer followed it around and got in one burst from almost dead astern. The plane smoked, and there was a small burst of flame from its engine. He passed the Zeke and never witnessed its fate. Singer dived from 7,000 feet to 3,000 and then tried a violent right turn. As he pulled out, his windshield fogged. He could barely see another Zeke coming head-on through the condensation.

Singer fired and the Zeke exploded. One wing fell off and the fuselage broke off back of the cockpit, a mass of flames. "All of a sudden, he just popped like a balloon," Davis recalled. Singer then pulled up alongside Davis, having destroyed two Zekes, with two other probables to his credit. Davis spotted the signature mustache of Singer draping down the sides of his jaws. "He was sitting there grinning like crazy," Davis recalled.[24]

Singer signaled for Davis to lead them to the *Essex* squadron rendezvous location. During their return flight to the fleet, Davis and Singer shepherded another shot-up F6F to his own flight deck before they took their place in the *Essex* landing circle. Since their Hellcats were undamaged, the VF-15 duo allowed their air group comrades to trap first. Last to land just after 0930, Davis found the flight deck crowded with returned planes. As he climbed out of his cockpit, he paused with only one foot out on his wing. It was 0938, and several ships within Task Group 38.3 had suddenly opened fire on an airplane plunging out of the low cloud level about a mile away. "He was coming straight down, and I stopped and watched him," Davis remembered.

The bandit, identified as a Japanese Judy bomber, had slipped all the way up on the carriers before abruptly plunging on the light carrier *Princeton*. Its 550-pound bomb smacked almost dead center on *Princeton*'s flight deck, exploding in the lower decks. "He must have hit the magazine," Davis recalled, "because it erupted." Fires in the hangar deck soon began cooking off torpedoes loaded on ready Avengers. One of the ensuing explosions tossed the carrier's twenty-five-foot-square forward elevator masthead high before it dropped back down in the pit. Within thirty minutes, *Princeton* was so ravaged by fires that Captain William Buracker ordered unneeded sailors to abandon ship.

Valiant efforts were made to contain the blazes on *Princeton* through the afternoon, but secondary explosions eventually negated this work. A massive explosion at 1524 caused extensive casualties and damage to the cruiser USS *Birmingham* (CL-62), which had drawn alongside *Princeton* to effect rescues and fight fires. More than seven hundred men on *Princeton* and *Birmingham* were killed or wounded as a result. That evening, Rear Admiral Sherman was forced to reluctantly pass the orders to scuttle his TG 38.3 carrier.

Davis was thoroughly exhausted from the flight. Having witnessed the start of *Princeton*'s misery, he headed belowdecks. He made his way into VF-15's ready room, which was noisy with excited pilots relating their attack stories. When Lieutenant McReynolds approached him to take his statement, Davis waved him away. "I've gotta have a cigarette first," he explained.

"I'll go on to someone else and come back to you," the intelligence officer said.

Davis leaned back in his leather chair and exhaled on his cigarette, calming his worn nerves. He had survived the gauntlet of antiaircraft fire and brushes with Japanese Zeros. By this point he had all but forgotten about dropping his bomb on *Zuiho*. He still had no idea if he had scored a hit or not. And then he was startled by division mate Doyle Bare slapping him on the back.

"Dick, you really put that one right down the stack," Bare exclaimed. "That carrier really blew like I've never seen anything blow in my life!"

Davis suddenly felt recharged. Months later he would be pinned with a Navy Cross for his accomplishments this day.

Strike coordinator McCampbell remained over Ozawa's fleet as the action tapered off. Aside from the loss of John Strane, the balance of the first *Essex* strike group returned to base.

But the assault on Ozawa's carrier force was just beginning.

ADMIRAL HALSEY HAD taken Vice Admiral Kurita's offered bait. Even as his first Task Force 38 carrier strike groups were approaching Ozawa's carriers, the Japanese Center Force was bearing down on Rear Admiral Clifton Sprague's Task Unit 77.4.3, code-named "Taffy 3."

Sprague's group consisted of six escort carriers, screened by three destroyers and three destroyer escorts. Kurita's battleships, cruisers, and destroyers passed through San Bernardino Strait in the early hours of October 25 and steamed southward along the coast of Samar Island. By dawn, two dozen Japanese warships were within twenty miles of Taffy 3 when an anti-submarine patrol launched from the escort carrier USS *St. Lo* (CVE-63) spotted them. At about 0700, the mighty battleship *Yamato* opened fire with her massive guns. The other battleships—*Nagato*, *Haruna*, and *Kongo*—quickly followed suit.

Kurita excitedly believed at first that he had Mitscher's main TF 38 fleet carriers under his guns. Sprague's escort carriers hurriedly launched all available aircraft as Japanese shells began exploding around his ships. His destroyers began laying down smoke screens to help disguise his small carriers while the smaller destroyer escorts charged toward the Japanese cruisers and battleships to attack. The valiant USS *Hoel* (DD-533), USS *Heermann* (DD-532), and USS *Samuel B. Roberts* (DE-413) were pounded by Kurita's warships as they made their last stand.

The Battle off Samar was devastating for Taffy 3. Several escort carriers were hit, and USS *Gambier Bay* (CVE-73) became the only U.S. carrier sunk by naval gunfire in World War II. *St. Lo* escaped serious damage during the surface battle, but her flight deck was crashed hours later by a kamikaze pilot. The resulting explosions and fires forced *St. Lo* to be abandoned by 1100, and she slipped beneath the waves a half hour later. The destroyers *Hoel* and USS *Johnson* (DD-557) and destroyer escort *Samuel B. Roberts* were sunk by Japanese warships on the morning of October 25.

The surface fight's drama played out over the radio for other task groups to hear. Shortly after 0800, Vice Admiral Thomas Kinkaid announced, "My situation critical." He called for fast battleships and air strikes to help defend his escort carriers off Samar. During the next hour, Kinkaid made repeated urgent calls for help. Admiral Chester Nimitz, some 3,500 miles away in Pearl Harbor, monitored the desperate calls from Taffy 3. His communication team sent a terse message to Halsey: "Where is TF 34?"

Halsey, of course, was on his battleship flagship, overseeing Mitscher's carriers in their assaults on Ozawa's carrier decoy force. As per normal routine, Nimitz's communication team padded dispatches with nonsense phrases to complicate enemy decryption efforts. His radio message to Halsey was padded on either end with the phrases "Turkey trots to water" and "The world wonders." The radioman decoding the message in Halsey's fleet failed to remove the trailing padding. The result played out within the Seventh Fleet as a seemingly stinging rebuke of Halsey's mistakes.

"Where is TF 34? The world wonders."

WHILE SPRAGUE'S TAFFY 3 was being pounded by Kurita's warships, Dave McCampbell and a wingman were still circling above Ozawa's carrier fleet after 0900. Task Force 38's first strike group had cleared the scene, but a smaller Strike No. 2 was approaching. As strike coordinator, McCampbell remained to direct their efforts.

Strike No. 2 included only twenty-nine planes. First to arrive within sight of Ozawa's force at 0945 were six Helldivers and six VT-13 TBMs launched from *Franklin* in TG 38.4. Minutes later, TG 38.3's contribution arrived in the form of seven *Lexington* VT-19 Avengers, with ten VF-19 Hellcats as cover. McCampbell assigned Strike 2's divisions to work over the less damaged warships to the north. *Chitose*, the carrier most heavily assaulted by Strike 1, had slipped beneath the waves before Strike 2 arrived.

The *Franklin* and *Lexington* Avengers made their runs on *Zuikaku* and *Chiyoda*, but Japanese records do not credit any torpedo hits during this attack. The battleship *Ise* logged many bomb near misses, and one small five-hundred-pound bomb exploded on top of her turret No. 2. Beginning at 0959, the carrier *Chiyoda* was attacked by several groups of dive-bombers. A series of damaging near misses and at least one direct 1,000-pound-bomb hit on her flight deck created fires within *Chiyoda*.[25]

Her damage control teams flooded her magazines, creating a 13-degree list to starboard. Water flooded her starboard engine room, leaving *Chiyoda* dead in the water by 1018. During the next two hours, efforts were made to take *Chiyoda* under tow while task force destroyers scurried about to pick up survivors from the sunk *Chitose* and the destroyer *Akitsuki*. McCampbell remained over the Japanese carrier fleet only long enough to assign targets to this group. Having been in the air since daybreak, he then turned for home with his wingman. They trapped on *Essex* at 1055, a full hour and a half after their first strike group had returned.

Lieutenant John Strane had a front-row view of the morning attacks. Since parachuting out of his blazing Hellcat following Strike 1, he had had time to take stock of his provisions before Strike 2 arrived on the scene. His one-man yellow raft had emergency gear, including a Very signaling pistol with star shells. At one point he fired his pistol at low-flying American planes, but the star shell was apparently unseen due to the bright sunlight.

Nursing his burned legs, Strane lay back in his raft after the second strike group turned for home. With damaged Japanese ships visible on the horizon, he hoped his fortunes would change for the better.

Certainly, Admiral Mitscher is going to keep pounding these carriers, he reasoned. *Someone will spot me eventually.*

THE FIRST HOUR after returning to *Essex,* CAG McCampbell was busy assessing the reports from his various pilots. Although he had not lingered over Ozawa's force long enough to see all the results of Strike 2, he knew that it had not included nearly enough planes to finish knocking out the Japanese carrier fleet.

He lobbied for follow-up strikes, but Task Group 38's brass was already thinking the same thing. Over the next hour, plane handlers and ordnancemen worked swiftly to refuel and rearm strike planes for the third strike. Intelligence officer Bob McReynolds and his team gathered input from the morning strikers as the VF-15 pilots were briefed on their next assignments. This time there would be no circling ahead of the task force while awaiting reports from search planes. Ozawa's carriers had been firmly located, and TF 38 was continuing to close the distance between the opposing fleets.

Lieutenant (jg) Duz Twelves was ready. His division leader, Lieutenant Commander George Duncan, had been assigned to lead the fighter cover for the next *Essex* strike force. Ensign Larry Self, assigned to fly wing on Duncan, planned to make his bomb count. As the minutes ticked away in the ready room, he was still chastising himself for his feeble bombing efforts against the Japanese battleship the previous day.[26]

I'm going to put my bomb in a goddamned carrier or I'll fly my plane right into it, one or the other, Self thought.

Officially dubbed Strike 3, the next Task Force 38 strike force included 164 planes launched from Ted Sherman's TG 38.3 and Admiral Ralph Davison's TG 38.4. This time Commander McCampbell would remain on board ship, and Commander Pedro Winters would act as strike coordinator.

Winters had not slept well the night before, eagerly anticipating his next chance to hit the Japanese fleet. He was still angry that his *Lexington* group had gone in on *Musashi* the previous afternoon without torpedoes or armor-piercing bombs. To top things off, he had sat out the first carrier strike that morning while McCampbell was given the lead. "I was whizzed off, a little of it carrying over from yesterday, and tired to boot," Winters admitted.[27]

By 1145, the carriers of both task groups were steaming into the wind, sending combat teams off their decks. Winters led seventy-nine strikers from *Essex*, *Lexington*, and *Langley*. Acting commander of AG-20, Commander Daniel "Dog" Smith, took the lead of his *Enterprise* force, and other strike TG 38.4 planes launched from *Franklin*, *San Jacinto*, and *Belleau Wood*. The flight into the target area would be only an hour after rendezvous, as TG 38.3 had narrowed the gap between fleets to 110 miles.

En route, Strike 3 first found the crippled *Chiyoda*. Several warships were milling about her, attempting to take her in tow. For the moment, Commander Winters was intent on first knocking out the least damaged flattops. "We wanted *all* the carriers, with maybe a BB or CA for the cherry on top," he recalled. Bypassing the *Chiyoda* group, Winters spotted *Zuiho* heading north at about 20 knots with a clear white wake. The big *Zuikaku*, also speeding to the north, was the most desired by Winters. "There was rivalry between *Lexington* and *Essex*, and Dave had had his way on the first strike of the morning," Winters remembered. "I was glad he had left the *Zuikaku* for us and had only nicked her, as indicated by a long thin line of oil in her wake."[28]

The *Lexington*, *Essex*, and *Langley* pilots had the advantage of a thin broken cloud layer to help disguise their advance. Winters divided his groups, remaining high to observe at first while sending his *Lexington* planes against the larger *Zuikaku*.

The *Langley* Avengers and their covering fighters went in on a light cruiser and a nearby destroyer, but they failed to score any torpedo hits. Dog Smith and the TG 38.4 strikers were split between *Zuiho*, *Zuikaku*, the battleships, and other warships. The *Essex* group was ordered to concentrate on *Zuiho*. Lieutenant Roger Noyes led the first six VB-15 Hell-divers directly in from 9,000 feet altitude while the other nine SB2Cs climbed for more altitude before diving.

During the approach to the ship, Winters directed Lieutenant Commander Duncan's fighter divisions to various ships. But Duncan, under directions from Rear Admiral Sherman, had his sights set only on hitting the biggest carrier he could find. When Winters called for Duncan to send a division down on another warship, Duncan recalled, "I wasn't going to pay any attention to him." He simply replied with "Roger."[29]

As Noyes approached, Duncan's division of VF-15 Hellcats went in first to strafe *Zuiho* and drop their five-hundred-pound bombs. Duncan landed his bomb in the middle of the flight deck. Behind him, Duz Twelves watched the carrier materialize below him as he dived through a cloud layer. "Everything in the fleet was shooting at us," he recalled. "My plane was being buffeted and was bouncing a lot." Realizing he was still unhit, Twelves pressed home his attack, squeezing his gun trigger as the flight deck grew larger. Pilots observing this attack later credited Duz with landing his bomb just inside the port catwalk on the flight deck near amidships.[30]

Bringing up the rear of the division, Larry Self was still smarting from the previous day's events. Under orders to release at about 3,000 feet, he decided to press it even lower. The altimeter on his Hellcat read 2,000 feet before Self pickled his bomb and pulled back hard on the stick. As he zoomed out low on the water, he was confident.

"I knew I had a hit," he recalled. "I knew where it was going. It had to. It couldn't go anyplace else." Sure enough, Self was credited with landing his quarter-ton bomb right on the after flight deck, just to starboard of center and just forward of *Zuiho*'s fantail markings. As he climbed back for altitude, Self was pleased to hear orders being called to the other *Essex* strikers to shift over to *Zuikaku*. He had helped ensure the demise of this flattop, vindication for the day before.[31]

Noyes dived in with six SB2Cs right behind Duncan's Hellcats. They claimed four direct hits as *Zuiho* ran to the southeast. Lieutenant Robert Cosgrove led in four VT-15 Avengers against *Zuiho*, in company with a pair of *Lexington* VT-19 TBMs, and claimed a direct hit amidships.

Six other VT-15 pilots carried 2,000-pound "blockbuster" bombs. Five of them went in on the big *Zuikaku*, accompanied by a division of VF-15 and the remaining nine VB-15 Helldivers, each toting 1,000-pound armor-piercing bombs. The VF-15 division went in first, strafing all the way down until releasing their five-hundred-pound bombs. One Hellcat pilot made a near miss within twenty feet of *Zuikaku*'s stern, and Bob Fash was seen to plant his bomb amidships on the flight deck. Close behind the *Essex* fighters, Lieutenant Dick Mills and six other VB-15 pilots claimed direct hits on *Zuikaku*.

Lieutenant (jg) Harry Goodwin led five of his VT-15 Avengers down and claimed three direct hits. *Zuikaku* was burning heavily by this point, with black smoke belching from numerous holes in her flight deck. The final VF-15 division, led by Lieutenant (jg) Red Voorhest, made strafing-and-bombing runs on a destroyer. Three five-hundred-pounders were near misses, but Voorhest was credited with a direct hit on the destroyer's bow. His target warship was seen to lose speed and fall behind the rest of the formation.

As the *Lexington*, *Essex*, and *Langley* groups completed their attacks, Commander Winters coached the *Enterprise*, *Franklin*, *Belleau Wood*, and *San Jacinto* divisions onto a variety of targets. Dog Smith's *Enterprise* group claimed four more bomb hits and two torpedo hits on *Zuiho*, which was also attacked by most of the *Belleau Wood* and *San Jacinto* Avengers. Winters had good reason to be pleased with his *Lexington* group: their 1,000-pounders and torpedo hits had wrecked the big flattop before other small groups of Strike 3 pilots continued to add to the Pearl Harbor attack veteran's misery.

Japanese records show that *Zuikaku* was caught by torpedo bombers executing hammer-and-anvil attacks. At 1315 the first torpedo hit her port side but failed to explode. Simultaneously, two Mark 13s exploded in her starboard side, flooding her No. 3 boiler room. During this same period, at least three bombs landed on the after portion of her flight deck, starting fires in the hangar deck. By 1321, *Zuikaku* had been ripped by three more torpedo explosions and a bomb that struck her flight deck between her middle and rear aircraft elevators.[32]

Within three minutes of these last torpedo hits, *Zuikaku* went dead in the water. With both of her sides ripped open, she began to settle with only a slight list. At 1327, Captain Takeo Kaizuka ordered all hands to move to the flight deck to prepare to abandon ship. He addressed his brave crew from the island structure, stating that he was going to go down with the ship. All hands saluted the formal lowering of the naval ensign as a bugler played "Kimigayo," the national anthem of Japan. The American warplanes had turned for home by the time Kaizuka ordered his men to abandon ship at 1358 as *Zuikaku*'s list increased to 23 degrees.

Zuiho had also been pounded. She was slowed at 1317 by a torpedo that exploded in her starboard bow, directly under the forward compass bridge. Within seconds, a smaller bomb hit her after elevator. By 1330, *Zuiho* had taken another torpedo, a direct bomb hit, and numerous near misses. The light carrier remained under nearly constant attack for the next half hour; even the bombs that missed exploded close enough to cause flooding belowdecks. By 1410, as the American warplanes ceased their attacks, *Zuiho*'s speed had dropped to 12 knots. Her internal flooding was faster than the sailors manning emergency pumps could contain. Listing to starboard, *Zuiho* maintained some speed until 1445, when her port engine room was also completely flooded.[33]

Commander Winters remained over the fleet to assess the damage as the carrier groups headed for home. After checking on the half-converted battleships fleeing toward the north, he returned in time to see *Zuikaku* going down at 1414. She half rolled on her port side and sank stern first, carrying down Captain Kaizuka, forty-eight officers, and 794 enlisted men. The destroyers *Wakatsuki* and *Kuwa* moved in to rescue more than 850 officers and men, including the *Zuikaku* Air Group 601 commander, Lieutenant Commander Takahide Aido.[34]

Pedro Winters saw no large explosions, nor fire or smoke. "Just a few huge bubbles," he recalled. "Quietly, and it seemed to me, with dignity. I was very glad she waited for us to return."[35]

GEORGE DUNCAN'S FIGHTERS were back over *Essex* at 1430, lining up for landings, along with their dive-bombers and torpedo planes. Warm smiles and congratulations met each returning pilot as he made his way toward his respective ready room.

Duz Twelves still had no idea where his five-hundred-pound bomb had landed. Upon pullout, he had used every bit of his mental energy to jink and dodge blossoming geysers from Japanese shells fired into the ocean. During his debriefing, he was quizzed by Lieutenant McReynolds, the VF-15 ACIO.[36]

"Did you hit the ship?"

"I wasn't about to look back," Twelves confessed. "All I was interested in was getting the heck out of there as fast as I could. I probably missed it. Don't put me down for a hit."

Five minutes later, he had made his way back to his stateroom and was hanging his sweat-soaked flight gear up to dry out. Over the squawk box, he was surprised to hear a VB-15 officer announce his congratulations for Lieutenant Twelves for scoring a direct bomb hit on the Japanese carrier. He was further stunned to hear that he was being recommended for a Navy Cross for his efficient bombing run.

By the time Duncan's flight was safely back on board *Essex*, all four Japanese carriers had been stopped. One was gone, and two others were dead in the water. The fourth, *Zuiho*, was badly crippled but still limping along when last seen. During the return of Strike 3, a fourth and smaller group of planes had been dispatched to mop up on Ozawa's fleet. It included only fifteen planes from *Lexington* and *Langley* of Rear Admiral Sherman's TB 38.3 and eighteen strikers from *Franklin* in Davison's TG 38.4. They arrived over the target area at 1415.

The *Lexington* and *Franklin* dive-bombers swarmed onto *Zuiho*, which had just gone dead in the water during their approach. Captain Kuro Sugiura, wounded by the air assaults, recorded ten near misses that inflicted additional flooding damage. By 1500, *Zuiho*'s list had increased to 23 degrees and Sugiura ordered the emperor's portrait transferred to the destroyer *Kuwa*. Ten minutes later he gave the order to abandon ship, and by 1526, *Zuiho*'s stern was dipping under the waves. She slid backward out of sight, without fire or explosion, losing only 215 officers and men.[37]

The fourth American strike made additional runs on nearby battleships but inflicted little lasting damage. Their reports, and those of Commanders Winters and Smith, would be enough to prompt one more air strike that afternoon to mop up on the crippled carriers.

JOHN STRANE HAD been watching the show. Since making a forced water landing with his VF-15 fighter around 0900, he had spent the past seven hours bobbing about in the swells in his yellow life raft. Throughout the day, he had fired his Very pistol three times at low-flying aircraft without success due to the bright sunlight.

By the time the fourth U.S. carrier strike group departed, Strane had watched more than 350 planes pass near his area as they continued to pound Ozawa's force. Trying to avoid sunburn as much as possible, the lieutenant shielded his face and dozed off for a while in the afternoon.

Unknown to Strane, a group of U.S. warships had been detached from Admiral Halsey's Task Force 34 when it turned south around 1115 on October 25. Under command of Rear Admiral Laurence DuBose, the cruisers USS *Santa Fe* (CL-60), USS *Mobile* (CL-63), USS *Wichita* (CA-45), and USS *New Orleans* (CA-32) were ordered to maintain a northerly course with their destroyers. At 1415, Halsey ordered this cruiser group to overtake any crippled ships from Admiral Ozawa's carrier force.[38]

Among the destroyers racing north with DuBose's cruisers was the busy USS *Cotten*. The previous afternoon, *Cotten*'s crew had rescued the VB-15 skipper, Commander Jim Mini, and his gunner, Arne Frobom, after they were forced to ditch their crippled Helldiver. At 1457 on October 25, her lookouts spotted a life raft with a lone occupant and left the screen to effect a rescue. It proved to be Lieutenant Strane of VF-15.[39]

Strane had spotted the approaching warships minutes before. He broke out his signal mirror and began using the bright sun to flash them. When the cruisers and destroyers were about 9,000 yards from him, he finally succeeded in getting a "roger" from one of the tin cans. At 1505, *Cotten* maneuvered alongside his raft and helped him on board. Strane was more than a little surprised to see another friendly face from his own carrier *Essex* looking over the rails.

Jim Mini called to him, "Welcome aboard, John!"[40]

Strane was stunned to learn how fortunate he had been in having his signal mirror spotted. "The boy that saw me was sitting on the aft 5-inch gun mount, peeling potatoes," he recalled. "Had the sun been on the other side of the destroyer, he would never have seen the reflection from the mirror. So, this boy got my flight suit, my life raft, and everything I had with me."

Just ten minutes after recovering Strane, *Cotten*'s busy crew maneuvered to pick up another downed aviator drifting in a life raft. This man proved to be Ensign George Denby of *Enterprise*'s VF-20, who had been forced to ditch eight hours earlier after having his F6F shot up by Zekes over Ozawa's fleet. Less than an hour after recovering the two downed fighter pilots, *Cotten* and her task group were within sight of Ozawa's cripples.

Pedro Winters, who had served as one of the strike coordinators, was returning to his own *Lexington* when he sighted DuBose's cruisers and destroyers on the horizon. Winters coached the U.S. warships toward the crippled carrier *Chiyoda*, still dead in the water with escorting vessels around her. DuBose sent his ships to general quarters at 1615 and raced forward. By 1633 they had *Chiyoda* in sight about 19,500 yards away.

By that point the cruisers *Wichita* and *New Orleans* had already commenced firing on *Chiyoda* with their main batteries. Within minutes the disabled Japanese carrier was smoking heavily after taking numerous shell hits, and she began settling in the water. At 1645, two destroyers were sent with torpedoes, but *Chiyoda* slipped under the waves at 1651 before they could fire. The battered flattop rolled on her starboard beam, hung for a few minutes, and then disappeared bow down, carrying most of her crew with her.

Mini and Strane had a close view of the action as *Cotten* passed within 8,000 yards of *Chiyoda* as she sank. For Strane, it was quite gratifying to know that the carrier his Air Group Fifteen had crippled earlier in the day was no longer a menace. But the ace's firsthand experience with surface combat was far from over.

NINETY MINUTES AFTER recovering Strike Group 3, *Essex* and her task group were pointed back into the wind to launch what would be recorded as Strike Group 5.

Nearly half of the eighty-nine warplanes were from Air Group Fifteen.

Fifteen Helldivers and ten Avengers were off the deck by 1612, making their rendezvous with four VF-15 divisions. *Lexington* contributed seventeen dive-bombers and a dozen Hellcats, while *Langley* added three torpedo-loaded Avengers. The sole contribution from Task Group 38.4 was sixteen fighter-bombers led by the tireless *Enterprise* acting air group commander, Dog Smith, making his third flight against the Japanese carriers of the day. The distance to the enemy force was now only one hundred miles.

Skipper Jim Rigg led the VF on this flight, although the Air Group 44 commander, Malcolm Wordell, would serve as target coordinator. Two VF-15 planes developed engine trouble after takeoff and were forced to return to the ship, leaving Rigg with thirteen fighters and one photo Hellcat. As they neared Ozawa's fleet, Wordell's strike planes passed over Admiral DuBose's warship force minutes after they had polished off the carrier *Chiyoda* with gunfire.

Several Japanese warships were still fleeing the approaching American cruisers and destroyers. Wordell pushed on and soon found that all four Japanese carriers were gone. His primary focus for this attack became the next most valuable targets: the converted battleship-carriers *Ise* and *Hyuga*.

Beginning around 1726, the battleship *Ise* was swarmed by *Essex*, *Langley*, and *Lexington* dive-bomber and torpedo planes. At least thirty-four bombs were listed as near misses by the Japanese crew, although many were close enough to rip open hull plates near the waterline and cause *Ise* to slow as water flooded into her port boiler rooms. Officially, she logged only one direct bomb explosion, while jubilant American aviators believed they had scored more than a dozen hits.[41]

Rigg took all four divisions down on *Ise*, strafing and unleashing their five-hundred-pound bombs before pulling out. Ted Overton, Warren Clark, and Dick Fowler were each credited with landing direct hits amidships in *Ise*'s superstructure antiaircraft gun mounts. The lone VF-15 photo Hellcat remained high to photograph the action with wingman Kent Lee, who opted to jettison his bomb to conserve fuel.

Bert Morris led his division down for additional runs, strafing the cruiser *Oyodo* from bow to stern. As they swept over the ship, Morris and his comrades noted a series of flashes, four in a line, similar to rockets being fired from amphibious rocket ships. Morris then led his combat team down to make strafing runs on a pair of Japanese destroyers before heading to the rendezvous site. *Oyodo* reported light damage from a close bomb near miss and a pair of five-inch rocket hits from American Hellcats.[42]

With dusk approaching, Commander Wordell led his strike group back for Task Force 38. When last seen, the damaged battleship *Ise* was beginning to pick up speed again and limp away from the scene. Two damaged planes, one from *Lexington* and one from *Enterprise*, were forced to make water landings near Rear Admiral DuBose's warships, which quickly recovered the three aviators. Jim Rigg and his *Essex* strikers were in the groove over their home base around 1800, just as the sun was dipping below the horizon.

For Kent Lee, the landing was a nervous experience. "I had never made a night carrier landing, nor had any night carrier landing practice," he recalled. He followed the photo F6F into the groove, carefully watching LSO Roy Bruninghaus in his lighted suit. Lee was much relieved to land without incident, chalking up his first night landing as a success.[43]

JOHN STRANE AND Jim Mini had long since relinquished thoughts of sleeping anytime soon. Their destroyer and Rear Admiral DuBose's other cruisers and destroyers had pounded the carrier *Chiyoda* under the waves. Racing forward, they swept past floating debris and Japanese survivors as their offensive continued.

At 1835, Japanese warships were picked up on radar at a distance of 28,500 yards. DuBose poured on the steam, and by 1853 the cruisers *Wichita* and *New Orleans* had opened fire on a Japanese vessel, the destroyer *Hatsuzuki*. For nearly an hour the sky was illuminated by the gunfire of cruisers and destroyers. The cruiser *Isuzu*, straddled by shells on either side of her bow, turned and made high speed to clear the area. As the distance to *Hatsuzuki* narrowed, DuBose sent three of his destroyers to race forward and fire torpedoes. At 2043 a large explosion was observed on the enemy ship. Two minutes later, DuBose's cruisers began firing star shells to illuminate the stricken vessel for a torpedo attack.[44]

Cotten was 10,000 yards from the scene when the crippled Japanese warship was finally seen to sink. *Hatsuzuki*'s last stand had allowed other Japanese warships to escape, but only eight sailors from the brave destroyer crew would be rescued. Having successfully polished off two of Ozawa's warships, DuBose finally turned his force back.

In the *Cotten* wardroom that evening, the rescued Air Group Fifteen officers were invited to take part in a special celebration meal that had been prepared. This day just happened to mark the one-year anniversary since *Cotten* had sailed from San Diego in October 1943 to join the Pacific Fleet. "They had a birthday party, and they dedicated it to Jim Mini and myself," Strane recalled. "We had the best meal we had had for many months on the *Cotten*."[45]

When Mini and Strane drifted off to sleep in the officers' quarters of their destroyer, they knew they had witnessed a surface action few of their Air Group Fifteen comrades would have believed.

TWENTY-TWO

THE "DUFFY WEAVE"

Jim Duffy struggled to sleep. Since his early months of training with VF-15, he had flown wing on Lieutenant John Strane on almost every mission, through numerous air battles and island strikes.[1] But he had become separated from Strane during their carrier attack and never saw him again. Duffy returned to *Essex*, but his division leader did not. *I failed him*, he thought. He felt overwhelming guilt, and on the morning of October 26 he had no flight duty to otherwise distract these feelings. Task Group 38.3 had made rendezvous with four fleet oilers, and the warships were spending the better part of the day refueling.

A bright spot came during the morning when Rear Admiral DuBose's cruisers and destroyers appeared on the horizon, fresh from their overnight gun battles against Ozawa's crippled ships. The destroyer *Cotten* flashed word that she was carrying three recovered Air Group Fifteen aviators and was ready to return them in exchange for the customary five gallons of ice cream per flyboy rescued. At 1510, *Cotten* snugged up alongside *Essex* and three smiling faces were soon swinging across the waves via breeches buoy baskets: Bombing 15 skipper Jim Mini, ARM1c Arne Frobom, and VF-15's John Strane.

Duffy was overjoyed to see his division leader. Strane shared his adventures in the sea and the task group's sinking of *Chiyoda* and another warship. He never questioned Duffy as to why he had become separated before their tangle with Zekes. But the unspoken still bothered Duffy greatly. "I never brought it up because I was so ashamed of it," he recalled. "He acted as though nothing had ever happened."

That day, the *Essex* air group enjoyed some rare downtime while other task groups carried the burden of fighter sweeps and search flights to continue working over any of the retreating Japanese warships. But the following morning, October 27, it was business as usual for Dave McCampbell's pilots. At 0600, Jim Duffy was launched with three divisions to search over the area from Manila to Coron in the Philippines. Five of the VF-15 Hellcats carried five-hundred-pound bombs, while the other seven lugged six HVARs each.

Lieutenant Bert Morris led the division assigned to the 250- to 260-degree sector. Off Burias Island, three of his F6Fs attacked a 2,000-ton Japanese freighter. Roughly a dozen of their five-inch rockets were seen to strike the merchant ship and create fires. Morris then led his division on strafing runs at Legaspi Field, shooting up a half dozen parked planes. During their return, his division salvoed their final rockets against a pair of destroyers.

Lieutenant (jg) Duz Twelves led the 260- to 270-degree three-hundred-mile search. On the first leg of the search, at 0730, Bill Deming tallyhoed a Fran down at 1,000 feet on an opposite course, heading toward the enemy disposition. Deming made a sharp turn to intercept, with his wingman on his tail. Deming opened fire at about six hundred feet and flamed the Fran's port engine. The fire spread to the wing tank. The starboard wing tank was then flamed by Deming's wingman, Lieutenant (jg) Monk Gunter. The Fran was seen to continue into a shallow glide until it hit the water and exploded on impact.

Two of Twelves's fighters attacked a 10,000-ton troop transport in Manila Bay, east of Corregidor Island. They fired rockets and strafed, noting the ship's weather decks to be crowded with uniformed soldiers. Leaving this ship damaged, Twelves continued across the bay and tallyhoed a Betty bomber about a mile east of Corregidor. Duz exploded the heavy bomber at low altitude, and Ensign Self soon destroyed a torpedo-carrying Kate off Cape Santiago.

Duffy was part of the third fighter search team, covering the 270- to

280-degree sector. With Lieutenant Strane still recovering from his rescue ordeal, Lieutenant (jg) Ken White led the division.

White's team encountered a pair of Betty bombers, one some distance behind the other one. White led his division down on the leading Betty, but it immediately dived for the wave tops and poured on the speed. "We were off to the races!" recalled Duffy. Gunning his throttle, he pulled out ahead of White and Ensign Don Gonya. Duffy and Gonya bracketed the first Betty, but found it to be in a terrific defensive position. "No one could get underneath it, and with its deadly rear guns, no one wanted to get close," said Duffy. His team made several flat-side firing passes, but the Betty pilot made small skids and slight but abrupt climbs to throw off their aim. Gonya finally got hits in the Betty's cockpit. It burst into flames and hit the water.[2]

The other Betty started making a run for its base. With full power, Duffy soon caught up and made hits in its port engine. It began smoking, followed by flames pouring from its engine and wing root. The bomber steadily lost altitude. "The gunners must have been scared to death, as they shot wildly," recalled Duffy. Their tracers arced straight up into the air, none passing anywhere close to his Hellcat. The Betty continued downward, finally crashing against the sea surface and cartwheeling in flames.

White's team continued its search, although one fighter developed engine trouble and was forced to turn back toward base. On the return leg, this pilot observed a crash-diving Japanese submarine and dropped his five-hundred-pound bomb on the swirling wake.

While these three teams were busy, *Essex* had launched four fighters to handle a relay CAP east of Luzon. Flying in two-plane sections, the VF-15 pilots had been assigned to serve as communications relay teams between their carrier task group and the longer-ranging scout teams.

Lieutenant George Crittenden's section took up station one hundred miles from TG 38.3. They duly orbited for the next four hours but had no enemy encounters. Farther out, handling relay duties at two hundred miles from the fleet, was the team of Lieutenants (jg) Swede Thompson and wingman Ken West. Their experiences were quite different.

Shortly after 0735, Thompson's section boldly slashed into a formation of thirty or more Japanese warplanes. Thompson engaged one Zeke head-on, sending it into the ocean, and shortly thereafter fired enough lead into another Zeke until its pilot was seen to bail out of his blazing fighter. Wingman West was credited with a probable on the first Zeke he attacked and a certain kill on another. Thompson and West made repeated passes throughout the enemy formation. They damaged other planes, but, in the swirling melee, none were observed directly to crash. In the end, West was credited with one Zeke kill, two probables, and a fourth Japanese fighter damaged.

As the raid was beginning to break up, many of the Japanese planes were seen to jettison their bombs and torpedoes. At that time, a Zeke came up and scored damaging hits on West's F6F in his engine, oil line, wings, tail, and fuselage. West's windshield was covered with oil. He called to Thompson, and they assumed a defensive formation and headed back to base. Although a half dozen Japanese planes pursued them, Thompson was able to ward them off West's crippled fighter. One Tony began closing on West's tail, but he was able to outdistance it by using full water injection speed.

West was forced to make an emergency landing on *Lexington*. After temporary repairs, he was able to return to *Essex* later in the day. Their attacks had been successful, but the VF-15 pair was lucky indeed to return against such heavy odds against them.

One final fighter mission was launched at 1007 on October 27. Skipper Jim Rigg led four divisions in company with another dozen *Lexington* Hellcats to attack Japanese warships reported off Semirara Island in the Visayan chain. For its part, VF-15 was assigned to hit a destroyer already beached due to damage it had sustained. Nine near misses were chalked up and Lieutenant (jg) Bill Anderson was credited with the only hit, a thousand-pound bomb seen to explode amidships on the destroyer, between the bridge superstructure and the No. 1 stack.

After strafing the burning destroyer thoroughly, Rigg brought his combat teams back to base without loss. The greatest sea battle in history off the Philippines had been concluded, and Air Group Fifteen had contributed its fair share to the victory.

Task Group 38.3 commander Ted Sherman informed Admiral Halsey that his crews were exhausted and his carriers were in need of replenishing weapons for their air groups. Halsey responded by ordering the task group back to Ulithi for reprovisioning. En route, Commander McCampbell learned that his air group was due for rotation. Having departed Pearl Harbor in early May, the *Essex* squadrons had completed six months of combat duty—considered the standard period after which air groups should be sent back for rest. As the news made the rounds, scuttlebutt was rampant. With the impending return to Ulithi, and then the expected rotation back to the States, VF-15's longer-tenured pilots anticipated a return to their families. But not all pilots would be granted such a luxury.

Ensign Dick Davis was among the *Essex* Hellcat pilots who had made a five-hour morning search flight for the Japanese fleet. Shortly after trapping and making his way to the VF-15 ready room, he received surprising news from skipper Jim Rigg. "Davis, get your bags," said Rigg. "You're going to the *Enterprise*. They're short of fighter pilots."[3]

The Navy's sixth aircraft carrier, *Enterprise* was a seasoned ship whose crew had been in the Pacific War fight since December 7, 1941. But her current Air Group 20 was still young on its combat tour, which had commenced on August 31 with strikes on the Bonin Islands. By comparison, the *Essex* Air Group Fifteen had been in combat since May and was one of the few air groups to have participated in both Philippine Sea battles in June and October.

By late October, *Enterprise*'s VF-20 squadron, under Commander Fred Bakutis, had suffered many losses in terms of F6Fs and pilots. With months to go on AG-20's tour, replacements were sorely needed. As TG 38.3 moved toward Ulithi, Commander McCampbell was requested to off-load twenty-two of his Hellcats and a dozen spare pilots to continue in service with VF-20. McCampbell and Rigg reviewed their roster and made the tough choices. Not wishing to burden any of the pilots who had been with VF-15 since joining *Essex* at Pearl Harbor, they instead tapped a dozen ensigns who had come into the unit as replacements between June and September: Paul Bugg, Dusty Craig, Dick Davis, Wayne Dowlen, Herman Foshee, Don Gonya, Jerry Lathrop, Earl Lewis, Dick McGraw, Jim Mooney, Bob Sprankle, and Jack Taylor.

During the afternoon of October 27, the transfer pilots were shuffled via destroyer to the carrier *Franklin*, where they remained overnight. At 0552 the following morning, the destroyer USS *Brush* (DD-745) came alongside and took on board passengers, including the VF-15 pilots, via breeches buoys. Several hours later, *Brush* in turn moved alongside the port quarter of *Enterprise* and off-loaded her new VF-20 replacement pilots.

Jack Taylor took his new assignment to VF-20 in stride. With four months of service in VF-15, he felt like a veteran as he entered the *Enterprise* ready room. "We acted like we were part of their air group," he recalled, "but we thought we were better than them, because we had been out longer than them." Taylor quickly blended into the *Enterprise* air group and would soon develop a certain pride in being on board the veteran carrier "Big E."[4]

As their own *Essex* headed in to Ulithi, the *Enterprise* air group continued flying support missions for three days over Leyte Island to protect the troops battling ashore and the vulnerable Allied ships anchored near shore. Japanese kamikazes were a continual menace. On October 29, *Intrepid* was damaged by a suicide plane that slammed into one of her port-side gun positions. The following day was even more devastating for TF 38 carriers.

Around 1400 on October 30, bogeys began to appear on TG 38.4 radar screens. Combat air patrols surged out to greet them, but at least four bandits managed to slip past to attack the task group at 1425. One Zeke dived straight into *Franklin*, steaming 4,000 yards to the port side of *Enterprise*. Three minutes later a second Zeke plowed through the antiaircraft fire to drop a bomb well forward of *Franklin*. This Zeke climbed for altitude and then turned to dive on *Belleau Wood*, hitting its after flight deck with a powerful explosion. Two more Zekes next attacked *San Jacinto* and *Enterprise*. Streaming AA fire splashed the first kamikaze short of *San Jacinto*, but the last attacker came in fast, diving toward the Big E's starboard side. Every 40mm and 20mm gun that was operable opened up.

A half mile out, the AA fire started a fire in the Zeke's port wing. It continued diving in as tracers poured into it. A quarter mile out, the Zeke began to roll. It nearly made a direct hit. It went fifteen feet above the flight deck, narrowly missing parked and fueled aircraft before exploding in the sea fifteen yards to port. Pieces of its wing landed in the port catwalk. Ensign Jim Mooney, watching this kamikaze attack from topside, noted that the pilot had his canopy open during the run. The whole event took only seconds, but Mooney was close enough to see that the pilot had his goggles pushed up on his head. "Within five seconds, he was in the water at about three hundred knots," Mooney recalled.[5]

KAMIKAZES WERE FAR from his thoughts as Duz Twelves rode a launch in toward the beach at Ulithi. Several of his friends had been detached for service on the Big E, but Twelves was hopeful that his carrier would soon be homeward bound, where he could reunite with his fiancée, Rhea. Soon after *Essex* and her task group dropped anchor in Ulithi's harbor on October 30, Twelves was among the fortunate aviators able to go ashore for drinks at the base O Club.

Dave McCampbell passed the word that Air Group Fifteen would indeed be rotated home soon. *Essex* took on fuel and supplies on October 31, along with a mass of new aviators. The return trip to Pearl Harbor would still include regular flight duties and combat air patrols for Satan's Playmates, which required a complete roster. Therefore, McCampbell and Jim Rigg were issued a baker's dozen of temporary replacement fighter pilots. During the morning and afternoon of October 31, they came over in groups from the escort carrier USS *Steamer Bay* (CVE-87).

Fighting Fifteen yeoman duly recorded their names onto the squadron roster: Ensigns William Allen, Reune Bertschi, Edward Bomar, James Butters, Galen Eaholtz, Robert Erickson, James Forsyth, Gene Langston, Leonard Lemley, Lyle Maxey, Bill Riffle, Thomas Tidwell, and John Whiteside. The following morning, *Essex* took on replacement aircraft for the trip, including thirty new F6Fs.[6]

Raised in Oakland, California, Ensign Lemley had a background similar to those of the other newbies. He enlisted shortly after the Pearl Harbor attack and proceeded into civilian pilot training in late 1942 before being sworn in as a naval aviation cadet. As he swung across to *Essex* in a bosun's chair on October 31, he marveled at the length of the fleet carrier's flight deck. "It was a monster," Lemley recalled. "We had little training on carrier operations. It was like on-the-job training [when] we joined Air Group Fifteen."[7]

One of the first duties for Lemley and his fellow rookie VF-15 pilots was to go onto the flight deck and warm up some Hellcats. Using a shotgun shell, each plane captain would fire it to start the Pratt & Whitney engines. Each pilot was given a plane number, but Lemley was assigned to fire up the CAG plane. "I asked what it was," he recalled, as older hands laughed.

By 1620 on November 1, Ted Sherman's TG 38.3 was underway from Ulithi. Its force included the carriers *Essex*, *Lexington*, and *Langley*, four cruisers, and sixteen destroyers bound for Manus Island in the Admiralties. Only three hours later, Sherman received orders to wheel his task group about and make its best speed toward the central Philippines area to intercept Japanese forces reported to be approaching that vicinity. Recent kamikaze attacks had damaged several of Pete Mitscher's carriers, so *Essex* simply could not be spared for the moment.

The news hit hard with the veteran pilots, who were already imagining Hawaii and California again. "It seemed reasonable to assume that we would be the next group relieved to go home," recalled division leader Baynard Milton. "But we had no idea when that would happen. Continuing delays kept dashing our great expectations and gnawing at our morale."[8]

Task Group 38.3 refueled in the Philippine Sea on November 3 before beginning a high-speed run to the west to participate in air strikes on Luzon and western Leyte. Ted Sherman's task group had been joined by a new fleet carrier, USS *Ticonderoga* (CV-14), about five hundred miles east of Leyte. En route that night, the cruiser *Reno* was struck by two Japanese submarine torpedoes, marking the first time in nearly two years that an I-boat had successfully attacked a warship operating with the American fast carriers. Dead in the water, with forty-six sailors killed, the cruiser was towed 1,500 miles back to Ulithi for repairs.

On the evening of November 4, Commander McCampbell and Jim Rigg briefed their pilots on raids scheduled for the following morning. At 0615 on November 5, Rigg led four divisions off the deck for a fighter sweep over Manila on Luzon. His group flew in company with fighter elements from *Lexington*, *Ticonderoga*, and *Langley*. Two VF-15 divisions remained on high cover while the other two went in to strafe aircraft on Nichols Field.

"Manila was a hellhole for antiaircraft fire," recalled fighter-bomber pilot Bill Anderson. Surrounded by hills, the area bristled with gun emplacements.[9]

Fifteen aircraft were strafed on the runway aprons and in their revetments, although only four of the larger transport planes caught fire from the bullets. Flying high cover at 11,000 feet, Lieutenant Ted Overton tallyhoed a pair of bogeys below his division. Overton reached 300 knots before he was able to blast down one of the Oscars from short range. After strafing Nichols Field, Doyle Bare flamed a lone Lily that slammed into the ground.

By the time the early VF sweeps had cleared the air over Nichols Field, a main strike group of SB2Cs and TBMs from Air Group Fifteen moved in over the base. CAG Dave McCampbell served as target coordinator for this strike group and a second one that followed. Dashing Dave's division was unable to locate a carrier that had been reported near Subic Bay, but he did tallyho a lone Val dive-bomber low on the water. Through numerous deflection shots, McCampbell raised smoke from the Val's engine, but it did not appear to be handicapped. Finally, a stern run knocked out the bomber's engine and forced it into the water.[10]

En route to the rendezvous area for Strike 2, McCampbell tallyhoed two Zekes at 12 o'clock on an opposite course. He and his wingman rolled over on them and stayed on their tails until both were destroyed. "Many gun stoppages plus four burnt-out barrels somewhat delayed the kill, although he never once was able to shake me off his tail by his violent maneuvers," CAG reported. McCampbell, down to only his outboard port gun being operational, delivered a short burst. He watched as the Zeke pulled up into a loop starting at three hundred feet altitude and then dived straight into the ground, exploding on impact.

"Eight other Zekes were observed over the rendezvous area but were not aggressive," McCampbell related. "No attempt was made to engage them since all my guns had stopped firing and my wingman had only two good guns left."

In the meantime, Roy Rushing had pursued and shot down the other Zeke even though only his starboard wing guns were operational. Rushing and his commander then rejoined their second section and returned to *Essex* with their air group. About the same time they were completing their Zeke kills, the *Essex* strike group had arrived over Luzon's bay. Two divisions under George Crittenden and John Strane escorted the bombers and torpeckers, adding their share of damage via rockets and strafing against revetments. En route to their rendezvous area, Strane's second division of VF-15 was jumped by about five Oscars and a pair of Kawasaki Ki-45 Kai Hei night fighters (code-named "Nicks").

Before launching, Lieutenant Strane and his wingman, Jim Duffy, had discussed their plans. Over Admiral Ozawa's carrier fleet on October 25, Duffy had weaved and zigged frantically while in pursuit of Zekes. Strane had coolly picked off the enemy fighters as his wingman employed what he had later jokingly dubbed the "Duffy weave." Heading for their planes before launching on November 5, Duffy had declared to Strane that he would not be used for bait again that day. "He just smiled and winked at me as we made our way across the deck to our Hellcats," Duffy remembered.[11]

The enemy, having waited for the Americans to complete their attacks, were first noticed by Strane at 12,000 feet. As two Oscars came in behind the *Essex* Helldivers, Strane and his wingman drove them off. Having lost his division leader on October 25, Duffy had vowed never to make that mistake again. "I stayed glued to John's wing," he recalled. He now found his division facing an odd combination: a twin-engine Nick fighter trailing behind a much slower Oscar fighter. The two enemy planes pressed home their attacks, diving down on Lieutenant Ken White and his wingman.

As White's section commenced their defensive Thach weave maneuvers, Strane and Duffy dived in to assist. Strane poured lead into the Oscar's engine. It made only a lazy half roll before continuing on its back until it slammed to earth and exploded. Duffy fired into the Nick in a head-on run. As his opponent started to pull out, Duffy noted its starboard engine aflame. The Japanese pilot pulled up and flashed over Duffy before falling off to starboard and crashing. Having lost two of their planes, the remaining Japanese strikers chose not to attack the *Essex* group any further. By the time this strike group returned to base, *Essex* had just completed the launch of another seven VF-15 fighters for an additional sweep over Luzon.

George Duncan was flight leader and Bert Morris had the second division. Right off the bat, one plane from Morris's division was forced back to base with a canopy that refused to close. Morris continued on with only his wingman, following Duncan's division toward the Manila area. Duncan and Morris took their six Hellcats down to strafe a dozen single-engine planes on Malvar North Field before proceeding to Clark Field. "We wound up there right at the tail-end of a strike on Clark Field from this other carrier task group," Duncan recalled.[12]

As the *Lexington* planes cleared the Japanese airfield, the *Essex* F6Fs prepared to sweep right in behind them. But Duncan's luck was not with him that day. Bert Morris and his wingman were forced to drop out of the formation, one F6F suffering from a side panel blown out of its canopy and the other having depleted its oxygen supply. Any attempt Morris made to notify Duncan that his section was returning to base was lost, as Duncan's division had dropped right into a hornet's nest.

Nothing was going as planned. A two-division sweep was already down to five planes. "This was a fighter sweep and we didn't expect much," Duncan recalled. "I had a new kid on my wing we were just breaking in." Ensign Reune Bertschi had been with the squadron for only a few days, but he was eager enough to make his first combat. A group of Zekes, Tonys, and Tojos was lying in wait for the four VF-15 pilots, and the action immediately became heated.

The Tojos attacked first, and as they pulled out of their firing runs, Duncan got a short burst on one. As a Zeke made a run on his port quarter, he pulled out, noting Bertschi finish off one of the Tojos with a head-on run.

Duncan made a low side run on a Zeke, flaming its engine with direct hits. With Bertschi back on his wing, the two warded off further enemy attacks. Duncan had his hands full trying to get his rookie wingman to properly execute a Thach weave. With Zekes and Tonys swirling about, Bertschi was wide-eyed. They climbed back to high altitude with fighters climbing after them, but the Japanese pilots wisely headed for the safety of cloud cover when Duncan's section turned back into them. By the time they headed for the rendezvous spot, Ensign Bertschi was now fully into his Thach weave, zigging madly. "I couldn't get him to stop," Duncan recalled.[13]

As he circled the rendezvous spot, Duncan had only his rookie wingman. Bert Morris's section had disappeared before the fight even began.

Oh, hell! he thought. *I can't go back home like this. My second section is nowhere to be seen. And I've lost the movie star and his two other boys. I'm in real trouble!*[14]

DUZ TWELVES, LEADING Duncan's second section, was fighting for his life. He and his wingman, Ensign Larry Self, had been jumped by a pair of Tojos as they flew over Clark Field to scout for parked aircraft.

Twelves and Self turned into them, deploying in a weave position, when two more Tojos began firing deflection shots. Just as Duz faced the new arrivals, four Zekes joined the assault on the American fighters. Twelves got in a deflection burst on one Zeke and saw hits land in its engine. He watched it long enough to note the Zeke crash and burn.

He was startled by the thumping of slugs ripping through his F6F. Other tracer bullets zipped by just over his port wing. Twelves pulled up steeply and began evasive action. Assistance was not available from his wingman, as Self's engine chose this inopportune moment to begin malfunctioning. His Hellcat fell back astern, leaving Duz jinking for his life. He found himself against three Zekes up high and another pair level with his altitude.

One of the latter fighters turned toward Twelves. As Duz met the Zeke nearly head-on, the Japanese pilot began firing. His aim was just off as Twelves continued straight at a slight downward angle. The Zeke pulled up steeply to a point about 3,000 feet above Twelves before rolling over to come down. Duz decided his only choice was to pull up sharply, almost straight up and right into the Zeke.

The American and Japanese pilots fired directly at each other. Duz's wing guns set the Zeke's engine on fire. Twelves narrowly recovered, whipping through two or three spin turns before he leveled out again. He caught only a brief view of his opponent as the Zeke continued down and crashed in flames.

The Zeke's wingman was now coming in. Twelves switched on water injection and hit his flap switch. *I'll have to dogfight my way out of this one*, he realized. With flaps down, he found that his F6F performed "beautifully" with a Zeke. In one turn, Duz pulled too tight and snap-rolled. As his opponent responded with a perfect slow roll, Twelves seized the chance to pour on full throttle and escape the fray with his battered Hellcat.

Larry Self, struggling with an F6F that could only muster two-thirds of its power, was behind the main fight that Twelves was engaged in. Challenged by four Tonys, Self pulled up abruptly and fired straight into one of the fighters. The Tony's engine flamed, black smoke poured forth, and a wing root erupted in flames. "We were never supposed to shoot head-on at an enemy airplane," Self recalled. "We were supposed to get on his tail."[15]

The enemy fighter exploded with enough force that fragments slammed into Self's cockpit canopy, blowing out its side panels. A shard of shrapnel or chunk of his canopy slashed Self's forehead above his left eye. Streaming blood, the lone pilot found himself in the fight of his life as the remaining three Tonys stayed after him. Self used every defensive maneuver in his trick bag. With a fouled engine, and unsure how serious his head wound was, he knew he had no chance to dogfight them. Self pushed into a steep dive, reaching 250 knots. Spotting a low cumulus bank, he zoomed into it and switched to flying on instruments. When he finally emerged from the clouds, he was relieved to find the sky clear of bandits. He wiped the blood from his face and headed for home.

Duncan and Bertschi managed to rendezvous with Twelves and Self. Two of their Hellcats were badly battered, but VF-15 mechanics would restore them to service. Duncan had his own challenges: he had lost the entire division of Lieutenant Morris during the flight and had not heard from them.

Called to the bridge after landing on *Essex*, Duncan made his report to Rear Admiral Ted Sherman.

"How many did you shoot down?" Sherman asked.[16]

"Just one," Duncan replied with disgust.

He was more concerned with the other pilots who had been lost. But his worries vanished when he entered the ready room and spotted Bert Morris.

"George!" Morris called. "I've been back forty-five minutes. Where the hell you been?"

"I could have killed him," Duncan recalled. He felt in hindsight that his badly scattered combat team had done well indeed to claim five enemy fighters killed.

John Strane and Jim Duffy were in high spirits by the time they returned to the VF-15 ready room. Strane had recorded his thirteenth aerial victory, and he had witnessed his wingman's Oscar also crash.

"Boy, you got one, huh!" Strane announced.[17]

"I did?" Duffy asked.

Strane just smiled and replied, "You sure did! Way to go, ace!"

His Oscar shoot-down on November 5 officially pushed Duffy to ace status. "It was a really good feeling," he recalled. "Not because I was one of twenty-six aces from VF-15 during our seven months in combat; I felt good because he didn't use me as bait that time."

THE NEXT *Essex* strike group on November 5 found plentiful shipping to attack in Manila Bay. Eleven F6Fs under Ted Overton chased away four Zekes. Lieutenant John Brodhead's seven Helldivers claimed three direct hits on the cruiser *Nachi*, while VeeGee Lambert's Avengers claimed a pair of torpedo hits. Overton's Hellcats strafed the cruiser and its nearby destroyer, *Akebono*, additionally pounding both vessels with direct rocket hits. *Nachi* was maneuvering radically at more than 20 knots when attacked, with bomb explosions fountaining the sea around her.

From VF-15, Overton, Dick Fowler, Rod Johnson, and rookie ensign Ed Bomar were credited with damage against *Nachi*, while Bob Fash scored a damaging near miss against the escort vessel. Following the *Essex* attacks, *Nachi* was assaulted by two waves of *Lexington* Helldivers and Avengers that hit the cruiser with rockets, bombs, and torpedoes. She was left dead in the water in a sinking condition, her bow blown off by torpedo explosions and her after magazine slammed by another torpedo. As the

Essex planes made their poststrike rendezvous at 1445, *Nachi* exploded, sending a cloud of red smoke high into the air.

By the time this group headed back to *Essex*, a fourth strike force was already well on its way toward Manila Bay. Jim Rigg led in the eight VF armed with five-hundred-pound bombs under each wing. Two of his men strafed and bombed a destroyer, claiming one hit on her quarterdeck. Another division made strafing runs on a second destroyer. The three pilots ahead of Ensign Kent Lee in Lieutenant (jg) Gunter's division missed the speeding warship.

Flying tail-end Charlie, Lee was confident he would score a hit. "I had him right in my sights, pickled the bomb, and nothing happened," he recalled. When Lee pulled out his division leader pulled alongside, staring at his five-hundred-pound bomb. "I could just see what he was thinking: 'That dumb-ass ensign.'"[18]

Frustrated, Lee called, "Let's make another run. Let me drop my bomb."

Lee's division went in for a second strafing run on the destroyer, which was smoking from numerous .50-caliber hits. Once again Lee pulled out, confident his dive had been perfect enough to score a hit. By this point, Gunter had had enough with his wingman's errant bomb. He led his men on additional strafing runs before heading back to base. After landing on *Essex*, Lee made a point of inspecting his F6F with several ordnancemen. "The bomb rack was not hooked up," Lee found. "Otherwise, I would have gotten myself a destroyer."

While *Essex* awaited the return of her strike groups in the early afternoon of November 5, Lieutenant George Crittenden was scrambled at 1347 with two divisions to intercept an enemy air raid on Task Group 38.3. The Hellcats were still clawing for altitude when the warships began firing on a pair of twin-engine medium bombers. The intensity of the fire forced Crittenden to have his CAP retire outside the screen at 3,000 feet to await orders.

The scrambled fighters dumped their loads of depth charges and were vectored out to intercept a bogey. Crittenden's radio failed as they approached a lone Judy, so he turned the lead over to Lieutenant (jg) Swede Thompson. As the VF-15 quartet bracketed the enemy plane, Crittenden landed enough hits in the Judy's engine and wing roots to send it flaming into the drink.

For those riding out the Japanese air strikes on November 5, there were plenty of close calls. One suicide plane hit *Lexington*'s signal bridge and another crashed right alongside *Ticonderoga*. With kamikazes lurking about the task force, *Essex* remained at general quarters throughout the night. Some aviators simply went to their ready room, too tense for any good sleep.

TWENTY-THREE

"I'VE GOT THREE MEATBALLS CORNERED"

November 6, 1944

Jake Hogue and Kester Roberts hit the night sky via cat shots at 0230. With Air Group Fifteen slated to make multiple strikes on Manila this day, Ted Sherman wanted to suppress the kamikaze threat. The pair of VF-15 night fighters was loaded with 250-pound bombs to help crater the runways as they strafed the parked planes.

After multiple strafing runs, Lieutenant Hogue and Ensign Roberts rendezvoused over Laguna de Bay without lights, preparing to return to base. At a nearby airfield, Roberts exploded an enemy aircraft just as it cleared the runway. At 0615 the bat men reached *Essex*, where they circled for a half hour as *Essex* launched a dozen other Hellcats of VF-15 for a morning sweep over Luzon.

At Nichols Field, George Duncan's group strafed two Betty bombers in "ready" condition on the ground; they were set ablaze. Duncan fired at a Fran just as it launched from the field; he scored hits in its starboard engine, wing root, and fuselage. The Japanese pilot attempted to return to base, but his plane ground-looped violently and burst into flames. Continuing on to Clark Field, Duncan's flight found no enemy aircraft and a ceiling too low to prevent effective strafing.

Ted Overton led two divisions of VF-15 to escort VB-15 and VT-15 planes for a strike against shipping in Manila Harbor. Antiaircraft fire was terrific, forcing Lieutenant (jg) Bill Rising of VB-15 to make a water landing. Overton flew cover over him until Rising settled his Helldiver into the ocean twenty-six miles from Sampaloc Point. Later in the day, two VB-15 pilots dropped rafts and supplies to Rising and his gunner and assisted with directing in a rescue submarine. The first strike returned with damage claims to a half dozen Japanese ships.

Lieutenant Bert Morris led the fighter escort for the second *Essex* strike of the day, against shipping near Subic Bay. Their force would return to the ship having contributed to the sinking of three enemy vessels. Morris and wingman Reune Bertschi bombed a minelayer near the bay's entrance, leaving it in sinking condition after Morris's five-hundred-pounder created a large explosion. Monk Gunter and Howard Smith each damaged a freighter/transport ship, while John Collins took his division down on a 3,000-ton auxiliary transport.

Collins's bomb exploded against the ship's side, while Bill Anderson landed a hit on the stern and Rod Johnson made a direct hit that created a brilliant explosion. This ship was seen to sink within minutes. Against another transport ship, Doyle Bare was credited with a five-hundred-pound hit on the forward deck. Two additional bombs dropped by Lieutenant (jg) Marshall Deputy of VB-15 left this vessel settling by the stern as its skipper headed the auxiliary ship toward the beach to save it.

At 1103, Ted Overton led nineteen pilots of VF-15 for a second fighter sweep over Manila. His F6Fs strafed Nichols Field and Clark Field, burning a dozen brand-new Betty bombers dispersed on the ground. Rookie pilot Leonard Lemley was new to aerial rockets, but he fired his into a hangar building and retired under heavy AA fire—close enough that one round penetrated his fuselage without exploding. After the sweep turned to return to base, one division headed to the mouth of Manila Bay to help cover the rescue work of a lifeguard submarine attempting to pick up a downed VB-15 aircrew.

By the time the sub was reported to be only fifteen minutes away from the location, Ensign Bill Riffle's Hellcat was desperately low on fuel. His division headed for *Essex*, but his F6F ran out of gas around 1638, just a mile short of the task force's destroyer screen. Riffle made a successful water landing and was soon spotted by the destroyer USS *Dortch* (DD-670), which was returning from rescuing a *Lexington* Avenger crew.

Dortch slowed to collect Riffle from his life raft and continued on toward its radar picket station duty area.

Essex ran through a heavy storm on November 8 that curtailed flight duty. The following day, orders were received for the ship to proceed to Guam, but during the night the orders changed. *Essex* began a high-speed run toward Leyte. "Dugout Dug (General MacArthur) spotted a Jap whale boat and needs the aid of the whole navy," mechanic Elmer Cordray wrote with disgust in his diary.[1]

November 11, 1944

At 0640, *Essex* launched four two-plane fighter teams on scouting missions for Japanese shipping in the Sibuyan, Visayan, and Camotes Seas. Each sector covered a 10-degree area, out as far as 350 miles from the ship. An additional four F6Fs were deployed in teams of two, one orbiting one hundred miles and the other two hundred miles, to relay back any contact reports from the search teams.

Lieutenant (jg) George Carr and his wingman sighted an enemy convoy of four large freighters with a half dozen escorting destroyers attempting to reach Ormoc Bay. Five Zekes were observed to be airborne, but they did not attack while Carr's section held the convoy under surveillance until 1015. When Carr finally turned for home, strike teams were already inbound to attack these ships.

Two of the other search teams found little of interest save for a demolished enemy destroyer beached on Semirara Island. Lieutenant (jg) Bill Deming's fourth search team observed four seventy-five-ton luggers and strafed them, leaving three burning furiously. When the team continued on to reconnoiter an airfield, Deming's plane was hit by AA fire. A large hole was ripped through the underside of his fuselage, and a fire started close to his seat. Although his plane was still somewhat airworthy, Deming was blinded by choking smoke, even after thrusting open his canopy.[2]

Deming glided down toward the waves just off the coast in Albay Gulf and made a successful water landing. But his F6F sank quickly. As it bubbled beneath the surface, Deming frantically tried to extract his life raft and survival gear, which had become snagged. By the time his Hellcat was ten feet underwater, he gave up the fight and kicked toward the surface. He succeeded in inflating his life jacket.

Lieutenant (jg) Bill Deming, seen in 1945, was shot down on November 11, 1944, and escorted to safety by Filipino guerrillas.   Mark Deming

As Deming's comrades circled the site of his crash, they saw native outrigger canoes paddling furiously toward the scene. Good fortune continued to shine on "Wild Bill": the canoes were full of friendly locals who had a healthy hatred for the Japanese, who had invaded their homeland. The natives smiled and waved to the *Essex* fighters circling above until they headed back for base.

Over the next two weeks, Deming was moved through the jungles and mountains of Luzon. At one point the Filipinos captured a young Japanese soldier. The guerrillas brought the prisoner before Lieutenant (jg) Deming and offered to let the American pilot execute their former tormentor with a .45-caliber pistol. Deming politely declined, saying he could not take the "honor" away from the locals, who had been so badly abused by the enemy military forces. Thankfully, Deming never learned of the final fate of this soldier.

LIEUTENANT JOHN COLLINS, handling the two-hundred-mile relay team duties over southwestern Samar and northern Leyte with his wingman, Swede Thompson, was confronted with three planes around 0940. Although Collins originally thought they were friendly P-47s due to their paint scheme, he finally spotted red meatballs on the wings.

Both the American and the Japanese fighters dropped their belly tanks and commenced a vicious dogfight. Collins and Thompson each downed an Oscar. Weaving defensively with each other, Thompson scored a second Oscar kill as Hellcat No. 1, piloted by Collins, was stitched by another Oscar. Yet another Oscar latched onto Thompson's tail and scored damaging hits before Collins could drive the Japanese plane away from his comrade's F6F. This Oscar was last seen smoking and was chalked up as a probable for Collins.

Thompson's Grumman was smoking heavily. Collins put bursts into the fuselage of two more of the attacking Oscars but watched in horror as Thompson's F6F soon nosed out of control into the ocean with a tremendous impact. Spotting two more Oscars in his rearview mirror, Collins pushed his throttle forward and raced for cloud cover at 320 knots with Oscars in pursuit. When he emerged from the clouds, he had shaken his enemy. It was time to head for the base.

The morning's actions had cost VF-15 two Hellcats and the life of Swede Thompson.

THE ENEMY CONVOY located by George Carr's search team caused a frenzy within Task Force 38. Less than thirty minutes after the ships were reported, *Essex* launched a deckload strike. Within forty-five minutes of the intelligence, Task Force 38 carriers—operating about two hundred miles east of San Bernardino Strait—had launched some 347 strike planes.

Officially listed as TA No. 3, the convoy included five troop transport ships carrying soldiers and munitions: *Taizan Maru, Mikasa Maru,*

Celebes Maru, Seiho Maru, and *Tensho Maru.* The transports were steaming near Ormoc in the company of the destroyers *Hamanami, Wakatsuki,*
Shimakaze, Naganami, Asashimo, and *Minesweeper No. 30.* The soldiers
and heavy equipment of the Japanese Army's 26th Division never had a
chance to make it ashore to Leyte.[3]

Dave McCampbell led the *Essex* parade with sixteen Hellcats accompanying twenty SB2Cs of VB-15 and eleven bomb-armed Avengers. *Ticonderoga* contributed another forty-four strike planes, with the collective
group of ninety-one planes under the direction of CAG McCampbell. Approaching Ormoc Bay off Leyte at 14,000 feet, McCampbell's pilots spotted the convoy rounding Apale Point into the bay, only about five miles
from the anchorage. Time was of the essence.

Lieutenant (jg) Jigs Foltz, flying a photo Hellcat with Ensign Merwin
Frazelle on his wing, dropped down first to photograph the enemy fleet
before the attacks commenced. CAG McCampbell and his wingman, Roy
Rushing, remained at 8,000 feet to direct the attacks. He assigned Bomb-
ing 15 to attack the leading transport as their primary target, while other
APs and destroyers were delegated to other carrier groups.

The *Essex* pilots were the first to hit convoy TA No. 3. Commander Jim
Mini's first division of VB-15 commenced their dives from 15,000 feet on
the Japanese transport. They each toggled a 1,000-pound bomb and a pair
of 250-pound GP wing bombs. Mini, Lieutenant Richard Glass, and Lieutenant (jg) Loren Nelson were credited with enough direct hits that the
merchant ship was immediately left in sinking condition.

The rest of Air Group Fifteen was coached on to other targets. Lieutenant John Brodhead and his Helldivers pilots claimed numerous bomb hits
on the second transport, followed by Charlie Sorenson's bomb-laden
Avengers sweeping in to add more hits. Also diving on this ship were skipper Jim Rigg and his wingman, Monk Gunter. They strafed all the way
down and dropped their five-hundred-pound bombs on the ship's bow
and amidships on the starboard side. The devastation was so complete
that coordinator McCampbell shifted the balance of his air group to the
next target.

As Baynard Milton's division came in to strafe, Ensign Leonard Lemley saw the second transport explode and sink, disappearing beneath the

waves in a massive sheet of flame. Having been with VF-15 for only a week, Lemley had never practiced skip bombing techniques, but he did his best when so ordered. Leveling off, Lemley toggled his bomb just forward of amidships on his target and then cleared the area. Afterward, he had to ask Milton where their bombs had landed.[4]

A Japanese convoy under attack in Leyte's Ormoc Bay on November 11, 1944. In this photo taken by VF-15's Jigs Foltz, a Japanese transport ship explodes during attacks by Essex *aircraft.*   U.S. Navy

On its own, Air Group Fifteen had quickly disposed of two Japanese transports piled high with ammunition and troops, *Tensho Maru* and *Taizan Maru.* The tail-end Charlie pilot of Jim Rigg's division quickly shifted targets. He was one of the new boys, Ensign Bob Erickson from Minnesota. Erickson adjusted his aim to hit one of the escorting destroyers in his path. His five-hundred-pound bomb was a direct hit, causing a large explosion.

The third transport in column was attacked by five SB2Cs led by Lieutenant Dick Mills. He, Dave Hall, and a third Helldiver pilot planted 1,000-pounders squarely onto the fleeing ship. Right on their tails, five TBMs piled on more direct hits and near misses that added to the transport *Mikasa Maru*'s misery. Finally, seven VF-15 Hellcats made strafing-and-bombing runs. Direct five-hundred-pound hits were credited to four of Satan's Playmates: Milton, Roy Nall, Carl White, and new pilot Galen Eaholtz.

The last two VF-15 pilots shifted to the fourth transport, *Seiho Maru*, in company with a pair of VT-15 crews. Lieutenant (jg) Norm Berree claimed a hit on the port side of the hull, while the *Essex* Avengers landed only four near misses with their five-hundred-pounders. As the *Essex* quartet continued on, their transport was still underway, but McCampbell coached in other air groups to finish it off.

The VF-15 divisions of Rigg, Milton, and White followed up with strafing runs on the destroyers before moving out toward the *Essex* air group's rendezvous area. The Japanese convoy had put up stiff antiaircraft fire throughout these attacks, and their gunners had proven to be quite efficient. Bombing Squadron Fifteen paid a heavy price.

Lieutenant (jg) John Foote's Helldiver, hit in the bomb bay as he pulled out of his freighter attack, plunged into the ocean with no survivors. Two other VB-15 dive-bomber crews, those of Ensigns John Avery and Melvin Livesay, were also lost after being hit by AA fire and slamming into the sea. Lieutenant (jg) Dave Hall's Helldiver was also hit, but he and his gunner were seen to scramble into their life raft after ditching. Lieutenant James Barnitz had his gunner wounded by AA fire and was forced to fly to Tacloban Airfield on Leyte to seek medical attention for him.

Fighting Fifteen suffered from both enemy AA fire and a dozen Oscars that swooped down on them after recovering from their strafing runs. Ensign Erickson's F6F was hit by a 40mm AA round and a burst of 7.7mm machine-gun fire. Flames erupted in the accessories section on his Hellcat's starboard side, beneath the hydraulic service cover. Erickson prepared to bail out, but he paused when his flames died off. He immediately departed for the task force, hoping to coax his fighter as close as possible to a friendly ship.

The other eleven *Essex* Hellcats battled their way through a swarm of Oscars. Rigg had only a brief glimpse of them at 6,000 feet before they descended on his divisions. "We were at a disadvantage but were able to proceed to the rendezvous area while fighting them off," Rigg recounted.[5]

Rigg landed damaging hits on one of the attacking Oscars before he was forced to pull out and take up a defensive weave on one of his squadron mates. The persistent Oscar soon dived back in, passing in front of

Rigg. He followed it down and gave it a long burst, sending it slamming into the water in a vertical dive.

Baynard Milton and Roy Nall each destroyed an Oscar. Nall's section leader, Norm Berree, raked another Oscar's entire fuselage with his bullets and sent it nosing into the ocean. Ensign Howard Smith, struggling with a fogged windshield after diving on a ship, was jumped by Oscars as he approached the rendezvous area. Turning into one head-on, he delivered enough lead to send it into the waves. Another Oscar then turned in front of Smith. He delivered enough rounds to cause the Japanese fighter to roll onto its back and nose into the water "like an arrow."[6]

Ensign Lemley, heading toward the rendezvous site with Milton, could see planes looping around in the distance. His radio suddenly crackled with a Mayday distress call from the dive-bombers. As they entered the fray, he saw Milton go after an Oscar. As another plane broke from the group, Lemley spotted the telltale red meatballs on its fuselage. *It's a Jap!* he thought. *Get the bastard!*[7]

As the Oscar flashed toward him, Lemley pulled hard on his stick and watched the enemy fighter flash under his cowling. "I missed him by about 25 feet," he recalled. Seconds later he went in pursuit of another Oscar that zipped past him. It was heading for the water, jinking heavily to avoid American gunfire. Only a couple of hundred yards behind, Lemley pursued until the Japanese pilot pulled into a 90-degree turn. "He pulled right into my gunsights," he remembered. "I just gave him a blast, then he stopped, and just went right into the water."

The dogfighting Hellcats prevented any more SB2Cs from being lost to enemy fighters. For their part, the stable VB-15 rear seat gunners countered the assault well with their .50-caliber machine guns. Aviation Radioman 3c Peter Trombina in Ensign George Oakman's SB2C was credited with downing one Oscar and scoring damaging hits on a second enemy fighter. Three VT-15 TBMs suffered AA damage over the Japanese convoy, but none were lost to the enemy fighters.

Commander McCampbell's section, which had been circling at 8,000 feet while the convoy attacks commenced, tallyhoed a lone Oscar passing directly overhead at Angels 11. The *Essex* CAG and wingman Rushing immediately pursued. They had little trouble in overtaking the bandit. "After about three minutes and when he saw us closing fast from astern, he did a half roll and remained on his back for about fifteen seconds before diving out," McCampbell stated.[8]

Due to the extreme range, CAG held his fire until the Oscar started down. McCampbell then nosed over and opened fire, raising smoke in its engine. Putting *Minsi III* into a half roll, he followed the Oscar as it spiraled to the left. Dave got in another short burst from astern before having to pull up to keep from overrunning his target. As the Oscar reappeared on the other side of a thin overcast layer, McCampbell got in a third burst. This apparently killed the pilot, as the fighter flew into the ground with a big explosion and flash of flames.

The Navy's top ace had just run his victory total to thirty-three kills.

Jigs Foltz, having completed his last photo run, picked up word that many rats were in the rendezvous area. He and his wingman, Ensign Frazelle, headed toward the area and tallyhoed an Oscar at 8,000 feet. Three Japanese fighters were spotted, and Foltz suddenly wished for the extra protection of the other half of McCampbell's CAG section.

"Come on over, Dave," he called over the radio. "I've got three meatballs cornered over here!"[9]

Foltz's transmission would later be the source of much kidding within VF-15. For the moment, two Hellcats versus three Tony fighters was enough to make the photo pilot understandably anxious. There was no time to wait for McCampbell and Rushing to arrive. Foltz turned into the first Oscar and scored damage with several seconds of .50-caliber bursts. But his attention was quickly diverted to another Oscar attacking him from astern.

Foltz turned and met this attacker head-on, level, and slugged it out until the Oscar's engine caught fire. The fire went out, but Foltz's opponent was seen to crash in the water. Frazelle caught another Oscar heading in toward Foltz. He doggedly pursued it, and Frazelle's two firing bursts proved enough to cause the Oscar to flip onto its back and dive straight into the water from 2,000 feet.

The main group of the battered *Essex* strike force, minus five Helldivers, regrouped and headed for home once the fighter assault had been quelled. Bob Erickson urged his crippled F6F close to TG 38.3 before he was forced to make a water landing shortly after 1230. Lieutenant (jg) Bob Brice was similarly forced to ditch his VB-15 Helldiver to AA fire. The crew of the destroyer USS *Clarence K. Bronson* (DD-668) efficiently scooped up both VB-15 airmen and Ensign Erickson of VF-15.[10]

Dave McCampbell and Roy Rushing remained over convoy TA No. 3 for another half hour, assigning the most valuable remaining ships to other TF 38 carrier groups. By the time they departed for home in company with strike planes from *Bunker Hill* and *Hornet*, the *Essex* CAG reported that seven of the enemy ships had been sunk, including all four troop transports.

Among the secondary waves of strikers arriving from TG 38.4 was *Enterprise*'s Air Group 20, led by Commander Dog Smith. The skies were so crowded above the convoy that Smith circled his planes for twenty minutes before starting down. Smith split his troops between three destroyers and the last transport, *Seiho Maru*, still limping along.[11]

Among the VF-20 fighters was a division comprising former VF-15 fighter pilots, with Ensign Jim Mooney as the acting combat team leader. The *Enterprise* dive-bombers, joined by VT-20 Avengers and a division of fighters, quickly knocked out two of the destroyers with bombs, torpedoes, and bullets. One tin can, likely *Hamanami*, absorbed as many as six bomb hits and one torpedo before rolling over and sinking. Another, *Shimakaze*, was disabled by bombing and strafing. Ablaze and dead in the water, *Shimakaze* drifted for some time after the attack until she exploded and sank.[12]

Two other destroyers went down in more spectacular fashion. *Naganami* exploded amidships and sank after many hits. *Enterprise* and *Yorktown* planes pounced on *Wakatsuki*, which absorbed bomb and torpedo hits. *Wakatsuki* was burning from bow to stern as Mooney's VF-20 division continued strafing it. Mooney made five runs on one destroyer that was circling wildly to evade bombs. On his fifth pass, the destroyer held a steady course, and Mooney finally released his five-hundred-pound bomb. "It hit on the fantail where all the depth charges are," he recalled. The destroyer erupted.[13]

Meanwhile, aerial witnesses saw *Wakatsuki* disintegrate in a spectacular double explosion. Fire and clouds of black smoke rose high as debris peppered the ocean surface for half a mile. By the conclusion of Task Force 38's strikes, four transports, four destroyers, and the minesweeper were gone. A single destroyer, *Asashimo*, had somehow survived the onslaught, the sole survivor of convoy TA No. 3's disaster.[14]

Closer to home, the action had been quite tame through most of the day. Three *Essex* CAP teams had returned without contact, but Lieutenant (jg) Bob Stime's fourth CAP team was finally given a vector at 1430. He tallyhoed a Judy at 6,000 feet and put his division into bracket formation. As they pursued, the pilots noted white smoke pouring from cylinders astern, possibly from rocket or jet propulsion units. Even at full throttle, the Hellcats were unable to close on the fleeing bandit. The jet blast lasted approximately seven minutes and kept the Japanese plane out of reach until its pilot made the mistake of employing jinking maneuvers. This allowed Stime's division to close in enough for all four pilots to make firing passes. In short order, the plane was riddled with .50-caliber holes. "We were close enough to see the many holes, but it did not burn, except for small bursts of flames which extinguished themselves," Stime reported. The Judy finally lost altitude slowly until it hit the sea, skipped once, and crashed. The division gave the kill credit to Ensign James Forsyth, one of the newly received replacement pilots for VF-15.[15]

Air Group Fifteen's success in destroying the convoy did little to console Bombing Squadron Fifteen's enlisted men for their heavy losses. The gunners revolted that evening and refused to fly again, having lost three popular comrades in one day. Several rear seat men announced that they would not fly again under those conditions, as they had done their tour of duty for six months and they should not be subjected to more losses. Skipper Jim Mini went to Commander McCampbell to inform him of the mutiny, a potential court-martial offense that could have had severe consequences.[16]

"I would take away their flight skins," McCampbell advised his VB-15 commander. By removing their flight orders, the SB2C rear gunners would not earn combat pay. McCampbell was irked. "We don't really need them anyway," he told Mini. "We haven't lost any of our bomber planes in air-to-air combat. So, let's send them up and put them with deck crews, plane handlers, for a while."[17]

In order not to make the event official, McCampbell let Mini return on deck and advise his enlisted men of their options. In addition to losing flight pay, the gunners would not have the privilege of returning home soon with the air group. Their pilots would continue to fly combat missions but without the protection of a trained rear gunner. After several tense minutes, the VB-15 gunners decided to revoke their threat and return to duty. The near mutiny was thus subdued, and the incident was never officially reported to *Essex* high command.[18]

November 12, 1944

Still smarting from the insurrection within VB-15, Dave McCampbell was troubled by another realization. His air group was apparently not being relieved anytime soon, and he had handed over a dozen of his more seasoned VF-15 pilots to *Enterprise*'s VF-20 two weeks prior. Conferring with Jim Rigg, he decided it was time to get them back. The Big E could have the batch of replacement rookies he had received days after sending off his more tenured bunch.

Orders were typed up during the evening, and on the morning of November 12 the mass reshuffling commenced. Admiral Mitscher's task group spent the day refueling at sea, affording McCampbell the perfect opportunity for the swap. At 0740, the destroyer *Clarence K. Bronson* pulled alongside *Essex* to take on board officers and their baggage. From VF-15, Lieutenant Commander Rigg released eleven of his latest replacement pilots: Ensigns Bill Allen, Reune Bertschi, Ed Bomar, Jim Butters, Galen Eaholtz, Jim Forsyth, Gene Langston, Leonard Lemley, Lyle Maxey, Tom Tidwell, and John Whiteside. Another of these newbies, Ensign Bob Erickson, was already on board *Bronson*, having been recovered from the ocean the previous day.

The replacement VF-15 pilots, including Erickson, reported to VF-20 for duty. Meanwhile, the more seasoned VF-15 pilots were delivered back to *Essex*: Jack Taylor, Dick Davis, Dusty Craig, Paul Bugg, Bob Sprankle, Don Gonya, Earl Lewis, Jim Mooney, Herman Foshee, Jerry Lathrop, Dick McGraw, and Wayne Dowlen. These men would now receive the benefit of liberty back home when their air group was eventually reassigned.

The dozen replacement pilots given to *Enterprise* would continue in service with VF-20 for months, some even remaining with the squadron until war's end in April 1945. But Ensign Erickson had no such luck. On his first mission with VF-20, he was forced to make another water landing during strikes on Manila. Erickson announced that he was heading back to the ship, but no trace of him was ever found after he ditched.[19]

All this shuffling complete, it was back to business for Air Group Fifteen the following day. *Essex* turned into the wind around 0600 on November 13 and began launching an early strike to destroy enemy shipping and dock facilities in Manila Bay off Luzon. Commander McCampbell was first off with his division to serve as target coordinator. Fighter skipper Jim Rigg followed with three more VF-15 divisions to cover fifteen VB-15 Helldivers and a dozen VT-15 Avengers. The combined TG 38.3 strike force also included elements from the air groups of *Ticonderoga*'s AG-80 and *Langley*'s AG-44.

Arriving around 0800, McCampbell assigned VB-15 to hit five freighters in Manila Bay, three of which were sunk. Jim Rigg took his Hellcat divisions down to strafe miscellaneous shipping, including seven small boats. One disintegrated under their bullets, two were left burning fiercely, and four were heavily damaged.

The only loss for McCampbell's squadrons was the TBM flown by Lieutenant (jg) Otto Bleech. Hit by antiaircraft fire over Manila Bay, Bleech was forced to make a water landing in the northern part of the bay. Several motorboats that headed his way were diverted by strafing from Rigg's fighters. But when last seen, Bleech and his two airmen were in their rubber raft with four small sailboats approaching them.

Only one Japanese aircraft was encountered, a Tony tallyhoed by photo Hellcat pilot Jigs Foltz at 0830. John Strane's division pushed over to attack, landing some damaging hits on the enemy fighter plane. As the Tony pilot turned away, he crossed right into the path of Foltz, who set it afire almost immediately. It crashed in the bay, and Jigs Foltz was celebrated as VF-15's newest ace pilot.

———

Lieutenants George Crittenden and Baynard Milton's divisions launched at 0828 on November 13 for a sweep over Luzon's Clark Field in company with sixteen *Ticonderoga* Hellcats. *No big problem, no particular sweat,* thought Milton. *Air resistance by the Japanese in the Philippines has been reduced to a minimum and is no longer any great concern.*[20]

Over Clark Field and Clark Field North, Crittenden's flight found only what appeared to be parked dummy aircraft. Moving on to Mabalacat Airfield, they noted many single- and twin-engine aircraft, some under camouflage netting and some out in the fields.

Critt led the pilots down to strafe on three runs. Two twin-engine medium bombers were set afire and others were damaged. "We destroyed some planes on the ground, which I'm reasonably sure had been reported as 'destroyed' several other times during the last few weeks," recalled Milton. He then turned with his division to make one more farewell pass over the enemy field.

As Milton raced across the field, firing into a hangar, his plane was hit. His left wing dropped dangerously and his plane went into a wild, high-speed, uncontrolled left turn, barely above the ground. He was able to regain control by kicking the right rudder full forward and slamming the stick all the way over and back. He avoided hitting the ground, then struggled to maintain his bearing while climbing for altitude.

Taking a quick damage assessment, Milton saw a large, ragged hole through his port wing. Experimenting, he found that he could barely turn to starboard. His plane had developed a natural tendency to go into a slight downward spiral to port. Milton struggled to gain altitude to clear the mountainous terrain ahead. His wingman, Lieutenant (jg) George Pigman, eased up alongside. Pigman tried calling him on the radio, but Milton found that his receiver was dead. Pigman circled Milton's F6F and assessed the damage.

From Pigman's hand signals, Milton learned that in addition to the big hole in his wing, he had landing gear problems. His port wheel was loose and only partially extended, and his starboard wheel was fully extended.

Lieutenant (jg) Baynard Milton (left) was escorted back to Essex *by his wingman, Lieutenant (jg) George Pigman (right), after his F6F was badly shot up on November 13.*   Doyle Bare collection, courtesy of Rita Bare

His efforts to fix this situation had no effect, as his hydraulic system was out of commission. He did find that his flaps and tailhook were operating fine. *Things aren't a complete washout,* he thought. *Some luck is still riding with me.*[21]

Having gained enough altitude to clear Luzon, Milton and Pigman started for home. With the constant pressure he was applying to the rudder and stick, his right leg and arm began to tire severely, resulting in cramps. Each time Milton released the two controls to restore circulation, his plane descending in a lazy spiral to the left. This made for a slow return to *Essex*. "My plans, at least for the moment, were to land aboard," Milton recalled. "No bailing out or ditching for me. I had already ditched twice in the Solomon Islands!"[22]

As they approached the fleet around 1200, Milton saw Pigman communicating with the ship via radio. Milton's wingman finally related via hand signals that the carrier wanted him to make a forced water landing in the ocean near the task group. Although he could not receive radio communications, Milton was able to transmit.

"Porkchop, old buddy, are you asking me which I want to do—bail out or ditch in the ocean?" he called.

Pigman nodded yes.

"I plan to do neither," Milton replied. "I plan to land on board!"

Pigman then called *Essex* and received permission for Milton to attempt his one-wheel landing. Milton keyed his mike and called the ship.

"Rebel Base, this is Rebel Six. Request permission to bring her aboard if possible."

A minute later Pigman signaled to his wing mate with a thumbs-up. Milton entered the groove, intending to fly in faster than usual, hoping to use his left wing, right wheel, and tailhook touching first to minimize the chances of cartwheeling across the deck. But at the last instant, the *Essex* LSO, Roy Bruninghaus, gave him a wave-off.[23]

On Milton's next pass, former VF-15 pilot Bruninghaus gave him a cut. As his F6F slammed down, his extended right wheel snapped off and went bouncing down the flight deck. The instant his Hellcat skidded to a stop, a deckhand jumped up on the wing and began helping Milton out of his harness. The flight surgeon, Doc Maness, and Bombing 15 skipper Jim Mini crowded up on the wing, wanting to know if the pilot was hurt.

"The hell with that," snapped the airedale. "There's still a possibility of fire."

There was no fire, but Milton, Mini, and Maness scrambled away from the crashed plane. Milton paused only long enough to grab his navigation board from the cockpit before heading below. A short time later he was advised in the ready room that his plane was being scrapped. He was told if he wanted to see his plane one last time, he had better hurry.

Milton raced topside and gave his trusted Grumman one last look. "Wounded and broken as she was, she had brought me safely home," he recalled. "They splashed her, and she started that last final dive to the bottom of the ocean. I was glad she was making the rest of the trip alone."[24]

LIEUTENANT (JG) DUZ Twelves, part of the next *Essex* strike group, had a return to the carrier almost as dramatic as Milton's.

His division leader, George Duncan, led ten VF-15 Hellcats off the deck at 1153 on November 13. They escorted a dozen VB-15 Helldivers and nine bomb-armed VT-15 Avengers toward Luzon, keeping company with similar strike groups from *Ticonderoga* and *Langley*. Upon arriving over Manila Bay, strike coordinator VeeGee Lambert assigned various targets to his divisions. Several of his TBMs blasted piers and a small boat basin while the rest of the *Essex* bombers assaulted warships and merchant ships in the bay.

Lieutenant Frank West and two other VB-15 pilots nailed a *Nagara*-class cruiser with their 1,000-pound bombs, leaving it settling by the stern. Lieutenant (jg) Don McCutcheon landed his bombload on a nearby destroyer, but the antiaircraft fire from these warships was intense. Lieutenant Roger Noyes's Helldiver was hit during his dive; his plane slammed straight into the harbor with no survivors. Another SB2C failed to make it back to *Essex*, but Lieutenant (jg) Bill Moore and his gunner were rescued by a task group destroyer.

Lieutenant Commander Duncan's divisions strafed miscellaneous shipping in Manila Bay and escaped largely unscathed. The sole exception was Duz Twelves, whose F6F had both wings ripped by antiaircraft fragments. His return flight to base was a struggle with a shot-up fighter. Limping along behind the others in the *Essex* air group, Twelves suddenly spotted a U.S. dive-bomber smoking heavily and losing altitude. Forgetting his own dilemma, he immediately turned to offer whatever assistance he could to his fellow carrier pilot.

The damaged Helldiver was flown by Lieutenant (jg) Edward F. Anderson of *Yorktown*'s VB-3. During his attack on merchant ships in Manila Bay, Anderson's SB2C was hit in the engine by an AA round. His engine flamed and smoked heavily but quickly died out. Anderson was able to rejoin his *Yorktown* group temporarily, but his engine continued to smoke intermittently. His cylinder head temperatures were high, and oil was streaming over both wing roots and through his bomb bay. Anderson opted to break away from VB-3 and head in search of a lifeguard ship.

Although Anderson's radio was out, he and Duz were able to communicate via hand signals. Anderson climbed through a cloud layer over Polillo Island, to the east of Luzon, and soon spotted a U.S. warship. With his Helldiver gradually losing altitude, Anderson made a forced landing near the destroyer USS *Maddox* (DD-731) as his engine finally conked out. He and his gunner were soon pulled on board *Maddox*.[25]

Seeing the *Yorktown* pilot make a safe landing, Duz Twelves turned for home. By the time his Task Group 38.3 appeared on the horizon, his division and the rest of the *Essex* strikers had already landed. On board ship, word was passed that a badly shot-up VF-15 Hellcat was entering the groove. Joe Rosenthal, a thirty-three-year-old Associated Press photographer traveling on *Essex* to document Task Force 38's combat, seized his camera and moved out onto the flight deck in wait.

Unknown to Twelves, the shrapnel damage his plane had sustained had carried away the dashpot that locked his tailhook in place. Due to this damage, his hook simply bounced free of the first arresting cable and then the next. Twelves stood on the brakes, but his Hellcat still plowed heavily into the crash barrier. His F6F pitched forward on its nose, with his props curling back around the cowl as they made impact. Rosenthal snapped pictures of the spectacular crash.

Emergency crews ran forward to hose down the fighter's engine and extract Duz, whose legs were badly bruised when his plane struck the barrier. He was assisted below for Doc Maness's inspection while airedales worked to clear the mess of his fighter. Eventually deciding the F6F to be unworthy of heavy repair work, the airedales pushed it over the side into the ocean.

In his diary that evening, Twelves matter-of-factly recorded the event: "Had my first accident. Crashed on deck and washed out the plane."[26]

JIM RIGG LED one more fighter sweep over the area near Clark Field on the afternoon of November 13. At Bamban Field, his F6Fs found twenty aircraft on the strip, although most had already been destroyed. Half of them, including several dummy planes, were well camouflaged. Their strafing efforts managed to set only one plane ablaze.

The pilots who flew four total CAP missions from *Essex* that day found better aerial action. One of the early divisions, led by Lieutenant Jack Symmes, received a vector at 0730. They soon tallyhoed a Jake flying at about 4,000 feet and bracketed it. Lieutenant (jg) Bill Anderson scored damaging hits from a high-side run. Ensign Herman Foshee followed closely from the opposite beam, raking the Jake's engine and cockpit and sending it into the sea thirty miles from the task force.

The day's second CAP team had no action, but George Carr's CAP No. 3 received a vector at 1400. Fifteen miles from the task force, they intercepted a Nakajima C6N Saiun reconnaissance plane (code-named "Myrt") at Angels 18. The pilots saw a torpedo or a very long belly tank slung underneath it. Carr and his wingman, Jack Taylor, bracketed the plane, both making half high-side runs with damaging hits. They followed with a second pass, during which Carr started a fire in the starboard wing root. Taylor's bursts at last caused the Myrt to explode.

Lieutenant (jg) Jake Lundin was leading the high division of CAP No. 4 when they received a vector and intercepted a Myrt about 1740, seven miles distant. Lundin's division chased it for about fifteen minutes without closing. For some unknown reason, the Myrt pilot then cut his speed sharply and Lundin's team closed. His wingman missed, but Lundin exploded the Japanese plane with a ten-second burst.

After splashing this Myrt, Lundin's team was immediately given another vector. In less than five minutes they tallyhoed two Frans down at Angels 24 heading for the task force. The Japanese planes broke in opposite directions and nosed down, very fast. Norm Berree pursued the northern bandit and sent it into the drink after four firing runs. Merwin Frazelle and Roy Nall teamed up on the second Fran, and it soon exploded at about 14,000 feet.

Ensign Dusty Craig, freshly returned from his stint on *Enterprise*, made two combat flights on November 13. He returned from the early-morning strike without incident, but his F6F was hit by an antiaircraft round during his late-afternoon CAP duty. "Very badly shot up," Craig noted in his flight book. "Horizontal stabilizer shot off at tip." His controls felt mushy, but Dusty was able to nurse his Hellcat back to *Essex*. LSO Roy Bruninghaus gave him a cut on his first pass. Craig was much relieved when his tailhook snagged a cable and jerked his F6F to a halt. Airedales cleared his Hellcat from the landing area, but Craig was surprised to see a deck officer later give orders to have it pushed over the side.[27]

DUZ TWELVES REMAINED grounded on November 14 with sore legs from his barrier crash. His division, led by George Duncan, was among four to launch at dawn in company with Air Group Fifteen bombers and torpedo planes to attack shipping and facilities in Luzon again. CAG Dave McCampbell flew as strike coordinator with a photo Hellcat and wingman as his second section. Upon arriving over Manila Bay, he assigned VB-15 and VT-15 to hit the boat basin, piers, and freighters in the harbor.

Most of the shipping had been previously damaged, but the *Essex* Helldivers dumped more bombloads on the hapless shipping. Antiaircraft fire claimed the SB2C of Lieutenant (jg) Raymond Turner, whose plane spun out of control into Manila Bay. During the bombing runs, McCampbell's four-plane team remained high to assess the damage and for him to assign targets for the *Essex*, *Ticonderoga*, and *Langley* planes.

McCampbell and Rushing dropped lower at one point to cover his photo VF-15 section after he ordered them to take damage assessment photos of ships inside the breakwater. As his section descended to parallel the photo plane's run, McCampbell spotted two Oscars on a converging course and turned into them. The leading Oscar dived down under him, out of sight, so McCampbell lined up on the second fighter.[28]

One long burst from *Minsi III*'s wing guns ripped through the Nakajima Ki-43, and it dived away to the right. As McCampbell turned to follow, another Oscar passed close overhead. Then Dave spotted another half dozen fighters staged above. He opened up on his radio, calling to Rushing: "Roy, I'm going to make a run for it toward Corregidor."

McCampbell nosed over to make speed, with Rushing snugged up on his wing. At full throttle and WEP, the CAG section easily outdistanced the Oscars before any could get a shot at them. While retiring at high speed, they met a Judy on their same level nearly head-on. "I took a crack at him without stopping to note the results," said McCampbell.

After making rendezvous with the photo F6F section, McCampbell led his division toward Laguna de Bay. There, he tallyhoed another Oscar below. McCampbell's first shots caused the enemy pilot to split-S away. Dave followed him in a long spiral and got in a long burst from astern before he had to pull out to avoid overrunning his target. "Since the plane never re-covered from the spiral and crashed to earth in a burst of flame, it is quite possible that my first burst of fire killed the pilot," McCampbell related.[29]

After this short action, McCampbell's division rendezvoused with the main combat team and he continued his work as target coordinator. Al-though George Duncan's fighters heard many tallyhos from other strike groups, they maintained high cover to successfully protect their bombers.

The final *Essex* strike for November 14 was launched at 1125. Lieutenant George Crittenden headed the VF-15 contingent, but they found no aerial opposition. Targets were becoming scarce by this point, so Air Group Fif-teen's bombers worked over an already disabled merchant ship in Cavite Harbor and nearby shore installations.

The *Essex* air group returned from its final combat hop of the tour without loss. Crew chief Chet Owens was already working to add one final Rising Sun flag to CAG Dave McCampbell's *Minsi III* command Hellcat. His victory tally now stood at thirty-four aerial kills, placing him solidly in the number one position as the U.S. Navy's top gun.

McCampbell was officially number two in the U.S. military's ace race of World War II. Dick Bong was two planes up on him and would wrap up his final combat on December 17 with forty kills to his wartime credit. Bong's record was contested by his buddy Tommy McGuire, whose tally as of November 12 stood at twenty-eight. McGuire would add another ten kills during the month of December. His chase ended on January 7, 1945, during a fighter sweep over northern Negros Island in the central Philip-pines, when he was killed while battling an Oscar fighter.

McGuire was posthumously awarded the Medal of Honor, and Bong was pinned with his own Medal of Honor by General Douglas MacArthur in December before being sent home for good. The U.S. Navy's top brass already had plans to bestow similar honors on its own leading ace, Dash-ing Dave McCampbell.

EPILOGUE

November 17, 1944

Duz Twelves, dressed in khakis with his cap at a rakish angle, stood alongside the sea-blue fuselage of Dave McCampbell's *Minsi III* Hellcat. Beneath the F6F's cockpit was the Air Group Fifteen CAG's final tally of Rising Sun emblems for all to see: thirty-four total victories achieved by the U.S. Navy's top ace pilot.

With thirteen kills to his own credit, Twelves was part of an elite group. To his left stood Larry Self, a double ace who had donned a bandanna beneath his cap to help disguise head wounds he had sustained in his final combat flight. To the right of Duz was his buddy Art Singer, another double ace, who sported a wide grin below his dark mustache. Navy photographers snapped images of the VF-15 pilots on the *Essex* hangar deck as they proudly stood behind their squadron battle flag with Commander McCampbell to its left. The broad white banner, emblazoned with the Satan's Playmates logo, sported 310 Rising Sun emblems—one for every Japanese aircraft VF-15 pilots had destroyed in aerial combat.

Two dozen seasoned Hellcat pilots posed for their picture. Each man was considered an ace, with at least five aerial kills to his credit. It was not lost on Duz Twelves that several others should have been present for this photo. Spike Borley, shot down in October and recovered by a U.S. submarine, had not been able to rejoin the team. Also absent were three VF-15 aces who would not be returning from the war: Ken Flinn, Bud Plant, and former skipper Charlie Brewer.

Fighting Fifteen pilots pose for the final squadron photo with their battle flag in November 1944 on the hangar deck of USS Essex *in front of CAG Dave McCampbell's Hellcat,* Minsi III
Front row, left to right: *Don Gonya, Robert Sprankle, Ernie Roycraft, Jake Hogue, Sam Lundquist, Larry Self, Dusty Craig, Kester Roberts, Jim Mooney, Doyle Bare, Dick Davis, and Merwin Frazelle.*
Second row, left to right: *Harold Seigler (aviation specialist [AVS]), Roy Nall, John Hoffman (AVS), Bob McReynolds (AVS), Joe O'Brien (AVS), Captain Carlos Wieber (Essex skipper), Jim Rigg, Dave McCampbell, George Duncan, Roy Rushing, George Pigman, Bob Fash, and Art Singer.*
Third row, left to right: *Inman Brandon (AVS), Earl Lewis, Carl White, Bert Morris, George Tarleton, Jack Symmes, Ted Overton, George Crittenden, John Strane, Bob Stime, Ken West, Jake Lundin, George Carr, Norm Berree, Jim Duffy, John Collins, Warren Clark, Howard Smith, and Baynard Milton.*
Fourth row, left to right: *Red Voorhest, Tom Hoey, Bill Anderson, Kent Lee, Monchie Gunter, Jerry Lathrop, Roy Bruninghaus (LSO), Dick McGraw, Dick Fowler, Ralph Foltz, Wayne Dowlen, Jack Taylor, Paul Bugg, Duz Twelves, Herman Foshee, Al Slack, Bob Johnson, and Ed Mellon.* Enterprise Holdings

In addition to the group photo of the aces, McCampbell and Jim Rigg had the entire squadron, pilots and enlisted personnel included, pose in front of his *Minsi III.* Excitement was in the air. Admiral Sherman's Task Group 38.3 was headed for Ulithi, where Air Group Fifteen would be officially relieved. Anti-submarine flights and CAP duty were a thing of the past, at least for a while. Air Group Four was coming on board *Essex* to officially relieve AG-15. Late that afternoon, the carrier *Bunker Hill* slipped into the lagoon and began off-loading ammunition for other warships to repurpose. *Bunker Hill* was slated to return for an overhaul at Navy Yard Puget Sound in Bremerton, Washington.

Dave McCampbell's heroes were honored on the flight deck in an awards ceremony. That evening the pilots packed all their personal possessions and were transferred the following day, November 18, by an LST across the harbor to *Bunker Hill*. Dave McCampbell went with a brown paper bag containing a bottle of Scotch given to him by his buddy Dave McDonald, the *Essex* XO. There they would pass the next two days waiting for their carrier to get underway for the States. Some sunbathed on the flight deck while others dashed off letters home.

On November 20 at 1404, *Bunker Hill* weighed anchor and set sail for Pearl Harbor in company with the destroyer USS *Downes* (DD-375) and a Liberty ship, designated as Task Unit 30.9.9. The trip was uneventful aside from routine CAP duty flown by Duz Twelves and others. For many it was a time to reflect on their personal blessings: being alive and en route back to their families. Twenty-six pilots who had flown with VF-15 between March and November 1944 were never coming home.

From Bombing Squadron Fifteen, seventeen pilots and fifteen rear seat gunners did not survive their tour of duty with Air Group Fifteen. Torpedo Fifteen suffered eight pilots and seventeen enlisted men killed or missing in action. During the return trip to Pearl Harbor, McCampbell wrote a full assessment of his air group's performance. He offered recommendations for future groups, including a need for more VHF combat channels for strike groups.[1]

McCampbell also believed air groups were being kept out for "unreasonable and deleterious lengths of time." After seven months of constant combat, two of his AG-15 pilots had been lost due to combat fatigue. He recommended that no air group should be required to remain in the combat zone for more than six months under any conditions. For any air group that saw continuous combat without extended relief, McCampbell felt this time period should be reduced to four months.[2]

On November 29, *Bunker Hill* rounded Oahu and steamed up the channel into Pearl Harbor. As *Bunker Hill* moored in Berth F-13 at Ford Island, newly promoted Lieutenant (jg) Dick Davis spotted a pair of familiar faces waving on the dock. John Van Altena, rescued by the submarine *Sailfish*, had been dropped off at Saipan and thereafter made his way to Pearl Harbor. Spike Borley had been longer in making his return, having ridden out the balance of a submarine war patrol on board his savior vessel, *Sawfish*.

Lieutenant (jg) Al Slack was amused to see a third pilot, his buddy Johnny Brex. Standing with a wide smile beneath a Filipino straw hat, Brex had a pair of souvenir Japanese boots dangling from one shoulder. Slack was also happy to reunite with Borley, whose personal effects he had had the grim task of inventorying when Borley failed to return from his flight in October. There were many handshakes, hugs, and survival stories to exchange when some of VF-15's pilots managed to secure liberty from *Bunker Hill* that afternoon. After weeks of eating scant provisions such as powdered eggs and dehydrated potatoes, the fighter pilots headed into Honolulu together. "The first thing we did in town was order the biggest steak we could get," Davis remembered.[3]

Bunker Hill remained in Pearl Harbor another day off-loading supplies and preparing for her return to the mainland for overhaul. Lines were cast the following morning, December 1, and the carrier was underway from Ford Island at 0705. Five days later, on December 6, *Bunker Hill* slipped into Puget Sound and anchored at Sinclair Inlet. The veteran airmen of AG-15 who returned from the war zone were now all on home soil—except one.[4]

Last to reach the United States was Lieutenant (jg) Bill Deming. Forced to ditch on November 13, Deming spent two weeks in the mountains of Luzon with Filipino guerrillas and local natives. He was warmly greeted in each village he visited, and was showered with gifts ranging from sandals to wicker baskets. Around the first of December, his guerrilla teams moved him from Luzon to Leyte Island in a fishing boat. Because they had to skirt Japanese patrols and aircraft, the voyage took a full week. There, Deming reported to American forces and eventually secured flights back to California. His fiancée was in distress during this time, as the Deming family had been notified that he was officially missing in action. She went to New York in mid-December, hoping to find out any news from Commander McCampbell.[5]

The return of Bill Deming to his Washington, Connecticut, home was a tearful reunion. Weeks later he married his fiancée in New Jersey on January 10, 1945. As fate would have it, his closest VB-15 buddy, Dave Hall, fell in love with the sister of Bill's wife, and they were also married in 1945. Discharged at the end of the war, Deming earned his degree in international relations from Yale and began a long and successful career in New York and Latin America.

FIGHTING FIFTEEN HAD shattered records during its combat cruise on the carrier *Essex*. With 26 aces and 310 aerial victories, VF-15 was the top-scoring carrier-based U.S. Navy fighter squadron of World War II. On the ground, AG-15 had destroyed another 348 planes positively wrecked (according to photo intelligence), had probably destroyed another 161 planes, and claimed an additional 129 as damaged. Between May and November 1944, VF-15 established a one-tour record for both Navy and Marine Corps fighter squadrons. The only Navy fighter squadron to tally more kills in World War II was VF-17 with 313 victories, but this was accomplished in two combat tours, not one.[6]

In terms of shipping, in seven months of combat, Dave McCampbell's air group sank thirty-eight cargo ships, probably sank ten more, and damaged another thirty-nine ships of 1,000 tons or larger size. Air Group Fifteen also assisted in the sinking and damaging of numerous Japanese warships, including the super-battleship *Musashi*, four aircraft carriers in Leyte Gulf, and many other cruisers and destroyers. On June 12, VF-15 Hellcats had achieved the unique honor of sinking the 960-ton destroyer–torpedo boat *Otori* solely with the use of their machine guns. It was little wonder that the pilots of McCampbell's air group would later be referred to as the "Fabled Fifteen."

Dashing Dave returned to the United States a war hero, the U.S. Navy's top fighter ace. His record of thirty-four aerial victories was third best of any American pilot in history, and he remains the Navy's "top gun" of all time. McCampbell's actions on October 24, 1944, at Leyte Gulf were legendary; on that day he downed nine enemy aircraft in defense of his carrier task force. He had already been written up for the Medal of Honor, and that recognition was in the works when *Bunker Hill* returned to Washington State.

McCampbell's reunion with his family was hindered. During December 1944, he found himself swept up in a whirlwind of military publicity stops. From Seattle, he was sent first to New York City to appear at an event for the National Association of Manufacturers show at the Waldorf-Astoria hotel. McCampbell spent several weeks in New York, guided by a Navy public relations official who kept him busy with appearances and radio shows. He enjoyed his newfound celebrity, eating big at clubs each night and being wined and dined, many of his expenses being covered by Grumman, the manufacturer of the F6F Hellcat, which had helped him achieve his success.[7]

He spent Christmas in West Palm Beach with his young daughter, Frances, and ex-wife, Susan, before beginning a tour of naval air bases. His visit in Florida also offered him the chance to visit his girlfriend Jill Heliker, with whom he had remained in correspondence throughout his combat tour. Soon after New Year's, McCampbell was notified that he would be receiving the Medal of Honor and was scheduled to appear at the White House.

The ceremony took place on January 10, 1945. McCampbell was called into President Franklin Roosevelt's office for his presentation. Accompanying him were his mother, LaValle McCampbell, and his sister, Frances— the latter being the mother-in-law of Dave's squadron mate Bert Morris. Dave's father, Andrew, was not present due to a recent injury.[8]

President Roosevelt, dressed in a dark suit and bow tie, was seated at his desk. His health was on the decline, and he was a man with only months of life remaining. McCampbell felt FDR's body looked frail, shrunken from weight loss, and his sunken eyes were surrounded by black rings. Still, the excitement of the moment caught the former CAG-15 aviator at a loss for words.

"Well, Dave, aren't you going to introduce your mother and sister to me?" the president asked.

Dave laughed nervously and then introduced his family. Roosevelt spoke to LaValle McCampbell and then handed her the medal. Mrs.

McCampbell draped the medallion and its pale blue ribbon around her son's neck, and Dave's sister, Frances, beamed as White House photographers snapped photos. Following the presentation, McCampbell's family was escorted into an anteroom to mingle with top military brass. "It was quite a thrill," McCampbell recalled of meeting General George C. Marshall, chief of staff of the U.S. Army; General Henry "Hap" Arnold, commanding general of the Army Air Forces; and Admiral Ernest King, chief of naval operations.[9]

"Then came the worst part of my whole experience," McCampbell said. Following the White House ceremony, he was sent by the Navy on a tour of the United States. Flown from city to city in a twin-engine Beechcraft SNB, the hero traveled with a copy of the new film *The Fighting Lady*, a color motion picture shot on board the carrier *Yorktown* in 1944. In each town, the movie was screened, followed by talks from McCampbell and other heroes. Their circuit included Glenview, Illinois; Ottumwa, Iowa; Los Angeles; San Diego; Oklahoma City; Dallas; Corpus Christi; New Orleans; Jacksonville; Melbourne; Fort Lauderdale; the University of Georgia; Chapel Hill, North Carolina; and then back to Washington.[10]

The most enjoyable stop for McCampbell was a visit to Leroy Grumman's aircraft factory, where he spoke to the workers who built the fighter planes that had made him famous. Following this extended trip, McCampbell married Jill Heliker on February 18, 1945, in Washington, DC. They had two sons, David Perry McCampbell and John Calhoun McCampbell. Son David would follow his father's path by serving in the U.S. Navy, from which he would eventually retire as a commander.

After his 1945 publicity tour, McCampbell was assigned as deputy chief of staff for the Commander Fleet Air Atlantic. McCampbell would remain in the U.S. Navy until his retirement on July 1, 1964. From 1948 to 1951, he served as the senior naval aviation adviser to the Argentine navy, stationed at Buenos Aires. After a year as executive officer of the carrier *Franklin D. Roosevelt* during the Korean War, McCampbell was promoted to captain. In the 1950s, he would command both the fleet oiler USS *Severn* (AO-61) and the aircraft carrier USS *Bon Homme Richard* (CV-31). His final assignment prior to retirement was that of assistant deputy chief of staff for operations to the commander in chief, Continental Air Defense Command.

As a well-known Medal of Honor recipient, Captain McCampbell was frequently asked to attend and speak at military engagements and organizational reunions. He willingly signed photos and books for fans, but for moneymaking professional collectors he often omitted his surname and signed only as "Dashing Dave."[11]

Today, his name is not forgotten. In 1988, the David McCampbell Terminal was dedicated at Palm Beach International Airport. A collection of McCampbell's personal aviation memorabilia is on display in Colorado Springs at the National Museum of World War II Aviation. The National Naval Aviation Museum in Pensacola has an F6F-5 Hellcat on display that is painted in the scheme of his famous *Minsi III* fighter.

McCampbell passed away in a nursing home in Florida on June 30, 1996, at age eighty-six. Days later, an honor guard stood at David Mc-Campbell Terminal in Palm Beach as his body was flown to Washington for burial in Arlington National Cemetery. In 2000, an *Arleigh Burke*–class guided missile destroyer was named in his honor, and USS *McCampbell* (DDG-285) was commissioned in 2002.

IN A 1983 book by Edwin P. Hoyt, the pilots of VF-15 were dubbed "Mc-Campbell's Heroes." In one combat cruise, Fighting Fifteen had produced twenty-six aces. At Los Alamitos, VF-15 was reorganized in early 1945. Lieutenant Commander George Duncan became the new skipper, although he relinquished that role in March when he was accepted to pursue his master's degree in aeronautical engineering. Many former *Essex* officers remained in service under the new VF-15 skipper, Lieutenant Commander Gordon Firebaugh: Warren Clark, George Crittenden, Wayne Dowlen, Jim Duffy, Ralph Foltz, Dick Fowler, Don Gonya, Dick McGraw, Bob McReynolds, Ed Mellon, Roy Nall, Ted Overton, Ernie Roycraft, Roy Rushing, John Strane, George Tarleton, Jack Taylor, and Duz Twelves. Returning to serve with VB-15 were former VF-15 fighter-bomber pilots Bill Anderson, John Van Altena, and Red Voorhest. The new fighter-bomber unit, officially VBF-15, included a half dozen Satan's Playmates veterans: Spike Borley, Paul Bugg, Dusty Craig, Dick Davis, Jerry Lathrop, and Jim Mooney.

The new VF-15 was still in training when the war ended, and the unit was decommissioned in Hawaii on October 20, 1945. Many VF-15 veterans would continue in naval service for many years. Two former pilots, Kent Lee and Dick Fowler, rose to the rank of rear admiral. Fowler, who later commanded the carrier *Ticonderoga*, flew with VF-32 in Korea from the carrier USS *Leyte*. He was nicknamed "Dad" by his younger pilots.

Flight service came with its costs: George Carr was killed in a flight accident in 1967, and John Brex perished in a postwar crash off Florida while flying night fighters. Al Slack, who served with Brex in both VF-15 and VF-152, named his son Robert Brex Slack in honor of his lost buddy. George Duncan very nearly lost his own life on June 23, 1951, in a violent flight deck crash of a new Grumman F9F Panther on board the carrier USS *Midway* (CV-41). Duncan commanded Air Group Five during the Korean War and later served as skipper of the carrier USS *Ranger* (CV-61). He retired as a captain in 1968, earned his law degree from George Washington University, and established a law practice.[12]

Bert Morris, released from active duty on October 17, 1945, returned to being movie star Wayne Morris in Hollywood. He filmed *Task Force* in 1949 and several Westerns in the early 1950s, and had minor roles in other films through the 1950s. On September 14, 1959, Morris was invited by his former air group commander, Dave McCampbell, to tour the carrier *Bon Homme Richard*. Morris suffered a heart attack while on board and was rushed to a hospital in Oakland, where he died at age forty-five. His ashes were buried at Arlington National Cemetery.

McCampbell's favored wingman, Roy Rushing, returned to the States in 1945, touring several cities and appearing on radio programs to help sell war bonds. He was discharged in December 1949 and then worked at the Pine Bluff Arsenal in Arkansas. Rushing died in the 1980s in Arkansas. Ralph Foltz flew Corsairs with VF-64 over Korea from the carrier USS *Boxer* and later served as commanding officer of VF-141 on *Lexington*. He retired from the Navy in 1970 as a commander and spent many years as a civilian flight instructor. Wendell "Duz" Twelves, later inducted into the Utah Aviation Hall of Fame, passed away in 1991 at the age of seventy.

Art Singer remained in the Naval Reserve until 1956 and subsequently earned his doctorate degree. He became a professor at San Diego State University, teaching education, and passed away in 2004. John Strane commanded Corsair squadron VF-113 on the carrier USS *Philippine Sea* (CV-47) during the Korean War. He also served as air officer on the carrier *Yorktown* and as commander of the utility wing, Pacific Fleet. He retired as a captain in 1972 after thirty-one years of service. George Pigman was called back into service during the Korean War and served as a flight instructor. He then used the G.I. Bill to attend Tulane University and became an accomplished lawyer in New Orleans.

Jack Taylor's fiancée, Mary Ann, came out to California during the period of Air Group Fifteen's re-formation and the two were married. After the war, Taylor returned to St. Louis. In 1957, he started Executive Leasing Company, but when he expanded his car leasing business to Atlanta, he found another company was using the same name. Already sporting an "E" logo, he decided to rename his company after one of the two carriers he had flown from, *Essex* or *Enterprise*. "Essex is kind of a ponderous name," Taylor recalled. "So, we started talking about the name Enterprise, and Enterprise has an upbeat, positive image." By 1996, Enterprise Rent-A-Car had surpassed $2 billion in revenues. After Taylor's passing in 2016, his son, Andrew, assumed the duties of executive chairman of Enterprise.[13]

The longest-living aces of VF-15 were Clarence "Spike" Borley and Jim Duffy. After the war, Duffy graduated from the University of Southern California with a degree in chemical engineering and started his own successful business. He enjoyed flying until the age of eighty-nine and in May 2015, he and Borley were among thirty-seven aces (out of seventy-five still living) who traveled to Washington, DC, to be honored at the U.S. Capitol. Each of the elite pilots was presented with a Congressional Gold Medal for having achieved ace status in combat. Duffy passed away at age ninety-seven on November 25, 2017. Borley, who retired as a commander, passed away on July 9, 2019, at the age of ninety-four.

Dave McCampbell, Air Group Fifteen, and Fighting Fifteen have each been immortalized in print in past decades. During their seven-month tour on board the carrier *Essex*, Satan's Playmates became the most successful U.S. Navy fighter squadron in history, shattering records for numbers of planes destroyed in the air, on the ground, and in shipping destruction. "We did a good job," George Duncan recalled. "We didn't lose a bomber or a torpedo plane to enemy air action while they were on board with us. We had a perfect score."[14]

Commander McCampbell was interviewed in November 1944 while traveling back to the United States from his tour of duty as the *Essex* CAG. Although aware of the ace race with Dick Bong and others, he insisted he was not on a personal quest to be the military's best. "The Admiral disliked very much that I shot down planes," McCampbell quipped. In his defense, Dave said that he "just happened to be lucky" to be around when enemy aircraft showed up. "If you get jumped by a plane or if you run on to a plane, there isn't any point in turning the other way. You may as well hit him."[15]

McCampbell's Fabled Fifteen did just that, more efficiently than any other carrier-based squadron in World War II.

Simply put, they were the U.S. Navy's top guns.

Fighting Fifteen (VF-15) Roster for USS *Essex* Deployment

MH	Medal of Honor	SS	Silver Star
NC	Navy Cross	LM	Legion of Merit
DFC	Distinguished Flying Cross	WIA	Wounded in Action
AM	Air Medal	KIA	Killed in Action
PH	Purple Heart	MIA	Missing in Action

Original Roster: May 3, 1944

Name	Rank	Awards	Notes
Bare, James Doyle	Ens./Lt. (jg)	AM (2)	
Barry, John Edmund, Jr.	Lt.	AM	KIA 9/9/44
Berree, Norman Rahn	Ens./Lt. (jg)	DFC, AM	
Borley, Clarence Alvin	Ens.	NC, DFC, PH	Joined 3/44
Brewer, Charles Walter	Lt. Cdr./Cdr.	NC	KIA 6/19/44
Bruce, James Lester	Ens./Lt. (jg)	AM	KIA 6/23/44
Burnam, Wesley Thomas	Ens.	AM	KIA 5/19/44
Butler, George Francis	Ens.		KIA 4/1/44
Carr, George Raines	Lt. (jg)	NC, DFC (2), AM	
Clark, Warren James	Ens./Lt. (jg)	NC	
Collins, John Joseph	Lt.	PH, AM, DFC	WIA 5/23/44
Crittenden, George Ralph	Lt.	PH, DFC, AM	WIA 6/15/44
Duffy, James Edward	Ens.	AM	
Duncan, George Chamberlain	Lt. Cdr.	NC, DFC (3), SS	
Flinn, Kenneth Ashton	Ens.	DFC (3), AM	KIA 10/13/44
Foltz, Ralph Emmett	Ens./Lt. (jg)	DFC (2)	Joined late 1943
Fowler, Richard Easton, Jr.	Ens./Lt. (jg)	NC, SS, DFC	

Name	Rank	Awards	Notes
Henning, William Victor	Lt. (jg)	AM	KIA 9/12/44
Hoffman, John Robert	Lt. (jg)/Lt.		Nonflying material officer
Ivey, John Randolph	Lt. (jg)	DFC	WIA and KIA 6/16/44
Johnson, David Edward, Jr.	Ens.	DFC	KIA 7/24/44
Johnson, Wallace Robert	Ens.	DFC, AM	
Jones, Alfred Alexander	Lt. (jg)	AM	KIA 6/15/44
Kenney, Leo Thomas	Lt. (jg)	PH, AM	WIA 5/20/44; KIA 6/11/44
Lundin, Walter Axel	Lt. (jg)	AM, DFC	
McCampbell, David	Cdr.	MH, LM with Valor, NC, SS, DFC (3), AM (2)	Promoted to CAG-15
McReynolds, Robert	Lt.		ACIO
Mellon, Glenn Edward, Jr.	Ens./Lt. (jg)	NC, AM	
Milton, Charles Baynard	Ens./Lt. (jg)	NC, DFC, AM	
Morris, Bert DeWayne, Jr.	Lt.	AM, DFC (2)	
Nall, Royce Lowell	Ens./Lt. (jg)	DFC, AM	Joined 4/44
O'Brien, Joseph James	Lt.		Nonflying admin. officer
Overton, Edward White, Jr.	Lt.	NC (2), AM	
Pigman, George Wood, Jr.	Ens./Lt. (jg)	DFC, AM	
Plant, Claude William	Ens.	DFC (2), SS, AM	KIA 9/12/44
Power, Joseph William, Jr.	Ens.	DFC	WIA 6/19/44; KIA 6/20/44

Original Roster: May 3, 1944 (cont.)

Name	Rank	Awards	Notes
Rader, George Harold	Ens.	AM	KIA 6/19/44
Rigg, James Francis	Lt./Lt. Cdr.	NC, DFC, AM	
Roach, Melvin Cleveland	Lt.		KIA 6/12/44
Rushing, Roy Warrick	Ens./Lt. (jg)	NC, DFC (2)	
Singer, Arthur, Jr.	Ens./Lt. (jg)	PH, NC, DFC (2)	WIA 6/24/44
Slack, Albert Cairrel	Ens./Lt. (jg)	SS, AM	
Stearns, Robert Lloyd	Lt.	NC, PH, AM	WIA 5/19/44; KIA 6/23/44
Stime, Robert Norwood, Jr.	Ens./Lt. (jg)	DFC, AM	
Strane, John Roberts	Lt.	NC, DFC (3), AM	WIA 10/24/44
Symmes, John Carlos Cleves	Lt. (jg)	NC, DFC (2)	
Tarr, Thomas, Jr.	Ens.	AM	KIA 6/19/44
Thompson, Thorolf Erling	Ens./Lt. (jg)	NC, DFC, AM (3)	MIA 11/11/44
Twelves, Wendell Van	Ens./Lt. (jg)	PH, NC, SS, DFC(2), AM	WIA 6/15/44
West, Kenneth Bradford	Lt. (jg)	AM	
White, Carleton	Ens./Lt. (jg)	AM	

VF-15 Replacement Pilots Received During Essex Cruise

Name	Rank	Awards	Date Joining Squadron/Notes
Allen, William Ward	Ens.		10/31/44 to 11/12/44
Bertschi, Reune Willard	Ens.		10/31/44 to 11/12/44
Bomar, Edward Tschirn	Ens.		10/31/44 to 11/12/44
Brex, John William	Ens.	AM	6/27/44; WIA
Bugg, Paul	Ens.	AM	9/11/44
Butters, James Anthony	Ens.		10/31/44 to 11/12/44

Name	Rank	Awards	Date Joining Squadron/Notes
Catterton, William Emmitt	Ens.		6/26/44; injured 7/1/44
Craig, Minor Alexander	Ens.	AM	6/27/44
Davis, Richard Lee	Ens.	NC, AM	6/20/44
Davis, Richard Wilbur	Lt. (jg)/Lt.		6/20/44; KIA 9/10/44
Dorn, Charles Adam	Ens.	AM (2)	6/20/44; KIA 10/12/44
Dowlen, Wayne Lewis	Ens.		6/26/44
Eaholtz, Galen Martin	Ens.		10/31/44 to 11/12/44
Erickson, Robert Waldemar Norbom	Ens.		10/31/44; KIA 11/11/44
Fash, Robert Paul	Lt. (jg)	NC, AM (2)	9/11/44
Forsyth, James Alvan	Ens.		10/31/44 to 11/12/44
Foshee, Herman Lee	Ens.	AM	9/44
Frazelle, Merwin Hobbs	Ens.		6/20/44
Gonya, Donald Elmer	Ens.		9/11/44
Green, Howard Charles	Ens.		6/20/44; KIA 9/10/44
Hamblin, Len Spencer	Ens.	AM	5/44; KIA 9/8/44
Langston, Gene Clair	Ens.		10/31/44 to 11/12/44
Lathrop, Jerome Lee	Ens.	AM	9/11/44
Lemley, Leonard Andrew	Ens.		10/31/44 to 11/12/44
Lewis, Earl Dilbon	Ens.		9/11/44
Maxey, Lyle Allan	Ens.		10/31/44 to 11/12/44
McGraw, Richard Herbert	Ens.	AM	6/20/44
Mooney, James David, Jr.	Ens.	AM	9/11/44
Riffle, William Byron	Ens.		10/31/44
Self, Larry Russel	Ens.	NC, DFC (2), AM	6/20/44
Smith, Howard Stratton	Ens.	DFC, AM	9/11/44
Sprankle, Robert Varian	Ens.		9/16/44

VF-15 Replacement Pilots Received During Essex Cruise (cont.)

Name	Rank	Awards	Date Joining Squadron/Notes
Taylor, Jack Crawford	Ens.	DFC	6/20/44
Tidwell, Thomas Wesley	Ens.		10/31/44 to 11/12/44
Whiteside, John Richard	Ens.		10/31/44

VBF Detachment of VF-15 Received from VB-15 on August 29, 1944

Name	Rank	Awards	Notes
Anderson, William Hill	Lt. (jg)	DFC, AM (2)	
Deming, Wilbur Stone, Jr.	Lt. (jg)	NC, AM	
Gaver, Henry Clayton	Ens.		KIA 9/24/44
Gunter, Monchie Middleton, Jr.	Lt. (jg)	AM (2)	
Hoey, Thomas Granville	Ens.		
Kramer, Henry Harold	Lt.		KIA 9/8/44
Lee, Kent Liston	Ens.	AM	
Van Altena, John Paul	Lt. (jg)	DFC, AM (3)	
Voorhest, Homer Burnett	Lt. (jg)	DFC, AM (3)	

VF(N)-77 Detachment, USS Essex (Blended into VF-15 on 9/25/1944)

Name	Rank	Awards	Notes
Brandon, Inman	Lt.		Nonflying AVS officer
Davis, Bonner Arlander	Ens.		KIA 5/23/44

Name	Rank	Awards	Notes
Freeman, Robert Mark	Lt. Cdr.	DFC	Transferred 10/1/44; one kill with VF(N)-77
Hogue, "J" "C"*	Lt.	NC, AM	
Kelly, Daniel Brady	Ens.		KIA 6/10/44
Lundquist, Samuel, Jr.	Lt.		
Roberts, Kester Merton	Ens.		One kill with VF-15
Roycraft, Ernest	Ens.	DFC	
Seigler, Harold Courtney	Lt.		Nonflying AVS officer
Tarleton, George Lester	Ens.	DFC	Two kills with VF(N)-77

* Initials such as "J" and "C" indicate a man whose birth certificate had no formal given first or middle name.

Top-Scoring Pilots of Fighting Fifteen (VF-15)

Name	Rank	Kills	Notes
McCampbell, David	Cdr.	34	ace in a day twice
Duncan, George Chamberlain	Lt. Cdr.	13.5	
Strane, John Roberts	Lt.	13	
Twelves, Wendell Van	Ens./Lt. (jg)	13	
Rushing, Roy Warrick	Ens./Lt. (jg)	13	ace in a day
Carr, George Raines	Lt. (jg)	13	ace in a day
Rigg, James Francis	Lt./Lt. Cdr.	11	ace in a day
Singer, Arthur, Jr.	Ens./Lt. (jg)	10	
Berree, Norman Rahn	Ens./Lt. (jg)	9	
Pigman, George Wood, Jr.	Ens./Lt. (jg)	8.5	
Plant, Claude William	Ens.	8.5	
Self, Larry Russel	Ens	8.5	
Morris, Bert DeWayne, Jr.	Lt.	7	
Brewer, Charles Walter	Lt. Cdr./Cdr.	6.5	
Fowler, Richard Easton, Jr.	Ens./Lt. (jg)	6.5	
Lundin, Walter Axel	Lt. (jg)	6.5	
Bare, James Doyle	Ens./Lt. (jg)	6	
Slack, Albert Cairrel	Ens./Lt. (jg)	5.5	
Symmes, John Carlos Cleves	Lt. (jg)	5.5 plus 5.5 kills with VF-21 in 1943	
Borley, Clarence Alvin	Ens.	5	
Duffy, James Edward	Ens.	5	
Flinn, Kenneth Ashton	Ens.	5	
Foltz, Ralph Emmett	Ens./Lt. (jg)	5	

Name	Rank	Kills	Notes
Johnson, Wallace Robert	Ens.	5	
Milton, Charles Baynard	Ens./Lt. (jg)	5	
Overton, Edward White, Jr.	Lt.	5	
Crittenden, George Ralph	Lt.	4.5	
Frazelle, Merwin Hobbs	Ens.	4	
Nall, Royce Lowell	Ens./Lt. (jg)	4	
Thompson, Thorolf Erling	Ens./Lt. (jg)	4	
Collins, John Joseph	Lt.	3	
Fash, Robert Paul	Lt. (jg)	3 plus 3 kills with VF-50 in 1944	
Gunter, Monchie Middleton, Jr.	Lt. (jg)	3	
McGraw, Richard Herbert	Ens.	3	
Mellon, Glenn Edward, Jr.	Ens./Lt. (jg)	3	
Smith, Howard Stratton	Ens.	3	
Van Altena, John Paul	Lt. (jg)	3	
Taylor, Jack Crawford	Ens.	2.5	
White, Carleton	Ens./Lt. (jg)	2.5	
Brex, John William	Ens.	2	
Deming, Wilbur Stone, Jr.	Lt. (jg)	2	
Power, Joseph William, Jr.	Ens.	2	
Stime, Robert Norwood, Jr.	Ens./Lt. (jg)	2	
Henning, William Victor	Lt. (jg)	1.5	
Johnson, David Edward, Jr.	Ens.	1.5	

Plus twenty-five other kills made by twenty-four pilots, including four by VF(N)-77 pilots operating from USS Essex.

ACKNOWLEDGMENTS

Because its cast of aces is no longer among us, writing a fresh view of the "fabled" Fighting Fifteen took on new heights. Fortunately, enough sources to fill a squadron roster stepped forward to share insightful material and images. I must first thank numerous family members of the Satan's Playmates pilots. Van Twelves and his sister, Valerie Twelves Gillen, supplied volumes of material and photos from their archives of their ace father, Wendell Van "Duz" Twelves. John Barry III, who has written his own book about his father's service with VF-15, was a steady supporter throughout this process. John allowed me to quote from his father's wartime diary and offered many rare photos and other material.

Many other children and relatives of VF-15 pilots contributed stories, articles, memoirs, and photos of their loved ones. They include David P. McCampbell, Kathy Duffy Kalohi, Mark Deming, Chris Foltz, Joe Foltz, Harry Pigman, Wayne Hornblow, Rita and James D. Bare Jr., Pam Morris Friedman, Robert Borley, Roger Overton, Debbie Fowler Baatstad, Richard Fowler, Bob Fash Jr., Bob Gorman, Thomas Strane, Bobbi Greenstreet, Sheri Uhrin, Marsha Craig Kuhnert, and Lieutenant Commander David Craig, USN.

Aviation authors Barrett Tillman and Thomas McKelvey Cleaver helped steer me toward various sources and holdings for material. For details on pilot Jack Taylor, I thank archivist Diane M. Everman of Enterprise Holdings. She assisted with edits and obtaining approval from Andy Taylor and his sister, Jo Ann Taylor Kindle, to provide photos and papers from the Jack Taylor collection. POW expert Katie Rasdorf shared files and other material regarding VF-15 pilots who were taken prisoner in 1944. Professional researcher Susan Strane was again vital to me in obtaining requested photos and documents from the National Archives. Renah Miller, A/V Photo Archivist at the American Heritage Center, also provided papers of U.S. fighter aces.

A number of museum archivists and employees deserve praise for their help in unearthing important documents. Jim Klages and Gene Pfeffer of the National Museum of World War II Aviation in Colorado Springs allowed me to review and copy material from their collection on VF-15 ace Walter "Jake" Lundin. Archivist Jared Galloway provided papers and links to VF-15 sources housed in the National Naval Aviation Museum in Pensacola. Nicole Davis sent VF-15 papers and links to oral histories held by the Museum of Flight in Seattle.

Randy Wilson and Hank Coates of the Commemorative Air Force in Dallas allowed me to review oral histories captured decades ago by their staff and volunteers. Randy went above and beyond in allowing me to dive through boxes and filing cabinets in search of desired materials. David Hanson, curator of the USS *Midway* Museum in San Diego, reviewed donated collections for relevant material. Mark Herber, a researcher dedicated to preserving the story of USS *Essex*, kindly shared *Essex* deck logs that he copied in the National Archives. Patricia Nava and Sonja Gaither provided various naval aviation documents from the History of Aviation Archives at the University of Texas at Dallas's Eugene McDermott Library.

My friend and literary agent, Jim Donovan, helped review and improve the manuscript. My Penguin Random House editor, Grace Layer, once again guided me through the publishing process with keen professionalism. Dashing Dave McCampbell and his Satan's Playmates remain the U.S. Navy's top guns of carrier aviation, but this fresh look into their legendary exploits was made possible only with the assistance of the above-named contributory aces.

GLOSSARY OF TERMS

AA:	Antiaircraft fire.
Angels:	Fighter direction code for altitude in thousands of feet.
Bandit:	Aircraft identified as a hostile.
Betty:	IJN Mitsubishi G4M Navy Type 1 land-based attack bomber.
Bogey:	Unidentified aircraft.
CAG:	Commander, air group.
CAP:	Combat air patrol.
Chandelle:	A steep climbing turn, usually started at high speed.
CIC:	Combat information center.
Deflection shot:	A technique of shooting ahead of a moving target so a projectile intercepts a target at a predicted point; also known as leading the target.
Dinah:	JAAF Mitsubishi Ki-46 Army Type 100 reconnaissance airplane.
Division:	A formation of four planes.
Emily:	IJN Kawanishi H8K Navy Type 2 large flying boat.
FDO:	Fighter director officer; also FIDO.
Fran/Frances:	IJN Yokosuka P1Y Ginga twin-engine fighter-bomber. The pilots always shorted "Frances" to "Fran," which was the formal code name.
Hamp:	IJN Mitsubishi A6M3 Navy Type 0 Model 32 carrier fighter.
High-side run:	A fighter attack pattern using a steep dive from the side.
HVAR:	High velocity aircraft rocket.
IJN:	Imperial Japanese Navy.
Irving:	IJN Nakajima J1N Navy Type 2 night-reconnaissance fighter.

JAAF:	Japanese Army Air Force.
Jack:	IJN Mitsubishi J2M Navy interceptor fighter.
Jake:	IJN Aichi E13A Navy Type 0 reconnaissance seaplane.
Jill:	IJN Nakajima B6N Navy carrier attack bomber.
Judy:	IJN Yokosuka D4Y Navy Type 2 carrier attack bomber.
Kate:	IJN Nakajima B5N Navy Type 97-1 carrier torpedo bomber.
Lily:	JAAF Kawasaki Ki-48 Army Type 99 twin-engine light bomber.
LSO:	Landing signal officer.
Lufbery circle:	A defensive air combat tactic where multiple aircraft form a horizontal circle in the air when attacked, allowing armament of each aircraft to protect other planes in the circle.
Mavis:	IJN Kawanishi H6K Navy Type 97 large flying boat.
Myrt:	IJN Nakajima C6N Navy carrier reconnaissance aircraft.
Nate:	JAAF Nakajima Ki-27 Army Type 97 fixed-gear fighter.
Nick:	JAAF Kawasaki Ki-45 Army Type 2 two-seat, twin-engine fighter.
Oscar:	JAAF Nakajima Ki-43 Army Type 1 fighter.
Overhead:	A steep diving run from directly above target.
Pete:	IJN Mitsubishi F1M Navy Type 0 observation seaplane.
Sally:	JAAF Mitsubishi Ki-21 Army Type 97 heavy bomber.
Scramble:	Launch of aircraft as soon as possible.
Section:	Two-plane tactical fighter unit.
Split S:	A violent roll to an inverted position, often made rapidly from level flight into a vertical dive.
Tail-end Charlie:	The rearmost plane of a formation.
Tojo:	JAAF Nakajima Ki-44 Army Type 2 fighter.
Tony:	JAAF Kawasaki Ki-61 Army Type 3 fighter.
Topsy:	Twin-engine Mitsubishi Ki-57 transport aircraft.
Val:	IJN Aichi D3A Navy Type 99 fixed-gear dive-bomber.
VBF:	Prefix for fighter-bomber squadron.
VF:	Prefix for fighter squadron.
VF(N):	Prefix for night-fighter squadron.
VT:	Prefix for torpedo bomber squadron.
Water injection:	Used for short-term emergency power; water is metered and mixed with the F6F's fuel.
WEP:	War emergency power; a throttle setting for use in desperate situations, producing more than 100 percent of an engine's normal rated power for a limited number of minutes.
Zeke/Zero:	IJN Mitsubishi A6M Navy Type 0 carrier fighter.

NOTES

CHAPTER ONE: DASHING DAVE

1. McCampbell, *Reminiscences*, 101.
2. Ibid., 102.
3. Ibid., 103–4.
4. Ibid., 105.
5. Ibid., 21.
6. Ibid., 1–10.
7. Ibid., 10–11.
8. Wittels, "4-F Hero," 109.
9. McCampbell, *Reminiscences*, 15–21.
10. Wittels, "4-F Hero," 109.
11. McCampbell, *Reminiscences*, 36, 47.
12. Ibid., 55–56.
13. Ibid., 67–68.
14. Ibid., 99.
15. Ibid., 110.
16. Cleaver, *Fabled Fifteen*, 59.
17. Interview with Michael and Caroline Hornblow.
18. Wittels, "4-F Hero," 110.
19. Cleaver, *Fabled Fifteen*, 60.

CHAPTER TWO: DUZ, DUFFY, AND JIGS

1. Wendell Van Twelves oral history, 1.
2. Ibid., 2.
3. Ibid., 1.
4. Ibid., 2–3.
5. Ibid., 3.

6. Ashcroft, *We Wanted Wings*, 33–35; Grossnick, "The History of Naval Aviator," 44.
7. Twelves oral history, 3.
8. Duffy interview with Collier.
9. Del Calzo and Collier, *Wings of Valor*, 63.
10. Duffy interview with Collier.
11. Guttman, "Ace Profile: Ralph Foltz of Fabled 15," 12.
12. Chris Foltz interview with author, September 14, 2022.
13. Twelves oral history, 3; Duffy interview with Collier.
14. Twelves oral history, 4.
15. Guttman, "Ace Profile: Ralph Foltz of Fabled 15," 13.
16. Twelves oral history, 4.

CHAPTER THREE: HELLCATS AND SATAN'S PLAYMATES

1. John Strane, American Fighter Aces Association Oral Interviews, pt. 1, 1.
2. McCampbell, "Carrier Air Group Fifteen," 1.
3. Fold3, "Biography of Arend Grothaus."
4. Cleaver, "Jim Duffy and the 'Duffy Weave,'" 44.
5. George Duncan oral history, 1–2.
6. Ibid., 3.
7. Ibid., 4.
8. Walter Lundin oral history, 2.
9. Ibid., 4–5.
10. Twelves oral history, 4.
11. James Duffy oral history; Duffy interview with Collier.
12. Foltz letter to William Coombes III, August 18, 1998.
13. Busha with Duffy, "Satan's Playmate," 73–74.
14. Albert Slack, American Fighter Aces Association Oral Interviews, pt. 2, 4.
15. Ibid., pt. 2, 4–5.
16. Ibid., pt. 2, 6.
17. McCampbell, *Reminiscences*, 113.
18. Tillman, *Hellcat*, 7–11.
19. Van Twelves email, September 9, 2022.
20. Barry, *Why Can't I*, 11–30.
21. Ibid., 31–33.
22. Ibid., 19–20, 35–36.
23. Cleaver, *Fabled Fifteen*, 64.
24. Lundstrom, *The First Team and the Guadalcanal Campaign*, 291–92.
25. Harry Pigman interview.
26. Fighting Fifteen War Diary, pt. 2: Narrative, 4.
27. Cleaver, *Fabled Fifteen*, 65.
28. Ibid., 63.
29. McCampbell, *Reminiscences*, 117.
30. Owens, "Remembering a Top Ace—David McCampbell."
31. Cordray, "My Diary," Introduction, 8.

32. Busha with Duffy, "Satan's Playmate," 74.
33. Ibid., 73.
34. Fighting Fifteen War Diary, pt. 2: Narrative, 6.
35. Barry, *Why Can't I*, 41–46.
36. Cordray, "My Diary," Introduction, 8.
37. Cleaver, *Fabled Fifteen*, 67.
38. McCampbell, *Reminiscences*, 112; Duncan oral history, 8.
39. Barry, *Why Can't I*, 50.
40. Ibid., 51–52, 55.
41. VB-15 War History, 11.
42. Cleaver, *Fabled Fifteen*, 69; Duncan oral history, 8.
43. Barry, *Why Can't I*, 57.
44. McCampbell, *Reminiscences*, 130.

CHAPTER FOUR: CAST ASHORE

1. Barry, *Why Can't I*, 61.
2. McCampbell, *Reminiscences*, 118–19.
3. Ibid., 121.
4. Ibid., 136; Cleaver, *Fabled Fifteen*, 63.
5. McCampbell, *Reminiscences*, 137.
6. Ibid., 122.
7. George Duncan and John Strane, American Fighter Aces Association Oral Interviews, 5.
8. McCampbell, "Simulated Attack on Panama Canal," 1–2.
9. Duncan oral history, 8.
10. McCampbell, *Reminiscences*, 140.
11. Cordray, "My Diary," March 5, 1944, 2.
12. Barry, *Why Can't I*, 77–79.
13. Ibid., 82.
14. Duncan and Strane, American Fighter Aces Association Oral Interviews, 18.
15. Ibid., 7.
16. Tillman, "Dashing Dave McCampbell: The Navy's Top Hellcat Ace," 82; McCampbell, *Reminiscences*, 148.
17. McCampbell, *Reminiscences*, 84–85.
18. Cleaver, *Fabled Fifteen*, 49, 55, 59, 71.
19. Barry, *Why Can't I*, 90.
20. McCampbell, *Reminiscences*, 139.
21. Barry, *Why Can't I*, 92.
22. VF(N)-77 war diary, December 1943–February 1944.
23. Barry, *Why Can't I*, 93.
24. Bruning, *Race of Aces*, 350–51.
25. Tillman, *Wildcat Aces of World War 2*, 27, 59; Tillman, *Hellcat Aces of World War 2*, 19.
26. Tillman, *Hellcat Aces of World War 2*, 21.

CHAPTER FIVE: FIRST COMBAT

1. Tillman, *Clash of the Carriers*, 22.
2. Barry, *Why Can't I*, 106.
3. McCampbell, *Reminiscences*, 154.
4. Cleaver, *Fabled Fifteen*, 77.
5. McCampbell, *Reminiscences*, 157.
6. Ibid., 162.
7. Cleaver, *Fabled Fifteen*, 77.
8. Duffy interview with Humphrey, May 14, 2006.
9. Twelves diary, May 19, 1944.
10. Barry, *Why Can't I*, 107.
11. USS *Sturgeon*, "Tenth War Patrol Report," 7–8.
12. Wittels, "4-F Hero," 109.
13. McCampbell, *Reminiscences*, 123.
14. Ibid., 158.
15. Find a Grave, "Joseph Prentice Willetts."
16. Twelves diary, May 20, 1944.
17. Barry, *Why Can't I*, 108.
18. Cordray, "My Diary," May 20, 1944, 5.
19. Barry, *Why Can't I*, 110–11.
20. McCampbell, *Reminiscences*, 192.
21. Commander Carrier Air Group Fifteen, Secret Memorandum, 5–6.
22. Busha with Duffy, "Satan's Playmate," 74.

CHAPTER SIX: TO THE MARIANAS

1. Barry, *Why Can't I*, 112–13, 116–17.
2. Tillman, *Clash of the Carriers*, 50–51.
3. Barry, *Why Can't I*, 118.
4. Tillman, *Clash of the Carriers*, 55.
5. Barry, *Why Can't I*, 118–19.
6. Tillman, *Clash of the Carriers*, 55.
7. McCampbell, *Reminiscences*, 149.
8. Morris, transcript of U.S. Navy interview, 20.
9. Tillman, *Clash of the Carriers*, 62.
10. Casse et al., "IJN *Kokko Maru*."
11. VF-15 air combat action report (hereafter abbreviated "ACA") No. 15, June 12, 1944, 4.
12. Slack, American Fighter Aces Association Oral Interviews, pt. 1, 19.
13. Barry, *Why Can't I*, 119–20.
14. Ibid.
15. Duncan oral history, 11.
16. Slack, American Fighter Aces Association Oral Interviews, pt. 1, 10; pt. 2, 14.
17. VF-15 ACA No. 18, June 13, 1944, 4A.

18. Barry, *Why Can't I*, 121–22.
19. Bridgers, "The Bent Pinkie: Operation Forager," 3.
20. VF-15 ACA No. 22, June 13, 1944, 3; Bridgers, "The Bent Pinkie: Operation Forager," 4.
21. Y'Blood, *Red Sun Setting*, 64–65.
22. Ibid., 66.
23. Barry, *Why Can't I*, 124.
24. VF-15 ACA No. 23, June 15, 1944, 4A.
25. Barry, *Why Can't I*, 126.
26. Y'Blood, *Red Sun Setting*, 66–67.
27. Ibid., 74–76.
28. Duffy interview with Collier.
29. Ibid.
30. Tillman, *Clash of the Carriers*, 102.
31. Ibid., 107–8.

CHAPTER SEVEN: TURKEY SHOOT'S
FIRST RAIDS

1. Strane, American Fighter Aces Association Oral Interviews, pt. 1, 6.
2. Oleson, *In Their Own Words*, 94.
3. Strane, American Fighter Aces Association Oral Interviews, pt. 1, 5. In his 1989 oral history interviews, Strane said that his dive-bomber companion on this flight was Ensign Wilfred Bailey. The VF-15 action reports, documented on the day of the flight, instead show the VB-15 pilot to be Lt. (jg) Donald McCutcheon. VF-15 ACA No. 28 and VB-15 ACA No. 26, June 19, 1944, 1–3.
4. Ibid., pt. 1, 6.
5. Ibid., pt. 1, 7.
6. Ibid., pt. 2, 7–8.
7. Tillman, *Clash of the Carriers*, 129–31, 137.
8. Duncan oral history, 20.
9. Tillman, *Clash of the Carriers*, 138–39.
10. Ibid., 145.
11. Oleson, *In Their Own Words*, 19.
12. Tillman, *Clash of the Carriers*, 147–50.
13. Ibid., 153, 162.
14. Oleson, *In Their Own Words*, 92.
15. Ibid., 94.
16. Hammel, *Aces Against Japan II*, 209–10.
17. Slack, American Fighter Aces Association Oral Interviews, pt. 1, 5.
18. Hammel, *Aces Against Japan II*, 210; Oleson, *In Their Own Words*, 93.
19. VF-15 ACA No. 30, June 19, 1944, 4A.
20. Ibid.
21. Oleson, *In Their Own Words*, 93.
22. Guttman, "Ace Profile: Ralph Foltz of Fabled 15," 15.
23. VF-15 ACA No. 30, June 19, 1944, 4D–4E.
24. Oleson, *In Their Own Words*, 95.

25. Ibid., 95.
26. Slack, American Fighter Aces Association Oral Interviews, pt. 2, 9.
27. Hammel, *Aces Against Japan II*, 210.
28. Slack, American Fighter Aces Association Oral Interviews, pt. 1, 6; pt. 2, 9.
29. Hammel, *Aces Against Japan II*, 211.
30. Tillman, *Clash of the Carriers*, 165.
31. Ibid., 173.
32. Ibid.

CHAPTER EIGHT: A RESCUE AND A TRAP

1. Barry, *Why Can't I*, 128.
2. Ibid., 129.
3. Cordray, "My Diary," June 19, 1944, 8.
4. Barry, *Why Can't I*, 129.
5. Hammel, *Aces Against Japan: The American Aces Speak*, vol. 1, 200.
6. Y'Blood, *Red Sun Setting*, 136.
7. VF-15 ACA No. 31, June 19, 1944, 4.
8. McCampbell, *Reminiscences*, 128–29, 180.
9. Ibid., 4.
10. Duffy interview with Humphrey, May 29, 2006.
11. Ibid.; Busha with Duffy, "Satan's Playmate," 75.
12. Ibid.
13. VF-15 ACA No. 31, June 19, 1944, 4.
14. Naval History and Heritage Command, *"Montpelier II."*
15. Hammel, *Aces Against Japan: The American Aces Speak*, vol. 1, 200.
16. Duncan oral history, 20.
17. Hammel, *Aces Against Japan: The American Aces Speak*, vol. 2, 201.
18. Ibid., 202.
19. Van Twelves, Aviation Hall of Fame Induction Address. Van Twelves later provided gun camera footage of this incident to the author.
20. Sakaida to Twelves, December 30, 1990; Sakaida, *Imperial Japanese Navy Aces of World War II*, 265.
21. Komachi to Twelves, May 7, 1991; Komachi to Sakaida, December 16, 1990.
22. Hammel, *Aces Against Japan: The American Aces Speak*, vol. 1, 203.
23. Ibid., 204.
24. Ibid.
25. Cordray, "My Diary," June 19, 1944, 9.
26. Strane, American Fighter Aces Association Oral Interviews, pt. 2, 8.
27. Slack, American Fighter Aces Association Oral Interviews, pt. 1, 8–9.
28. McCampbell, *Reminiscences*, 180.
29. Strane, American Fighter Aces Association Oral Interviews, pt. 2, 8.
30. Ibid.
31. VF-15 ACA No. 32, June 19, 1944.
32. Strane, American Fighter Aces Association Oral Interviews, pt. 2, 8.
33. Barry, *Why Can't I*, 129.
34. Twelves to Sakaida.

35. Van Twelves, Aviation Hall of Fame Induction Address.
36. Twelves oral history, 12.
37. Twelves diary, June 19, 1944.
38. Tillman, *Clash of the Carriers*, 194–99.
39. Ibid., 194–96.

CHAPTER NINE: NIGHT FIGHTERS AND THE NEW BOYS

1. VFN-77 ACA Report No. 1, June 20, 1944, 8.
2. Ibid., 6.
3. Ibid., 6–7.
4. Ibid., 8.
5. Ibid., 9.
6. Twelves diary, June 20, 1944.
7. Gray, *Jack Taylor: The Enterprise*.
8. Jack Taylor oral history with Winkler, 4.
9. Ibid., 5.
10. Ibid., 6.
11. Dick Davis, Veterans History Project interview.
12. Ibid.
13. Richard L. Davis oral history; USS *Essex* deck log, June 20, 1944.
14. Magee, "Combative Pilot Records Checkered Career," C1.
15. Taylor, National WWII Museum oral history.
16. Barry, *Why Can't I*, 130.

CHAPTER TEN: MOPPING UP IN THE MARIANAS

1. Twelves diary, June 21, 1944; Twelves oral history, 9.
2. Cleaver, *Fabled Fifteen*, 114.
3. VF-15 ACA No. 37, June 23, 1944, 4A.
4. McCampbell, *Reminiscences*, 182.
5. Ibid., 183.
6. VF-15 ACA No. 40, June 23, 1944, 4A.
7. USS *Essex* deck log, June 26, 1944.
8. Undated newspaper clipping from Minor A. Craig papers, courtesy of Lt. Cdr. David Craig.
9. Craig, interview with Minor Craig Jr.
10. Slack, American Fighter Aces Association Oral Interviews, pt. 1, 15.
11. Craig, interview with Minor Craig Jr.
12. Hallas, *Saipan: The Battle That Doomed Japan in World War II*, 198, 277.
13. Cordray, "My Diary," June 27, 1944, 10.
14. Twelves oral history, 10; Cleaver, *Fabled Fifteen*, 118; McCampbell, *Reminiscences*, 188.
15. Barry, *Why Can't I*, 134.
16. *Essex* Action Report, June 1944, 10.
17. McCampbell, *Reminiscences*, 184–85.

18. *Essex* Action Report, June 1944, pt. 7, Air Operations, 10; Hoyt, *McCampbell's Heroes*, 121–22.
19. Barry, *Why Can't I*, 138.
20. Ibid., 135–38.

CHAPTER ELEVEN: *MINSI II*

1. McCampbell, *Reminiscences*, 189.
2. Cordray, "My Diary," July 6–9, 1944, 10–11.
3. Twelves diary, July 19, 1944; Cordray, "My Diary," July 19, 1944, 12.
4. Twelves diary, July 21, 1944.
5. Hornfischer, *The Fleet at Flood Tide*, 254.
6. Clifton, *The Life and Legacy of Albert Slack*, 47.
7. Slack, American Fighter Aces Association Oral Interviews, pt. 1, 9–10.
8. Twelves diary, July 24, 1944.
9. Craig, interview with Minor Craig Jr.
10. Twelves diary, July 24, 1944.
11. Magee, "Combative Pilot Records Checkered Career"; VF-15 ACA No. 68, July 24, 1944; USS *Essex* deck log, July 24, 1944.
12. Magee, "Combative Pilot Records Checkered Career."
13. Barry, *Why Can't I*, 131, 156.
14. Cordray, "My Diary," July 28, 1944, 13; Duncan oral history, 13.
15. Ibid., July 31, 1944, 13–14.
16. Barry, *Why Can't I*, 167.
17. Ibid., 168.
18. Commander Carrier Air Group Fifteen, Comments and Recommendations on Air Operations for Period 18 July to 8 August 1944, 16 August 1944, 1.
19. Ibid., 3.
20. Ibid., 6.
21. Barry, *Why Can't I*, 170, 175.
22. Ibid., 176.

CHAPTER TWELVE: FIGHTER-BOMBERS

1. Lee, *Reminiscences*, vol. 1, 1–12.
2. Ibid., 42.
3. Ibid., 77.
4. Ibid., 80.
5. Mark Deming email to author, February 9, 2023.
6. Cordray, "My Diary," August 19, 1944, 14.
7. Lee, *Reminiscences*, vol. 1, 81.
8. Barry, *Why Can't I*, 180.
9. Twelves diary, August 19–24, 1944.
10. Owens, "Remembering a Top Ace—David McCampbell," 65.
11. Lee, *Reminiscences*, vol. 1, 83.
12. Anderson, Veterans History Project interview; Lee, *Reminiscences*, 83.
13. Cleaver, *Fabled Fifteen*, 124, 127.

14. Ibid., 127–28.
15. Enterprise archives; Barry, *Why Can't I*, 189.
16. Barry, *Why Can't I*, 190.
17. Ibid., 190–92; Twelves diary, August 31–September 1, 1944.
18. Taylor, National WWII Museum oral history.
19. Barry, *Why Can't I*, 196.
20. Taylor, National WWII Museum oral history.
21. Barry, *Why Can't I*, 197.
22. Lee, *Reminiscences*, vol. 1, 84.

CHAPTER THIRTEEN: TRIUMPHS AND TRAGEDIES OFF MINDANAO

1. McCampbell, *Reminiscences*, 155.
2. Ibid., 156.
3. Ibid.
4. Slack, American Fighter Aces Association Oral Interviews, pt. 1, 13.
5. Barry, *Why Can't I*, 215.
6. Ibid., vii–viii.
7. Twelves diary, September 9, 1944.
8. VF-15 ACA No. 102, September 9, 1944, 4.
9. USS *Bashaw*, "Third War Patrol Report," 14–20.

CHAPTER FOURTEEN: "A BUNCH OF HORNETS"

1. Robert Gorman email to author, February 14, 2023.
2. James Mooney oral history, 2–3, 23–24.
3. Ibid., 18.
4. Duncan and Strane, American Fighter Aces Association Oral Interviews, 24.
5. Winters, *Skipper*, 84.
6. VF-15 ACA No. 106, September 12, 1944, 4.
7. Winters, *Skipper*, 84.
8. VF-15 ACA No. 106, September 12, 1944, 4A.
9. Ibid., 4C.
10. Duncan and Strane, American Fighter Aces Association Oral Interviews, 22.
11. Winters, *Skipper*, 85.
12. McCampbell, *Reminiscences*, 273.
13. VF-15 ACA No. 107, September 12, 1944, 4.
14. Ibid., 4A.
15. VF-15 ACA No. 110, September 13, 1944, 4A–4D.
16. Aircraft action report addendum to VF-15 ACA No. 110; Dick Davis, Veterans History Project interview.
17. Second Emergency Rescue Squadron. "Mission Report—Rescues—03."
18. VF-15 ACA No. 110, September 13, 1944, 4C.
19. Duncan and Strane, American Fighter Aces Association Oral Interviews, 23.
20. Tillman, *Hellcat*, 124.
21. Dick Davis, Veterans History Project interview.
22. VF-15 ACA No. 110, September 13, 1944, 4E.

23. Ibid., 4D.
24. Ibid., 4.
25. Busha with Duffy, "Satan's Playmate," 76.

CHAPTER FIFTEEN: FIRST STRIKES IN THE PHILIPPINES

1. Hackett et al., "IJN Escort *CD-5*."
2. VF-15 ACA No. 121, September 21, 1944, 3.
3. Busha with Duffy, "Satan's Playmate," 76.
4. Hackett et al., "IJN Escort *CD-5*."
5. Cleaver, *Fabled Fifteen*, 143.
6. McCampbell, *Reminiscences*, 274.
7. VF-15 ACA No. 123, September 22, 1944, 4; McCampbell, *Reminiscences*, 274.
8. Twelves diary, September 24, 1944.
9. Duncan and Strane, American Fighter Aces Association Oral Interviews, 35.
10. Ibid., 36.
11. Twelves diary, October 3, 1944.
12. Cleaver, *Fabled Fifteen*, 146.

CHAPTER SIXTEEN: "A REAL CRAP SHOOT"

1. VB-15 ACA No. 104, October 10, 1944, 2.
2. McCampbell, *Reminiscences*, 154.
3. Cleaver, *Fabled Fifteen*, 149.
4. Winters, *Skipper*, 98.
5. Cleaver, *Fabled Fifteen*, 149.
6. Ibid.
7. Taylor oral history with Winkler.
8. Twelves oral history, 6.
9. Cleaver, *Fabled Fifteen*, 152.
10. Lee, *Reminiscences*, 85–86.
11. Ibid., 87.
12. Borley, statement, 6.
13. Dillon, interview with author, September 2021.
14. VF-15 ACA No. 141, October 12, 1944, 4.

CHAPTER SEVENTEEN: SILENT SERVICE SURVIVORS

1. Cleaver, *Fabled Fifteen*, 155.
2. Ward, interview with Clay Blair.
3. Richard L. Davis oral history.
4. Ibid.
5. VF-15 ACA No. 145, October 13, 1944, 4.
6. Twelves diary, October 13, 1944.
7. Owens, "Remembering a Top Ace—David McCampbell," 65.
8. Morison, *History of United States Naval Operations in World War II*, vol. 12, 94.
9. Borley, statement, 10.

10. Mooney oral history, 7.
11. Craig, interview with Minor Craig Jr.
12. Morison, *History of United States Naval Operations in World War II*, vol. 12, 98–100.
13. Ibid., 100–3.
14. Borley, statement, 11.
15. Cleaver, *Fabled Fifteen*, 160.
16. Borley, statement, 12.
17. Cleaver, *Fabled Fifteen*, 160.
18. Borley, statement, 13.
19. USS *Sawfish*, "Eighth War Patrol Report," 21.
20. Ibid., 29.
21. Cleaver, *Fabled Fifteen*, 161.
22. USS *Sawfish*, "Eighth War Patrol Report," 21.

CHAPTER EIGHTEEN: "LOOKS LIKE I'VE SHOT MY BOLT"

1. Twelves diary, October 19–20, 1944.
2. Wittels, "4-F Hero," 110.
3. VF-15 ACA No. 150, October 21, 1944, 4.
4. Clifton, *The Life and Legacy of Albert Slack*, 51.
5. Craig, interview with Minor Craig Jr.
6. Tillman, *U.S. Navy Fighter Squadrons in World War II*, 43, 128.
7. Duncan oral history, 14.
8. Hoyt, *The Battle of Leyte Gulf*, 102.
9. Ibid., 102–3.
10. Tillman, *Hellcat*, 136.

CHAPTER NINETEEN: "I WAS READY TO GO"

1. McCampbell, *Reminiscences*, 200.
2. Hoyt, *McCampbell's Heroes*, xii.
3. McCampbell, *Reminiscences*, 201.
4. Lundin oral history, 12–13.
5. VF-15 ACA No. 155, October 24, 1944, 4.
6. McCampbell, *Reminiscences*, 144–45.
7. Lundin oral history, 13.
8. Ibid., 13.
9. Russell, *David McCampbell*, 6.
10. McCampbell, *Reminiscences*, 203.
11. Ibid.
12. Hoyt, *McCampbell's Heroes*, xiv; McCampbell, *Reminiscences*, 204.
13. McCampbell, *Reminiscences*, 203; USS *Langley* war diary, 29–30.
14. Lundin oral history, 13–14.
15. Ibid., 4A.
16. McCampbell, *Reminiscences*, 204.

17. USS *Langley* war diary, 29–30.
18. McCampbell, *Reminiscences*, 301.

CHAPTER TWENTY: BATTLE OF THE SIBUYAN SEA

1. Tillman, *Hellcat*, 138.
2. Bradshaw and Clark, *Carrier Down*, 59.
3. Hackett and Kingsepp, "IJN Battleship *Musashi*."
4. VF-15 ACA No. 156, October 24, 1944, 4.
5. Morris, transcript of U.S. Navy interview, 21.
6. Winters, *Skipper*, 124.
7. Bridgers, "Where's Point X-Ray?"
8. Hackett et al., "IJN Battleship *Nagato*."
9. Taylor, National WWII Museum oral history.
10. Hackett and Kingsepp, "IJN Battleship *Musashi*."
11. Hackett and Kingsepp, "IJN Battleship *Yamato*."
12. Winters, *Skipper*, 126.
13. Duncan oral history, 14–15.
14. Magee, "Combative Pilot Records Checkered Career."
15. Mark Deming email to author, February 9, 2023; Albert Slack, American Fighter Aces Association oral history, circa 1980s, 20.
16. Craig, interview with Minor Craig Jr.
17. Hackett and Kingsepp, "IJN Battleship *Yamato*."
18. Hackett and Kingsepp, "IJN Battleship *Musashi*."
19. McCampbell, *Reminiscences*, 206.
20. Magee, "Combative Pilot Records Checkered Career."

CHAPTER TWENTY-ONE: CARRIER STRIKES OFF CAPE ENGAÑO

1. Morison, *History of United States Naval Operations in World War II*, vol. 12, 193.
2. McCampbell, *Reminiscences*, 206.
3. Morison, *History of United States Naval Operations in World War II*, vol. 12, 322.
4. McCampbell, *Reminiscences*, 207.
5. Tully, "IJN *Zuikaku*."
6. Richard L. Davis oral history; Dick Davis, Veterans History Project interview.
7. McCampbell, *Reminiscences*, 207.
8. Ibid.
9. Tully, "IJN *Chitose*."
10. VT-15 ACA No. 120, October 24, 1944, 4G–4H.
11. Dick Davis, Veterans History Project interview.
12. Ibid.
13. Ibid.; Richard L. Davis oral history.
14. Duffy interview with Humphrey, May 29, 2006.
15. Tully, "IJN *Zuiho*."
16. VT-19 ACA No. 53-44, October 25, 1944, 3; Tully, "The Sinking of *Akizuki*."

17. Hackett and Kingsepp, "IJN *Oyodo*"; Hackett and Kingsepp, "IJN *Hyuga*"; Hackett et al., "IJN *Ise*."
18. Busha with Duffy, "Satan's Playmate," 74.
19. Ibid.
20. Duffy interview with Humphrey, May 29, 2006; Busha with Duffy, "Satan's Playmate," 74.
21. Busha with Duffy, "Satan's Playmate," 74.
22. Duncan and Strane, American Fighter Aces Association Oral Interviews, 33.
23. Richard L. Davis oral history.
24. Dick Davis, Veterans History Project interview.
25. http://www.combinedfleet.com/Ise.htm; http://www.combinedfleet.com/Chiyoda.htm; accessed February 3, 2023.
26. Magee, "Combative Pilot Records Checkered Career."
27. Winters, *Skipper*, 130.
28. Ibid.
29. Duncan oral history, 16.
30. Twelves oral history, 8.
31. Magee, "Combative Pilot Records Checkered Career."
32. http://www.combinedfleet.com/Zuikak.htm, accessed February 4, 2023.
33. http://www.combinedfleet.com/Zuiho.htm, accessed February 4, 2023.
34. http://www.combinedfleet.com/Zuikak.htm, accessed February 4, 2023.
35. Winters, *Skipper*, 133.
36. Twelves oral history, 8.
37. http://www.combinedfleet.com/Zuiho.htm, accessed February 4, 2023.
38. Morison, *History of United States Naval Operations in World War II*, vol. 12, 331.
39. USS *Cotten* war diary, 1.
40. Duncan and Strane, American Fighter Aces Association Oral Interviews, 34.
41. Hackett et al., "IJN *Ise*."
42. Hackett and Kingsepp, "IJN *Oyodo*."
43. Lee, *Reminiscences*, 95.
44. USS *New Orleans* war diary, 1.
45. Duncan and Strane, American Fighter Aces Association Oral Interviews, 34.

CHAPTER TWENTY-TWO: THE "DUFFY WEAVE"

1. Duffy interview with Humphrey, May 14, 2006.
2. Busha with Duffy, "Satan's Playmate," 76.
3. Dick Davis, Veterans History Project interview.
4. Taylor, National WWII Museum oral history.
5. Stafford, *The Big E*, 422; Mooney oral history, 8.
6. USS *Essex* deck log, October 31, 1944.
7. Leonard Lemley, Veterans History Project interview.
8. Hammel, *Aces in Combat: The American Aces Speak*, 111.
9. Anderson, Veterans History Project interview.

10. VF-15 ACA No. 167, November 5, 1944, 14.
11. Busha with Duffy, "Satan's Playmate," 76.
12. Duncan and Strane, American Fighter Aces Association Oral Interviews, 16.
13. Ibid.
14. Ibid., 17.
15. Magee, "Combative Pilot Records Checkered Career."
16. Duncan and Strane, American Fighter Aces Association Oral Interviews, 17.
17. Busha with Duffy, "Satan's Playmate," 76.
18. Lee, *Reminiscences*, 92–93.

CHAPTER TWENTY-THREE: "I'VE GOT THREE
MEATBALLS CORNERED"

1. Cordray, "My Diary," November 10, 1944, 20.
2. Mark Deming email to author, February 9, 2023.
3. Nevitt, "The TA Operations to Leyte, Part II."
4. Lemley, Veterans History Project interview.
5. VF-15 ACA No. 179, November 11, 1944, 4B.
6. Ibid., 4C.
7. Lemley, Veterans History Project interview.
8. VF-15 ACA No. 179, November 11, 1944, 4A.
9. Duncan and Strane, American Fighter Aces Association Oral Interviews, 17.
10. United States Pacific Fleet, Task Force Thirty-Eight Point Three war diary, November 12, 1944, 19.
11. Stafford, *The Big E*, 428.
12. Nevitt, "The TA Operations to Leyte, Part II."
13. Mooney oral history, 10.
14. Nevitt, "The TA Operations to Leyte, Part II."
15. VF-15 ACA No. 178, November 11, 1944, 4A.
16. Cleaver, *Fabled Fifteen*, 202.
17. McCampbell, *Reminiscences*, 218.
18. Cleaver, *Fabled Fifteen*, 203.
19. Air Group 20 ACA No. 115, November 13, 1944.
20. Hammel, *Aces in Combat: The American Aces Speak*, vol. 1, 110–11.
21. Ibid., 112.
22. Ibid., 113.
23. Ibid., 114.
24. Ibid., 115.
25. USS *Maddox* war diary, 1.
26. Twelves diary, November 13, 1944.
27. "After Crash Landing Minor Craig Watched Plane Pushed Overboard," 1, 7.
28. VF-15 ACA No. 185, November 14, 1944, 4.
29. Ibid.

EPILOGUE

1. Commander Carrier Air Group Fifteen, Comments and Recommendations on Air Operations for Period 6 September to 18 November 1944, 28 November 1944, 3.
2. Ibid., 1–2.
3. Slack, American Fighter Aces Association Oral Interviews, pt. 1, 16; Dick Davis, Veterans History Project interview.
4. USS *Bunker Hill* war diary, 1–2.
5. Mark Deming email to author, February 9, 2023.
6. Tillman, *U.S. Navy Fighter Squadrons in World War II*, 43, 46–47, 118.
7. McCampbell, *Reminiscences*, 221–22.
8. Ibid., 221–26.
9. Ibid., 225.
10. Ibid., 222–23.
11. Tillman, "Dashing Dave McCampbell: The Navy's Top Hellcat Ace," 85.
12. Slack, American Fighter Aces Association Oral Interviews, pt. 1, 15–16.
13. Taylor oral history with Winkler, 23.
14. Duncan oral history, 9–10.
15. McCampbell, transcript of U.S. Navy interview, 25.

BIBLIOGRAPHY

INTERVIEWS AND CORRESPONDENCE

Bare, Rita. Telephone interview with author, December 2, 2022. Rita and her husband, James D. Bare Jr., also supplied his father's wartime VF-15 photos.

Borley, Robert. Telephone interview with author, August 22, 2022.

Craig, Lt. Cdr. David. Email exchanges of Minor Craig flight log, papers with author.

Deming, Mark. Telephone interview, February 8, 2023, and email correspondence with author.

Dillon, William J. Personal interviews with author, September 2021 to June 2022.

Foltz, Chris. Telephone interviews with author, September 14 and 22, 2022.

Foltz, Joseph. Telephone interviews with author, September 11 and 13, 2022.

Fowler, Richard. Telephone interviews with author, September 28 and October 15, 2022.

Friedman, Pam Morris. Telephone interview with author, September 10, 2022.

Gillen, Valerie Twelves. Written correspondence, telephone interviews, and email correspondence with author, August to December 24, 2022.

Gorman, Robert. Telephone interviews, February 7 and 14, 2023, and email correspondence with author, February 14, 2023.

Hornblow, Michael and Caroline. Telephone interview with author, September 10, 2022.

Kalohi, Kathy Duffy. Telephone interview, September 10, 2022, and email correspondence with author.

Kuhnert, Marsha Craig. Telephone interview with author, February 7, 2023.

Overton, Roger. Telephone interview with author, September 24, 2022.

Pigman, Harry. Telephone interview with author, September 14, 2022.

Strane, Thomas. Telephone interview, October 6, 2022, and email correspondence with author.

Twelves, Van. Written correspondence, telephone interviews, and email correspondence with author, August 2022 to March 17, 2023.

ORAL HISTORIES, MEMOIRS, AND DOCUMENTARIES

Anderson, William H. Veterans History Project interview. Library of Congress, AFC/2001/001/48956.

Craig, Minor A., Sr. Audiotaped interview with Minor A. Craig Jr., November 21, 2004.

Davis, Dick. Veterans History Project interview. Library of Congress, AFC/2001/001/16736.

Davis, Richard L. Oral history memoir no. 1151. American Air Power Heritage Foundation, Commemorative Air Force. May 15, 1992, interview with George W. Coombes.

Duffy, James E. Interview with Peter Collier, circa 2015, for *Wings of Valor*. Courtesy of Kathy Duffy Kalohi.

———. Oral history memoir no. 2002-0258. American Air Power Heritage Foundation, Commemorative Air Force. October 6, 2002, interview with Ron E. Larson.

———. Videotaped interviews with Richard Humphrey, May 14 and 29, 2006.

Duncan, George Chamberlain. Oral history, October 9, 1994, National Museum of the Pacific War.

———. University of North Texas Oral History Collection, no. 1030. October 9, 1994, interview with Calvin Christman.

———, and John R. Strane. The American Fighter Aces Association Interviews. Interview with Eugene Valencia. Circa 1960s.

Foltz, Ralph. Oral history memoir no. 1796. American Air Power Heritage Foundation, Commemorative Air Force. April 4, 1994, interview with Sara Cartwright.

Gray, Tim, dir. *Jack Taylor: The Enterprise*. South Kingston, RI: World War II Foundation, 2022.

Lee, Kent L. *Reminiscences of Vice Admiral Kent L. Lee, USN (Ret.)*, vol. 1. Oral history interview by Paul Stillwell. Annapolis, MD: U.S. Naval Institute, 1990.

Lemley, Leonard Andrew. Veterans History Project interview. Library of Congress, AFC/2001/001/26603.

Lundin, Captain Walter "Jake." Oral history and personal papers collection, National Museum of World War II Aviation.

McCampbell, David. *The Reminiscences of Capt. David McCampbell, USN (Ret.).* Oral history interview by Paul Stillwell. Annapolis, MD: U.S. Naval Institute, 2010.

McCampbell, Commander Dave. Transcript of U.S. Navy interview, November 29, 1944.

Mooney, James. Oral history, recorded May 14, 2011. National Museum of the Pacific War.

Morris, Lt. Wayne. Transcript of U.S. Navy interview, November 29, 1944.

Slack, Albert C. The American Fighter Aces Association Oral Interviews. Museum of Flight, Seattle, WA. Parts 1 and 2, 1989.

Strane, John R. The American Fighter Aces Association Oral Interviews, Museum of Flight, Seattle, Washington. Pt. 1, December 1989; pt. 2, January 1990.

Taylor, Jack. Enterprise Rent-a-Car Archives, Jack Taylor personal papers.

———. National WWII Museum Oral History. National Museum of the Pacific War oral history.

———. Oral history conducted with David F. Winkler, PhD, July 9, 2001. Naval Historical Foundation Oral History Program.

Twelves, Wendell Van. Oral history memoir. American Air Power Heritage
    Foundation, Commemorative Air Force. May 26, 1991, interview with Colonel John
    S. Harris.
——. Personal diary, 1944. Courtesy of National Naval Aviation Museum.
——. Personal papers. Courtesy of Van Twelves and Valerie Twelves Gillen.
Ward, Robert M. Interview with Clay Blair Jr.

OFFICIAL STATEMENTS AND MILITARY DOCUMENTS

Air Group 20 Action Reports, November 13, 1944.
Borley, Ensign C. A. Statement, December 16, 1944.
Commander Carrier Air Group Fifteen. Comments and Recommendations on Air
    Operations for Period 18 July to 8 August 1944, 16 August 1944.
——. Comments and Recommendations on Air Operations for Period 6 September to
    18 November 1944, 28 November 1944.
——. Secret Memorandum #1-44, 31 May 1944. Report of Air Operations on Marcus
    and Wake, 19, 20, 23 May 1944.
McCampbell, David. "Carrier Air Group Fifteen (CVG-15)," 1 September 1943–6
    December 1944, pt. 2: Narrative.
——. "Report of Air Operations Conducted by Carrier Air Group Fifteen During the
    Period 11–18 June 1944," Commander Carrier Air Group Fifteen to Commander in
    Chief, United States Fleet, 5 July 1944.
——. "Simulated Attack on Panama Canal 18 Feb. 1944—Report on," 19 February 1944.
United States Pacific Fleet, Task Force Thirty-Eight Point Three. War diary, November
    1944.
USS Bashaw. "Third War Patrol Report," August 7 to October 4, 1944.
USS Bunker Hill. War diary, December 1944.
USS Clarence K. Bronson. War diary, October 25, 1944.
USS Cotten. War diary, October 25, 1944.
USS Essex. Action report, June 1944.
USS Essex. Deck logs, March–November 1944.
USS Langley. War diary, October 1944.
USS Maddox. War diary, November 13, 1944.
USS Montpelier. War diary, June 19, 1944.
USS New Orleans. War diary, October 25, 1944.
USS Sailfish. R. E. M. Ward, "Report of Twelfth War Patrol," December 11, 1944.
USS Sawfish. "Eighth War Patrol Report," September 9 to November 8, 1944.
USS Sturgeon. "Tenth War Patrol Report," May 20, 1944.
VB-15. Air combat action reports, May–November 1944.
VB-15. War history, September 1, 1943–December 6, 1944.
VF-15. War diary and air combat action reports, May–November 1944.
VF(N)-77. War diary, December 1943–February 1944.

ARTICLES, UNPUBLISHED MEMOIRS, AND LETTERS

"After Crash Landing Minor Craig Watched Plane Pushed Overboard." Democrat,
    April 4, 1990, 1, 7.

Bridgers, John D. "The Bent Pinkie: Operation Forager." Accessed April 8, 2023. http://www.tk-jk.net/Bridgers/NavyYears/TheBentPinkie-OperationFo.html.

———. "Where's Point X-Ray? The Battle of Leyte Gulf." Accessed April 8, 2023. http://www.tk-jk.net/Bridgers/NavyYears/WheresPointX-Ray TheBattle.html.

Busha, James P., with Lt. Cdr. James E. Duffy (USN). "Satan's Playmate: Creation of an Ace." *Flight Journal*, Special Interest "Hellcat" issue (Summer 2006): 72–77.

Cleaver, Thomas McKelvey. "Jim Duffy and the 'Duffy Weave': On-the-Job Training Yields a Tactical Advantage." *Flight Journal*, no. 6 (June 2017): 43–51.

Cordray, Elmer. "My Diary." Unpublished VF-15 memoirs, courtesy of Kathy Duffy Kalohi.

Find a Grave. "Joseph Prentice Willetts." Accessed February 20, 2023. https://www.findagrave.com/memorial/82018316/joseph-prentice-willetts.

Fold3. "Biography of Arend Grothaus (1917–1944). Accessed November 12, 2022. fold3.com/memorial/653585883/arend-grothaus/stories.

Grossnick, Roy A. "The History of Naval Aviator and Naval Aviation Pilot Designations and Numbers, the Training of Naval Aviators and the Number Trained (Designated)." *United States Naval Aviation, 1910–1955.* Washington, DC: Naval Historical Center, 1997.

Guttman, Jon. "Ace Profile: Ralph Foltz of Fabled 15." *Bulletin of the American Fighter Aces Association* 29, no. 2 (2012): 12–16.

Hackett, Bob, and Sander Kingsepp. "IJN Battleship Musashi: Tabular Record of Movement." Accessed April 8, 2023. http:// www.combinedfleet.com/ musashi.htm.

———. "IJN Battleship *Yamato*: Tabular Record of Movement." http://www.combinedfleet.com/yamato.htm.

———. "IJN Hyuga: Tabular Record of Movement."Accessed February 3, 2023. http://www.combinedfleet.com/ Hyuga.htm.

———. "IJN *Oyodo*: Tabular Record of Movement." Accessed February 3, 2023. http://www.combinedfleet.com/oyodo_t.htm.

———. "IJN *Zuiho*: Tabular Record of Movement." Accessed February 3, 2023. http://www.combinedfleet.com/Zuiho.htm.

———. "IJN *Zuikaku* ("Happy Crane"): Tabular Record of Movement." Accessed February 1, 2023. http://www.combinedfleet.com/Zuikak.htm.

———. "The Sinking of *Akizuki*." Accessed February 3, 2023. http://www.combinedfleet.com/akizuki-mystery.html.

Hackett, Bob, Sander Kingsepp, and Lars Ahlberg. "IJN Battleship *Nagato*: Tabular Record of Movement." Accessed April 12, 2023. http://www.combinedfleet.com/nagatrom.htm.

———. "IJN *Ise*: Tabular Record of Movement." Accessed February 3, 2023. http:// www.combinedfleet.com/ Ise.htm.

Hackett, Bob, Sander Kingsepp, and Peter Cundall. "IJN *Escort* CD-5: Tabular Record of Movement." Accessed January 22, 2022. http://www.combinedfleet.com/CD-5_t.htm.

Magee, Jack. "Combative Pilot Records Checkered Career." *Times Press-Recorder*, August 17, 1988, C1.

Naval History and Heritage Command. "*Montpelier II* (CL-57)." Accessed January 3, 2022.

Nevitt, Allyn D. "IJN *Hatsuzuki*: Tabular Record of Movement." Accessed February 4,
    2023. http://www.combinedfleet.com/hatsuz_t.htm.
———. "The TA Operations to Leyte, Part II." Accessed December 21, 2022. http://www
    .combinedfleet.com/taops2.htm.
"Not Jap Zeros but Old Films Scared Flier Wayne Morris." *New York Daily News*,
    February 3, 1945, 42.
Owens, ADRC William Chester, USN (Ret.). "Remembering a Top Ace—David
    McCampbell." *Foundation* (Fall 1996): 64–65.
Sadamu, Komachi, letter to Wendell Van Twelves, May 7, 1991.
Sadamu, Komachi, letter to Henry Sakaida, December 16, 1991.
Sakaida, Henry, letter to Wendell Van Twelves, December 30, 1990.
Second Emergency Squadron. "Mission Report—Rescues—03: 17 November 1944."
    Accessed September 9, 2022. http://www.pbyrescue.com/Rescues/17nov44.htm.
Tillman, Barrett. "Dashing Dave McCampbell: The Navy's Top Hellcat Ace." *Flight
    Journal*, Special Interest "Hellcat" issue (Summer 2006): 78–85.
Tully, Anthony P. "IJN *Chitose*: Tabular Record of Movement." Accessed February 2,
    2023. http://www.combinedfleet.com/ChitoseCV_t.htm.
———. "IJN *Chiyoda*: Tabular Record of Movement." Accessed February 3, 2023.
    http://www.combinedfleet.com/Chiyoda.htm.
Twelves, Van. Aviation Hall of Fame Induction Address for Wendell V. Twelves. Hill Air
    Force Base, Ogden, UT, May 30, 2011.
Twelves, Wendell Van, letter to Henry Sakaida, February 15, 1991.
Wittels, David G. "4-F Hero." *Saturday Evening Post*, April 14, 1945, 107–10.

BOOKS

Ashcroft, Bruce. *We Wanted Wings: A History of the Aviation Cadet Program*. San
    Antonio: HQ AETC Office of History and Research, 2005.
Barry, John, III. *Why Can't I*. Bloomington, IN: Archway Publishing, 2020.
Blair, Clay, Jr. *Silent Victory: The U.S. Submarine War Against Japan*. Philadelphia:
    J. B. Lippincott, 1975.
Boyce, Col. J. Ward, USAF (Ret.) (ed.). *American Fighter Aces Album*. Mesa, AZ:
    American Fighter Aces Association, 1996.
Bradshaw, Thomas I., and Marsha L. Clark. *Carrier Down: The Sinking of the USS
    Princeton*. Austin: Eakin Press, 1990.
Bruning, John R. *Race of Aces: WWII's Elite Airmen and the Epic Battle to Become the
    Masters of the Sky*. New York: Hachette Books, 2020.
Campbell, Douglas E. *Save Our Souls: Rescues Made by U.S. Submarines During World
    War II*. Washington, DC: Syneca Research Group, 2016.
Cleaver, Thomas McKelvey. *Fabled Fifteen: The Pacific War Saga of Carrier Air Group 15*.
    Havertown, PA: Casemate, 2020.
Clifton, Sally. *The Life and Legacy of Albert Slack*. Coppell, TX: Privately published, 2024.
Del Calzo, Nick, and Peter Collier. *Wings of Valor: Honoring America's Fighter Aces*.
    Annapolis, MD: Naval Institute Press, 2016.
Fletcher, Gregory G. *Intrepid Aviators: The True Story of USS* Intrepid's *Torpedo
    Squadron 18 and Its Epic Clash with the Superbattleship* Musashi. New York: NAL
    Caliber, 2012.

Hallas, James H. *Saipan: The Battle That Doomed Japan in World War II*. Guilford, CT: Stackpole Books, 2019.

Hammel, Eric. *Aces Against Japan: The American Aces Speak*, vol. 1. Novato, CA: Presidio Press, 1992.

———. *Aces Against Japan: The American Aces Speak*, vol. 2. Pacifica, CA: Pacifica Military History, 2009.

———. *Aces Against Japan II: The American Aces Speak*, vol. 3. Pacifica, CA: Pacifica Press, 1996.

Hornfischer, James D. *The Fleet at Flood Tide: America at Total War in the Pacific, 1944–1945*. New York: Bantam Books, 2016.

Hoyt, Edwin P. *The Battle of Leyte Gulf: Disaster and Triumph in the Bloodiest Sea Battle of World War II*. Chicago: Playboy Press Paperbacks, 1972.

———. *McCampbell's Heroes*. New York: Avon Books, 1983.

Lundstrom, John. *The First Team and the Guadalcanal Campaign: Naval Fighter Combat from August to November 1942*. Annapolis, MD: Naval Institute Press, 1994.

Morison, Samuel E. *History of United States Naval Operations in World War II*, vol. 12: *Leyte, June 1944–January 1945*. Boston: Little, Brown, 1988.

Oleson, James A. *In Their Own Words: True Stories and Adventures of the American Fighter Ace*. Lincoln, NE: iUniverse, 2007.

Russell, David Lee. *David McCampbell: Top Ace of U.S. Naval Aviation in World War II*. Jefferson, NC: McFarland, 2019.

Sakaida, Henry. *Imperial Japanese Navy Aces of World War II*. Madrid: Ediciones del Prado, 1999.

Stafford, Edward P. *The Big E: The Story of the USS* Enterprise. Illustrated edition. Annapolis, MD: Naval Institute Press, 2015; originally published 1962.

Tillman, Barrett. *Clash of the Carriers: The True Story of the Marianas Turkey Shoot of World War II*. New York: NAL Caliber, 2005.

———. *Hellcat: The F6F in World War II*. Annapolis, MD: Naval Institute Press, 1979.

———. *Hellcat Aces of World War 2*. London: Osprey Publishing, 1996.

———. *U.S. Navy Fighter Squadrons in World War II*. North Branch, MN: Specialty Press, 1997.

———. *Wildcat Aces of World War 2*. London: Osprey Publishing, 1995.

Winters, Captain T. Hugh, USN (Ret.). *Skipper: Confessions of a Fighter Squadron Commander, 1943–1944*. Mesa, AZ: Champlin Fighter Museum Press, 1985.

Y'Blood, William T. *Red Sun Setting: The Battle of the Philippine Sea*. Annapolis, MD: Naval Institute Press, 1981.

INDEX

NOTE: *Italic page numbers* indicate photographs and maps.

ABOUT THE AUTHOR

Stephen L. Moore, a sixth-generation Texan, graduated from Stephen F. Austin State University in Nacogdoches, Texas, where he studied advertising, marketing, and journalism. He is the author of two dozen books on World War II, Vietnam, and Texas history, including *Patton's Payback*, *Beyond the Call of Duty*, and *Blood and Fury*. Parents of three children, Steve and his wife, Cindy, live north of Dallas in Lantana, Texas.